Work–Life Balance

In the rapidly changing modern work environment, time pressures seem ever increasing and new technology allows work to be conducted any time and anywhere. These are just two of the factors that make it more and more difficult for working men and women to integrate work and home life. Consequently, there is a need for flexible and innovative solutions to manage the work–home interface.

Work–Life Balance: A Psychological Perspective presents up-to-date information on work–home issues, including the latest research findings. The book's emphasis is strongly psychological, with a focus on practical solutions, and includes chapters that deal with psychological issues such as the conflict between work and family, how work stresses may affect partners, and recovery from work. It also includes sections on legal issues, as well as examples of initiatives being implemented by leading employers. Contributors are drawn from the leading researchers in their fields and reflect the international character of the current challenges facing employers and employees.

Its practical focus and innovative approach make this an essential book for managers, HR professionals and organizational psychologists, as well as students in these disciplines. The theoretical basis and research focus mean the book will also be invaluable for researchers investigating workplace issues.

Fiona Jones is a Senior Lecturer at the Institute of Psychological Sciences, University of Leeds, UK. She conducts research on the topic of stress, including the effects of work stress on marital partners and on health behaviors. Her publications include the book 'Stress: Myth, theory and research'. She is a Chartered Health Psychologist.

Ronald Burke is Professor of Organizational Behaviour at the Schulich School of Business, York University, Ontario, Canada. His work has focused on the relationship between the work environment and the individual's overall well-being. He has published over 500 articles and edited or co-edited 17 books, and is a Fellow of the Canadian Psychological Association.

Mina Westman is an Associate Professor at the Faculty of Management, Tel Aviv University, Israel. Her primary research interests include job and life stress, negative and positive crossover, work–family interchange and the effects of vacations and short business trips.

Work–Life Balance
A Psychological Perspective

DISCARD

Edited by Fiona Jones, Ronald J. Burke and Mina Westman

Ψ Psychology Press
Taylor & Francis Group

HOVE AND NEW YORK

First published 2006 by Psychology Press
27 Church Road, Hove, East Sussex BN3 2FA

Simultaneously published in the USA and Canada
by Psychology Press
711 Third Avenue, New York, NY 10017

Reprinted 2008

*Psychology Press is an imprint of the Taylor & Francis Group,
an Informa business*

First issued in paperback 2012

Typeset in Times by Garfield Morgan, Rhayader, Powys
Cover design by Sandra Heath

British Library Cataloguing in Publication Data
A catalogue record for this book is available from the British Library

Library of Congress Cataloging-in-Publication Data
Work-life balance : a psychological perspective / [edited by] Fiona
Jones, Ronald J. Burke, and Mina Westman.
        p. cm.
    Includes bibliographical references.
    ISBN 1-84169-529-7
    1. Work and family. I. Jones, Fiona. II. Burke, Ronald J. III.
Westman, Minah.
        HD4904.25.W736 2005
        331.25–dc22
                                                     2005016528

ISBN 978-1-84169-529-7 (hbk)
ISBN 978-0-415-65479-1 (pbk)

Contents

PART III
Relationships between work and home life

PART IV
Managing the work–home interface

Figures

Tables

Contributors

Richard N. Block, School of Labor and Industrial Relations, Michigan State University, East Lansing, Michigan, USA

Paula Brough, Faculty of Health Sciences, Griffith University, Brisbane, Queensland, Australia

Louis C. Buffardi, Department of Psychology, George Mason University, Fairfax, Virginia, USA

Ronald J. Burke, Schulich School of Business, York University, Ontario, Canada

Mark Cropley, Department of Psychology, Surrey Sleep Research Centre, University of Surrey, Guildford, UK

Jennifer C. Cullen, Department of Psychology, Portland State University, Portland, Oregon, USA

Tracy L. Dumas, Organizational Sciences, Columbian College of Arts and Sciences, The George Washington University, Washington, DC, USA

Paulette R. Gerkovich, Catalyst, New York, USA

Lisa M. Germano, Department of Psychology, Old Dominion University, Norfolk, Virginia, USA

Leslie B. Hammer, Department of Psychology, Portland State University, Portland, Oregon, USA

Angela Holt, Honeywell International, Inc., Phoenix, Arizona, USA*

---

* Ms Holt's contribution to this book was completed while she was a candidate for the Master of Labor Relations and Human Resources degree at Michigan State University and prior to her association with Honeywell International, Inc. This article has no relationship to her association with Honeywell International and was not endorsed by Honeywell International in any way.

Fiona Jones, Institute for Psychological Sciences, University of Leeds, Leeds, UK

Thomas Kalliath, School of Business and Information Management, Australian National University, Canberra, Australia

Gail Kinman, Department of Psychology, University of Luton, Luton, UK

Ellen Ernst Kossek, School of Labor and Industrial Relations, Michigan State University, East Lansing, Michigan, USA

Suzan Lewis, Department of Psychology and Speech Pathology, Manchester Metropolitan University, Manchester, UK

Debra A. Major, Department of Psychology, Old Dominion University, Norfolk, Virginia, USA

Martin H. Malin, Chicago–Kent College of Law/Illinois Institute of Technology, Chicago, Illinois, USA

Michael O'Driscoll, Department of Psychology, The University of Waikato, Hamilton, New Zealand

Nicola Payne, School of Health and Social Sciences, Middlesex University, London, UK

Nancy P. Rothbard, University of Pennsylvania, Philadelphia, Pennsylvania, USA

Margarita V. Shafiro, Department of Psychology, Portland State University, Portland, Oregon, USA

Cath Sullivan, Department of Psychology, University of Central Lancashire, Preston, UK

Lois E. Tetrick, Department of Psychology, George Mason University, Fairfax, Virginia, USA

Mina Westman, Faculty of Management, The Leon Recanati Graduate School of Business Administration, Tel Aviv University, Tel Aviv, Israel

Fred Zijlstra, Department of Psychology, Surrey Sleep Research Centre, University of Surrey, Guildford, UK

Acknowledgements

I would like to thank our international contributors for their efforts. In addition, working with Fiona Jones and Mina Westman has been a rewarding collaboration from the evening we first discussed this possibility in London a while back. As this collection demonstrates, family continues to be a source of satisfaction and inspiration for many. My children Sharon, Rachel and Jeff make every day worthwhile. Finally for my partner, Susan, behind every great love is a great story.

Ronald Burke

Introduction

Work–life balance: key issues

Fiona Jones, Ronald J. Burke and Mina Westman

Over the past two decades the issues of work–family and work–life balance have received extensive publicity and have been subject to increasing investigation (e.g., Hogarth *et al.*, 2000; Eby *et al.*, 2005). Concerns about work–life balance have become salient for a number of reasons. Demographic and social changes have resulted in more women entering the workforce, working mothers becoming the norm rather than the exception. Technological advancements (e.g., cell phones, e-mail, fax) have made it easier for work demands to intrude into family and personal life. Furthermore, the move towards global competition has increased pressure on organizations and individual employees alike to be more flexible and responsive to change. Over the past couple of decades there has been an increase in the proportion of employees working long hours in many developed countries (Kodz *et al.*, 2002). Kodz *et al.* found that employees frequently attribute this to increased workload (due to a range of factors including organizational changes, e-mail load and staff changes), job insecurity and long hours culture. Evidence relating to many of these issues is presented in Chapter 1. Reports of high levels of work stress and stress-related illness are commonplace and there is a perception that the workplace is becoming ever more stressful (Jones and Bright, 2001).

In this climate, managing the boundary between home and work is becoming more challenging. There is a need for employees and employers alike to find flexible and innovative solutions that maximize productivity without damaging employees' well-being, their family relationships and other aspects of personal life. Furthermore, the provision of work–life balance policies is likely to play a role in recruiting and retaining good-quality employees and maintaining a competitive edge in a demanding market-place.

This book aims to make a contribution to the work–family and work–life literature by presenting an overview of up-to-date research-based information, with an emphasis on the psychological perspective. The topics selected for inclusion are those that have been identified as likely to be relevant to students, academics, researchers, practitioners and managers working in this field. The implications for practice are highlighted wherever possible. For those interested in researching in this area it includes chapters on research perspectives and methods. For the practitioner and manager, there are chapters describing best practices and focusing on the importance of organizational values in promoting work–life balance. Overall, the book aims to provide a resource for all those interested in work–life issues to use in studying and working in this area. In the following section we provide a brief introduction to some of the issues and theories that are central to this area before laying out more fully the aims and structure of the book.

Work–life balance and conflict

A blurring of boundaries between work and home life and an increasing difficulty in maintaining a balance between these two domains is now increasingly recognized. Frequently this issue is seen as a difficulty in terms of maintaining 'work–*family* balance'. However, it is also increasingly recognized that people may be involved in multiple roles outside their family life, e.g., leisure roles, community roles, religious roles (Frone, 2003). The term 'work–*life* balance' is therefore seen as more inclusive. While the terms are seldom clearly defined, they are frequently conceptualized in terms of self-ratings of general perceptions of balance between roles. However, Marks and MacDermid (1996), measure role balance in terms of balance of *attention, satisfaction* and *effort* across roles (see Chapter 4). There is also now a move towards the use of the term 'work–life integration' (e.g., Lewis *et al.*, 2003) rather than 'balance', as balance implies a 50:50 investment or allocation, which may not be the desired situation for many people. However, these latter two terms are not clearly distinguished. For example, Kofodimos (1993), though she wrote about balance, defined it is a way that appropriately sums up the concept of work–life integration, that is:

> a satisfying, healthy, and productive life that includes work, play, and love; that integrates a range of life activities with attention to self and to personal and spiritual development; and that expresses a person's unique wishes, interests and values. It contrasts with the imbalance of a life dominated by work, focussed on satisfying external requirements at the expense of inner development, and in conflict with a person's true desires.
>
> (p. xiii)

The terms 'work–family balance', 'work–life balance' and 'work–life integration' are all used within this book depending on the emphasis of the chapter. For example, when describing existing good practice (Chapter 11), the term 'work–family' is seen as more accurate in describing policies for which there is current recognition as 'best practice'.

The potentially damaging effects of a lack of work–life balance are frequently investigated by researchers in terms of the ways in which activities and emotions in one domain spill over into another domain and the ways in which different domains conflict.

Researchers have been interested in the dual phenomenon of work–family conflict (work impacting on family life) and family–work conflict (family impacting on work life) for the past two decades (Eby *et al.*, 2005). Typically employees perceive work impacting more on home life than vice versa (e.g., Williams and Alliger, 1993). A range of negative outcomes of work–family conflict have been reported. These include negative effects on work performance, absenteeism and turnover, reduced marital satisfaction, depression and poor physical health (Allen *et al.*, 2000). These phenomena are discussed in further detail in Chapters 3 and 5.

The impact of work conflict and other manifestations of work stress are not restricted to the individual employee as there is now increasing evidence that it may affect partners and other family members – a phenomenon known as 'crossover', which is discussed in Chapter 7. A great deal of research effort has focused on investigating these negative effects of work on home life. However, it is also clear that not all psychological effects of work are bad. A working day in which much is achieved may lead to feelings of satisfaction that may spill over into home life and enhance contacts with others and promote enjoyment of outside activities. Increasingly researchers in the areas of role conflict and crossover are considering such positive effects (see Chapters 5 and 7). This may help in the development of positive interventions to improve working life.

However, overall evidence currently suggests that the demands of work and the resulting lack of work–life balance are having negative effects on both individuals and organizations. Reports of increasing stress levels are widespread (e.g., Smith *et al.*, 2000). For organizations this may translate into increased levels of illness, absenteeism and attrition. Media reports and anecdotal evidence suggest increasing numbers of women may be giving up high-powered jobs to care full time for children (e.g., Wallis, 2004). Furthermore, in the UK, highly qualified senior employees have been reported to be retraining as plumbers (O'Donnell, 2004), a career allowing the individual far greater control than corporate employment. Such extreme individual solutions are detrimental to company efficiency. Clearly, it is important that solutions are found that are consistent with individual, family and organizational well-being.

Conflicting organizational pressures

Over the past 10 years many organizations have tried to become more employee/family/personal life friendly. These efforts have typically involved the creation of policies supportive of work–family balance. Some of the best practices and organizations are considered in Chapter 11.

However, unfortunately, the presence of work–family or work–life policies does not guarantee that they will be utilized or that they will be effective. This may be a result of organization cultures or management practices that support long working hours and may discourage employees from taking advantage of these policies in subtle and not-so-subtle ways (see Chapter 10). Thus, while helpful to some people, new policies may have little benefit for the bulk of the working population. This may be the result of deeply held and long-standing assumptions built into the culture of many organizations that may cause resistance to these changes (see Chapters 10 and 12). These include the expectation that managers need to control the work, that the primary obligation of employees is to their employers, that men should invest more in work than at home and that women have the prime responsibility for the home. Furthermore, there is an assumption that home and work should be separate spheres and home is not the concern of the organization. Men and women who want to succeed may be expected to fit in with these cultural expectations.

On top of this, companies are likely to be experiencing new pressures that may be seen as conflicting with an emphasis on work–life balance. They are operating in a market-place that is ever more competitive and requires increasing efficiency, demanding more involvement from employees. While this has often resulted in more interesting and challenging work for employees, it may also require more time and energy. Thus work and home may be seen as conflicting or competing arenas. This view suggests that an emphasis on one detracts from the other. Thus, workers who are visible in the workplace from early in the morning until late at night are seen as committed and valuable, regardless of whether such visibility is conducive to productivity. In contrast, workers who would like to use work–life balance policies are likely to be discouraged and fear that their careers will suffer.

There is, therefore, a need to seek solutions that simultaneously meet the personal needs of employees and the business needs of employers and if possible to create synergies between work and personal life.

What needs to be done?

While much is known about the effects of lack of work–life balance, too little is yet known about how to improve it. However, some central findings from organizational psychology research do suggest major factors that are likely to be fundamental to improving work–life balance for employees.

A central requirement for work–life balance is that employees have high levels of discretion and control over the conditions of work (Bailyn, 1993). This is now well established as a crucial factor in both reducing stress and improving employee motivation (e.g., Karasek and Theorell, 1990; Jones and Fletcher, 2002). Furthermore, where control is given over timing and place of work this, by definition, gives employees scope to improve work–life balance (see Chapter 8). However, as indicated above, increased individual control will only be effective if organizational cultures support work–life integration. In turn, organizational change may need to be supported by changes in legislation and government policy.

Practical interventions, put in place at company level, are most likely to be successful if they stem from sound theoretical perspectives and rigorous research. Furthermore, they need thorough evaluation. Collections like the present book can contribute to these efforts by disseminating information to inform future developments.

AIMS OF THE BOOK

This book aims to pull together the current theoretical perspectives and research findings with up-to-date information on practical interventions. These are set in the context of introductory chapters on social and legal issues, to equip the reader with knowledge and information essential for an informed approach to involvement in developments in this area. Individual psychological factors are clearly critical to the ways that people perceive work–home problems, the way they negotiate solutions and the satisfaction and/or stress they derive from the integration (or lack of it) that they achieve. Thus, a distinctive feature of the book is its strongly psychological emphasis. However, it is also clear that work–life balance is an issue that affects both the individual and the organization. To encompass this, there is a mix of chapters, some focusing on individual issues and psychological effects, while others emphasize organizational concerns including organizational culture and policy issues and initiatives being implemented by leading-edge employers. The writers are drawn from the leading researchers in their fields and will reflect the international character of the challenges facing employers and employees. They bring together research findings as well as practical examples from Canada, the USA, Australia, Israel, New Zealand and Europe. The different chapters in the book reflect both the traditional emphasis on work–family balance and the move to the more recent recognition of wider work–life balance and integration issues.

The outline and organization of the book are described below.

The book is divided into four parts. Part I provides the background and context to the book by discussing the changing nature of work and the current legal and administrative context for work. Debra Major and Lisa Germano give an introductory view of the diverse impacts that have changed the nature of work in recent years. This includes discussion of the changing role of women and the impacts of technology in the workplace. In the second chapter, Richard Block, Martin Malin, Ellen Kossek and

Angela Holt focus on the role of legal and employer approaches in work–family issues. They describe and contrast approaches to leave and time off to meet family needs in the USA, Canada and the EU. They further highlight some examples of best practice in these areas. This will be of use to managers and human resources professionals as well as students.

Part II, on researching the work–home interface, provides an introduction to research theories and perspectives. It will therefore be of particular interest to those who want to conduct research in this area in either applied or academic contexts. Nancy Rothbard and Tracy Dumas (Chapter 3) give a historical perspective as well as outlining current theoretical and research perspectives. They introduce key theoretical constructs such as spillover and work–family conflict, which are explored in greater depth in subsequent chapters. These are useful overviews for the student and practitioner new to this area. The chapter also introduces some new and emerging perspectives. These include the potentially positive aspects of multiple roles and people's preferences and strategies for managing work–home boundaries.

This is followed by Lois Tetrick and Louis Buffardi's detailed review of current measures that will be invaluable for the researcher (Chapter 4). They examine both the conceptualization and measurement of important constructs in this area. It includes a review of measures of work–family conflict as well as some newer measures for examining positive effects of work on family and for looking at work–family balance. The chapter includes discussion of relationships between these constructs. The measures have been most frequently used in cross-sectional studies; however, the chapter concludes with a discussion of alternative approaches to assessing work–family behavior, for example, using experiential sampling methodology.

In Part III, current evidence from up-to-date research in this area is reviewed. It contains four chapters and draws on a diverse range of theoretical approaches to this area and highlights benefits as well as negative effects of work. Chapter 5 on role conflict and enhancement by Michael O'Driscoll, Paula Brough and Thomas Kalliath reviews in depth the extensive literature on work–family conflict and the factors that might moderate the relationship between conflict and psychological well-being. However, in his focus on enhancement, O'Driscoll *et al.* also consider more recent literature investigating positive effects, i.e., the notion that experiences and activities in work may enhance home life and vice versa.

Possibly nowhere is the issue of work–family conflict likely to be more apparent than when people work at home, yet this is a form of work often utilized to actually help manage the conflicting demands of home and work. Cath Sullivan and Suzan Lewis get to grips with the complex issues in this research area in Chapter 6. They focus on whether working at home facilitates the management of the work–home interface by increasing flexibility, or whether it may increase spillover and make satisfactory integration of work and home more difficult. They further consider issues surrounding gender and the management of domestic duties and evidence concerning the pros and cons of home-working for family functioning.

In Chapter 7, on crossover and contagion of work stress, Mina Westman discusses the ways in which job demands and strain are transmitted from job incumbents to their partners, affecting their psychological and physical health. Based on the crossover literature and on models of job stress and the work–family interface, Westman develops a comprehensive framework to integrate the literature conceptually, delineating the mechanisms that underlie the crossover process.

In the last chapter in this part, Chapter 8, Fiona Jones, Gail Kinman and Nicola Payne consider the potentially damaging effects of work on health behaviors. While clearly viewed as an occupational health issue by many organizations, this is seldom seen as a work–life integration issue. However, this chapter argues that increased work and home demands and poor work–life balance are likely to detrimentally affect a range of health behaviors including diet, exercise and substance use. On the other hand, if organizations positively support good health behaviors (such as exercise and healthy eating) this may help employees in coping with work demands. Furthermore, the adoption of unhealthy behaviors is a likely mechanism whereby poor work–life balance may lead to impaired physical ill health. Thus it is argued that work–life balance/integration programs need to support healthy lifestyles.

Part IV shifts its emphasis towards topics that suggest practical implications for managing the work–home interface. In the first of these chapters (Chapter 9) Fred Zijlstra and Mark Cropley consider new research looking at how people recover from the strain and fatigue of the working day. They explore to what extent family and domestic demands after work might facilitate or prohibit recovery. Furthermore, they shed light on the role of sleep and of leisure and the kind of activities the individual might use to recover. Finally they address the role organizations could play in promoting recovery.

The role organizations need to play in work–life integration is more exclusively the focus of the final chapters. In Chapter 10, Ron Burke examines the role of organizational culture on the success or otherwise of initiatives to facilitate work–life integration. He draws on research suggesting that work–family policies will not be successful without a culture that supports work–life balance.

In Chapter 11, Leslie Hammer, Jennifer Cullen and Margarita Shafiro use a case study approach to describe specific instances of current good practice in the field. They highlight specific companies that provide a range of different approaches all of which have received some award or recognition for commitment to work– family services. They further highlight the distinction between availability of services and their use, an important issue raised above and in Chapter 10. The kind of information given in this chapter is hard to obtain but likely to be very useful to the student and professional alike.

The last chapter in this part, Chapter 12 by Paulette Gerkovich, presents a radical approach to the need for change in organizations. She argues that too often flexible work arrangements are seen as 'women's issues'. As such they are likely to render women marginal in male-dominated organizations. She suggests that it is necessary to challenge the gendered nature of organizations and argues that work–life policies recognizing the needs of all employees, potentially play a part in this.

Finally, in the conclusion to the book the editors provide a brief summary of some overall themes and issues raised by the book and their implications for practice. It highlights what we still need to do in terms of both addressing the gaps in our knowledge and research and in creating practical and innovative solutions. These are needed so that individuals and organizations can achieve greater work–life integration to make both family and work environments function more effectively.

REFERENCES

Allen, T. D., Herst, D. E. L., Bruck, C. S., and Sutton, M. (2000). Consequences associated with work-to-family conflict: a review and agenda for future research. *Journal of Occupational Health Psychology*, 5, 278–308.

Bailyn, L. (1993). *Breaking the mold*. New York: The Free Press.

Eby, L. T., Casper, W. J., Lockwood, A., Bordeaux, C., and Brinley, A. (2005). Work and family research in IO/OB: content analysis and review of the literature (1980–2002). *Journal of Vocational Behavior*, 66, 124–197.

Frone, M. (2003). Work–family balance. In J. C. Quick and L. E. Tetrick (eds), *Handbook of occupational health psychology* (pp. 143–163). Washington, DC: American Psychological Association.

Hogarth, T., Hasluck, C., Pierre, G., Winterbotham, M., and Vivian, D. (2000). *Work–life balance 2000: Results from the baseline study*. London: Department of Education and Employment.

Jones, F., and Bright, J. (2001). *Stress: Myth, theory and research*. London: Prentice Hall.

Jones, F., and Fletcher, B. C. (2002). Job control, physical health and psychological well-being. In M. J. Shabracq, J. A. Winnubst and C. L. Cooper (eds), *Handbook of work and health psychology* (2nd edn). Chichester: Wiley.

Karasek, R. A., and Theorell, T. (1990). *Healthy work: Stress, productivity and the reconstruction of working life*. New York: Basic Books.

Kodz, J., Davis, S., Lain, D., Sheppard, E., Rick, J., Strebler, M., Bates, P., Cummings, J., Meager, N., Anxo, D., Gineste, S., and Trinczek, R. (2002). Working long hours in the UK: a review of the research literature, analysis of survey data and cross-national organizational case studies (Employment Relations Research Series No.16). Retrieved 26 April 2005 from http://www.dti.gov.uk/er/emar/longhours.htm

Kofodimos, J. (1993). *Balancing act*. San Francisco: Jossey-Bass.

Lewis, S., Rapoport, R., and Gambles, R. (2003). Reflections on the integration of paid work with the rest of life. *Journal of Managerial Psychology*, *18*(8), 824–841.

Marks, S. R., and MacDermid, S. M. (1996). Multiple roles and the self: a theory of role balance. *Journal of Marriage and the Family*, *58*(2), 417–432.

O'Donnell, F. (2004). From city suit to boiler suit. *The Scotsman*, 17 August.

Smith, A., Johal, S., Wadsworth, E., Davey Smith, G., and Peters, T. (2002). *The scale of occupational stress: The Bristol Stress and Health Study*. London: Health and Safety Executive.

Wallis, C. (2004). The case for staying home. *Time*, 22 March.

Williams, K. J., and Alliger, G. M. (1994). Role stressors, mood spillover, and perceptions of work–family conflict in employed parents. *Academy of Management Journal*, *37*, 837–868.

Part I
Background and context

The two opening chapters together set the scene for the rest of the book and provide background information that should be useful to both practitioners and researchers. In Chapter 1, Debra Major and Lisa Germano examine, in detail, the changing nature of work, addressing the wide range of economic, social and demographic factors that have occurred in recent years. They suggest that these have had major impacts on employment relationships and led to increasingly blurred boundaries between home and work for many people. These offer both threats and opportunities in terms of maintaining a satisfactory work–life balance.

The changes in employment relationships, outlined in Chapter 1, are reflected in a wide range of complex legislation, the nature of which varies greatly between countries. Some understanding of these legal issues is needed by those interested in research or practice in this field. While it is not possible to provide in-depth coverage of legislation worldwide, Richard Block, Martin Malin, Ellen Kossek and Angela Holt, in Chapter 2, provide a useful source of reference for practitioners and researchers in the USA and EU. For all readers they provide a summary of the diverse approaches taken to legislation, reflecting the differing cultural values in different parts of the world.

1 The changing nature of work and its impact on the work–home interface

Debra A. Major and Lisa M. Germano

The changing nature of work is widely discussed among organizational scholars and in the popular media. In this chapter, we focus on the changes that are especially likely to affect the work–home interface. The chapter is divided into four sections. In the first, we discuss changes in workforce demographics, including the participation of women in the labor force, working mothers and rising eldercare responsibilities. In the second section, factors influencing the changing nature of work are examined, including globalization, the rise of the service industry and advances in information technology. In the third section, we consider major changes in the nature of employment relationships. Finally, we conclude with a discussion linking changes in the nature of work to blurred work–family boundaries and highly individualized work–life management strategies.

CHANGES IN WORKFORCE DEMOGRAPHICS

Women's increasing labor force participation

In industrialized nations around the world, women's labor force participation has increased steadily over the last century. Women now constitute the majority of the American workforce (Fitzgerald and Harmon, 2001) and nearly half the workforce in New Zealand and the UK (Statistics New Zealand, 2001b; National Statistical Coordination Board, 2002). In the USA, the overall participation rate of women reached 60% in 2000 (Toossi, 2002). Canadian women's labor force participation reached a record level of 61.2% in 2003 (Statistics Canada, 2004). In Australia, 64% of women aged 15–64 years were employed in 1999 (Commonwealth Office of the Status of Women, 2001). In Israel, women's labor force participation has risen steadily to 44% in 1998 (Israel Central Bureau of Statistics, 2000).

One influence on women's increased labor force participation is the rising education levels of women in many countries. In Israel, for example, the rate of schooling for Jewish women caught up with that of Jewish men in the 1990s. Between 1988 and 1998, the median years of schooling increased

37% for non-Jewish women but only 16% for men (Israel Central Bureau of Statistics, 2000). In the USA, statistics from the 2002 *National Study of the Changing Workforce* (*NSCW*), a project based on interviews with 3052 employees representing a cross-section of the American workforce, show that from 1977 to 2002 women's educational attainment increased more rapidly than men's. In 2002, 31% of women compared to 27% of men had completed four years or more at college (Bond et al., 2002).

In addition to women's rising education levels, the expansion of jobs in traditionally female-dominated fields, including social work, nursing, education, retail trade and personal services, has contributed to women's increased labor force participation in the USA (Appelbaum, 2003). Health and community services and education are the predominant industries of paid employment for women in New Zealand (Statistics New Zealand, 2001b). In Israel, women are more likely than men to work in education and health, welfare and social-work services (Israel Central Bureau of Statistics, 2000). Similarly, in 1999, Australian women held 78% of all health and community services jobs and 67.2% of all jobs in education (Commonwealth Office of the Status of Women, 2001). The highest representation of Canadian women continues to be in clerical personnel (66.7%) and intermediate sales and service personnel (65.3%; Human Resources Development Canada, 2001). In the UK in 2001, a quarter of the female employees held jobs doing administrative or secretarial work (National Statistical Coordination Board, 2002).

Women in managerial positions

Despite other advancements (e.g., educational attainment), women are still less likely to hold managerial positions than men. At the beginning of the 1990s, the number of women at the senior management level of top US corporations had increased less then 2%. White men held 95% of all top managerial positions. Likewise, in the federal government, women held only 6.4% of executive manager positions (Gutek, 1993). More recent findings reveal that the situation has not improved dramatically. While American women (38%) were more likely to work in managerial or professional occupations than men (28%) in 2002, men (42%) were still more likely than women (33%) to supervise other employees as a major part of their jobs (Bond *et al.*, 2002).

The underrepresentation of women in management is not unique to the USA. Canadian statistics indicate that in 2000 only 10.8% of employed women held a management position, and only 19.1% of senior-level managers were women (Human Resources Development Canada, 2001). In New Zealand, only 11% of women in paid employment work as legislators, administrators and managers, compared to 15% of the men. Compared to women in 2001, men in the UK were most likely to be managers, senior officials or work in skilled trades (National Statistical Coordination Board,

2002). Australian statistics reveal that in 1999 only 3.6% of employed women held positions as managers and administrators, compared to 9.5% of employed men (Commonwealth Office of the Status of Women, 2001). In Israel, only 22% of the country's managers are women, and of that number only 8% are CEOs or directors-general. In contrast, 33% of male managers are CEOs/directors-general (Israel Central Bureau of Statistics, 2000).

Part-time employment

In considering women's increased labor force participation, it is important to note that women work part time more often than men. This trend is evident across the globe. In the USA, 19% of women work part time, while only 8% of men work part time. In Canada, 27% of women work part time, while 10% of men work part time (United Nations Statistics Division, 2000). In Israel, twice as many women as men engage in part-time labor (Israel Central Bureau of Statistics, 2000). In Australia, 44% of women work part time compared to only 12% of men (Commonwealth Office of the Status of Women, 2001). In 2001, 36% of women worked part time while only 12% of men worked part time in New Zealand (Statistics New Zealand, 2001b). In 2001, almost half of the jobs held by women in the UK were part time (National Statistical Coordination Board, 2002).

Women with children in the labor force

In most industrialized nations, women with young children are remaining in the workforce and re-entering the workforce soon after childbirth. The labor force participation rate of mothers in the USA with non-adult children was 71.8% in 2002 (US Department of Labor, Bureau of Labor Statistics, 2003). For women with children younger than six, workforce participation rates increased from 39% to 64.9% between 1976 and 2000. For those women with infants, the increase was from 31% to 55.2% over the same time period (Bachu and O'Connell, 2001). In 2002, 49.2% of women in Australia with children younger than five remained in the workforce (Australian Bureau of Statistics, 2003a). For both New Zealand and the UK, the age of a woman's youngest child is a critical factor in determining her participation in the workforce. In 1996, women in New Zealand whose youngest child was less than a year old had a workforce participation rate of 36.5%. However, their workforce participation rate more than doubled (78.1%) when their youngest child was between the ages of 13 and 17 (Statistics New Zealand, 1996). In the UK, 55% of women with children younger than five remained in the workforce in 2003. However, workforce participation rates increased to 73% when the youngest child was between the ages of five and 10 and further increased to 80% when the youngest child was between 10 and 15 years old (National Statistics Online, 2004).

Whether a cause or a consequence of women's increased participation in the labor force, it appears that perceptions regarding mothers' employment are also changing. In Britain, Germany and the USA, the proportion of people who believe that women's employment has negative effects on family and children has declined (Scott *et al.*, 1996). Men's attitudes, in particular, are changing as illustrated in the 2002 *NSCW* report. In 1977, 74% of men felt that men should support the family financially and that women should stay at home taking care of the children and the housework. In 2002, only 42% of the men supported this view.

Of course, perceptions of working mothers are culturally influenced. Treas and Widmer (2000) examined attitudes toward married women's employment across countries and classified them into three major groups. Work-oriented countries such as Canada, Germany (East), Israel, the Netherlands, Norway, Sweden, and the USA are least likely to recommend that married women stay home, even when they have a preschooler. The family accommodating countries, including Australia, Austria, Germany (West), Great Britain, Italy, Japan, New Zealand, Northern Ireland and Russia, place less emphasis on married women's labor force participation and are likely to support part-time rather than full-time employment even once children are grown. Finally, motherhood-centered countries like Bulgaria, the Czech Republic, Hungary, Ireland, Poland, Slovenia and Spain support full-time work before children are born and after they are grown. These countries prefer that women with preschool children stay at home. It is notable that in most industrialized nations there is at least some acceptance of mothers participating in the labor force. Attitudes across countries appear to support full-time employment prior to childbirth and support at least part-time work after children are grown.

Motherhood, in contrast to fatherhood, seems to have some bearing on the position one assumes in the labor force (Friedman and Greenhaus, 2000). For instance, in a sample of government relations managers in the USA, a significantly higher proportion of the women than men reported having no children (Scott, 2001). Further, among those with children, women were more likely than men to have only one child. Compared to their male coworkers, women devoted three times as much time to child-care. In the UK, women without children are more likely than women with children to hold managerial or administrative positions (Wheelock and McCarthy, 1997). Research shows that the majority of professional women do marry and have children, however these events occur later in life than for women working in nonprofessional positions (Fitzgerald and Harmon, 2001). In the USA, some expect to see an increase in managerial and professional women who drop out of the labor force for extended periods of time (i.e., five years or more), then return to work (Wallis, 2004). Many professional women are finding that the demands of their high-profile positions cannot easily be scaled back to accommodate family. Thus, it is not purely a desire to raise children that may drive more professional women out of the workforce. Instead, long work hours and constraints of the work environment may push women to choose between work and family. When unable to achieve the work–family balance they desire, women whose circumstances give them a choice about working (e.g., a spouse earning an adequate income for the family) may be increasingly likely to quit.

Men and women with eldercare responsibilities

Declining birth and fertility rates coupled with increasing life expectancies have created a rapidly growing global elderly population. For most developed countries, life expectancy ranges from 76 to 80 years (Kinsella, 2000). This increases the likelihood that more and more employees will have living parents and young children that require care simultaneously. Like childcare, the majority of caregiving to the elderly is informal and the responsibility of women relatives (Johnson and Climo, 2000).

Employees with eldercare responsibilities are more likely to report difficulties in balancing work and home responsibilities than those with no eldercare commitments (Neal *et al.*, 1990). Eldercare responsibilities often lead to interruptions at work, partial absences and having to change work schedules (Barling *et al.*, 1994). In the 2002 *NSCW*, 35% of those interviewed said that they provided eldercare to someone in their family who was 65 years or older. Of this 35%, 36% indicated that providing care took time away from work (Bond *et al.*, 2002). Furthermore, eldercare responsibilities have the potential to be more stressful than childcare responsibilities as they are sometimes unexpected and often intensify as time goes on (Barling *et al.*, 1994).

FACTORS INFLUENCING THE CHANGING NATURE OF WORK

Although the rapidity of change is one of the hallmarks of work today, the major influences on the changing nature of work have been operating for some time. For more than a decade, globalization has been redefining what it takes for organizations to be viable and competitive in the market-place. The service industry has been growing since the 1970s, resulting in the self-perpetuating, 24/7, service-on-demand model we see today. Technological advancements have impacted how, when and where work gets done, while also making it easier to stay in touch with friends and family. Each of these major influences on the changing nature of work is discussed in more detail below.

Globalization

Organizational theorists argue that global competition is a driving force behind current business strategies aimed at reducing costs in order to be successful in the world market. Businesses strive to be lean, focused and responsive. Organizations attempting to be flexible in order to respond quickly to changing market conditions expect their employees to be likewise adaptable (Hall and Moss, 1998). In some respects, employees now work in an environment characterized by a permanent state of flux (Sparrow, 2000).

The business strategies many companies have pursued to become globally competitive have resulted in the centralization of infrastructural business components (e.g., administration, human resources), a consolidation around core businesses, delayering (i.e., a reduction in the number of organizational levels), outsourcing and offshoring, downsizing and understaffing (Dunford, 1999; Sparrow, 2000). In turn, employees of these companies and their families face fear of job loss and unemployment, low wages, increased work hours, more demanding workloads and a diminishing sense of control over work (Grosswald *et al.*, 2001; Sparks *et al.*, 2001). In the USA, the percentage of the workforce with long-tenure jobs (i.e., those of 10 years or more) declined slightly from the late 1970s to 1993, and then fell sharply to its lowest level in 20 years of comparable data by 1999 (Cappelli, 1999). Today's employees find that their loss of job security is coupled with greater pressure for flexibility.

Organizational restructuring had a substantial impact on middle managers who found themselves unemployed as the result of downsizing and delayering (Dunford, 1999). In some respects, middle managers became symbolic of the 'fat' businesses were striving to cut. For those who lost their jobs as well as the survivors of the cuts, one of the most psychologically difficult aspects of this process was the fact that being laid off or fired had little to do with performance (Hall and Moss, 1998).

Rise of the service industry

Since the 1970s, most job growth in the USA has been in the service sector. This trend is expected to continue as non-household service-producing jobs are projected to increase by 17.6 million between 1996 and 2006 (US Department of Labor, 1999). One force contributing to this trend has been the shift from work done in the home by family members to work done in the market. American workers are increasingly buying time-saving products (i.e., fast food) and 'contracting out' household work (i.e., housekeeping, gardening, live-in childcare) that they used to do themselves (US Department of Labor, 1999).

Competition can be fierce in the burgeoning service sector (Patterson, 2001; Schaaf, 1995). When your business is providing a service, competitive advantage is gained through developing high-quality relationships with your customers. This entails being acutely focused on customers' needs and expectations and ensuring that they are met in a timely and satisfactory way (Patterson, 2001; Schneider and Bowen, 1995). In an effort to meet the needs and expectations of more customers, businesses are offering their services through multiple channels. The customer now has the option of shopping online, through mail-order catalogs, over the telephone or in brick-and-mortar stores. Smart retailers collect information about their customers' tastes and purchase histories. Learning how their customers behave across all channels facilitates the development of long-term relationships and enhances the customer's experience (Spector, 2002).

In concert with technological advancements, which are described in the next section, the demands of the service industry have resulted in the increasing need for a 24/7 workforce (i.e., staffing 24 hours a day, seven days a week). For example, the Internet provides its users with access to services around the world. The Internet is not restricted by traditional business hours or time zones. Therefore, in order to remain competitive in a global market-place, a business's website needs constant customer service support (Spector, 2002).

The 24/7 economy also means that people work non-standard business hours, creating a greater need for services to be available at a wider variety of times. Some services have become automated, such as banking automatic teller machines (ATMs) and vending machines for various supplies (e.g., postage stamps). Automated services benefit the customer because they are always uniform and provide 24-hour uninterrupted service, with no breaks or shift changes. While automated services free humans from boring and unpleasant work (Gutek and Welsh, 2000), not all services lend themselves to automation. Twenty-four-hour grocery stores, pharmacies, convenience stores and mail services must be staffed. Consequently, a 'vicious circle' is created. Global competition and technological advancement demand that employees be more flexible and work non-standard business hours. In turn, these employees now expect service providers to reciprocate and offer their services during extended hours, requiring them to hire employees to work non-standard business hours.

Technological advancements

Computers, cellular phones, pagers, videoconferencing and other advances in information technology have contributed to the capacity for some work to be performed 24/7 from virtually anywhere (Kalleberg and Epstein, 2001). Computers are simply endemic to business today. The Current Population Survey (CPS) in the USA in September of 2001 included a supplement on computer use. Results of the CPS revealed that 72.3 million people (53.5% of the total employed population) used a computer at work (US Department of Labor, Bureau of Labor Statistics, 2002a). Canadian data show that in 2001 81% of all private sector businesses used computers (Peterson, 2001).

Similarly, statistics from Australia indicate that 84% of all businesses utilized computers in 2002 (Australian Bureau of Statistics, 2002). In New Zealand, 99% of large businesses (i.e., 50 or more full-time employees) and 86% of firms with fewer than 20 full-time employees regularly use computers in the conduct of business (Statistics New Zealand, 2002).

Not only are these technologies pervasive in the workplace, but they are also common in the home. In their review of the impact of computers and the Internet on the family, Hughes and Hans (2001) reported that 51% of all US households had a computer and 42% had Internet access, based on US Department of Commerce data from 2000. Statistics from other western countries are similar. For instance, New Zealand's 2001 Household Economic Survey showed that 47% of households had a home computer, and according to New Zealand's 2001 Census 37% had access to the Internet (Statistics New Zealand, 2001a, 2001c).

Results of the 2002 *NSCW* show substantial technology use in the workplace and at home (Bond *et al.*, 2002). In the overall sample, 57% reported using a computer for personal things several times per week. Of managers and professionals in the sample, 62% use a computer at home for job-related work and 39% use a computer at home for reading and sending work-related e-mail outside of regular work hours.

Heavy reliance on other communication technologies, such as cellular phones and pagers, is also notable. In New Zealand, for instance, 58% of households had at least one mobile phone in 2001 (Statistics New Zealand, 2001c). Along with computers, these communication technologies also appear to increase employers' access to their employees outside of the workplace. In the *NSCW* interviews, 32% of employees indicated that they are regularly contacted outside of work hours about work matters. The frequency of contact seems to be particularly high among managers and professionals. Of the managers and professionals in the sample, 28% indicated that they were contacted *several times* per week about work-related matters outside normal work hours, compared to only 13% of other employees (Bond *et al.*, 2002).

THE CHANGING NATURE OF EMPLOYMENT RELATIONSHIPS

Employee–employer relationships of this decade have been described as a 'paradoxical combination of high hopes and declining trust' (Mir *et al.*, 2002, p. 188). While downsizing has created an atmosphere of wariness in which employees no longer necessarily expect job security, employees nonetheless have high expectations regarding equitable treatment, access to training and development, feedback for growth and development, proper resources and tools to perform their work and appropriate rewards for their performance. We anticipate that this is a trend that will continue. Current and future arrivals into the workforce who saw their parents betrayed in the 1980s and 1990s are likely to be more demanding of employers and less willing to sacrifice work–life balance than employees of their parents' generation (Loughlin and Barling, 2001). Though it is common for the changing nature of work to be described in terms of its negative effects on employees, some have characterized it as an opportunity for a 'new covenant' of shared responsibility between employers and employees, under which opportunities for creativity, challenge, maturity and freedom flourish in work organizations (Dunford, 1999). Flexible and family-friendly organizations have the potential to be a positive influence on the work–family interface.

The new psychological contract

A great deal has been written about the changing psychological contract between employees and employers (e.g., Cavanaugh and Noe, 1999; Hall, 1996; Hall and Moss, 1998; Rousseau and Schalk, 2000; Schalk and Rousseau, 2001; Sparrow, 2000). The rise in global competition and advances in information technology are considered to be two of the major forces behind the new contract (Schalk and Rousseau, 2001). In order to determine what may have changed, it is important to understand the basis for comparison. The 'old' psychological contract was characterized by the paternalism of employers toward their employees (Cavanaugh and Noe, 1999). Under the traditional arrangement, which is essentially non-existent today, employers offered a lifetime career in a single organization in exchange for continued loyal service (Hall and Mirvis, 1995, 1996; Sparrow, 2000). Some have argued that the old contract is more mythical than real. Hall and his colleagues (Hall and Mirvis, 1996; Hall and Moss, 1998) contend that lifetime employment was never the norm in the USA or elsewhere. Regardless, there is substantial agreement that today's psychological contract is characterized by a recognition that the employee and employer share responsibility for maintaining the relationship for as long as it is mutually beneficial (Altman and Post, 1996; Sparrow, 2000). Both the employer and the employee are invested in maintaining the employee's employability inside and outside the organization (Dunford, 1999).

When the new psychological contract is operationalized well, it satisfies the needs of both employers and employees. Businesses have the skilled adaptable workforce they need to be competitive, and employees have the developmental experiences they need to maintain their marketability. Some have argued that the new psychological contract has created a crisis of commitment (see Dunford, 1999), but loyalty is still possible under the new contract. Instead of being based on more traditional factors, such as length of service, loyalty stems from development and performance (Hall and Moss, 1998). Some employers fail to recognize the nature of the exchange (i.e., development opportunities and flexibility in exchange for performance and adaptability) and assume that individual employees are to be completely responsible for their own career development. Employers unwilling to bear any of the responsibility for employees' professional development are likely to find themselves in violation of the psychological contract.

Research shows that high levels of psychological contract violations have a number of potentially negative repercussions, including increased likelihood of exit, voice, and neglect behaviors and decreased demonstrations of loyalty. Exit behaviors include actively searching for a new job or quitting. Voice behaviors frequently involve direct appeals to higher authorities in an effort to repair the employment relationship. Lateness, conducting personal business at work and wasting time at work are examples of neglect behaviors (Turnley and Feldman, 1999). In their study involving a sample of 800 managers, Turnley and Feldman found that employees were especially likely to look for another job in response to high levels of contract violation when procedural justice was perceived to be low, when justification for violations was insufficient and other job alternatives were available. Other research has demonstrated that met expectations positively influence organizational commitment and intentions to remain in the organization (Flood *et al.*, 2001). In their study of high-technology workers, Flood *et al.* found that perceived equity and meritocracy were both positively associated with met expectations.

Interestingly, research suggests that what employees have come to expect is shaped by their work experiences. Cavanaugh and Noe (1999) found that having experienced involuntary job loss, downsizing and organizational restructuring were associated with having beliefs congruent with the new psychological contract (e.g., personal responsibility for career development, expectation of job insecurity, commitment to type of work over specific employer). Moreover, these beliefs mediated the relationship between work experiences and intentions to remain with the current employer and job satisfaction. Similarly, Edwards *et al.* (2003) found that greater belief in employee self-reliance reduced the degree to which lay-offs were seen as a breach of the psychological contract.

Schalk and Rousseau (2001) note a push for more explicit communication between employers and employees regarding the specifics of today's psychological contract. They argue that greater *transparency* in psychological contracts has become more accepted and valued because (1) there is a realization that reading and relying on subtle cues in culturally heterogeneous societies is difficult, (2) contracts are likely to be of shorter duration and (3) contracts increasingly cross cultural boundaries.

Family-friendly benefits

There are a variety of perspectives regarding the true goals of family-friendly policies and practices. Perhaps the most cynical view is that the purpose of most family-friendly programs is to accommodate business needs and that such policies do not, in fact, help employees find work–life balance but instead ensure that employees are able to adjust their family lives in order to meet work demands and to be available to work longer hours (Grosswald *et al.*, 2001; Lambert, 1993). In support of this view, research has shown that the extent to which family life interferes with work is the most consistent predictor of parents' importance ratings regarding six different family-friendly programs, while work interference with family fails to significantly predict importance ratings (Frone and Yardley, 1996). A more moderate view holds that family-friendly programs are mutually beneficial to employers and employees. Employees benefit from programs that increase flexibility and support home life. Employers profit because offering desirable benefits enhances their efforts to recruit, retain and motivate valued employees and, in addition, serves as a valuable public relations tool (Nord *et al.*, 2002). In either case, it seems clear that the changing nature of work has had an impact on family-friendly organizational policies.

The 2002 *NSCW* data show gains in the family-friendliness of US organizations since 1992 (Bond *et al.*, 2002). For example, the percentage of respondents indicating that there are unwritten rules indicating you should not take care of family needs on company time has declined from 36% to 32%. The percentage of respondents indicating that supervisors are fair in responding to work–family needs has increased from 78.5% to 82%. In addition, more employees now feel comfortable bringing up personal or family issues at work, 73% up from 63%. Analyses also show that when the workplace culture and supervisors are supportive of work–family needs, employees are significantly more satisfied with their jobs, more committed to the organization and more likely to plan to remain with the employer. In addition, employees also experience less work–family conflict, report less negative spillover from work to home, have better mental health and are more satisfied with their lives. These findings are consistent with previous research indicating that family-supportive policies are associated with reduced work–family conflict, enhanced organizational commitment, increased job satisfaction and other positive outcomes (Allen, 2001; Lambert, 2000; Thomas and Ganster, 1995; Thompson *et al.*, 1999) and that the association depends on a workplace culture and supervisors that support the programs and encourage employees to utilize them (Allen, 2001; Thompson *et al.*, 1999).

In terms of specific programs offered, some things have changed and others have not. For instance, the *NSCW* results show that the percentage of employers offering onsite childcare in 2002 is the same as 1992: about 10%. On the other hand, the percentage of employers offering some type of eldercare benefits has more than doubled in a decade, rising from 11% to 24% (Bond *et al.*, 2002). It is important to keep in mind that the existence of work–life programs does not guarantee use. One reason for this disconnect is that employees are often unaware that certain programs exist, and that they are eligible to use them. For example, in *The Cornell Couples and Career Study*, 71% of the sample was either unaware or mistaken about at least one work–life practice or policy (Still and Strang, 2003). Supervisor support is another key determinant of the disconnect between benefit availability and use. As Nord *et al.* (2002) concluded based on their study of work–family program implementation, 'In subtle and not-so-subtle ways, immediate supervisors often communicate the "real" outcomes of taking part in WLB [work–life balance] programs, particularly when participation was inconsistent with deeply held cultural beliefs of the organization' (p. 229).

Finally, although the changing nature of work has certainly influenced family-friendly program availability, a great deal of variation can be attributed to cross-national differences. The USA has the distinction of providing the least support to working parents. For example, according to a 1998 United Nations study, the USA was one of only six countries out of 152 surveyed that did not, and still does not, have paid maternity leave (Olson, 1998). The Family and Medical Leave Act of 1993 provides eligible employees with up to 12 weeks of unpaid job-protected leave in a 12-month period to care for newborn or adopted children, relatives with medical conditions and their own health problems (Ruhm, 1997; for further details also see Chapter 2). Although the UK is often criticized along with the USA for not doing more to support working parents, recent government reforms suggest progress. Effective April 2003, the Maternity and Parental Leave (Amendment) Regulations 2002 extended the maternity pay period from 18 to 26 weeks and increased the standard rate of statutory maternity pay (SMP). Women also may opt to take an additional 26 weeks of unpaid leave. Fathers are allowed two weeks of statutory paternity pay following the birth or adoption of a child at the same rate as SMP (Department of Trade and Industry, 2003). However, in Scandinavia parental leave is substantially more generous (see Hayden, 2003). For instance, in Sweden parents can take up to 15 months of job-protected leave per child at up to 80% of their previous pay. The leave can be taken flexibly, at any time, until the child reaches 8 years of age. In Norway, parents can take 42 weeks of leave at 100% of their previous wage or 52 weeks at 80%. (For further discussion of legal entitlement in the USA, UK and Europe see Chapter 2.)

Flexible working arrangements

While globalization and the rise of the service industry have created a business need for flexible work schedules, advances in information and communication technologies have made them possible. The increase in alternate work schedules is largely attributable to the aftermath of organizational downsizing and restructuring and to the desire on the part of employers to have greater flexibility in controlling labor costs (Armstrong-Stassen, 1998). Under ideal circumstances, alternate work schedules have

Table 1.1 Schedule flexibility statistics from the 2002
         NSCW (Bond *et al.*, 2002)

Frequency	Control over work schedule	
	Start time	*Quit time*
Occasionally	29%	43%
Daily	18%	23%
Complete schedule control	30%	36%

the potential to give employees more control over their schedules and greater flexibility to manage work and family life. However, when the scheduling is involuntary and the worker does not have a choice regarding the time and the days worked, working a non-standard shift can add to the imbalance of work–life demands (Tausig and Fenwick, 2001).

Using data from the May 1997 Supplement to the Current US Population Survey (CPS), Golden (2001) determined that more than 27% of the US workforce is able to alter work start and end times. In addition, 47.9% of managers in the CPS reported having flexible schedules. The report of the most recent *NSCW* data does not single out managers but does provide additional detail regarding the frequency and types of flexibility found in the US labor force. Statistics are summarized in Table 1.1.

Some research suggests that flexible work schedules are most important to women and those with children. In their sample of managers, Scandura and Lankau (1997) found that women who reported that their employers offered flexible work hours had greater job satisfaction and organizational commitment than women who said their employers did not offer flexibility. A similar pattern of results was found for managers with children under the age of 18. Both sets of results applied regardless of whether or not the managers actually used the benefit. For men, there were no differences in satisfaction or commitment based on the availability of flexible hours.

Unfortunately, research shows that there is considerable disparity regarding who has access to flexibility. For instance, Golden's (2001) analysis of data from the May 1997 Supplement to the CPS showed that the odds of having flexibility are greatly increased for those who are self-employed, in college, married, working part time or working more than 50 hours per week. Analyses also demonstrate that flexibility is significantly less likely for women, non-whites and the less educated. There is substantial agreement in the literature that, although many organizations offer flexible scheduling, most employ arbitrary strategies for determining who is able to take advantage of the flexibility. This lack of a systematic process creates inequities and fails to provide the majority of employees with their preferred schedule (Armstrong-Stassen, 1998; Nord *et al.*, 2002; Valcour and Batt, 2003). It seems that human resource policies have not kept pace with the demand for flexibility, not only in terms of determining individual schedules, but also in terms of training, evaluating and compensating those working alternate schedules (Nord *et al.*, 2002). In addition, many employees engage in a trade-off between working long hours and flexibility (Golden, 2001). The *NSCW* data show that average weekly work hours have increased from 70 to 82 hours for dual-earner couples over the past 25 years (Bond *et al.*, 2002). Other estimates show a steady increase since the early 1970s in the number of hours Americans work annually, specifically 1878 hours in 2000, up from 1679 hours in 1973 (Schor, 2003). In the USA both men and women work more hours than in the past. If work schedule flexibility is coupled with a high number of required work hours and a demanding workload, then flexibility is unlikely to contribute to greater work–family balance.

Working longer hours is no longer a trend in other countries. In Australia between 1982 and 1994, the average number of hours worked by full-time employees increased from 42 to 45 hours per week. However, this trend leveled off in the late 1990s and since 2000 has dropped to approximately 44 hours per week (Australian Bureau of Statistics, 2003b). A similar pattern is evident in New Zealand; the average number of hours worked per week slowly increased in the early 1990s, peaked in 1995 and has since decreased gradually (Statistics New Zealand, 2001d). In the UK the number of people working over 45 hours per week rose steadily from 1992 until it peaked in 1997. Since 1997, the average number of hours worked per week declined until 1999, leveled off through 2001 and then declined into 2003 (National Statistics Online, 2003).

RAMIFICATIONS FOR THE WORK–FAMILY INTERFACE

Globalization, the expansion of the service industry and advances in technology have contributed to the changing nature of work, resulting in new relationships between employees and their employers. These macro- and more micro-level changes have implications for the work–family interface, in particular greater boundary permeability between the two domains and more individualized work–life management strategies. Each is discussed in detail below.

Blurred work and family boundaries

Many of the repercussions from the changing nature of work have resulted in greater permeability of work into the family domain. Telework is an excellent example of the manner in which advances in communication technologies have impacted how, where and when work gets done, infiltrating space and time more typically reserved for family and personal life. Alternate work schedules and advancements in information technology create tensions between greater flexibility and continuous accessibility. In other words, having the means to work 24/7 can be accompanied by pressure to do so. Yet, the same technological tools that enable work can also be used to facilitate family life.

Telework

The terms telework and telecommuting tend to be used broadly to refer to working outside of the traditional office through the use of one or more communication technologies (Nilles, 1998). Sparrow (2000) reports that at the beginning of this century, between 10% and 30% of large organizations in the USA, Canada, northern Europe and Australia used telework as an employment arrangement. Harpaz (2002) indicates that the USA has the greatest percentage of teleworkers in its labor force (i.e., more than 25%), followed by Finland with approximately 17%, Sweden at about 15%, the Netherlands at about 14%, Denmark with just over 10%, the UK with around 7%, and Germany with about 6%. In Spain, Italy, Ireland and France, less than 5% of the labor force telecommutes.

In 2001, 19.8 million Americans reported that they did some work at home as part of their primary jobs. Half of these workers were employed in managerial and professional occupations, while one in five worked in sales occupations (US Department of Labor, Bureau of Labor Statistics, 2002b). Similarly, among occasional teleworkers in the UK, 91% fall into three occupational groups: managers (37%), professionals (37%), and associate professional and technical occupations (17%; HOP Associates, 2002). While equal numbers of men and women are teleworking in the USA (US Department of Labor, Bureau of Labor Statistics, 2002b), 67% of the teleworkers in the UK are men. The gender difference in the UK is related to the jobs that teleworkers hold. Jobs that are more conducive to tele-working (e.g., managers, professionals and information technology work-ers) are predominantly occupied by men (HOP Associates, 2002).

For both organizations and individuals, a consistent set of potential telework advantages are discussed in the literature. From the organiza-tional perspective, the potential advantages include increased productivity, increased human resources, decreased absenteeism and tardiness, savings in direct expenses, increased motivation and satisfaction, and creation of a positive organizational image (Harpaz, 2002; Sparrow, 2000). Potential advantages to the employee include flexibility, autonomy and independence, control over time, savings in travel time and commuting expenses, oppor-tunity to work with fewer distractions and greater availability to family (Harpaz, 2002; Kurland and Bailey, 1999). In a survey of 9000 employees of a large multinational corporation, US employees reported numerous bene-fits associated with telework (Sparrow, 2000). Of those employees engaged in telework, 75% felt that it had a positive impact on their productivity, 60% reported an improved ability to concentrate, 66% reported a positive effect on morale and 48% indicated a heightened commitment to their employer.

Notably, the largest percentage, 80%, agreed that telework had improved their work–life balance.

Potential disadvantages of telework are also discussed in the literature. Teleworking employees may experience social isolation, lack of professional support and visibility, impeded career advancement, difficulty in separating work and family, and over-availability (Cooper and Kurland, 2002; Grosswald *et al.*, 2001; Harpaz, 2002; Hughes and Hans, 2001). Organizations may find that their teleworking employees feel less committed, that it is difficult to create team synergy and that non-teleworkers are resentful (Kurland and Bailey, 1999; Nord *et al.*, 2002). The extent to which either these disadvantages or the aforementioned advantages are realized probably depends a great deal on the frequency of telework (Bailey and Kurland, 2002; Harpaz, 2002; Kurland and Bailey, 1999). For instance, professional and social isolation are unlikely when telework is relatively infrequent but more likely when an employee is engaged in telework full time. Kurland and Bailey (1999) argue that a key advantage of occasional telework is that it may provide employees with a distraction-free environment away from phones, co-workers and office demands. The need for freedom from distractions is apparently great. According to the 2002 *NSCW* report, 43% of the sample said that frequent interruptions during the work day make it difficult to get work done (Bond *et al.*, 2002). However, home may not provide a distraction-free environment when it is a full-time workplace. For full-time teleworkers, there is less opportunity to separate work and personal life, as well as the potential for friends, relatives and neighbors to equate being home with being available. (For further discussion of the evidence relating to teleworking, see Chapter 6.)

Like other types of alternate and flexible working arrangements, organizations currently appear to lack clear policies and procedures for implementing telework (Kurland and Bailey, 1999). Access to telework, its frequency and the conditions under which it occurs are often negotiated between employees and their supervisors. Thus, telework accessibility and arrangements can vary a great deal even within the same work environment. For the individual employee, creating desirable telework arrangements may hinge on the quality of the relationship with the supervisor and his or her own negotiation skills.

Is there time for anything other than work?

While it is clear that the changing nature of work has blurred the boundaries between work and family life, it is less clear whether the effects are positive or negative from a family perspective. For instance, although the 80% of teleworkers in Sparrow's (2000) sample indicated that the practice improved work–life balance, only 33% felt they were involved in their children's educations, 40% indicated that they had difficulty managing work–life, 50% reported feeling drained at the end of the day and 62% said they simply had too much work to do. Data from the 2002 *NSCW* tell a similar story (Bond *et al.*, 2002). In that sample, 35% indicated that they are overwhelmed by the amount of work they have to do, and 45% reported that they experience some or a lot of work interference with family (an increase from the 34% reporting the same levels in 1977), despite increased flexibility.

A recent review of the occupational health literature concludes that choice regarding work hours is a key factor in promoting well-being (Sparks *et al.*, 2001). Yet, there is evidence of large disparities between how much people would like to work and how much they actually do work. The *Cornell Couples and Career Study* shows that across every life stage at least 75% of men and women are working more hours than they would like (Clarkberg and Merola, 2003). Moreover, the gap between actual and preferred work hours is substantial with a median from 9 to 15 hours too much per week across all groups. These data suggest that alternate work schedules and greater flexibility have not been coupled with the reduction in work hours that most people desire. Several studies suggest that overwork is particularly high among well-educated professionals and managers (e.g., Clarkberg and Merola, 2003; Clarkberg and Moen, 2001; Jacobs and Gerson, 1998) and that this group is also most likely to experience negative spillover from work to family (Grzywacz *et al.*, 2002).

Work–family researchers posit that assumptions about how work must be structured, organizational demands and lack of negotiation account for rising time pressures experienced by employees. According to one participant in Nord *et al.*'s (2002) study, 'It seems that the general perception is that working exorbitant hours is a good thing. Our director makes comments about working 20-h days, and it gives the impression that if you are not working that many hours, there is something wrong with you. Lack of efficiency is rewarded more often than efficiency in working' (p. 229). Clarkberg and Moen (2001) contend that employer demands and institutionalized features of the work environment have conspired to create work in pre-packaged units where 0 and 40+ are the most common options. In interviews with their sample, Clarkberg and Merola (2003) discovered that most professionals never imagined that they might be able to negotiate a different work arrangement than they currently had. They seemed to perceive that excessive hours were simply an inherent part of the job.

Of course, work hours are influenced by societal factors as well as organizational norms. Differences in national economic and political conditions create large cross-cultural disparities in work time. For instance, in the Netherlands, Norway, France and Germany there is a strong commitment to work-time reduction. From 1979 to 2000, these countries have experienced work-time reductions of 10% or more (Hayden, 2003). Compared to the USA, work hours have also fallen in South Korea and Japan. Several countries, including France, Denmark, Norway and Belgium, have reduced the standard workweek to below 40 hours per week (Hayden,

2003). Consistent efforts to reduce the workweek are also underway in Portugal, Greece and Spain (Hayden, 2003). Work-time reduction has failed to gain political support in the USA (Fagan, 2001). American employees have the distinction of being 'world leaders' in hours worked (Hayden, 2003; Olson, 1999).

The situation is similar when it comes to vacation and leisure time. European Union Working Time Directives require a minimum of four weeks paid leave for all employees each year and some European countries require five weeks by law (Hayden, 2003). In large multinational corporations, it is not uncommon to find that American employees are getting one or two weeks of vacation time while their counterparts doing the exact same jobs in Europe and Australia receive a minimum of four to six weeks (Robinson, 2003).

Technology's influence on family life

It is perhaps ironic that the same technology that makes it possible for people to work longer hours also facilitates personal and family life. According to the 2000 US Department of Commerce statistics reported by Hughes and Hans (2001), among those who have a computer in the home, 96.6% of women and 93.6% of men employ it to communicate with friends and family. Other technologies are used similarly. The *NSCW* data show that 70% of all employees sometimes use a cellular phone or pager to keep in touch with friends and family, and 43% do so on a daily basis (Bond *et al.*, 2002). Moreover, 55% of the sample indicated that these technologies help them manage their work, personal and family lives 'a lot better' and 27% said they 'helped some', yielding a total of 82% of respondents indicating that technology improves the work–family interface. Those who are most overworked may be making the greatest use of technology. *NSCW* results show those who experience high levels of negative spillover from their jobs to their home lives use these technologies the most (Bond *et al.*, 2002).

Professionals taking part in the *Cornell Couples and Career Study* likewise emphasized the importance of information and communication technologies, including cellular phones, pagers, computers and the Internet, in managing work and family life (Chesley *et al.*, 2003). For example, 36.7% of women and 47.8% of men reported sending e-mail to family at home from work. In addition, 48.2% of women and 50.1% of men indicated that they used pagers and/or cellular phones to keep in touch with family. Those making the greatest use of information technologies tended to be younger, more highly educated and more affluent. Men and women both use communication technologies to keep in touch with family. For both men and women, education was the strongest predictor of using a computer to manage work and home. Similar to the 2002 *NSCW* results, Chesley *et al.* (2003) found a positive relationship between the number of information technologies used and the level of negative spillover from work to family.

Interestingly, for women, higher levels of technology use were also associated with greater *positive* work-to-family spillover.

These results paint a picture of hard-working professionals who use technology at home in order to work, and likewise use technology at work to manage things at home. The same technologies that make it possible to work anytime and anywhere also appear to make it easier to maintain ties with friends and families, despite greater work demands. Many of the more negative repercussions of the changing nature of work, however, are not universal. Cross-national comparisons reveal that, in terms of work hours and leisure time, American employees are the 'poster children' for overwork.

Individualized work–life management strategies

Many have argued that, especially in the USA, large-scale governmental intervention is needed to protect families in the face of the changing nature of work (e.g., de Graaf, 2003; Heymann, 2002; Martin, 1997; Moen, 2003). In the meantime, employees and their employers are left to grapple with the work–family interface.[1] Under the new psychological contract, employees must take responsibility for ensuring the viability of home life, in much the same way they have become responsible for managing their own careers. This is not to say that individuals were not responsible for managing home life in the past. Rather, long work hours and work's infiltration into time and space typically reserved for family constitute a potential threat to family life which must be actively managed. Although it is arguably the employer's obligation to provide resources that facilitate management of the work–family interface (Roman and Blum, 2001), the employee must nonetheless be proactive in seeking out, utilizing, negotiating for and, in some cases, even demanding, employer accommodations for family.

Research on flexible and alternate work schedules illustrates the idiosyncratic nature of today's employment relationships. Most organizations lack clear criteria, policies and procedures for deciding who gets accommodations, which often means that employees are left to bargain with their individual supervisors for the best 'deal'. As Schalk and Rousseau (2001) note, there is substantial individual variation in the new psychological contract, even within a given organization, as top performers with highly sought after skills become increasingly aware of their leverage in employment negotiations. Those with superior negotiation skills and those who have developed good relationships with their immediate supervisors are likewise likely to wield considerable influence over their own employment arrangements. Clear priorities and an understanding of what one is willing to 'trade' are important, and there are already signs that employees are willing to trade compensation for a higher-quality personal life (Mir *et al.*, 2002). According to retired General Electric CEO Jack Welch, 'Most bosses are perfectly willing to accommodate work–life balance challenges if you've earned it with performance. The key word here is: *if*' (McGinn, 2005, p. 48).

The above description shares striking parallels with the circumstances that have always been faced by employees whose families have 'special needs'. Consider, for example, the employed parents of children who are disabled or chronically ill. These employees know first hand that there is no standard procedure for obtaining the family accommodations they need; there is no single best way to cope with the competing demands of work and family. Instead, they recognize that their dynamic work and family circumstances require engaging in a continuous process of role negotiation in order to best manage the work–family interface (Major, 2003). It is perhaps not too far-fetched to argue that, given the changing nature of work, all employees must now consider the 'special needs' of their families as well as develop the advocacy and negotiation skills necessary to meet them.

CONCLUSION

Implications of the changing nature of work for the work–family interface are perhaps best described as a paradoxical combination of opportunity and threat. On one hand, employers need highly skilled professionals who are flexible and adaptable, and they will go to considerable lengths to recruit and retain them. Family-friendly benefits, flexible work arrangements and personalized accommodations are some of the organizational offerings that savvy professionals can seek and use to their advantage in managing the work–family interface (see Chapter 11). On the other hand, long work hours and technological 'tethers' that link individuals to work 24/7 are realities confronted by employees and their families, especially those in the USA. It is rather ironic that in this discussion of the changing nature of work the one thing that has not changed is the notion that work–family balance is the employee's problem to solve. Until social and political movements aimed at reducing work hours and protecting personal time gain greater momentum, it is up to individual employees to be their own best advocates in pursuing accommodations that create a desirable work–family interface.

NOTES

1 For examples of employer best practices in provision of work–life programs see Chapter 11.

REFERENCES

Allen, T. D. (2001). Family-supportive work environments: the role of organizational perceptions. *Journal of Vocational Behavior*, *58*, 414–435.

Altman, B. W., and Post, J. E. (1996). Beyond the 'social contract': an analysis of the executive view at twenty-five large companies. In D. T. Hall (ed.), *The career is dead–long live the career: A relational approach to careers* (pp. 46–71). San Francisco: Jossey-Bass.

Appelbaum, E. (2003, June). *The transformation of work and employment relations in the U.S.* Paper presented at the NICHD conference, Workforce/Workplace Mismatch? Work, Family, Health, and Well-Being, Washington, DC.

Armstrong-Stassen, M. (1998). Alternative work arrangements: meeting the challenges. *Canadian Psychology, 39*, 108–123.

Australian Bureau of Statistics (2002). Business use of information technology, Australia. Retrieved 16 January 2004 from http://www.abs.gov.au/Ausstats/ABS@.nsf/0/9c7742890adec989ca2568a900139423?OpenDocument

Australian Bureau of Statistics (2003a). *Australian social trends. Work: National summary tables.* Retrieved 16 March 2004 from http://www.abs.gov.au/Ausstats/abs%40.nsf/94713ad445ff1425ca25682000192af2/9d281183ed41f104ca256d39001bc350!OpenDocument

Australian Bureau of Statistics (2003b). *Australian social trends. Work: Paid work: Longer working hours.* Retrieved 16 March 2004 from http://www.abs.gov.au/Ausstats/abs%40.nsf/94713ad445ff1425ca25682000192af2/f46f5073e7cd46e4ca256d39001bc354!OpenDocument

Bachu, A., and O'Connell, M. (2001). *Fertility of American Women: June 2000.* US Census Bureau, Current Population Reports, P20-543RV. Historical tables: Table H5. Retrieved 15 September 2003 from http://landview.census.gov/population/socdemo/fertility/tabH5.pdf

Bailey, D. E., and Kurland, N. B. (2002). A review of telework research: findings, new directions, and lessons for the study of modern work. *Journal of Organizational Behavior, 23*, 383–400.

Barling, J., MacEwen, K. E., Kelloway, E. K., and Higginbottom, S. F. (1994). Predictors and outcomes of eldercare-based interrole conflict. *Psychology and Aging, 9*, 391–397.

Bond, J. T., Thompson, C., Galinsky, E., and Prottas, D. (2002). *Highlights of the national study of the changing workforce.* New York: Families and Work Institute.

Cappelli, P. (1999). *The new deal at work: Managing the market-driven workforce.* Boston: Harvard Business School Press.

Cavanaugh, M. A., and Noe, R. A. (1999). Antecedents and consequences of relational components of the new psychological contract. *Journal of Organizational Behavior, 20*, 323–340.

Chesley, N., Moen, P., and Shore, R. P. (2003). The new technology climate. In P. Moen (ed.), *It's about time: Couples and careers* (pp. 220–241). Ithaca, NY: ILR Press.

Clarkberg, M., and Merola, S. S. (2003). Competing clocks: work and leisure. In P. Moen (ed.), *It's about time: Couples and careers* (pp. 35–48). Ithaca, NY: ILR Press.

Clarkberg, M., and Moen, P. (2001). The time-squeeze: is the increase in working time due to employer demands or employee preferences? *The American Behavioral Scientist, 44*, 1115–1136.

Commonwealth Office of the Status of Women (2001). *Women in Australia 2001: Section 3 – Statistical appendix.* Retrieved 13 March 2004 from http://www.osw.dpmc.gov.au/pdfs/wia_2001_part4.pdf

Cooper, C. D., and Kurland, N. B. (2002). Telecommuting, professional isolation, and employee development in public and private organizations. *Journal of Organizational Behavior, 23*, 511–532.

de Graaf, J. (ed.) (2003). *Take back your time: Fighting overwork and time poverty in America*. San Francisco: Berrett-Koehler.

Department of Trade and Industry (2003). *Balancing work and family life: Enhancing choice and support for parents*. Retrieved 23 March 2004 from http:// dti.gov.uk/er/individual/balancing.pdf

Dunford, R. (1999). 'If you want loyalty get a dog!': loyalty, trust and the new employment contract. In S. R. Clegg, E. Ibarra-Colado and L. Bueno-Rodriquez (eds), *Global management: Universal theories and local realities* (pp. 68–82). London: Sage.

Edwards, J. C., Rust, K. G., McKinley, W., and Moon, G. (2003). Business ideologies and perceived breach of contract during downsizing: the role of the ideology of employee self-reliance. *Journal of Organizational Behavior, 24*, 1–23.

Fagan, C. (2001). The temporal reorganization of employment and the household rhythm of work schedules: the implications for gender and class relations. *The American Behavioral Scientist, 44*, 1199–1212.

Fitzgerald, L. F., and Harmon, L. W. (2001). Women's career development: a postmodern update. In F. T. L. Leong and A. Barak (eds), *Contemporary models in vocational psychology* (pp. 207–255). Mahwah, NJ: Lawrence Erlbaum Associates.

Flood, P. C., Turner, T., Ramamoorthy, N., and Pearson, J. (2001). Causes and consequences of psychological contracts among knowledge workers in the high technology and financial services industries. *International Journal of Human Resource Management, 12*, 1152–1165.

Friedman, S. D., and Greenhaus, J. H. (2000). *Work and family – allies or enemies? What happens when business professionals confront life choices*. Oxford: Oxford University Press.

Frone, M. R., and Yardley, J. K. (1996). Workplace family-supportive programmes: predictors of employed parents' importance ratings. *Journal of Occupational and Organizational Psychology, 69*, 351–366.

Golden, L. (2001). Flexible work schedules: which workers get them? *American Behavioral Scientist, 44*, 1157–1178.

Grosswald, B., Ragland, D., and Fisher, J. M. (2001). Critique of U.S. work/family programs and policies. *Journal of Progressive Human Services, 12*, 53–81.

Grzywacz, J. G., Almeida, D. M., and McDonald, D. A. (2002). Work–family spillover and daily reports of work and family stress in the adult labor force. *Family Relations, 51*, 28–36.

Gutek, B. A., and Welsh, T. (2000). *The brave new service strategy: Aligning customer relationships, market strategies, and business structures*. New York: Amacom.

Gutek, B. A. (1993). Changing the status of women in management. *Applied Psychology: An International Review, 42*, 301–311.

Hall, D. T. (ed.) (1996). *The career is dead–long live the career: A relational approach to careers*. San Francisco: Jossey-Bass.

Hall, D. T., and Mirvis, P. H. (1995). Careers as lifelong learning. In A. Howard (ed.), *The changing nature of work* (pp. 323–361). San Francisco: Jossey-Bass.

Hall, D. T., and Mirvis, P. H. (1996). The new protean career. In D. T. Hall (ed.),

The career is dead–long live the career: A relational approach to careers (pp. 15–45). San Francisco: Jossey-Bass.

Hall, D. T., and Moss, J. E. (1998). The new protean career contract: helping organizations and employees adapt. *Organizational Dynamics, 26*, 22–37.

Harpaz, I. (2002). Advantages and disadvantages of telecommuting for the individual, organization and society. *Work Study, 51*, 74–80.

Hayden, A. (2003). Europe's work-time alternatives. In J. de Graaf (ed.), *Take back your time: Fighting overwork and time poverty in America* (pp. 202–218). San Francisco: Berrett-Koehler.

Heymann, J. (2002). *Can working families ever win?* Boston: Beacon Press.

HOP Associates (2002). *Telework in the UK: Who's doing it?* Retrieved 9 January 2004 from http://www.flexibility.co.uk/flexwork/location/telework-2002.htm

Hughes, R., Jr, and Hans, J. D. (2001). Computers, the Internet, and families: a review of the role new technology plays in family life. *Journal of Family Issues, 22*, 776–790.

Human Resources Development Canada (2001). *Annual Report: Employment Equity Act 2001.* Retrieved 9 January 2004 from http://www.hrsdc.gc.ca/asp/gateway.asp?hr=len//p//o///swe/we/ee_tools/reports/annual/2001/2001annualrep08shtml&hs=wzp

Israel Central Bureau of Statistics (2000, July). Prime Minister's Office. *Women and men in Israel.* Retrieved 29 September 2003 from http://www.cbs.gov.il/statistical/women_e.pdf

Jacobs, J. A., and Gerson, K. (1998). Who are the overworked Americans? *Review of Social Economy, 56*, 442–459.

Johnson, N. E., and Climo, J. J. (2000). Aging and eldercare in more developed countries. *Journal of Family Issues, 21*, 531–540.

Kalleberg, A. L., and Epstein, C. F. (2001). Temporal dimensions of employment relations. *American Behavioral Scientist, 44*, 1064–1075.

Kinsella, K. (2000). Demographic dimensions of global aging. *Journal of Family Issues, 21*, 541–558.

Kurland, N. B., and Bailey, D. E. (1999). Telework: the advantages and challenges of working here, there, anywhere, and anytime. *Organizational Dynamics, 28*, 53–68.

Lambert, S. J. (1993). Workplace policies as social policy. *Social Service Review, 67*, 237–260.

Lambert, S. J. (2000). Added benefits: the link between work–life benefits and organizational citizenship behavior. *Academy of Management Journal, 43*, 801–815.

Loughlin, C., and Barling, J. (2001). Young workers' work values, attitudes, and behaviours. *Journal of Occupational and Organizational Psychology, 74*, 543–558.

Major, D. A. (2003). Utilizing role theory to help employed parents cope with children's chronic illness. *Health Education Research: Theory and Practice, 18*, 45–57.

Martin, G. T. (1997). An agenda for family policy in the United States. In T. Arendell (ed.), *Contemporary parenting: Challenges and issues* (pp. 289–324). Thousand Oaks, CA: Sage.

McGinn, D. (2005, 4 April). Leadership for the 21st century: Jack on Jack – his next chapter. *Newsweek*, 41–48.

Mir, A., Mir, R., and Mosca, J. B. (2002). The new age employee: an exploration of changing employee–organization relations. *Public Personnel Management, 31,* 187–200.

Moen, P. (2003). Epilogue: toward a policy agenda. In P. Moen (ed.), *It's about time: Couples and careers* (pp. 333–337). Ithaca, NY: ILR Press.

National Statistical Coordination Board (2002). *The jobs people do.* Retrieved 29 September 2003 from http://www.statistics.gov.uk/cci/nugget.asp?id=ll

National Statistics Online (2003). *Hours worked: Further fall in long hours working.* Retrieved 16 March 2004 from http://www.statistics.gov.uk/cci/nugget.asp?id=341

National Statistics Online (2004). *Work and family.* Retrieved 16 March 2004 from http://www.statistics.gov.uk/CCI/nugget.asp?ID=436&Pos=8&ColRank=2& Rank=1000

Neal, M. B., Chapman, N. J., Ingersoll-Dayton, B., Emlen, A. C., and Boise, L. (1990). Absenteeism and stress among employed caregivers of the elderly, disabled adults, and children. In D. E. Biegel and A. Blum (eds), *Aging and caregiving: Theory, research, and policy* (pp. 160–183). Newbury Park, CA: Sage.

Nilles, J. M. (1998). *Managing telework: Strategies for managing the virtual workforce.* New York: Wiley.

Nord, W. R., Fox, S., Phoenix, A., and Viano, K. (2002). Real-world reactions to work–life balance programs: lessons for effective implementation. *Organizational Dynamics, 30,* 223–238.

Olson, E. (1998, 16 February). U.N. surveys paid leave for mothers: U.S. among nations without a policy. *New York Times,* A5.

Olson, E. (1999, 7 September). Americans lead the world in hours worked. *New York Times,* C9.

Patterson, F. (2001). Developments in work psychology: emerging issues and future trends. *Journal of Occupational and Organizational Psychology, 74,* 381–390.

Peterson, G. (2001). Electronic commerce and technology use. In G. Sciadas (ed.), *Connectedness series,* No. 5. Ottawa, Ontario: Science, Innovation and Electronic Information Division.

Robinson, J. (2003). The incredible shrinking vacation. In J. de Graaf (ed.), *Take back your time: Fighting overwork and time poverty in America* (pp. 20–27). San Francisco: Berrett-Koehler.

Roman, P. M., and Blum, T. C. (2001). Work–family role conflict and employer responsibility: an organizational analysis of workplace responses to a social problem. In R. T. Golembiewski (ed.), *Handbook of organizational behavior* (2nd edn, pp. 415–444). New York: Marcel Dekker.

Rousseau, D. M., and Schalk, R. (eds) (2000). *Psychological contracts in employment: Cross-national perspectives.* Thousand Oaks, CA: Sage.

Ruhm, C. J. (1997). Policy watch: the family and medical leave act. *Journal of Economic Perspectives, 11,* 175–186.

Scandura, T. A., and Lankau, M. J. (1997). Relationships of gender, family responsibility and flexible work hours to organizational commitment and job satisfaction. *Journal of Organizational Behavior, 18,* 377–391.

Schaaf, D. (1995). *Keeping the edge: Giving customers the service they demand.* New York: Dutton.

Schalk, R., and Rousseau, D. M. (2001). Psychological contracts in employment. In N. Anderson, D. S. Ones, H. K. Sinangil and C. Viswesvaran (eds), *Handbook of industrial, work and organizational psychology* (Vol. 2, pp. 133–142). London: Sage.

Schneider, B., and Bowen, D. E. (1995). *Winning the service game*. Boston: Harvard Business School Press.

Schor, J. (2003). The (even more) overworked American. In J. de Graaf (ed.), *Take back your time: Fighting overwork and time poverty in America* (pp. 6–11). San Francisco: Berrett-Koehler.

Scott, D. B. (2001). The costs and benefits of women's family ties in occupational context: women in corporate–government affairs management. *Community, Work and Family*, *4*, 5–27.

Scott, J., Alwin, D. F., and Braun, M. (1996). Generational changes in gender-role attitudes: Britain in cross-national perspective. *Sociology*, *20*, 471–492.

Sparks, K., Faragher, B., and Cooper, C. L. (2001). Well-being and occupational health in the 21st century workplace. *Journal of Occupational Psychology*, *74*, 489–509.

Sparrow, P. R. (2000). New employee behaviours, work designs and forms of work organization: what is in store for the future of work? *Journal of Managerial Psychology*, *15*, 202–218.

Spector, R. (2002). *Anytime, anywhere: How the best bricks-and-clicks businesses deliver seamless service to their customers*. Cambridge, MA: Perseus.

Statistics Canada (2004). Latest release from the labour force survey. Retrieved 10 January 2004 from http://www.statcan.ca/english/Subjects/Labour/LFS/lfs.pdf

Statistics New Zealand (1996). *Paid employment lower for women with young children*. Retrieved 16 March 2004 from http://www.stats.govt.nz/domino/external/web/nzstories.nsf/092edeb76ed5aa6bcc256afe0081d84e/bc5af1087809f086cc256b180007fcad?OpenDocument

Statistics New Zealand (2001a). *2001 census snapshot 2 (Who has access to the Internet?)*. Retrieved 16 January 2004 from http://www.stats.govt.nz/domino/external/pasfull/pasfull.nsf/web/4C2567EF00247C6ACC256B7500141AB1

Statistics New Zealand (2001b). *2001 census snapshot 11 (Women)*. Retrieved 29 September 2003 from http://www.stats.nz/domino/external/pasfull/pasfull.nsf/web/Media+Release+2001+Census+Snapshot+11+Women

Statistics New Zealand (2001c). *Household economic survey year ended 30 June 2001*. Retrieved 16 January 2004 from http://www.stats.govt.nz/domino/external/pasfull/pasfull.nsf/web/Hot+Off+The+Press+Household+Economic+Survey+Year+ended+30+June+2001?open

Statistics New Zealand (2001d). *Part 07: Hours of work*. Retrieved 16 March 2004 from http://www.stats.govt.nz/domino/external/pasfull/pasfull.nsf/7cf46ae26dcb6800cc256a62000a2248/4c2567ef00247c6acc256c0700787245?OpenDocument

Statistics New Zealand (2002). *Information technology use in New Zealand* (Catalog No. 01.035.0001). Wellington, New Zealand: author.

Still, M. C., and Strang, D. (2003). Institutionalizing family-friendly policies. In P. Moen (ed.), *It's about time: Couples and careers* (pp. 288–309). Ithaca, NY: ILR Press.

Tausig, M., and Fenwik, R. (2001). Unbinding time: alternate work schedules and work–life balance. *Journal of Family and Economic Issues*, *22*, 101–119.

Thomas, L. T., and Ganster, D. C. (1995). Impact of family-supportive work variables on work–family conflict and strain: a control perspective. *Journal of Applied Psychology*, *80*, 6–15.

Thompson, C. A., Beauvais, L. L., and Lyness, K. S. (1999). When work–family benefits are not enough: the influence of work–family culture on benefit utilization, organizational attachment, and work–family conflict. *Journal of Vocational Behavior*, *54*, 392–415.

Toossi, M. (2002). A century of change: the U.S. labor force, 1950–2050. *Monthly Labor Review*, *125*, 15–28.

Treas, J., and Widmer, E. D. (2000). Married women's employment over the life course: attitudes in cross-national perspective. *Social Forces*, *78*, 1409–1436.

Turnley, W. H., and Feldman, D. C. (1999). The impact of psychological contract violations on exit, voice, loyalty, and neglect. *Human Relations*, *52*, 895–922.

United Nations Statistics Division (2000). *The world's women 2000: Trends and statistics*. Retrieved 18 January 2004 from http://unstats.un.org/unsd/demographic/ww2000/table5b.htm

US Department of Labor (1999). *Futurework – trends and challenges for work in the 21st century* (Ch. 4). Retrieved 14 January 2004 from http://www.dol.gov/asp/programs/history/herman/reports/futurework/report/chapter4/main.htm

US Department of Labor, Bureau of Labor Statistics (2002a). Computer and internet use at work in 2001. Retrieved 19 January 2004 from http://www.bls.gov/news.release/ciuaw.nr0.htm

US Department of Labor, Bureau of Labor Statistics (2002b). *Work at home in 2001*. Retrieved 11 January 2004 from http://www.bls.gov/news.release/homey.nr0.htm.

US Department of Labor, Bureau of Labor Statistics (2003). *Employment characteristics of families in 2002*. Retrieved 11 January 2004 from http://www.bls.gov/news.release/pdf/famee.pdf

Valcour, P. M., and Batt, R. (2003). Work–life integration: challenges and organizational responses. In P. Moen (ed.), *It's about time: Couples and careers* (pp. 310–331). Ithaca, NY: ILR Press.

Wallis, C. (2004, 22 March). The case for staying home. *Time*, 51–59.

Wheelock, J., and McCarthy, P. (1997). Employed mothers and their families in Britain. In J. Frankel (ed.), *Families of employed mothers: An international perspective* (pp. 3–34). New York: Garland.

2 The legal and administrative context of work and family leave and related policies in the USA, Canada and the European Union

Richard N. Block, Martin H. Malin,
Ellen Ernst Kossek and Angela Holt

INTRODUCTION

Countries and cultures vary in the extent to which government is viewed as playing a role in encouraging or mandating workplace practices to support work and family (Lewis and Haas, 2005). In a world in which corporations operate internationally, and in which employees and the unions that represent them find themselves in 'competition' with employees in other countries, it is important to understand international differences in social mores and employer implementation of work and family policies. For example, although over the last several decades the USA has generally become more accepting of women's participation in paid employment and of fathers' involvement in early child care, an implementation gap persists where many legal and employer practices related to work and family have not fully caught up to labor market and societal changes (Barnett, 1999; Lewis and Haas, 2005). In this chapter we describe and contrast legal and employer approaches to work and family supports related to leave and time off from work for family, pregnancy and caregiving, in the USA, Canada, the European Union (EU) and selected countries in the EU. While the field of work and family has now broadened to include eldercare and time off from work for all employees regardless of whether they have caregiving responsibilities (Kossek and Lambert, 2005), due to space limitations we focus our review on policies relating to leave and caregiving.

Table 2.1 provides an overview of the provisions of leave policies by country that we will draw upon throughout this chapter. As the table shows, for example, Canada and the countries of Europe have more extensive legally mandated family leave policies than the USA. As our review will suggest, these differences in policy may be attributed partly to several key differences in contextual and institutional contexts (Lipset, 1989; Block *et al.*, 2004). The differences between the USA and Canada and between the USA and the countries in Europe are consistent with the findings of other research that demonstrate that Canada and the EU provide higher labor standards to employees within their borders than the USA (Block, Roberts and Clarke, 2003; Block, Berg and Roberts, 2003).

Table 2.1 Characteristics of parental leave in the USA, Canada, UK, Germany, Norway and Sweden

Country	Title of legislation	Scope of coverage (benefit and eligibility)	Compensation rate	Duration	Job security
USA	Family and Medical Leave Act of 1993 (federal)	Eligible employees for an eligible employer;[a] birth or care of a child, adoption or foster care placement, care employee's spouse, parent or child or because of the employee's own illness	Unpaid	12 weeks	Entitled to same position or one that is equivalent in pay, benefits and other terms and conditions of employment
UK	No explicit family leave policy	There are maternity and parental (same for paternity) benefits	Maternity: paid (90% of salary for 6 weeks and then L100/week for 12 weeks). Parental: Unpaid	18 weeks maternity; 13 weeks unpaid parental	Entitled to same position as before leave
Canada	Employment Standards Legislation (federal); most Canadian provinces have separate Human Rights and Employment Standards Amendments	New mothers and parents are entitled to the leave; maternity leave benefits can be received after a 2-week waiting period	55% (maternity: 15 weeks; parental: up to 35 weeks)	17 weeks maternity leave; 12–52 weeks parental leave	Entitled to same position with equivalent terms and conditions of employment

Country	Law	Description	Payment	Maximum duration	Job protection
Germany	The Maternity Protection Act (Mutterschutzgesetz) and Child Benefit Act (Bundeserziehungsgeldgesetz)	Maternity and parental leave that protects employees from termination, grants income, entitles employees to their job upon return, and absence from work to raise a child	State benefits paid for up to 24 months; EUR460 ($544 US) 1st year and EUR307 ($363) 2 years	Maximum of 3 years	Entitled to return to same position the employee held before leave; may request a reduction in work hours after the birth of a child
Norway	N/A	Parental leave entitles either parent to leave if they have been employed or self-employed for 6 of the past 10 months; mothers who are not entitled to cash benefits receive a 'maternity grant'	100% for 42 weeks or 80% of salary for the full year	1 year; 3 years for single parent	Full job protection; entitled to return to same position the employee held before leave
Sweden	The Swedish Family Policy	All employees are entitled to this leave; family leave benefits allow for a reduced work schedule until a child is 8 years old	Paid (90% of pay for first 12 months and flat rate for additional 3 months)	Paid up to 15 months; extended leave up to 18 months	Entitled to same position employee held at commencement of leave

a 'Eligible employee' is an employee who has worked at least 12 months with 1250 hours of service to the employer; 'eligible employer' is any person engaged in commerce or in any industry or activity affecting commerce who employs 50 or more employees for each working day during each of 20 or more calendar workweeks in the current or preceding calendar year (Family and Medical Leave Act, 1993; www.dol.gov).

Also relevant, especially with respect to differences between the EU and USA, is the role of trade unions in creating social policy. In the EU unions are considered to be social partners with employers through corporatist arrangements and are full participants in the dialogue with employer groups and governments around social (including employment) policy. The USA in contrast, takes more of a minimalist market-based employer approach in which markets are assumed to be competitive and in which employers have wide latitude to determine the level of support they will provide for the family-related needs of their employees. There is little or no employee representation for work and family at the organizational level because of low unionization and the absence of employee representation at high governmental levels. Another contributing factor may be culturally based; consistent with its long-standing belief in individualism, the US culture tends to value approaches to employee caregiving determined by individual employees and individual employers, with a limited role for government regulation (Block *et al.*, 2004).

The chapter is organized as follows. In the next three sections we provide a review of the legal obligations and employer practices with a focus on family leave and time off from work for family, in the USA, then Canada, and the EU and selected EU countries. In each section we discuss the relevant legislation and policy and highlight some best employment practices, particularly in regard to paid and unpaid family leave, time off for pregnancy and caregiving. In the final section we summarize and provide directions for future research.

WORK AND FAMILY IN THE USA

In this section we first discuss legal obligations to provide support for work and family in the USA with a focus on the Family Medical Leave Act of 1993, as it represents the major US legislation. We then provide data on the prevalence of employee access to workplace policies addressing work and family.

Legal issues related to work and family in the USA

Employers in the USA have no legal obligation to provide direct support specifically for maternity or childcare. But under the Family and Medical Leave Act US employers do have legal obligations to provide unpaid leave and time off from work up to 12 weeks in any 12-month period for the birth or adoption of a child, for the employee's serious health condition, or to care for a spouse, parent or minor or disabled child who has a serious health condition.[1] The FMLA covers employers of 50 or more full- and part-time employees (see Walters v. Metropolitan Education Enterprise, Inc., 1997). The FMLA requires that employers continue employee health insurance coverage while an employee is on leave under the same conditions that would have occurred if the employee had continued working (US Department of Labor, undated-c).

An employee returning from FMLA leave has a right to be restored to the same or an equivalent position from which the employee took leave. The Department of Labor (DOL) regulations define an equivalent position as 'one that is virtually identical to the employee's former position in terms of pay, benefits and working conditions, including privileges, perquisites and status. It must involve the same or substantially similar duties and responsibilities, which must entail substantially equivalent skill, effort, responsibility, and authority' (Legal Information Institute, undated, Sec. 2614(a)(1)). The statute, however, provides that an employee is not entitled to any right or benefit to which the employee would not have been entitled had the employee not taken a leave (Legal Information Institute, undated, Sec. 2614(a)(3)).

Implementation trends[2]

The primary impetus for enactment of the FMLA was the need to enable employees to take time off from work following the birth or adoption of a child without worrying about job security or health insurance.[3] In practice, however, leave following birth or adoption of a child accounts for a small minority of FMLA leaves that are taken. The DOL's 2000 surveys, the most recent data available (Cantor *et al.*, 2000), summarize the reasons for taking leave during the previous 18 months. The most frequent reason for taking leave was one's own health, which comprised a majority (52.4%) of the respondents. The second most common reason, given by less than a fifth of the sample (18.5%), was to care for a newborn, newly adopted or newly placed foster child. The third most frequent reason, given by 13% of the sample, was to care for an ill parent, followed by an ill child (11.5%). Only 7.8% of all leaves were taken for maternity-related disability.

Because most leave is taken or sought for serious health conditions, most of the litigation has been over this issue. This is not surprising as the term 'serious health condition' is ambiguous. While the term clearly covers open heart surgery, and would clearly not cover a skinned knee, health conditions in between these two situations, such as a case of bronchitis or a child's ear infection, are often open to debate. A survey of appellate court FMLA decisions issued between December 1994 and October 1999 found that 25% concerned the seriousness of the employee's illness and 6% concerned the seriousness of the illness of the employee's family member (Wisensale, 2001, p. 172).

The FMLA allows an employer to require an employee to substitute applicable paid leave accrued under a collective bargaining agreement or under an employer's unilaterally adopted policies for FMLA leave.[4] Where the employer imposes such a requirement, the paid leave runs concurrently with the employee's statutory entitlement of 12 weeks of FMLA leave. Where the employer does not impose such a requirement, an employee may exhaust accrued paid leave and then take an additional 12 weeks of unpaid FMLA leave. An employer may also designate other unpaid leave taken by an employee for reasons covered by the FMLA as FMLA leave (US Department of Labor, undated-c).

Another DOL regulation provides '[i]f an employee takes paid or unpaid leave and the employer does not designate the leave as FMLA leave, the leave taken does not count against an employee's FMLA entitlement' (US Department of Labor, undated-d). But in Ragsdale v. Wolverine World Wide, Inc. (2002), the US Supreme Court held that this regulation could not be used to grant an employee who took 30 weeks of unpaid leave (because of an illness) an additional 12 weeks of unpaid FMLA where her employer had not informed her that the 30 weeks of leave would be considered FMLA leave. The court ruled that to give the employee an additional 12 weeks of leave when she had already taken 30 weeks was inconsistent with the FMLA's grant of only 12 weeks of leave. The court also observed that Ragsdale had not relied on her employer's failure to notify her of the designation of her leave as FMLA leave. There was no evidence that she would have acted differently had she received the designation notice.

Legal ambiguities

The FMLA has generated a great deal of litigation since it was enacted. This section will discuss some of the more important unresolved issues under the statute.

As noted, the FMLA requires employers to restore employees returning from leave to the same or positions equivalent to the positions they held prior to taking leave. The statute contains two exceptions to the job restoration requirement. The first enables an employer to deny job restoration to a salaried employee who is among the 10% highest paid within a 75-mile radius, if denial of job restoration 'is necessary to prevent substantial and grievous economic injury', the employer notifies the employee at the time it determines that such injury will occur and the employee refuses to return from leave (US Department of Labor, undated-e). There is evidence that this provision is rarely invoked. Gely and Chandler's (2004) survey of 136 childbirth leave cases decided between 1995 and 2003 found that employers raised the 'key employee' defense in only three cases.

More controversial, however, is the second exception, which provides '[n]othing in this section shall be construed to entitle any restored employee to . . . any right, benefit or position to which the employee would not have been entitled had the employee not taken leave' (Legal Information Institute, undated, Sec. 2614(a)(3)). DOL regulations appear to place the burden of proof on the employer to establish that the exception applies. The regulations provide '[a]n employer must be able to show that an employee would not otherwise have been employed at the time reinstatement is requested in order to deny restoration to employment' (US Department of Labor, undated-a). The regulations give an example of an employee on leave when a lay-off is conducted. They state, 'An employer would have the burden of proving that an employee would have been laid off during the FMLA leave period and, therefore, would not be entitled to restoration' (US Department of Labor, undated-a).

In the USA, where the unionization rate is low, employers generally have a great deal of flexibility to reallocate, transfer and lay off employees as their interpretation of business needs requires. Thus, substantial changes may occur at the workplace when an employee is away from work for up to 12 weeks. These changes have often found their way into court, and this exception to the 'job restoration' principle has generated some legal controversy regarding how it should be interpreted. Given an adverse job action, such as a lay-off, must the employee taking a leave prove that he or she suffered an adverse impact on the job because of the leave, or must the employer prove that the adverse impact would have occurred regardless of the leave? In Rice v. Sunrise Express, Inc. (2000), decided by the Seventh Circuit Court of Appeals,[5] Rice was one of the company's two billing clerks when she took an FMLA-protected leave. The employer laid her off effective the date she was scheduled to return from leave, retaining the other billing clerk, who had been with the employer less time than Rice. There was conflicting evidence concerning whether the employer would have laid off Rice rather than the other billing clerk, had Rice not taken leave. The court observed that the FMLA entitles an employee returning from leave to restoration to her former position or an equivalent position, but that a returning employee could not obtain a job or position that he/she would not have had if no leave had been taken.

In order to balance these two principles, the court ruled that this exception to the 'restoration' rule incorporated a discrimination requirement into the FMLA's job guarantee provision, i.e., the complaining employee must show that the change in the job status suffered by the employee was an act of discrimination taken against the employee due to the employee's leave.

Although other courts prior to *Rice* had adopted this discrimination analysis,[6] legal scholars have criticized this approach that requires *employees to prove* that their employers denied them job restoration because of their leave.[7] The Courts of Appeals for the Tenth and Eleventh Circuits have also disagreed with the discrimination analysis approach and have followed the DOL regulation and held that the employer has the burden of proving that the employee would not have occupied his or her pre-leave position even if he or she had not taken leave.[8] The issue is not likely to be resolved definitively unless the Supreme Court agrees to review it.

Questions about the rationale for an employer's action *vis-à-vis* an employee may also arise after the employee returns from leave. An employer may restore an employee to his or her former position when the employee returns from leave but subsequently take adverse action against the employee. The FMLA prohibits employers from interfering with, restraining or denying employees their FMLA rights (Legal Information Institute, undated). Thus, the relevant question is whether an employer's adverse action against an employee because who has taken leave interfered with the employee's leave rights. In cases such as this, the issue is whether the adverse action is due to the leaves or attendance and productivity problems associated with the absences. As with denials of job restoration, the courts have disagreed over how to analyze such claims.

In Bachelder v. America West Airlines, Inc. (2001) employee Bachelder had been a passenger service supervisor when the employer discharged her in April 1996. She had taken FMLA leave in 1994 and 1995. On 14 January 1996 she had a corrective action discussion with her manager, at which she was advised to improve her attendance. FMLA-protected and non-protected absences were cited. In February 1996 Bachelder was absent for three weeks for medical reasons. On 9 April she called in sick for one day to care for her child. She was terminated shortly after the last absence for being absent 16 times since the January counseling, failing to carry out certain job responsibilities and for below-par on-time performance.

Reversing the lower court, the Ninth Court of Appeals held that the discharge of Bachelder interfered with her FMLA rights. The court analogized the FMLA provision to the National Labor Relations Act, the law covering union–management relations, which prohibits employer interference with, restraint or coercion of employee rights to engage in concerted activity and which does not require a showing of discrimination. The court observed, 'As a general matter, then, the established understanding at the time the FMLA was enacted was that employer actions that deter employees' participation in protected activities constitute "interference" or "restraint" with the employees' exercise of their rights' (Bachelder v. America West Airlines, p. 1124). The court held that an FMLA plaintiff 'need only prove by a preponderance of the evidence that her taking of FMLA-protected leave was a negative factor in the decision to terminate her' (Bachelder v. America West Airlines, p. 1125).

Other courts have disagreed with this 'in-part test' and have held that the employee has the burden of proving that his or her FMLA-protected activity motivated the adverse employment action. For example, in Kohls v. Beverly Enterprises, Wisconsin, Inc. (2001) the court ruled for the employer, holding that the employee must prove that the employer would not have discharged her had she not taken the FMLA leave. In Burke v. Health Plus of Michigan, Inc. (2003) the court granted summary judgment against the plaintiff's FMLA claim. The court characterized the plaintiff's evidence as establishing, at most, that her employer was hostile to her because she was ill and would request FMLA leave after she exhausted her paid time-off benefits. In the court's view, the allegations of such a pre-emptive action were insufficient to establish a prima facie case of discrimination.

The requirement of a showing of intentional discrimination in FMLA interference claims has been severely criticized (Malin, 2003). As with the dispute over burdens of proof in denials of job restoration cases, the division in the courts over FMLA interference claims must probably await definitive action from the Supreme Court.

In the US federal system national law generally pre-empts state law in that a state may not validly enact a law that provides lesser coverage than national law, but states may enhance federally provided legal benefits. California is the only state in the country to have enacted a comprehensive paid family leave program. Under California's new Family Leave Law, effective 1 July 2004, workers will receive up to six weeks of paid leave per year to care for a new child (birth, adoption or foster care) or seriously ill family member (parent, child, spouse or domestic partner). The benefit will replace up to 55% of wages, up to a maximum of $728 per week in 2004. The maximum benefit will increase automatically each year in accordance with increases in the state's average weekly wage (California, undated).

Work and family at the workplace in the USA

As employers in the USA have no legal obligation to provide for employees' family needs beyond the requirement for unpaid leave in the FMLA, family-related benefits are provided to employees either by employer discretion or through collective bargaining. Although, as noted, work and family issues arise in a variety of work-related contexts, they are most clearly expressed in matters related to childcare. Table 2.2 presents data on the availability to employees of employer-provided childcare in the USA. Table 2.2 indicates that few employees have such services available to them. In 2003 only 8% of private employees had access to childcare services through their employer. This percentage was double the percentage in 2000, when only 4% of private employees worked for employers who provided childcare. In 1999, the percentage was 6%.

Employees in service industries are roughly twice as likely to work for employers who provide childcare as employees in goods-producing industries. In 2003 only 5% of employees in goods-producing industries had access to employer-provided childcare, while 9% of employees in service-producing industries had access to such services. This difference may be due to the higher percentage of female employees in the service-producing sector relative to the goods-producing sector. Between 1999 and 2003 the mean percentage of female employees in the service-producing sector was approximately 53%, while the mean percentage of female employees in the goods-producing sector was approximately 24% (US Bureau of Labor Statistics, undated-b).

It is interesting that union-represented workers in the USA are only slightly more likely to have access to employer-sponsored or financed childcare than non-represented workers. In 2003 10% of union-represented

Table 2.2 Percentage of employees in the USA with access to employer-provided childcare services, by industry, union representation and employer size, 1999, 2000, 2003

Year	Employer-provided funds or on-site or off-site child care	Resource and referral service	All	Employer-provided funds or on-site or off-site child care	Resource and referral service	All	Employer-provided funds or on-site or off-site child care	Resource and referral service	All
	By industrial sector			*By union representation status*			*By establishment employment*		
	All private industry			*Represented by a union*			*Establishments of fewer than 100*		
1999	6			5			3		
2000	4			8			1		
2003	8	10	18	10	15	25	4	3	7
	Goods-producing industries			*Not represented by a union*			*Establishments of 100 or more*		
1999	2			6			10		
2000	2			4			9		
2003	5	11	16	8	10	18	13	19	32
	Service-producing industries								
1999	7								
2000	5								
2003	9	10	19						

Source: US Bureau of Labor Statistics (undated-a).

workers had access to employer-sponsored childcare, while 8% of non-represented workers had such access. In 1999 the percentage of non-represented employees who had access to employer-sponsored childcare was similar to the percentage of union-represented employees who had such access; the percentages were 6% and 5%, respectively. In 2000 8% of union-represented workers had access to employer-sponsored childcare, as compared to 4% of non-represented workers.

These data suggest that while union-represented employees are slightly more likely to have access to employer-sponsored childcare than non-represented employees, the differences are not that great. If it is true that employer-sponsored childcare is provided in union-represented firms because employees and employers negotiate for it, the fairly low incidence of employer-sponsored childcare in non-represented firms suggests that employers resist providing such a benefit in negotiations and/or that most unions do not negotiate for such a benefit for the employees they represent. In a union-represented workplace, obtaining employer-sponsored childcare may mean that the union must sacrifice something else. Thus, it may be that most unions do not place a sufficiently high value on the benefit such that they are willing to give up something for it in collective bargaining negotiations. It may be that given a choice between employer-sponsored childcare or an increase in some other component of compensation, such as wages or health insurance, employees prefer the latter. One might suggest that this could be because childcare is a benefit that employees may need only for a short period of their working life; after the age of five, children attend school. Moreover, not all employees who require childcare would obtain it from the employer even if it was offered by the employer; there are often substitutes for employer-sponsored childcare. Therefore, at any one time, only a small percentage of employees in a bargaining unit are likely to have a need for employer-sponsored childcare. On the other hand, the need for increases in other types of compensation is likely to be widespread.[9]

It should also be observed, however, that in 2003 union-represented workers were 50% more likely than non-represented workers to have access to a childcare referral service.[10] This suggests that although unions were either unable to convince employers to provide childcare services or were unwilling to give up other benefits for employer-provided childcare, they are able to convince their employers to provide the relatively inexpensive childcare referral service. The data also suggest that unions were willing to raise childcare-related issues during collective bargaining negotiations, and were able to place childcare in the contract in many instances. As it is not unusual in collective bargaining for parties to introduce a benefit at a low level, and to build on that benefit in future negotiations, the small gap between union-represented and non-represented employees in access to employer-provided childcare may increase into the future.

The data also suggest that employees in larger establishments are substantially more likely than employees in smaller establishment to have access to childcare support through their employer. These data suggest that resources play a large role in the decisions of US employers to provide support for childcare. Larger employers generally have greater financial resources than smaller employers, and are likely to be able to afford childcare to a greater extent than small employers.

With respect to the matter of FMLA leave, as noted above, other accrued leave can be linked to FMLA leave to provide paid leave for employees. The two major types of paid leave in the USA are sick leave and vacation. Although employees in the USA are not legally entitled to sick leave or vacation (Block, Roberts and Clarke, 2003), it is not unusual for employees in the USA to have accrued such leave. Table 2.3 provides a sense of the percentage of employees in the USA who have access to such benefits. As can be seen, about half of all employees in the USA have access to sick leave and about 80% have access to vacations. These give employees some options with respect to maintaining income during an FMLA leave.

WORK AND FAMILY IN CANADA

National leave policy in Canada

Unlike the case in the USA, where there is no mandated pay for employees on FMLA leave, Canadian employees on approved family-related leave receive benefits through the federal Employment Insurance System, the system that is supported through taxes on employers and employees and is used primarily for compensating unemployed workers (Block, Roberts and Clarke; 2003, Human Resources and Skill Development Canada, undated).

Policies vary by province[11] and many provide more than required by the Employment Standards Legislation in Canada. The minimum national benefit rate is 55% of the employee's salary, with a maximum of $413 per week. An employee must accumulate 600 insured working hours in the previous 52 weeks to be eligible for maternity and parental benefits and must have suffered a loss of income of at least 40%. Biological and surrogate mothers are eligible to receive up to 15 weeks of maternity benefits, while parental benefits have a maximum of 35 weeks. The 35 weeks of parental benefits may be taken by one parent or shared between the two parents. Like maternity benefits, sickness benefits also may be received for up to 15 weeks. A combination of all three types of benefits can be taken for a maximum of 50 weeks. Aside from financial benefits, employees who take leave are entitled to their jobs upon return from leave (Human Resources and Skill Development Canada, undated).

Maternity benefits may be received by either a biological or surrogate mother for up to 15 weeks and for up to 52 weeks if the child is hospitalized. Parental benefits are payable for up to 35 weeks to either the biological or adoptive parents while caring for a newborn or an adopted child (Human Resources and Skill Development Canada, undated).

Table 2.3 Percentage of employees in the USA with vacation and sick leave time, by industry, union representation and establishment size, selected years

Year	Sick leave (all employees)	Vacations (all employees)	Sick leave (full-time/ part-time employees)	Vacations (full-time/ part-time employees)	Sick leave	Vacation	Sick leave	Vacation
	By industrial sector				By union representation		By establishment size	
	All private industry				*Represented by a union*		*Establishments, LT 100*	
1990							47	
1992							53	
1994							50	88
1996							50	86
1999	53	79	63/19	90/43	54	86	47	73
2000		80		91/39		93		73
2003		79		91/40		90		73
	Goods-producing industries				*Not represented by a union*		*Establishments GT 100*	
1991							67	
1993							65	97
1995							58	96
1997							56	95
1999	42	84			53	78	60	86
2000		89				79		89
2003		87				78		87
	Service-producing industries							
1999	57							

Source: US Bureau of Labor Statistics (undated-a).

A new type of federal benefit was added as of 4 January 2004. 'Compassionate Care' benefit entitles eligible employees in provinces that permit such leave to receive benefits for up to six weeks if the employee must be absent from work to care for a family member (a child or step-child, wife, husband or common-law partner, father or mother, step-parent, or the common-law partner of the employee's mother or father) with a significant risk of death within 26 weeks. Like maternity, parental and sickness benefits, the employee has to have accumulated at least 600 insured working hours in the previous 52 weeks. The care in question can be emotional support, direct assistance or the arrangement of care for the third party (Human Resources and Skill Development Canada, 2004).

An overview of work–family labor standards

In Canada the provinces have the sole authority to adopt labor standards for all employees within the province that do not work in industries that operate directly in interprovincial commerce. This latter group includes such industries as airlines, communications and banking. For the purposes of labor standards, these industries are under what is called the federal jurisdiction. Labor standards for the federal jurisdiction are established by the federal government through the Canada Labour Code. The three territories, Northwest Territories, Nunavut and Yukon, may adopt their own labor standards. In areas in which the territories choose not to legislate, the Canada Labour Code governs. Thus, within Canada, there are 14 governmental jurisdictions that adopt labor standards: the 10 provinces, the three territories and the federal government (Block, Roberts and Clarke, 2003).

Table 2.4 summarizes the relevant work–family legislation in the 14 Canadian jurisdictions. Despite the legal separation among the provinces, territories, and the federal jurisdiction, there is substantial uniformity among them. Of the 14 jurisdictions, 13 permit 17 or 18 weeks of maternity/pregnancy leave. Alberta permits 15 weeks. Most of the jurisdictions permit 35–37 weeks of parental leave, generally taken after the exhaustion of maternity/pregnancy leave benefits.

In general, Canada has developed an integrated system of work–family support, with responsibilities shared between the individual jurisdictions and the federal government. The jurisdictions provide the statutory authority to provide employees with the leave. The federal government, through the tax-supported Employment Insurance system, provides the financial support.

Work–family support at the Canadian workplace

Table 2.5 presents the percentage of Canadian employees overall, and by sector, union representation and establishment size, with access to employer-financed childcare. As indicated in Table 2.5, only 6% of Canadian

Table 2.4 Percentage of employees in Canada with childcare, 1998–99, by industry, union representation and employer size

	Men	Women
Overall	6	6.1
By industry		
Forestry, mining	3.3	7.2
Labor-intensive tertiary manufacturing	2.9	2.5
Primary product manufacturing	3.6	0.0
Secondary product manufacturing	2.9	2.7
Capital-intensive tertiary manufacturing	12.3	3.5
Construction	1.8	0.0
Transportation, storage	5.2	4.0
Retail trade and commercial services	2.3	1.2
Finance and insurance	3.9	5.8
Real estate, etc.	2.2	2.3
Business services	3.8	2.5
Education, health care	17.3	13.9
By union representation		
Represented	11.5	10.7
Not represented	3.7	4.5
By establishment size		
Fewer than 10 employees	1.0	1.6
10–49 employees	2.1	2.7
50–99 employees	2.5	3.2
100–499 employees	4.3	4.0
500–999 employees	11.7	9.1
1000 or more employees	24.0	23.0

Source: Comfort *et al.* (2003).

employees had access to employer-financed childcare in 1998–99, approximately the same level as the USA. On the other hand, there are greater differences within groups in Canada than in the USA. The largest differences can be seen by examining the industrial distribution of childcare services. Education and health care have by far the highest incidence of employer-provided childcare access. This is likely to be because both of these industries are part of the public sector in Canada, and are more likely to respond to political pressure than private employers. Unionization also appears to matter more in Canada than in the USA. Represented employees are two to three times as likely as non-represented employees to have access to employer-provided childcare. Establishment size and unionization, which are related, also appear to be associated with employer-provided childcare. These data suggest that Canadian unions have been more aggressive in pursuing and obtaining employer-provided childcare than their counterparts in the USA. One may speculate that part of the reason may be the different health insurance systems in the two countries. In the USA, unions must

Table 2.5 Canadian maternity/pregnancy leave requirements by province, 2004

	Weeks maternity/ pregnancy leave	Weeks parental leave	Period for completion of parental leave	Compassionate care leave	Family responsibility/ illness/emergency leave
Federal jurisdiction	17	37	Immediately after maternity leave	Yes	
Alberta	15	37	Immediately after maternity leave		
British Columbia	17	35 or 37	Immediately after maternity leave		
Manitoba	17	37	None		8 weeks
New Brunswick	17	37	Immediately after maternity leave	Yes	3 days
Newfoundland	17	35	Immediately after maternity leave	Yes	3 days
Northwest Territories	17	37	Immediately after maternity leave		
Nova Scotia	17	52	Immediately after maternity leave	Yes	Yes
Nunavut	17	29	Immediately after maternity leave	Yes	Yes
Ontario	17	35/37	Immediately after maternity leave		10 days
Prince Edward Island	17	35	Immediately after maternity leave	Yes	8 weeks
Quebec	18	52	Must end 70 weeks after birth	Yes	12 weeks
Saskatchewan	18	34/37	Immediately after maternity leave		
Yukon	17	52	Immediately after maternity leave	Yes	8 weeks

Source: Provincial and Canadian Government websites.

bargain for health insurance coverage; therefore, increases in health insurance must be diverted from other potential benefits. On the other hand, in Canada, where health insurance is provided by the government, unions need not negotiate for it; therefore, they can bargain for other benefits, such as employer-provided childcare.

WORK AND FAMILY IN EUROPE AND THE EUROPEAN UNION

Although the EU is not a sovereign country but a political union of sovereign countries, the EU has become increasingly politically integrated over the last 40 years. The directives issued by the European Council apply to all member states, and the EU acts in international bodies like a single entity (Block, Berg and Roberts, 2003). Thus, there is a basis for comparing the EU with the USA and Canada.[12]

Formal legislation

The directives that may be considered as addressing work and family can be conceptualized as tracking the creation of the family in the context of employment: they relate to pregnancy, return to work immediately after childbirth and childcare. Interestingly, these directives were not initially justified on the basis of work and family, as the EU has moved cautiously in issuing directives on social policy (Springer, 1994). Rather, these directives were premised on three widely held norms within the EU: (1) worker health and safety, including psychological health; (2) employment policy that would support the labor force participation of women; and (3) equal employment opportunities for women (Springer, 1994).

Thus, the earliest directive directly addressing employers and employees, Directive 92/85, issued in 1992, derived its authority from the Directive 89/391, issued in 1989 (European Council, 1992a). Directive 89/391 places a broad-based general duty on employers to safeguard the safety and health of their employees (European Council, 1989).

Specifically referring to Directive 89/391, Directive 92/85 requires employers to shield pregnant and breastfeeding workers from exposure to substances considered harmful to the fetus or infant. The directive requires the European Commission to make an assessment of those substances that are considered hazardous or harmful to pregnant and breastfeeding workers. Employers are obligated to take this assessment into account, to inform affected workers of the results of their assessment and to change the conditions of workers who are exposed to these substances. If appropriate changes in conditions cannot be made, employers are obligated to find the worker a different job, or failing that place the worker on leave. The directive also requires 14 weeks of maternity leave, prenatal leave as needed for care of the fetus, a prohibition on dismissal for pregnancy or breast-feeding. Payment for leave is to be in accordance with national laws and policies (European Council, 1992a).

Parental leave is addressed in Directive 96/34. This directive, extended to the UK in 1997,[13] grants men and women parental leave for up to three months during the first eight years of the child's life (European Council, 1996, 1997). Directive 2002/73 reaffirmed the principle, established in directives issued in 1976 and 1992, that women returning from maternity leave are to be returned to the position from which they took the leave or are to be provided a job that is equivalent to the job from which they took the leave (European Parliament and European Council, 2002). Thus women who take maternity leave may suffer no job disadvantage.

Indirectly related to work and family, but relevant, is the EU working time directive, Directive 93/104. This directive, although justified on the basis of worker health and safety, affects work and family issues by placing limits on the number of hours a person may work in specified time periods, thus permitting the employee some time to address family-related matters. The directive entitles the worker to at least 11 hours off within each 24-hour period and to 24 hours off in every seven-day period. The directive also limits the worker to an average of no more than 48 hours of work in each seven-day period over a reference period of not more than four months. Finally, the directive guarantees each worker in the EU a minimum of four weeks of annual leave per year (European Council, 1993).

Informal

In addition to the formality of binding legislation, the EU has also addressed work and family through informal means. A non-binding recommendation (European Union, undated) issued by the European Council encourages the member states to develop '[m]easures . . . to enable men and women to reconcile their occupational and family obligations' (European Council, 1992b). Among other recommendations, member states were encouraged to consider addressing childcare for parents who work or were in school, affordability of childcare and training for childcare workers.

Following the issuance of the 1992 recommendation, the Council shifted its approach and conceptualized childcare in the EU as a component of a full-employment strategy in the Community because it removes a barrier to female labor force participation. The Luxembourg Job Summit of 1997 announced a European Employment Strategy (EES) (European Commission, 2002a). As part of the EES, the European Council, meeting in Barcelona in 2002, stated in its conclusions that EU member states should strive toward the goal of childcare for 33% of all children under three years old, and for 90% of all children between three years old and mandatory

Table 2.6 Summary of status of selected EU members regarding 2002
European Council targets on childcare, 2002

	Exceeds or within 20% of Council targets, 1- to 3-year-olds	*Exceeds or within 20% of Council targets, 3 years to school age*
Austria (2000–01)		
Belgium (2001)		
Flemish	×	N/A
French		N/A
Denmark (2001)	×	×
Germany (1998)		×
Italy (1998)		
Netherlands (2001)		
Spain (2000–01)		×

Source: European Commission (2002a).

school age (European Council, 2002). In essence, the Council focused on numerical goals for childcare within each member country rather than recommending that the EU legislate for all member countries.

In its 2002 report to the Council, the European Commission examined childcare polices in various EU member states to determine how far the member states would be required to go to meet the Barcelona targets. Of the 15 states, seven provided data to the European Commission on the percentage of children in childcare by the relevant ages. These data are summarized in Table 2.6.

Based on these data, the Commission came to two conclusions. First, the Commission determined that most European states did not provide sufficient, affordable childcare services to meet the Council's targets. Second, the Commission determined that the lack of comparable data across member states would make it difficult to assess whether countries were meeting the targets (European Commission, 2002a).

Referring to the Luxembourg Summit on Employment Strategy in 1997, as well as previous and subsequent meetings, Eurostat, the data analysis agency for the EU and the European Commission, conducted a feasibility study in 2002 regarding the collection of childcare data in the EU. The study concluded that it was necessary to collect uniform data from the providers and the users (European Commission, 2002b).

Comparisons of national leave policies and best practices for selected EU countries

In addition to examining work and family at the EU level, it also seems useful to focus on the country level. To that end, this section will review national leave policies and examples of progressive firm-level practices for selected EU countries based on the availability of reliable research data.

Although this is not intended to be a complete survey of work–family practices in the EU countries, we hope this section will provide the reader a flavor of some national differences within the EU as well as what is possible under these national regimes.

United Kingdom

With respect to national policy, women on maternity leave are legally entitled to receive 26 weeks of ordinary maternity leave at all contractual benefits except wages and salary (UK Department of Trade and Industry, 2004). Women on ordinary maternity leave receive statutory maternity pay, which, since April 1993, is 90% of regular pay for the first six weeks and £100 or 90% of average weekly earnings, whichever is less, for the next 20 weeks (Department of Trade and Industry, 2004). Women who have been employed for 26 weeks or more are entitled to 26 weeks of additional maternity leave after the conclusion of ordinary maternity leave, with entitlement to benefits determined by the employment contract (UK Department of Trade and Industry, 2004). Men on paternity leave receive two weeks' leave at the same rate as statutory maternity pay for the last 20 weeks (Bowker *et al.*, 2003; UK Department of Trade and Industry, 2003).

As an example of practices in the UK, Wakefield Metropolitan District Council in West Yorkshire, which is a local council to over 300,000 people in the community, developed a work–life balance 'scheme' to create, attract and retain a more qualified and motivated workforce (Bigwood, 1996). Since the 1980s the council has implemented programs such as flexitime, job sharing and career breaks. Recently, labor and management worked jointly to form a group that developed leave options that the employees desired and that were feasible for the council. The result was four different options from which the employees could choose depending upon their needs. These included two types of leaves: *paid short-term leave*, allowing individuals to take up to a maximum of 15 days a year for dependant care; and open-ended *unpaid longer-term leave* as a supplement to the short-term leave. *Term-time working* allows employees to work only during school terms and be off when school is not in session, but they are still paid in installments throughout the year. The fourth option, *temporary negotiated hours*, allows employees and managers to establish working hours that are feasible for both the employee and the organization. Two other new work–life policies include formation of day-care clubs for children during school holidays and a computerized childcare information service to assist parents, childcare providers and employers (Bigwood, 1996).

The retailer Marks & Spencer increased its maternity leave options to include short enhanced leave that provides 18 weeks full pay and another 8 weeks of statutory maternity/adoption pay. M&S also added enhanced long leave whereby the employee receives 10 weeks at full pay, 16 weeks of statutory pay and 26 weeks of unpaid leave. Asda Group Unlimited, the UK's second largest food retailer, developed its 'Babies at Asda' program. Women receive 90% pay for the first six weeks and then statutory maternity pay for up to one full year and salaries return to 100% when they return to work. Paternity leave can be taken for two weeks at full pay. Both men and women can change their hours upon returning to work to accommodate their needs (Bowker *et al.*, 2003).

Germany

Regarding national policy, the Maternity Protection Act (*Mutterschutzgesetz*) and the federal Child Benefit Act (*Bundeserziehungsgeldgesetz*) are the statutory protections in Germany. These laws grant employees maternity leave and pay, the right to return to their job after leave and the right to be absent from work to raise the child. An employee cannot be dismissed during pregnancy or up to the end of the fourth month after the birth. The federal Child Benefit Act also protects employees from dismissal during their absence from work. In some exceptional cases, however, the employer is entitled to terminate the employment contract with the approval of a competent authority (Moll and Wojtek, 2003).

Pregnant women are not required to work six weeks before and eight weeks after childbirth. During this time they are entitled to receive maternity pay at 100% of average earnings, with the cost to be shared by the statutory health insurance policy and the employer if the person has statutory health insurance, or shared between the state and the employer if the person does not have statutory health insurance or private health insurance (Europa: Gateway to the European Union, undated; European Foundation for Employment and Living Conditions, undated-b). After the maternity pay period ends, a parent is entitled to childcare leave to the end of the month in which the child reaches 18 months of age. There is a childcare payment of DM600 per month (as of July 2004), which decreases after the seventh month at higher incomes and which is also coordinated with the maternity allowance (European Foundation for Employment and Living Conditions, undated-a). When returning to work after their absence, they may go back to their previous hours of employment and position as before the birth (Moll and Wojtek, 2003).

With respect to practice in Germany, RWE Net AG, which is the largest electricity distribution company in Europe, has a number of progressive policies such as a company kindergarten and on-site day care for children of employees, and three-year parental leave with the option of working part time when they return. Job sharing is also very common. RWE also has an employee involvement program where employees work in small teams to create solutions or suggestions regarding workplace issues of concern to them (Jones, 2003).

Sweden

With respect to policy, Sweden is by far the most progressive industrialized country in the area of family leave benefits. Employees receive 90% of pay for the first 12 months of leave and then a fixed benefit for an additional three months. This leave may be divided between parents however they choose, although there are incentives for fathers to take a substantial portion of it. Employees are entitled to their jobs upon return from the leave. There is extended parental leave until the child is 18 months of age and then the employee can work up to 6 hours a day and still receive benefits until the child is eight years old (Parry, 2001). Parental leave may be taken in quarter, half or full days in the years before the child completes his/her first year of school (Haas, 2003). With respect to practice, it must be noted that Sweden's federally mandated benefits are among the best in the world and are so comprehensive that organizations most likely do not find the need to increase benefit levels above those prescribed by national policy. Thus, firms in Sweden must provide substantial work–family benefits for their employees.

Norway

As Norway is not a member of the European Union, it is not obligated to comply with EU directives. Thus, it may act with complete sovereignty in work and family policy. As a Scandinavian country, Norway's work–family policy is similar to the policy in Sweden in providing generous leave benefits. In Norway either parent is eligible for leave. The parent must have been employed for at least six of the previous 10 months. Either parent may take up to 52 weeks of leave at 80% or 42 weeks at 100% pay. Single parents, however, are entitled to three years' leave. These cash benefits are for 'insured' parents. Maternity grants are available for women who cannot receive maternity benefits and also for adoptive parents (Jordan, 1999).

With respect to practice among Norwegian firms, the HAG Company, a furniture manufacturer, offers a generous maternity/paternity leave system. This is for either birth or adoption of a child and the employee is entitled to 42 weeks of leave at full pay or 52 weeks at 80% of his/her salary. New mothers also can take unpaid leave for up to another full year after the paid leave and are entitled to the same job upon return (Jones, 2003).[14]

COMPARING INSTITUTIONAL SUPPORT FOR WORK–FAMILY IN THE USA, CANADA AND THE EUROPEAN UNION

Structurally, the USA, Canada, and the EU have used a blend of legal and informal mechanisms to reconcile work–family conflicts. The main legal mechanism has been time off for family reasons with no long-term penalty to job status, with penalty defined as a job status different from what the employee would have experienced had he or she not taken the leave.

Differences among the USA, Canada, and the EU revolve around pay and related legal structures. Canadian workers receive pay provided through the Employment Insurance system while on family-related leave. Workers in the USA receive no paid leave for family purposes, although they may use any other paid leave, such as sick pay or vacation pay, that they have accrued. EU directives do not provide workers in EU countries maternity leave pay, although legislation in the individual countries may provide for pay from government sources.

Overall, it can be concluded that in these three western democracies there is a consensus that, at a minimum, employees are entitled to time off from work for maternity and childcare purposes with no loss of job status. Beyond this, however, there are differences with respect to pay and the amount of time to be taken.

Future research directions

The review in this chapter shows that there are policy differences across the three jurisdictions. Thus, a key question revolves around the economic and social costs of these varying policies. Do employers in countries that provide paid maternity, either directly or through relatively high payroll taxes, incur higher costs than employers in countries that do not provide such leave? If employers in paid-leave countries do incur relatively high costs, are they compensated in terms of greater productivity, lower turnover and higher morale? If their maternity leave costs are higher, do employers compensate by reducing costs in other employment-related areas, such as the number of employees or reduced supervisory costs?

Even if costs are higher associated with leave, does it make a difference? What is the overall increment to employment costs associated with work–family policies? If it is small, a country may decide that the improvement in the quality of life of its citizens is worth the cost. Even if it is not small, it may be asked whether these differences matter in terms of the economic health of the jurisdiction, as measured by such factors as employment growth and change in GDP. In other words, even if there are micro firm effects, are there macro effects?

Overall, it is hoped that this comparative overview will encourage researchers to think about different ways that capitalist systems can address the issue of work–family balance. This is likely to encourage research in ways that we cannot predict.

NOTES

1 For the text of the Family and Medical Leave Act, see Legal Information Institute (undated).

2 This section discusses only the most common problems. For example, the FMLA requires, whenever the need for leave is foreseeable based on the expected date of birth or adoption placement, that the employee provide the employer with at least 30 days' notice of the leave. Where the need to begin leave on a particular date is not foreseeable, the employee must provide as much notice as practicable. But a survey of 138 FMLA cases involving childbirth leave decided between 1995 and 2003 found that employers raised a defense of an employee's alleged failure to give sufficient notice only eight times (Gely and Chandler, 2004).

3 For example, although the House of Representatives and Senate committee reports accompanying the FMLA addressed the need for all types of leave covered by the Act, they devoted the majority of their discussions to the need for leave following birth or adoption of a child or to care for a seriously ill child (US Congress 1993a, 1993b, 1993c).

4 See Table 2.3 and the associated text for data on the prevalence of some paid leave in the United States.

5 The national legal system in the USA consists of 94 district courts, generally organized around state and regional boundaries, 12 circuit courts, or courts of appeals, organized geographically, each of which hears appeals from the district courts within its circuit, and one Supreme Court, which is the highest judicial body in the country. For a description of the national judicial system in the USA, see http://www.fjc.gov/federal/courts.nsf. For a listing of the districts and a map of the circuits, see http://www.law.emory.edu/FEDCTS/. Most states have analogous legal systems to decide questions of state law.

6 See, for example, Dollar v. Shoney's, Inc. (1997); Watkins v. J & S Oil Co. (1998); Marks v. School Dist. of Kansas City, Mo. (1996); Maxwell v. American Red Cross Blood Service (1996), Tuberville v. Personal Fin. Corp. (1996); Oswalt v. Sara Lee Corp. (1996, affirmed,1996).

7 See Hickox (2002) and Malin (2003).

8 Smith v. Diffee Ford-Lincoln Mercury, Inc. (2002); Strickland v. Water Works & Sewer Board of City of Birmingham (2001).

9 For example, employees may prefer an additional wage increase to employer-sponsored childcare. They can use the wage increase to purchase their own childcare.

10 A childcare referral service provides employees with the names of childcare providers. The providers may be 'approved' by the employer, or the providers may simply be those who meet state standards are located near the employer. The purpose of such a service is to facilitate the acquisition of childcare by the employee.

11 See pp. 000–000, below.

12 For a discussion of the theoretical differences among the governing structures of the EU, the USA and Canada, see Marleau (2003).

13 Under the 1992 Maastricht Treaty, because of the unwillingness of the UK to move forward on social issues as quickly as the other members of the EU, the EU modified its traditional unanimity rule for adopting directives on social issues. Under Maastricht, the UK could opt out of any directive on social issues with which it disagreed, thus permitting the directive to apply to the other EU members. When, as a result of a change in the UK government from conservative to labour, the UK later decided to 'opt in' on a directive from which it had previously 'opted out', it was necessary to issue a new directive (see Block et al., 2001).

14 Although this paper has focused on work and family issues leave on either side of the North Atlantic, the reader may also be interested in work and family legislation in Australia and New Zealand, English-speaking countries with cultural ties to Europe. In Australia, the Workplace Relations Act of 1996

provides parents who have been employed for 12 months with the same employer up to 52 weeks of unpaid parental leave associated with a newborn, provided that the parents may not take the leave simultaneously and the leave may be reduced by other leave taken or parental leave available to the employee through an arbitration award or state law. The employee on leave is generally entitled to return to the position he or she held prior to the leave (see Australia, Government of, undated). In New Zealand, as in Australia, parents may share up to 52 weeks of leave associated with the birth of a child. The parent must have been employed with the same employer for at least 12 months, worked at least 10 hours per week and not be self-employed. The parent who does not take leave is entitled to two weeks partner/maternity leave. The female employee is entitled to up to 12 weeks of a government payment, which may be transferred to a husband/spouse or partner of either gender. The payment replaces the employees' average weekly earnings up to a maximum. Effective 1 July 2004, the maximum was NZ $346.63 per week, with the payment made to the spouse/ partner on leave. Receipt of the statutory leave payment is not reduced by other payments received by the employee to which he or she is entitled (for example, from a collective bargaining agreement) (see New Zealand Department of Labour, undated, and Gravitas Research and Strategy, Limited, 2003).

REFERENCES

Australia, Government of (undated). *Commonwealth Consolidated Acts, Workplace Relations Act of 1996*. Retrieved 29 July 2004 from http://www.austlii.edu.au/au/legis/cth/consol_act/wra1996220/sch14.html

Barnett, R. (1999). A new work–life model for the 21st century. *Annals of the American Academy for Political and Social Sciences, 562*, 143–158.

Bigwood, S. (1996). The advantage of a caring approach. *People Management, 2*(10), 40–42.

Block, Richard N., Berg, P., and Belman, D. (2004). The economic dimension of the employment relationship. In J. A.-M. Coyle-Shapiro, L. M. Shore, M. S. Taylor and L. E. Tetrick (eds), *The employment relationship: Examining psychological and contextual perspectives* (pp. 94–118). Oxford, UK: Oxford University Press.

Block, R. N., Berg, P., and Roberts, K. (2003). Comparing and quantifying labour standards in the United States and the European Union. *International Journal of Labour Law and Industrial Relations, 19*(4), 441–467.

Block, R. N., Roberts, K., Ozeki, C., and Roomkin, M. (2001). Models of international labor standards. *Industrial Relations, 40*(2), 258–292.

Block, R. N., Roberts, K, and Clarke, R. O. (2003). *Labor standards in the United States and Canada*. Kalamazoo, MI: W. E. Upjohn Institute for Employment Research.

Bowker, G., Rotchell, D., and Frost, T. (2003, April). Hot topic: the UK's working parents move up the pay league. *Human Resources*, London.

California (undated). *California Unemployment Insurance Code, Part 2, Disability Benefits, Chapter 7, Paid Family Leave*, §§ 3300–3306. Retrieved 3 August 2004 from http://www.leginfo.ca.gov/cgi-bin/displaycode?section=uic&group=03001-04000&file=3300-3306

Canada, Government of (undated). *Compassionate Care Benefits*. Retrieved 4 January 2004 from http://www.hrdc-drhc.gc.ca/ei-ae/pubs/compassionate_care.shtml

Cantor, D., Waldfogel, J., Kerwin, J., McKinley Wright, M., Levin, K., Rauck, J., Hagerty, T., and Kudela Stapleton, M. (2001). *Balancing the needs of families and employers: The family and medical leave surveys.* Washington, DC: US Department of Labor. Retrieved at www.dol-gov/asp/fmla/main2000.htm

Comfort, D., Johnson, K., and Wallace, D. (2003). *Part-time work and family friendly policies in Canadian workplaces.* Ottawa: Statistics Canada and Human Resources Development Canada. Retrieved 4 April 2004 from http://www.statcan.ca/english/freepub/71-584-MIE/71-584-MIE03006.pdf

Employment Insurance Benefits (undated). Retrieved 15 December 2003 from www.hrdc-drhc.gc.ca/ae-ei/employment_insurance

Europa: Gateway to the European Union (undated). *European Commission – Social Protection in the EU – Germany.* Retrieved 27 July 2004 from http://europa.eu.int/comm/employment_social/missoc/2002/germany_en.pdf

European Commission (2002a). *Communication from the Commission to the Council – Draft Employment Report 2002,* SEC (2002) 1204. Retrieved 27 July 2004 from http://europa.eu.int/comm/employment_social/news/2002/nov/jer2002_en.pdf

European Commission (2002b). *Feasibility study on the availability of child care statistics in the European Union.* Working Paper, Directorate E, Unit E-2, Living Conditions, 3/2001/E/N°16. Retrieved 27 July 2004 from http://europa.eu.int/comm/eurostat/Public/datashop/print-catalogue/EN?catalogue=Eurostat&collection=12-Working+papers+and+studies&product=KS-CC-02-001-__-N-EN

European Council (1989). *Council Directive of 12 June 1989 on the introduction of measures to encourage improvements in the safety and health of workers at work.* Retrieved 27 July 2004 from http://europa.eu.int/eur-lex/en/search/search_lif.html

European Council (1992a). *Council Directive 92/85/EEC of 19 October 1992 on the introduction of measures to encourage improvements in the safety and health at work of pregnant workers and workers who have recently given birth or are breastfeeding* (Tenth Individual Directive within the meaning of Article 16 (1) of Directive 89/391/EEC). Retrieved 27 July 2004 from http://europa.eu.int/eur-lex/en/search/search_lif.html

European Council (1992b). *Recommendation of 31 March 1992 on child care (92/241/EEC).* Retrieved 28 July 2004 from http://europa.eu.int/smartapi/cgi/sga_doc?smartapi!celexapi!prod!CELEXnumdoc&lg=EN&numdoc=31992H0241&model=guichett

European Council (1993). *Council Directive 93/104/EC of 23 November 1993 concerning certain aspects of the organization of working time.* Retrieved 27 July 2004 from http://europa.eu.int/eur-lex/en/search/search_lif.html

European Council (1996). *Council Directive 96/34/EC of 3 June 1996 on the framework agreement on parental leave concluded by UNICE, CEEP and the ETUC.* Retrieved 27 July 2004 from http://europa.eu.int/eur-lex/en/search/search_lif.html

European Council (1997). *Council Directive 97/75/EC of 15 December 1997 amending and extending, to the United Kingdom of Great Britain and Northern Ireland, Directive 96/34/EC on the framework agreement on parental leave concluded by UNICE, CEEP and the ETUC.* Retrieved 27 July 2004 from http://europa.eu.int/eur-lex/en/search/search_lif.html

European Council (2002). *Presidency conclusions Barcelona 15 and 16 March.* Retrieved 8 July 2004 from http://ue.eu.int/newsroom/up.asp?MAX=&BID=76&DID=71025&File=/pressData/en/ec/71025.pdf&LANG=1

European Foundation for Employment and Living Conditions (undated-a).

Germany: Childcare payment. Retrieved 28 July 2004 from http://www.eurofound. eu.int/emire/GERMANY/CHILDCAREPAYMENT-DE.html

European Foundation for Employment and Living Conditions (undated-b). *Germany: Maternity protection.* Retrieved 28 July 2004 from http://www. eurofound.eu.int/emire/GERMANY/MATERNITYPROTECTION-DE.html

European Parliament and European Council (2002). *Directive 2002/73/EC of the European Parliament and of the Council of 23 September 2002 amending Council Directive 76/207/EEC on the implementation of the principle of equal treatment for men and women as regards access to employment, vocational training and promotion, and working conditions.* Retrieved 28 July 2004 from http://europa.eu.int/ eur-lex/en/search/search_lif.html

European Union (undated). *EU Law – Definitions: Secondary legislation.* Retrieved 28 July 2004 from http://europa.eu.int/eurlex/en/about/pap/process_and_players2. html

Gely, R., and Chandler, T. (2004). Maternity leave under the FMLA: an analysis of the litigation experience. *Journal of Law and Policy, 15,* 143–168.

Government of Alberta (undated). *Employment Standards Code,* Chapter E-9. Retrieved 15 December 2003 from http://www.qp.gov.ab.ca/documents/acts/ E09.cfm

Government of British Columbia (undated-a). Ministry of Skills Development and Labour, *Employment Standards: Parental Leave, ESA Section 51.* Retrieved 15 December 2003 from http://www.labour.gov.bc.ca/esb/igm/sections/sect_051. htm

Government of British Columbia (undated-b). Ministry of Skills Development and Labour, *Employment Standards: Pregnancy Leave, ESA Section 50.* Retrieved 15 December 2003 from http://www.labour.gov.bc.ca/esb/igm/sections/sect_050. htm

Government of Yukon (undated-a). *Compassionate Care Leave.* Retrieved 4 April 2004 from http://www.gov.yk.ca/depts/community/labour/compare.html

Government of Yukon (undated-b). *Maternity and Paternity Leave.* Retrieved 4 April 2004 from http://www.gov.yk.ca/depts/community/labour/matpat.html

Gravitas Research and Strategy, Limited (2003). *Evaluation of the Implementation of Paid Parental Leave.* Prepared for Employment Relations Service, New Zealand Department of Labour, 27 August. Retrieved 27 July 2004 from http://www.ers. govt.nz/parentalleave/pdfs/PPLevaluation/doc

Haas, L. (2003). Parental leave and gender equality: lessons from the European Union. *Review of Policy Research, 20,* 89–115.

Hickox, S. A. (2002). The elusive right to reinstatement under the family medical leave act. *Kentucky Law Journal, 91,* 477–522.

Human Resources and Skills Development Canada (2004) *Employment insurance (EI) compassionate care benefits.* Retrieved from http://www.hrsdc.gc.ca/asp/ gateway.asp?hr=en/ei/types/compassionate_care.shtml&hs=tyt

Human Resources Development Canada (undated). *Employment insurance: Maternity, parental, and sickness benefits.* Retrieved from http://www.hrdc-drhc.gc.ca/ae-ei/pubs/special_e.shtml

Jones, D. (2003). Europe taking lead in work–life balance. *Canadian HR Reporter, 16*(14), 6–7.

Jordan, L. (1999). *OLR Research Report: Background Information on European and*

Canadian Parental Leave Laws. Retrieved 7 April 2004 from http://www.cga. satate.ct.us/ps99/rpt/olr/htm/

Kossek, E. E., and Lambert, S. J. (eds) (2005). *Work and Life Integration: Organizational, Cultural and Individual Perspectives*. Mahwah, NJ: Lawrence Erlbaum Associates.

Legal Information Institute (undated). *US Code Collection: Title 29, Chapter 28*.

Lewis, S., and Haas, L. (2005). Work–life integration and social policy: a social justice approach to work and family. In E. Kossek and S. Lambert (eds), *Work–life Integration: Organizational, Cultural and Individual Perspectives*, pp. 349–379. Mahwah, NJ: Lawrence Erlbaum Associates.

Lipset, S. M. (1989). *Continental divide: The values and institutions of the United States and Canada*. Toronto and Washington, DC: C. D. Howe Institute and National Planning Association.

Malin, M. H. (2003). Interference with the right to leave under the Family and Medical Leave Act. *Employee Rights and Employment Policy Journal*, 7, 329–376.

Marleau, V. (2003). Globalization and the problem of compound decentralization: lessons from the Canadian labour relations setting. Paper presented at the *Decentralization of labour policies and collective bargaining, international seminar in commemoration of Marco Biagi*, Modena, Italy.

Moll, W., and Wojtek, H. K. L. (2003). *Labour and employee benefits: Germany*. Retrieved 3 October 2003 from http://www.practicallaw.com/scripts/topic.asp? Topic_ID=236&viewType=law

New Brunswick Department of Training and Employment Development (undated). *Employment Standards*. Retrieved from http://www.gnb.ca/0308/001e.htm

Newfoundland and Labrador (undated). *Labor Standards Act Amended: Chapter L-2*. Retrieved 4 January 2004 from http://www.gov.nf.ca/hoa/statutes/l02.htm#43.3

New Zealand Department of Labour (undated). *Information on taxpayer-funded paid parental leave*. Retrieved 29 July 2004 from http://www.ers.govt.nz/parental leave/71T.html

Northwest Territories (undated). *Consolidation of Labour Standards Act*. Retrieved 4 January 2004 from http://www.canlii.org/nt/sta/pdf/type169a.pdf

Nova Scotia Environment and Labour (undated). *Labor Standards Code*. Retrieved 8 April 2004 from http://www.gov.ns.ca/legislature/legc/statutes/labourst.htm

Ontario Ministry of Labour (undated). *Publications*. Retrieved 8 April 2004 from http://www.gov.on.ca/LAB/english/es/es_pubs.html

Parry, J. A. (2001). Family-leave policies. *NWSA Journal*, Fall, 78.

Prince Edward Island, Community and Cultural Affairs (2001). *Guide to employment standards*. Retrieved 15 December 2003 from http://www.gov.pe.ca/photos/ original/cca_2001guide.pdf

Province of Manitoba, Manitoba Labour and Immigration (undated-a). *Employment standards: Compassionate care*. Retrieved 15 December 2003 from http:// www.gov.mb.ca/labour/standards/pdf/compassionate_care_leave.pdf

Province of Manitoba, Manitoba Labour and Immigration (undated-b). *Employment standards: Maternity and parental leave*. Retrieved 15 December 2003 from http://www.gov.mb.ca/labour/standards/facts.html

Quebec, Commission des Nomes du Travail (undated). *Absences and leaves for family and parental matters*. Retrieved 5 April 2004 from http://canadaonline. about.com/gi/dynamic/offsite.htm?site=http%3A%2F%2Fwww.cnt.gouv.qc.ca% 2Fen%2Findex.asp

Saskatchewan Labour (undated). *Labour standards.* Retrieved 15 December 2003 from http://www.labour.gov.sk.ca/standards

Springer, B. (1994). *The European Union and its citizens: The social agenda.* Westport, CT, and London: Greenwood Press.

UK Department of Trade and Industry (2003). *Working fathers (PL517) rights to leave and pay: A guide for employers and employees: Introduction.* Retrieved 13 July 2004 from http://www.dti.gov.uk/er/individual/patrights-pl517a.htm

UK Department of Trade and Industry (2004). *Maternity rights (PL958 Rev 9): A guide for employers and employees: Section 4 maternity leave.* Retrieved 13 July 2004 from http://www.dti.gov.uk/er/individual/mat-pl958b.htm

US Bureau of Labor Statistics (undated-a). *Employee benefits survey – national compensation survey: Benefits.* Retrieved 11 May 2005 from http://www.bls.gov/ncs/ebs/home.htm

US Bureau of Labor Statistics (undated-b). *National employment hours and earnings.* Retrieved 12 May 2004 from http://www.bls.gov/ces/home.htm

United States Congress (1993a) House Committee on Education & Labor, H. Rep. No. 103-8(I).

United States Congress (1993b) House Committee on Post Office & Civil Service, H. Rep. No. 103-8(II).

United States Congress (1993c) Senate Committee on Labor & Human Resources, S. Rep. No. 103-3.

United States Department of Labor (undated-a). *The family and medical leave act of 1993: 29 CFR 825.216.* Are there any limitations on an employer's obligation to reinstate an employee? Retrieved from http://www.dol.gov/dol/allcfr/ESA/Title_29/Part_825/29CFR825.216.htm

United States Department of Labor (undated-e). *The family and medical leave act of 1993: 29 CFR 825.217.* What is a 'key employee?' Retrieved from http://www.dol.gov/dol/allcfr/ESA/Title_29/Part_825/29CFR825.217.htm

United States Department of Labor (undated-d). *The family and medical leave act of 1993: 29 CFR 825.700.* What if an employer provides more generous benefits than required by FMLA? Retrieved from http://www.dol.gov/dol/allcfr/ESA/Title_29/Part_825/29CFR825.700.htm

Wisensale, S. K. (2001). *Family leave policy: The political economy of work and family in America* (p. 172). Armonk, NY: M. E. Sharpe.

TABLE OF CASES

Bachelder v. America West Airlines, Inc., 2001, 259 F. 3rd 1112, 9th Circuit at http://caselaw.lp.findlaw.com/data2/circs/9th/9917458p.pdf

Burke v. Health Plus of Michigan, Inc. 2003, 2003 WL 102800, E.D. Mich.

Dollar v. Shoney's, Inc., 1997, 981 F. Supp. 1417, N.D. Ala.

Kohls v. Beverly Enterprises, Wisconsin, Inc. 2001, 259 F. 3rd 799, 7th Circuit at http://caselaw.lp.findlaw.com/scripts/printer_friendly.pl?page=7th/002064.html

Marks v. School Dist. of Kansas City, Mo. 1996, 941 F. Supp. 886, W.D. Mo.

Maxwell v. American Red Cross Blood Service, 1996, 3 Wage & Hour Cases 2d 633, N.D. Ala.

Oswalt v. Sara Lee Corp., 1996, 889 F. Supp. 253, N.D. Miss. 1995, affirmed, 1996,

74 F.3d 91, 5th Cir. at http://caselaw.lp.findlaw.com/scripts/printer_friendly.pl?page=5th/9560402cv0.html, August 4, 2004.

Ragsdale v. Wolverine World Wide, Inc., 2002, U.S. Supreme Court, 535 U.S. 81 at http://caselaw.lp.findlaw.com/scripts/printer_friendly.pl?page=us/000/00-6029.html, August 2, 2004.

Rice v. Sunrise Express, Inc., 2000, 209 F. 3rd 1008, 7th Cir. at http://caselaw.lp.findlaw.com/scripts/printer_friendly.pl?page=7th/973982.html

Smith v. Diffee Ford-Lincoln Mercury, Inc., 2002, 298 F. 3d 955, 10th Circuit at http://caselaw.lp.findlaw.com/scripts/printer_friendly.pl?page=10th/006362.html

Strickland v. Water Works & Sewer Board of City of Birmingham, 2001, 239 F. 3d 1199, 11th Circuit at http://caselaw.lp.findlaw.com/scripts/printer_friendly.pl?page=11th/9914103man.html

Tuberville v. Personal Fin. Corp., 1996, 3 Wage & Hour Cases 2d 882, D. Miss.

Walters v. Metropolitan Education Enterprise, Inc., U.S. Supreme Court, 1997, 519 U.S. 202, 1997 at http://caselaw.lp.findlaw.com/scripts/printer_friendly.pl?page=us/000/u9701010.html

Watkins v. J & S Oil Co., 1998, 977 F. Supp. 520, D. Me.

Part II

Researching the work–home interface

This part focuses on introducing the core theoretical constructs and measurement issues relevant to understanding and researching in the work–life context. As such it is likely to be of particular relevance to students and researchers. Chapter 3 by Nancy Rothbard and Tracy Dumas introduces the psychological models and approaches used in researching this area. It moves from a historical perspective outlining theories used in early studies to introducing emerging perspectives, including new research examining the ways in which work may enrich or enhance home life.

This theoretical introduction is complemented by Chapter 4, by Lois Tetrick and Louis Buffardi, which provides practical information about the ways in which core concepts are measured, from measures of conflict to those of perceived work–life balance. A particularly useful feature is the inclusion of full details of two important measures. In addition, there are descriptions and comparisons of many other widely used scales. Overall, this chapter will provide vital information for those conducting researchers, as well as helping the general reader to critically evaluate the evidence provided elsewhere.

3 Research perspectives: managing the work–home interface

Nancy P. Rothbard and Tracy L. Dumas

Managing the interface between work and home has emerged as a central topic for both management practitioners and academics. With the growing numbers of women in the workforce and the increase of dual-earner couples (Burke and Greenglass, 1987; Lambert, 1990; Voydanoff, 1987), today's organizations face the challenge of implementing practices that allow their employees to achieve at work, while also engaging meaningfully in their homes and communities (see Chapter 1). As juggling multiple roles has become more prevalent for both men and women, organizational scholars have focused more study on the relationship between work and home and the ways individuals enact and navigate their roles in the two domains. These scholars have drawn primarily from the disciplines of psychology and sociology to provide the theoretical basis for examining characteristics of work and home roles, and much of the research has considered how the work–home interface may be related to critical outcomes such as stress, role conflict and multiple role participation.

Past research has addressed the ways work and non-work roles might influence one another, building on psychological constructs such as affect, cognition and values (see Edwards and Rothbard, 2000, for a review). For example, researchers have asked whether negative affect at home spills over and negatively influences a person's work role, or whether a person compensates by throwing him or herself into the work role to escape such negative affect. Prior research also has been very concerned both with role stress and its antecedents (e.g., Edwards and Rothbard, 2005; Greenhaus and Parasuraman, 1986; Zedeck, 1992), focusing on role expectations (Higgins *et al.*, 1992), demands (Grandey and Cropanzano, 1999; Kopelman *et al.*, 1983, Frone *et al.*, 1992a) and fit between desired and actual environmental characteristics (Edwards and Rothbard, 1999). Moreover, a great many studies have focused on work–family conflict (Frone *et al.*, 1992a; see Chapter 5). Indeed a recent meta-analysis found a consistent negative relationship between work–family conflict and job and life satisfaction (Kossek and Ozeki, 1998).

Although much of past research in the work–family area focused on detrimental outcomes of actively participating in multiple roles such as stress and conflict, more recently work–family researchers have begun to consider the potentially enriching effects of multiple roles (Kirchmeyer, 1992; Rothbard, 2001; Ruderman *et al.*, 2002; see Chapter 5). Such recent studies have relied on psychological theories such as self-regulation and self-esteem to explain why positive experiences in one role might carry over and enhance functioning in another role (Rothbard, 2001). The crux of this argument is that psychological resources accrued in one role boost self-esteem and confidence and thus enhance functioning in another role (Rothbard, 2001; Ruderman *et al.*, 2002).

Further developments in work–family research center around people's strategies for managing the boundary between these roles (e.g., Kossek *et al.*, 1999; Rothbard *et al.*, 2005; see also Chapter 6). Whereas past researchers have considered the characteristics of the boundary between home and work roles (Dubin, 1973; Hall, 1972; Hall and Richter, 1988), more recent research has begun to examine how integration or segmentation strategies for navigating the work–family boundary may affect an individual's psychological experience of work and family roles (e.g., Kossek *et al.*, 1999; Nippert-Eng, 1995; Rothbard *et al.*, 2005).

Finally, whereas most research addressing the work–home interface has historically addressed the management of work and family demands, this area of inquiry is rapidly expanding to consider various other aspects of employees' non-work lives such as community involvement and racial identity. Similarly, many companies have expanded the focus of their human resources policies from that of work–family balance to work–life balance to reflect the variety of non-work roles that employees may hold and enact. Among the studies addressing non-family, non-work roles are those of Kingston and Nock (1992), who examined working couples' community involvement, and, more recently, Dumas' (2003) examination of workers' involvement in community music organizations. In a similar vein, Phillips *et al.* (2002) addressed the role of racial diversity as a factor in people's preference for role boundary management strategies. These studies and others reflect emerging directions and research perspectives in the study of the work–non-work interface.

As reflected in the variety of studies addressing the work–non-work interface, this is a dynamic area of research that has changed dramatically in the past decade. In this chapter we review the progression of research on the work–non-work interface and explicate links to psychological constructs that underpin this research. We also identify important new developments and future directions in this critical field of study.

DOMINANT MODELS IN WORK–FAMILY RESEARCH

Through the 1980s and the 1990s the amount of research on work and family roles increased substantially. This proliferation of research led to several models capturing the relationship between work and family roles. Edwards and Rothbard (2000) provide a review and integration of much of the existing research on the relationship between work and family roles. They identified six recurring linking mechanisms depicted in the work–family literature: spillover, compensation, segmentation, resource drain, congruence and work–family conflict. Of these six mechanisms, spillover, compensation, segmentation and congruence have been primarily used to explain observed relationships between work and family constructs, whereas resource drain and work–family conflict are primarily outcomes of work and family role enactment. Spillover, compensation and segmentation have emerged as the dominant models characterizing the linkage between work and non-work roles. Role conflict and stress have also emerged as dominant areas of research on the work–family interface. We first review spillover, compensation and segmentation and then turn to a discussion of work–family conflict and stress.

Spillover, compensation and segmentation

Spillover

Spillover is a process whereby experiences in one role affect experiences in the other, rendering the roles more similar. Research has examined the spillover of mood, values, skills and behaviors from one role to another (Edwards and Rothbard, 2000), although the majority of this research has focused on mood spillover. The spillover model is supported when there is a significant positive relationship between measures of work and non-work experiences (Edwards and Rothbard, 2000; Lambert, 1990; Staines, 1980). Congruence is also represented by a positive relationship between measures of work and non-work experiences, but is caused by a third factor affecting both the work and non-work roles (Edwards and Rothbard, 2000). Spillover can take two forms. One is characterized by similarity between a work construct and a related construct in the non-work role, as when someone who is highly satisfied with his or her work organization becomes highly satisfied with his or her experiences in the family role. The second form of spillover entails the transference of experiences intact between work and non-work domains, as when fatigue from work is displayed at home; however, this second form must also entail the fatigue affecting family functioning for it to constitute spillover (Edwards and Rothbard, 2000). Existing research finds significant evidence of spillover (Lambert, 1990). In a key study of spillover, Williams and Alliger (1994) used experience sampling methodology to examine mood-related spillover on a daily basis, finding that working parents in their sample were more likely to bring work-related emotions home than they were to transfer family-related emotions to the workplace.

Compensation

A second process by which work and family roles may be linked has been termed 'compensation'. Compensation refers to a relationship between work and non-work roles whereby people attempt to make up for deficiencies in one role through greater involvement in another role (Champoux, 1978; Edwards and Rothbard, 2000; Lambert, 1990; Zedeck, 1992), and entails a negative relationship between constructs in the two roles (Edwards and Rothbard, 2000). Individuals can compensate for dissatisfaction in one role in a number of ways: they can reduce the importance ascribed to a less rewarding role or they can seek rewards and invest more time and attention in an alternative role (Edwards and Rothbard, 2000). Evidence for compensation has been found in a number of studies. Evans and Bartolome (1984) found that managers temporarily sought fulfillment in their family lives when they faced disappointment with their experiences at work. Tenbrunsel *et al.* (1995) also found a compensatory relationship between work and family roles for employed men. More recently, Rothbard (2001) found that women who experienced negative affect from family were more engaged with their work, consistent with a compensation story.

Segmentation

Unlike the compensation and spillover models, the segmentation model posits no systematic relationship between work and non-work roles (Edwards and Rothbard, 2000). Instead, segmentation has been used to describe the separation of work and family, such that the two roles do not influence one another (Edwards and Rothbard, 2000; Staines, 1980; Zedeck, 1992). Initially, segmentation was viewed as the natural division of work and family due to the physical and temporal separation of the two roles and to their innately different functions (Blood and Wolfe, 1960; Dubin, 1973). However, given the more recent view that work and family are closely related domains of human life (Burke and Greenglass, 1987; Kanter, 1977; Voydanoff, 1987), segmentation has been reconceptualized as an active psychological process whereby people may choose to maintain a boundary between work and family (Eckenrode and Gore, 1990; Lambert, 1990; Morf, 1989; Near, 1984). For example, Piotrkowski (1979) found that some people may actively suppress work-related thoughts, feelings and behaviors while at home, and vice versa. Building on this notion of segmentation as an active psychological process, recent research has articulated the notion that segmentation may be a strategy for work and family boundary management (Kossek *et al.*, 1999; Rothbard *et al.*, 2005) for keeping work and non-work domains separate and maintaining an impermeable boundary between work and non-work roles (Nippert-Eng, 1995).

Work–family conflict and stress

Another research perspective on the work–family interface has examined the psychological consequences of actively participating in both work and family roles (see also Chapter 5). The majority of this research has examined the detrimental or depleting effects of actively participating in multiple roles (Rothbard, 2001). Research on work–family conflict and stress are situated solidly in this tradition, examining the conditions under which working parents or dual-income families are negatively affected by simultaneous work and home demands.

Role conflict remains of central concern to work–family researchers and has been documented in many working populations. Examining data from the 1977 Quality of Employment Survey, Pleck *et al.* (1980) found that many working adults experienced conflict between work and family roles. A decade later, Frone *et al.* (1992b) conducted structured interviews of 631 working adults in Erie County, New York, as part of a longitudinal study of stress processes. When asked about the prevalence of work–family role conflict in their lives, nearly 60% of the respondents reported that their work role interfered with their family role, and 22% reported that their family role interfered with their work role. In a related study, Frone *et al.* (1992a) found that high involvement in both work and family roles led to increased work–family role conflict.

Research on work–family conflict and stress has its roots in role theory (Merton, 1957) and incorporates notions of perception and cognitive appraisal. Borrowing from the role theory tradition, classic conceptualizations of work–family conflict (e.g., Kopelman *et al.*, 1983; Greenhaus and Beutell, 1985) suggest that an individual encounters role conflict when the sent expectations or demands from one role interfere with the individual's ability to meet the sent expectations or demands from another role (Kahn *et al.*, 1964; Katz and Kahn, 1966; Merton, 1957). An example of role conflict is that of an employee who is simultaneously pressured to work overtime while family members urge that employee to come home. In a seminal article, Greenhaus and Beutell (1985) pushed these notions of role conflict further and divided work–family conflict into three categories: time-based, strain-based and behavior-based (see Chapter 5). Time-based conflict occurs when time spent in one role precludes participation in another role. Strain-based conflict occurs when stressors arising in one role affect the individual's enactment of another role despite the fact that the roles may not conflict temporally. Behavior-based conflict stems from situations where expectations or norms for behavior in one role are incompatible with the expectations for behavior in the other role.

Work–family research has refined understanding of work–family conflict further by showing that role conflict is bidirectional (Crouter, 1984; Frone *et al.*, 1992a) and can be asymmetric or reciprocal (Tenbrunsel *et al.*, 1995). An example of asymmetric role conflict may be that of a working father who feels that his work role interferes with his family role, yet does not feel that his family role interferes with his work role. Alternatively, an example of reciprocal role conflict could be that of a working mother who feels that her work schedule interferes with time she would like to spend with her child – and also feels that household responsibilities take away from the resources she has to fulfill work responsibilities. In each case these individuals encounter role conflict, the experience of one role interfering with enactment of another role.

Several studies have also linked work–family conflict with role stress (Anderson *et al.*, 2002; Frone *et al.*, 1992a; Grandey and Cropanzano, 1999). For example, Frone *et al.* (1992a) found that job stress increased work-to-family conflict whereas family stress increased family-to-work conflict. Drawing on Hobfoll's (1989, 1998) conservation of resources theory, Grandey and Cropanzano (1999) examined the relationship between stress and conflict and also found that work-role stress increased work-to-family conflict, which in turn led to greater job distress, whereas family-role stress led to greater family-to-work conflict, which in turn led to greater family distress. Anderson *et al.* (2002) similarly found that greater family demands increased the experience of role conflict from work to family and from family to work. In this study, both work-to-family conflict and family-to-work conflict were predictors of stress for the employees and expectations regarding career outcomes were key factors shaping employees' psychological experience of stress.

Research on work–family conflict and stress draws on psychological traditions to understand these phenomena through incorporating notions of perception and cognitive appraisal into models of work–family conflict. Indeed, several studies of work–family conflict and stress emphasize perception as a key mediator of the relationship between stressors and strain (Kopelman *et al.*, 1983; Higgins *et al.*, 1992; Greenhaus and Parasuraman, 1986), reflecting the concept that objective stressors do not affect a person unless he or she perceives them subjectively (Kahn *et al.*, 1964; Lazarus and Folkman, 1984). A number of theoretical models and empirical studies have emphasized how individual demographic differences such as age and gender, and personal characteristics such as locus of control, type A behavior and self-esteem, influence these subjective assessments (e.g., Frone *et al.*, 1992a; Grandey and Cropanzano, 1999; Greenhaus and Parasuraman, 1986). Indeed psychological resources have been found to decrease work–family conflict and strain (Grandey and Cropanzano, 1999). Other sources of subjective perception that have been studied include coping resources and the availability of social support (Burke and Greenglass, 1987; Eckenrode and Gore, 1990; Greenhaus and Beutell, 1985; Voydanoff, 1987).

Research has also begun to incorporate the notion of cognitive appraisal into the study of work–family conflict and stress (see Edwards and Rothbard, 2005). Cognitive appraisal entails the evaluation of situational characteristics in relation to salient personal standards such as values, goals, needs or desires in order to assess whether a situation is beneficial or detrimental to the individual (Lazurus and Folkman, 1984). Building on stress research and person–environment fit theory, research on work–family conflict and stress has begun to examine how a person's assessment of fit or misfit in the environment influences stress and well-being in work and family roles (Edwards and Rothbard, 2005; Edwards and Rothbard, 1999). For example, Edwards and Rothbard (1999) found that well-being in both work and family roles increased as people's appraisal of their environment matched their desires.

Recent work on work–family conflict has also broken new ground by examining the individual's psychological decision processes when faced with competing role demands. Incorporating psychological constructs from research on stress, decision processes, self-esteem and identity into the study of work–family conflict and stress has yielded new insights into the nature of this relationship. In a cleverly designed vignette study, Greenhaus and Powell (2003) manipulated pressures applied by role senders for participating in competing work and family activities as well as the social support of role senders in each activity. They found that work and family pressures influenced participation choice as did the salience of the roles. Self-esteem also moderated the effect of role salience on activity choice.

GENDER DIFFERENCES AND THE WORK–HOME INTERFACE

Another important research perspective within the work–family literature has focused on gender differences. Gender has been found to affect career advancement (e.g., Stroh *et al.*, 1992), perhaps through differential access to valuable work networks (Ibarra, 1992), work and family time investment (Leete and Schor, 1994; Rothbard and Edwards, 2003), work–family conflict and role stress (e.g., Greenhaus *et al.*, 1987; Gutek *et al.*, 1991), and strategies for managing the work–family interface (Andrews and Bailyn, 1993).[1] These gender differences may be due to gender role socialization and different opportunity structures for men and women, which can lead men and women to have different psychological experiences of work and family roles (Rothbard and Brett, 2000).

Men and women have different perceptions of their work roles (Rothbard and Brett, 2000). Women's perceptions of their work role are often shaped by barriers to career advancement, compensation and networking opportunities (Rothbard and Brett, 2000). Such barriers start with sex typing of jobs (Blau and Ferber, 1992) and persist with differential access to development opportunities such as international assignments (Catalyst, 1996).

Men and women's experience of family roles is similarly affected by different sets of expectations for role enactment. Societal norms and gender role socialization suggest that women are expected to identify more with the family role (Aryee and Luk, 1996; Lobel, 1991) and spend more time on household activities (Bielby and Bielby, 1989; Hochschild, 1989). Indeed research suggests that there is a substantial gender gap in household work between men and women (up to 19 hours per week) such that women engage in household work to a much greater extent than do men (South and Spitze, 1994). Studies in the work–family arena also provide evidence for the idea that women participate more in the family role than men do. For example, a recent study of time investment in work and family roles found that women devoted 7 hours more per week to family than did men (Rothbard and Edwards, 2003).

Gender differences also exist in the ways that participation in work and family roles affects one another. For example, Tenbrunsel *et al.* (1995) found that, unexpectedly, men's work involvement increased their family involvement, but that women's work involvement had no effect on their family involvement. Rothbard and Edwards (2003) found that family time investment decreased work time investment for women, but did not affect work time investment for men.

Men and women also differ in the ways they manage the boundary between work and family roles. Men are more likely to segment or compartmentalize work and family roles, whereas women tend to integrate these roles (Andrews and Bailyn, 1993). This gender difference in management of the boundary between work and family is thought to stem from differences in mental models men and women have about work and family roles, as well as from different societal expectations regarding how men and women ought to handle work and family roles (Andrews and Bailyn, 1993; Rothbard and Brett, 2000).

Although much research has found gender differences in work–family relationships, it is important to note that some researchers have not found these differences. For example, Frone *et al.* (1992a) did not find significant gender differences in the antecedents and outcomes of work–family conflict. Likewise, Frone *et al.* (1992b) did not find gender differences in the permeability of the work–home boundary. Further, Anderson *et al.* (2002) did not find differences between men and women in the experience of work–family conflict. Thus, the gender findings are mixed, and require further study to understand the circumstances under which they emerge and those where they do not seem to be meaningful. Moreover, it is also important to note that much of the research that found gender differences has focused on the relationship between work and family roles rather than work and non-work community-based roles. Recent research that has considered other non-family aspects of the work–home interface has failed to find significant gender differences (Dumas, 2003; Phillips *et al.*, 2002). A fruitful avenue for future research should consider whether gender differences persist in the experience of work and non-work roles other than the family role.

EMERGING PERSPECTIVES ON THE WORK–HOME INTERFACE

Past research perspectives have contributed greatly to our understanding of the work–home interface, yet we still grapple with understanding the psychological and behavioral challenges people face when engaging in and navigating multiple roles. Further, new issues and challenges that warrant consideration are developing. As a result, several new streams of research have begun to emerge within the domain of the work–home interface. We address three new research perspectives that have emerged. First, we discuss a research perspective focusing on the potential enriching aspects of multiple roles – a perspective that emphasizes the notion of psychological resources that are accrued in role participation. This research perspective has been fueled by the question of how people respond to actively participating in multiple roles, and by a challenge to the work–family area's heavy emphasis on role conflict and stress. We next discuss an emerging research perspective that focuses on the strategies people use to manage the boundary between work and family roles. This research focuses on people's preferences for integrating or segmenting work and family roles. Finally, we address an emerging research perspective on role identity and identity navigation amongst multiple roles.[2]

Enrichment

Although role conflict and stress are possible psychological outcomes of participating in multiple roles, another potential psychological consequence of participating in multiple roles is enrichment. The enrichment perspective that has begun to emerge in the work–family literature (Rothbard, 2001; Ruderman *et al.*, 2002; see also Chapter 5) is based on the premise that roles provide individuals with psychological resources that can be beneficial to them in other life roles. This research builds on theoretical insights from sociologists Sieber (1974) and Marks (1977), who posited that individuals are likely to benefit from holding multiple roles.

Sieber's (1974) discussion of role accumulation suggests four mechanisms through which individuals benefit from holding multiple roles because they can (1) amass role privileges across their various roles, (2) achieve overall status security by allowing roles to serve as buffers or compensate for each other, (3) receive additional resources for status enhancement and improved role performance, and finally (4) experience personality enrichment and ego gratification through the psychological experience of occupying multiple roles. Marks (1977) goes further and posits an expansion model of human energy, allegiance and personal resources through enactment of multiple roles. He contends that individuals' enactment of multiple roles may actually create more energy or personal resources rather than deplete finite reserves. Combining these insights with theories of self-esteem and psychological resources, several recent studies have found evidence for the enriching aspects of multiple role enactment.

Foundational research on the enrichment perspective emphasized that participating in multiple roles can be beneficial to overall mental health. In two studies, Thoits (1983, 1986) found that individuals who hold multiple role identities report significantly less psychological distress. Similarly, Barnett *et al.* (1992) found that multiple roles can serve as buffers against psychological distress. Specifically, Barnett *et al.* (1992) interviewed female nurses and social workers in Massachusetts over a two-year period regarding their job role quality and psychological distress. They found that family roles buffered women from the negative effects of changes in job role quality on mental health. Barnett *et al.* (1992, p. 635) suggest that the multiple role involvement benefited these women because it gave them various sources of 'role-related rewards that directly influence psychological well-being'.

In another early study in this emerging research perspective, Kirchmeyer (1992) surveyed alumni of an undergraduate business program in a western Canadian university regarding their work and non-work roles. The 122 respondents held a variety of non-work roles including community work, recreation groups and families. In this study, Kirchmeyer (1992) found significant support for the enrichment model such that increased time spent in community work and parenting was associated with greater job satisfaction and organizational commitment. She also found that time devoted to community work was associated with greater job satisfaction and organizational commitment. In contrast, she found no support for the depletion model, noting that increased time and involvement with non-work activities did not reduce organizational commitment or job satisfaction. Additionally, Kirchmeyer's (1992) respondents reported that their participation in non-work roles yielded the benefits outlined in Sieber's (1974) model of role accumulation. More specifically, their involvement in multiple roles provided them with security against the failures and strains of work, enhanced their status and developed skills and perspectives useful for work. Kirchmeyer (1992) also found that resource enrichment from involvement in community and recreation roles was positively related to organizational commitment and job satisfaction.

More recently, research has begun to examine the psychological mechanisms by which one role might be enriching to another role. Examining whether engagement in work and family roles was enriching or depleting, Rothbard (2001) drew on psychological theories of emotion and self-esteem to explain why positive and negative affect in response to one role might carry over and increase or decrease engagement in another role. She surveyed workers of various types at a large public university in the USA. Overall, she found that both enrichment and depletion can occur as a result of engagement in multiple roles. She also found gender differences in the effects of engagement in work and family roles such that women's work-related negative affect was depleting to family engagement, whereas men's work-related positive affect was enriching to family engagement. Moreover, women's work engagement was positively influenced by both positive and negative family-related affect. Rothbard (2001) suggests that the affective experience of work and family roles are key determinants of whether holding multiple roles is enriching or depleting.

Ruderman *et al.* (2002) also examined the psychological mechanisms that determine whether holding multiple roles is beneficial for individuals. They conducted both an exploratory qualitative study as well as a quantitative survey examining how non-work roles contributed to women's managerial roles. Women managers interviewed by Ruderman and colleagues reported that their non-work roles provided them with better interpersonal skills and psychological benefits such as increased self-esteem and confidence. Further, Ruderman *et al.* (2002) found that commitment to multiple life roles was positively related to feelings of psychological well-being.

This more recent work examining the positive effects of participation in work and home roles is expanding the study of the work–home interface and providing more detailed explanations of the psychological mechanisms fostering enrichment. More specifically, recent work has built upon the earlier resource accumulation of multiple role theories to include the impact of affect, cognitive appraisal, emotion and self-esteem (Rothbard, 2001; Ruderman *et al.*, 2002).

Role boundaries and the work–home interface

A second emerging research perspective has focused on how individuals enact or manage the boundary between home and work. Whereas much of past research in this area addressed issues of the permeability of the boundary between home and work (Hall and Richter, 1988; Pleck *et al.*, 1980), this new perspective focuses explicitly on integration versus segmentation as strategies for coping with work and family roles (Ashforth *et al.*, 2000; Kossek *et al.*, 1999; Rothbard *et al.*, 2005). Segmentation is a strategy by which a person separates work and non-work time, artifacts and activities, whereas integration is a strategy whereby the person overlaps these role experiences (Nippert-Eng, 1995).

In an early study that focused explicitly on the strategies people use for managing their multiple roles, Hall (1972) examined female college students who were also wives and mothers. Among the role management strategies he observed were role integration and partitioning. He described role integration as 'redesigning roles so that they can be performed simultaneously in a mutually reinforcing manner' and role partitioning as choosing 'not to attend to one role while performing another' (Hall, 1972, pp. 476–477). Although this early study identified clear role management strategies, it was not until the 1990s that a new body of studies emerged to more fully examine this perspective.

Consistent with the findings in Hall's initial work, Nippert-Eng (1995) and Perlow (1998) also found evidence that people actively manage the work–non-work boundary using integration or segmentation. Nippert-Eng (1995) studied employees at a research and development firm. She found that the scientists and other professional workers led very integrated lifestyles. They handled personal matters such as paying bills or making doctors' appointments during work time. The scientists that Nippert-Eng studied took work home, kept many work-related materials such as journals in their homes and conversely received personal mail at their work addresses. Additionally, some reported that colleagues were indistinguishable from friends. Conversely, Nippert-Eng also found that other employees in the same organization segmented their work and non-work lives. These workers never mentioned their non-work activities at work, nor did they have pictures of family at work. Similarly, they did not see co-workers outside of work or take work home in any way. Perlow (1998) observed similar diversity of boundary management strategies among software engineers. Some took work home regularly and accepted phone calls at home in the evenings and at weekends, whereas other workers chose to leave all work activities in the workplace.

Expanding the body of research on boundary management strategies, Kossek *et al.* (1999) developed a theoretical framework synthesizing research on these strategies. They focused on choice of strategy, either segmentation or integration, as a dependent variable. They hypothesized that gender differences, personality, caregiving resources and organizational climate would influence a person's choice of role boundary management strategy.

More recent empirical work has built on these foundations and focuses on the outcomes of using either a segmenting or integrating boundary management strategy. These studies have focused on outcomes such as role conflict (Dumas, 2003), satisfaction (Dumas, 2003; Rothbard *et al.*, 2005), commitment (Rothbard *et al.*, 2005) and attraction to different organizational settings (Rau and Hyland, 2002). Many of these studies have taken a contingency approach to the effects of boundary strategy on various outcomes. For example, Rau and Hyland (2002) studied MBA students and found that those with low role conflict were more attracted to companies that offered telecommuting arrangements (a more integrating policy), whereas those with high role conflict were more attracted to companies that offered flexitime arrangements (a more segmenting policy). This is because integrating might exacerbate the effects of conflict when people have high degrees of role conflict. Other research on work–family boundary management has drawn on psychological concepts such as congruence and cognitive appraisal to explore the fit between strategy and preference. Individuals have preferences for boundary management strategies (Edwards and Rothbard, 1999; Rothbard *et al.*, 2005); however, these preferences may not be congruent with organizational policies (Rothbard *et al.*, 2005). In a survey study, Rothbard *et al.* (2005) found that when employee preferences for how they would like to manage the boundary between home and work were incongruent with company policies and practices – many of which foster a blurred boundary between home and work – employees experienced lower satisfaction and commitment.

Identity navigation

A third emerging research perspective revolves around role identity and the ways that people navigate multiple role identities. Individual identity is closely related to the roles people hold (Stryker and Serpe, 1982; Thoits, 1983). Further, the extent to which any individual identifies with a given role affects their enactment of that role (Lobel, 1991; Lobel and St Clair, 1992) as well as role outcomes (Frone *et al.*, 1995). Several studies have found support for the effect of role identification on role participation. For instance, Lobel and St Clair (1992) surveyed former students of an executive education course and found that those with a higher reported career identity salience reported greater work effort. Likewise, Rothbard (2001) found that identification with a role was associated with increased engagement in that role. Rothbard and Edwards (2003) surveyed employees at a public university, sampling a diverse population including both men and women, as well as a variety of job types. They found that increased identification with a family role was associated with greater time invested in the family role, and that increased work identification was associated with greater time invested in the work role.

The existing research described above has established role identification as a key factor affecting the outcomes of enactment of work and non-work roles. Recent studies have also progressed beyond examining absolute levels of role identification and have begun to explore a person's relative identification with work and non-work roles. Specifically, in a theoretical piece, Thompson and Bunderson (2001) assert that individuals identify unequally with work and non-work roles and that one role will serve as an anchor identity role. In other words, the anchor identity role is more salient and central to the individual's self definition than the other roles they may hold (Thompson and Bunderson, 2001). Further, these authors consider whether experiences in the anchor or non-anchor role are identity-affirming or identity-discrepant. They then predict different role outcomes depending on whether experiences in the non-anchor and anchor roles are identity-affirming or identity-discrepant. They theorize that when experiences in both the anchor and non-anchor roles are identity-affirming, the individual will experience increased enrichment and reduced conflict between roles. They also theorize that when the anchor role is identity-affirming, and the non-anchor role is identity-discrepant, the individual will retreat to the affirming anchor role.

In a recent study, Dumas (2003) also studied relative identification with work and non-work roles. Unlike Thompson and Bunderson's (2001) framework, Dumas (2003) allowed for the possibility that individuals might identify equally with their work and non-work roles. She then compared outcomes of those who identified equally and unequally with their work role and their role in a community-based volunteer orchestra. She hypothesized and found an interaction between the individual's relative identification and role boundary management strategy such that those who identified more equally with their work and non-work roles experienced greater role conflict when integrating rather than segmenting their roles.

Research on role identification underscores how an individual's sense of self may affect the work–non-work interface. Understanding how people navigate and make sense of multiple role identities is a central challenge for work–family and organizational scholars. This is especially true as organizations become populated by people with a diverse set of family and other non-work identities that can be salient and affect the way work gets done. Related to research on work and family identities is research on how non-work racial or ethnic identities might affect people's experience in the workplace.

Increased corporate globalization and advances in civil rights have boosted the racial and ethnic diversity of many corporations. The issue of role boundary management and identity navigation may be particularly useful for addressing the impact of demographic diversity on the work–home interface (Phillips *et al.*, 2002). As diverse groups of people come together, they often must decide how much of their 'selves' should be included in their work organizations (Berg, 2002). The reality of diversity poses many questions for scholars and practitioners. How do different cultural norms fit together in the workplace? How should those in the minority ethnic group balance their racial identity and community allegiance with their work 'selves'? How should individuals from minority religious traditions observe religious holidays and customs while also adhering to company policy? How does this influx of different cultures and norms affect the enactment of 'work self' for those of the dominant culture? A study by Phillips *et al.* (2002) partially addressed these questions with a survey of MBA students regarding their preferences for management of the work–home boundary, and the demographic diversity of their workgroups. Phillips *et al.* (2002) found that individuals in racially diverse groups reported greater preferences for segmentation of home and work roles. They argued that this result was due to the individual's need to preserve their racial identity through role segmentation.

CONCLUSION

The changing face of the workforce, particularly the increase in the number of employed women and dual-income families, was the impetus for work–family policies and much of the work–family research of the 1980s and

1990s. Researchers and organizations sought to understand how best to manage employees who had childcare or eldercare responsibilities. Accordingly many research questions and perspectives focused on the issue of managing the demands of work responsibilities and tasks with home caregiving tasks. Although there remains much to understand about how to help employees manage demands of their work and family roles, other societal changes have introduced additional challenges to managing the work–home interface that go beyond role conflict to identity navigation. Accordingly research on the work–home interface has begun to address these challenges through new research perspectives on role boundaries and the challenges and rewards of holding and navigating multiple role identities.

NOTES

1 Gender differences are considered in further detail throughout this volume; for example Chapters 5, 6, 7, 8 and 11.
2 Further discussion of the relationships between work–family 'enrichment' and the related concepts of 'facilitation', 'enhancement' and 'compensation' can be found in Chapter 5, as well as further relevant research findings.

REFERENCES

Anderson, S. E., Coffey, B. S., and Byerly, R. T. (2002). Formal organizational initiatives and informal workplace practices: links to work–family conflict and job-related outcomes. *Journal of Management, 28,* 787–810.

Andrews, A., and Bailyn, L. (1993). Segmentation and synergy: two models linking work and family. In J. C. Hood (ed.), *Men, work and family* (pp. 262–275). Newbury Park, CA: Sage.

Aryee, S., and Luk, V. (1996). Balancing two major parts of adult life experience: work and family identity among dual-earner couples. *Human Relations, 49,* 465–487.

Ashforth, B. E., Kreiner, G. E., and Fugate, M. (2000). All in a day's work: boundaries and micro role transitions. *Academy of Management Review, 25,* 472–491.

Barnett, R. C., Marshall, N. L., and Singer, J. D. (1992). Job experiences over time, multiple roles, and women's mental health: a longitudinal study. *Journal of Personality and Social Psychology, 62,* 634–644.

Berg, D. N. (2002). Bringing one's self to work: a Jew reflects. *Journal of Applied Behavioral Science, 38,* 397–415.

Bielby, W. T., and Bielby, D. D. (1989). Family ties: balancing commitments to work and family in dual earner households. *American Journal of Sociology, 54,* 776–789.

Blau, F. D., and Ferber, M. A. (1992). *The economics of women, men and work* (2nd edn). Englewood Cliffs, NJ: Prentice-Hall.

Blood, R. O., and Wolfe, D. M. (1960). *Husbands and wives*. New York: Macmillan.

Burke, R. J., and Greenglass, E. (1987). Work and family. In C. L. Cooper and I. T. Robertson (eds), *International review of industrial and organizational psychology* (pp. 273–320). New York: Wiley.

Catalyst (1996). *Women in corporate leadership: Progress and prospects*. Research report. Itasca, IL: Catalyst.

Champoux, J. E. (1978). Perceptions of work and non-work: a reexamination of the compensatory and spillover models. *Sociology of Work and Occupations*, *5*, 402–422.

Crouter, A. C. (1984). Spillover from family to work: the neglected side of the work family interface. *Human Relations*, *6*, 425–442.

Dubin, R. (1973). Work and non-work: institutional perspectives. In M. D. Dunnette (ed.), *Work and non-work in the year 2001* (pp. 53–68). Monterey, CA: Brooks/Cole.

Dumas, T. L. (2003). When to draw the line: effects of identity and role boundary management on interrole conflict. Unpublished doctoral dissertation, Northwestern University.

Eckenrode, J., and Gore, S. (1990). Stress and coping at the boundary of work and family. In J. Eckenrode and S. Gore (eds), *Stress between work and family* (pp. 1–16). New York: Plenum Press.

Edwards, J. R., and Rothbard, N. P. (1999). Work and family stress and well-being: an examination of person–environment fit in the work and family domains. *Organizational Behavior and Human Decision Processes*, *77*, 85–129.

Edwards, J. R., and Rothbard, N. P. (2000). Mechanisms linking work and family: clarifying the relationship between work and family constructs. *Academy of Management Review*, *25*, 178–199.

Edwards, J. R., and Rothbard, N. P. (2005). Work and family stress and well-being: an integrative model of person–environment fit within and between the work and family domains. In E. E. Kossek and S. J. Lambert (eds), *Work and life integration: Organizational, cultural and psychological perspectives in a global world*. Mahwah, NJ: Erlbaum.

Evans, P., and Bartolome, F. (1984). The changing pictures of the relationship between career and family. *Journal of Occupational Behavior*, *5*, 9–21.

Frone, M. R., Russell, M., and Cooper, M. L. (1992a). Antecedents and outcomes of work family conflict: testing a model of the work–family interface. *Journal of Applied Psychology*, *77*, 65–78.

Frone, M. R., Russell, M., and Cooper, M. L. (1992b). Prevalence of work–family conflict: are work and family boundaries asymmetrically permeable? *Journal of Organizational Behavior*, *13*, 723–729.

Frone, M. R., Russell, M., and Cooper, M. L. (1995). Job stressors, job involvement and employee health: a test of identity theory. *Journal of Occupational and Organizational Psychology*, *68*, 1–11.

Grandey, A. A., and Cropanzano, R. (1999). The Conservation of Resources model applied to work–family conflict and strain. *Journal of Vocational Behavior*, *54*, 350–370.

Greenhaus, J. H., Bedeian, A. G., and Mossholder, K. W. (1987). Work experience, job performance, and feelings of personal and family well-being. *Journal of Vocational Behavior*, 200–215.

Greenhaus, J. H., and Beutell, N. J. (1985). Sources of conflict between work and family roles. *Academy of Management Review, 10*, 76–88.

Greenhaus, J. H., and Parasuraman, S. (1986). A work–non-work interactive perspective of stress and its consequences. *Journal of Organizational Behavior Management, 8*, 37–60.

Greenhaus, J. H., and Powell, G. N. (2003). When work and family collide: deciding between competing role demands. *Organizational Behavior and Human Decision Processes, 90*, 291–303.

Gutek, B. A., Searle, S., and Klepa, L. (1991). Rational versus gender role explanations for work family conflict. *Journal of Applied Psychology, 76*, 560–568.

Hall, D. T. (1972). A model of coping with role conflict: the role behavior of college educated women. *Administrative Science Quarterly, 17*, 471–486.

Hall, D. T., and Richter, J. R. (1988). Balancing work life and home life: what can organizations do to help? *Academy of Management Executive, 2*, 213–223.

Higgins, C. A., Duxbury, L. E., and Irving, R. H. (1992). Work–family conflict in the dual-career family. *Organizational Behavior and Human Decision Process, 51*, 51–75.

Hobfoll, S. E. (1989). Conservation of resources: a new attempt at conceptualizing stress. *American Psychologist, 44*, 513–524.

Hobfoll, S. E. (1998). *Stress, culture, and community: The psychology and philosophy of stress.* New York: Plenum.

Hochschild, A. R. (1989). *The second shift.* New York: Avon.

Ibarra, H. (1992). Homophily and differential returns: sex differences in network structure and access in an advertising firm. *Administrative Science Quarterly, 37*, 422–447.

Kahn, R. L, Wolfe, D. M., Quinn, R. P., and Snoek, J. D. (1964). *Organizational stress: Studies in role conflict and ambiguity.* New York: Wiley.

Kanter, R. M. (1977). *Work and family in the United States: A critical review and agenda for research and policy.* New York: Russell Sage Foundation.

Katz, D., and Kahn, R. L. (1966). *The social psychology of organizations.* New York: Wiley.

Kingston, P. W., and Nock, S. L. (1992). Couples' joint work status and community and social attachments. *Social Science Quarterly, 73*, 862–875.

Kirchmeyer, C. (1992). Non-work participation and work attitudes: a test of scarcity vs. expansion models of personal resources. *Human Relations, 45*, 775–795.

Kopelman, R. E., Greenhaus, J. J., and Connolly, T. F. (1983). A model of work, family, and interrole conflict: a construct validation study. *Organizational Behavior and Human Performance, 32*, 198–215.

Kossek, E. E., Noe, R. A., and DeMarr, B. J. (1999). Work–family role synthesis: individual and organizational determinants. *International Journal of Conflict Management, 10*, 102–129.

Kossek, E. E., and Ozeki, C. (1998). Work–family conflict, policies, and the job-life satisfaction relationship: a review and directions for organizational behavior human resources research. *Journal of Applied Psychology, 83*, 139–149.

Lambert, S. J. (1990). Processes linking work and family: a critical review and research agenda. *Human Relations, 43*, 239–257.

Lazarus, R. S., and Folkman, S. (1984). *Stress, coping, and adaptation.* New York: Springer.

Leete, L., and Schor, J. B. (1994). Assessing the time-squeeze hypothesis: hours worked in the United States, 1969–89. *Industrial Relations*, *33*, 225–243.

Lobel, S. A. (1991). Allocation of investment in work and family roles: alternative theories and implications for research. *Academy of Management Review*, *16*, 507–521.

Lobel, S. A., and St. Clair, L. (1992). Effects of family responsibilities, gender, and career identity salience on performance outcomes. *Academy of Management Journal*, *35*, 1057–1069.

Marks, S. R. (1977). Multiple roles and role strain: some notes on human energy, time and commitment. *American Sociological Review*, *42*, 921–936.

Merton, R. K. (1957). *Social theory and social structure*. New York: Free Press.

Morf, M. (1989). *The work/life dichotomy*. Westport, CT: Quorum.

Near, J. P. (1984). Predictive and explanatory models of work and nonwork. In M. D. Lee and R. N. Kanungo (eds), *Management of work and personal life: Problems and opportunities* (pp. 67–85). New York: Praeger.

Nippert-Eng, C. E. (1995). *Home and work: Negotiating boundaries through everyday life*. Chicago: University of Chicago Press.

Perlow, L. (1998). Boundary control: the social ordering of work and family time in a high-tech corporation. *Administrative Science Quarterly*, *43*, 328–357.

Phillips, K. W., Rothbard, N. P., and Dumas, T. L. (2002). It's not that I don't like you: preferences for segmentation and engagement in organizational activities. Paper presented at the *Annual National Academy of Management meeting*, Denver, CO.

Piotrkowski, C. S. (1979). *Work and the family system*. New York: Free Press.

Pleck, J. H., Staines, G. L., and Lang, L. (1980). Conflict between work and family life. *Monthly Labor Review*, *103*, 29–32.

Rau, B. L., and Hyland, M. A. (2002). Role conflict and flexible work arrangements: the effects on applicant attraction. *Personnel Psychology*, *55*, 111–137.

Rothbard, N. P. (2001). Enriching or depleting? The dynamics of engagement in work and family. *Administrative Science Quarterly*, *46*, 655–684.

Rothbard, N. P., and Brett, J. M. (2000). Promote equal opportunity by recognizing gender differences in the experience of work and family. In E. A. Locke (ed.), *The Blackwell handbook of principles of organizational behavior*. Oxford, UK: Blackwell.

Rothbard, N. P., Phillips, K. W., and Dumas, T. L. (2005). Managing multiple roles: work–family policies and individuals' desires for segmentation. *Organization Science*, *16*, 243–258.

Rothbard, N. P., and Edwards, J. R. (2003). Investment in work and family roles: a test of identity and utilitarian motives. *Personnel Psychology*, *56*, 699–730.

Ruderman, M. N., Ohlott, P. J., Panzer, K., and King, S. N. (2002). Benefits of multiple roles for managerial women. *Academy of Management Journal*, *45*, 369–386.

Sieber, S. D. (1974). Toward a theory of role accumulation. *American Sociological Review*, *34*, 567–578.

South, S. J., and Spitze, G. (1994). Housework in marital and nonmarital households. *American Sociological Review*, *59*, 327–347.

Staines, G. L. (1980). Spillover versus compensation: a review of the literature on the relationship between work and nonwork. *Human Relations*, *33*, 111–129.

Stroh, L. K., Brett, J. M., and Reilly, A. H. (1992). All the right stuff: a comparison of female and male managers' career progression. *Journal of Applied Psychology*, 77, 251–260.

Stryker, S., and Serpe, R. T. (1982). Commitment, identity salience and role behavior: theory and research example. In W. Ickes and E. S. Knowles (eds), *Personality, roles and social behavior* (pp. 199–216). Springer-Verlag: New York.

Tenbrunsel, A. E., Brett, J. M., Maoz, E., Stroh, L. K., and Reilly, A. H. (1995). Dynamic and static work–family relationships. *Organizational Behavior and Human Decision Processes*, 63, 233–246.

Thoits, P. A. (1983). Multiple identities and psychological well-being: a reformulation and test of the social isolation hypothesis. *American Sociological Review*, 48, 174–187.

Thoits, P. A. (1986). Multiple identities: examining gender and marital status differences in distress. *American Sociological Review*, 51, 259–272.

Thompson, J. A., and Bunderson, J. S. (2001). Work–non-work conflict and the phenomenology of time: beyond the balance metaphor. *Work and Occupations*, 28, 17–39.

Voydanoff, P. (1987). *Work and family life*. Newbury Park, CA: Sage.

Williams, K. J., and Alliger, G. (1994). Role stressors, mood spillover, and perception of work–family conflict in employed parents. *Academy of Management Journal*, 37, 837–868.

Zedeck, S. (1992). Introduction: exploring the domain of work and family concerns. In S. Zedeck (ed.), *Work, families, and organizations* (pp. 1–32). San Francisco: Jossey-Bass.

4 Measurement issues in research on the work–home interface

Lois E. Tetrick and Louis C. Buffardi*

As we have seen in Chapter 3, there is a considerable body of literature on the interface between the work and non-work domains. Much of this research has focused on the work–family interface and has generally subscribed to a 'role scarcity' or negative spillover approach to the interaction of the work and family domains. As a result, much of the literature has focused on work–family conflict. Therefore, we will begin this chapter with a review of the conceptualization and measurement of work–family conflict. Then we will discuss recent developments in conceptualizing and measuring the work–family interface from a positive spillover or work–family facilitation perspective. After having considered both work–family conflict and work–family facilitation, we conclude the chapter with a discussion of conceptualizations of work–family fit and balance, and the resultant measurement and methodological issues associated with examining balance.

WORK–FAMILY CONFLICT

One of the most common constructs addressing the work–home interface is that of work–family conflict. The basic premise of the construct is that one's roles in the work and family domains are sometimes incompatible and interfere with full participation in both roles. Thus, role demands from one domain interfere with demands stemming from the other domain (Greenhaus and Beutell, 1985). Greenhaus and Beutell's (1985) influential theoretical article also articulated different categories of work–family conflict based on directionality and type.

* We thank Beth Kikta and Michael Ford for their assistance and contributions to this chapter.

Directionality and type of work–family conflict

The directionality dimension distinguished between the source of the conflict, i.e. work interfering with family and family interfering with work. However, most of the early research focused on either a broad measure of conflict that included both directions or just work interfering with family, with substantially less attention paid to family interfering with work. Indeed, Frone *et al.* (1992a) found that work interfering with family was reported nearly three times as often as family interfering with work.

In addition to these directionality distinctions among work–family conflict measures, Greenhaus and Beutell (1985) also argued for three types of work–family conflict: strain-, time- and behavior-based. Time-based conflict occurs when time devoted to one role makes it difficult to participate in another role, e.g., 'My work takes up time that I'd like to spend with family/friends' (Frone *et al.*, 1992b). Strain-based conflict reflects that strains experienced in one role interfere with participation in another role, e.g., 'I'm often too tired at work because of the things I have to do at home' (Gutek *et al.*, 1991). In contrast, behavior-based conflict occurs when the specific behaviors required by one role are incompatible with the behaviors expected in the other role, e.g., 'The problem-solving behaviors I use in my job are not effective in resolving problems at home' (Carlson *et al.*, 2000). As Carlson *et al.* (2000) indicate, crossing these three types of conflict with the two directions yields six unique categories of work–family conflict.

Many studies involving the work–family conflict construct, often using different measures, have appeared in the literature; enough so, in fact, that two meta-analyses have surfaced with respect to consequences associated with work–family conflict. The meta-analyses speak to the construct validity of general work–family conflict, although not to the construct validity of a specific instrument.

Meta-analyses of work–family conflict

Based largely on the directionality distinction, Kossek and Ozeki (1998) divided the work–family conflict literature according to three types of measures (work interfering with family, family interfering with work, and bidirectional measures that included items that mixed directions). No attempt was made to categorize results based on time, strain and behavior conflict distinctions as virtually all work–family conflict measures to that date included a mixture of item types, most frequently time and strain. They conducted a meta-analysis on the relationship of work–family conflict with two major outcomes: job satisfaction (46 correlations) and life satisfaction (26 correlations). They noted a wide range in the magnitudes of the correlations between these variables and suggest that some of this variation may be due to the differences in the measures used. That said, their results demonstrate that the relationship between job satisfaction and the various work–family conflict measures is strong and negative (–0.31, corrected across all measures). The relationship was strongest for the global measures (–0.31), followed by work interfering with family (–0.27) and family interfering with work (–0.18). This weaker relationship found for family interfering with work may be a function of differential permeability of the two domains – families may be much more willing to adjust to work pressures than organizations are willing to adjust to the family demands of their employees. In addition, if family is the source of the interference, one would expect that would have a weaker relationship with job satisfaction than if work were the source of conflict. The negative relationship between all measures of conflict and job satisfaction understandably were stronger (–0.37) for those in dual-career families, but the relationships were only marginally different for women (–0.35) than men (–0.29).

With respect to life satisfaction, the various measures of work–family conflict were strongly related (–0.36, corrected), with somewhat higher correlations for women (–0.42) than men (–0.32). Family interfering with work relations (–0.25) were somewhat weaker than either the global (–0.29) or the work interfering with family measures (–0.35).

In general, the meta-analysis supports the distinction of family interfering with work and work interfering with family. In terms of future research, Kossek and Ozeki (1998) suggest that most research has ignored jointly assessing work–family conflict, satisfaction and employer work–family supports. The Human Resource Management literature particularly is devoid of research on the effect of work–family policies on life satisfaction, perhaps reflecting a bias of employing organizations toward more job-related outcomes.

A more recent meta-analysis (Allen *et al.*, 2000) limited its focus to work interfering with family measures, while examining a wider array of consequences of conflict that included work-, non-work- and stress-related outcomes. They located a total of 67 articles across six major journals published between 1977 and 1998. Owing to the large amount of overlap of studies that were also referenced in Kossek and Ozeki's (1998) meta-analysis, Allen *et al.*'s findings with respect to job satisfaction (a work-related outcome) and life satisfaction (a non-work outcome) essentially duplicated the results of the previous meta-analysis.

With respect to other work-related outcomes, Allen *et al.* (2000) found that work interfering with family correlated highest with intentions to leave (weighted $r = 0.29$). Correlations with organizational commitment (–0.23) were similar to those with job satisfaction. Relatively few studies were done examining effects on behavioral outcomes such as absenteeism, job performance and actual turnover, and those correlations were typically weak (–0.02, –0.12, and 0.14, respectively).

Non-work outcomes studied included marital satisfaction ($r = -0.23$) and family satisfaction (–0.17), both somewhat weaker relationships than was found for life satisfaction (−0.28). Allen *et al.* reported that the results of studies of the former two variables were particularly inconsistent across samples.

A particularly wide array of stress-related outcomes have been studied in conjunction with work interfering with family, including general psychological strain, physical symptoms, depression, alcohol abuse, burnout, work-related and family-related stress. The strongest relationships are found with burnout (weighted $r = 0.42$) and work-related stress (0.41). Indeed, with the exception of alcohol abuse, Allen *et al.* (2000) report average weighted correlations ranging from 0.29 to 0.42 across the stress-related outcomes. However, they caution that the few studies using objective measure of health (e.g., blood pressure, cholesterol) typically yield lower correlations than when general self-report measures are used. In addition, they report that longitudinal studies are quite rare and, when done (e.g., Frone *et al.*, 1997), fail to show significant effects between work interfering with family and overall health, hypertension and depression. However, that same study indicated that family interfering with work did have longitudinal effects on those same outcomes and that work interfering with family was longitudinally related to heavy alcohol consumption.

As previously indicated, many different measures of work–family conflict have been used in contributing to the empirical literature. Indeed authors of both meta-analyses (Kossek and Ozeki, 1998; Allen *et al.*, 2000) indicate that differences among the measures used may be responsible for some of the variability in correlations of the construct with other outcomes. One of the purposes of this chapter is to identify the major measures of the construct and examine them in greater detail.

Summaries of the major measures of work–family conflict

Based on the measures cited in the above meta-analyses, a comprehensive list was developed and their corresponding reference articles noted. Also, two recent measures that developed separate scales to assess time-, strain- and behavior-based conflict (Stephens and Sommer, 1996; Carlson *et al.*, 2000) were added to the list, given that previous instruments generally overlooked such distinctions. Citation searches were conducted for each of the reference articles through September 2003. Each article identified by the citation search was examined to determine whether the work–family conflict measure was actually used in the study reported.

Lists of these measures and their respective citation counts (with respect to actual usage of the measure) before and after 1996, to determine the relative 'currency' of the measures, appear in Table 4.1. When the article reported usage of the conflict measure in question, reliabilities and correlations with the other study variables were recorded. Each of the five measures that continue to be used in the research on work–family conflict (Bohen and Viveros-Long, 1981; Kopelman *et al.*, 1983; Gutek *et al.*, 1991;

Table 4.1 Studies reporting use of work–conflict measure before and
after 1996

Work–family conflict measures	Number of studies using measure prior to 1996	Number of studies using measure after 1996
Holahan and Gilbert (1979)	6	1
Burke *et al.* (1979)	2	1
Bohen and Viveros-Long (1981)	14	10
Buetell and Greenhaus (1982)	0	0
Kopelman *et al.* (1983)	15	15
Bodin and Mitelman (1983)	0	0
Greenhaus and Buetell (1985)	1	0
Burley (1989)	2	0
Small and Riley (1990)	1	0
Gutek *et al.* (1991)	3	13
Frone *et al.* (1992b)	7	12
Netemeyer *et al.* (1996)	N/A	7
Stephens and Sommer (1996)	N/A	0
Carlson *et al.* (1998)	N/A	1
Carlson *et al.* (2000)	N/A	4

Frone *et al.*, 1992a, 1992b; Netemeyer *et al.*, 1996) and the two recently developed measures of some theoretical significance (Stephens and Sommer, 1996; Carlson *et al.*, 2000) will be evaluated in turn.

To facilitate the evaluation of these work–family conflict measures, Table 4.2 provides a listing by the six unique categories (2 directions × 3 types) suggested by Greenhaus and Beutell (1985). Table 4.3 summarizes estimates of internal consistency reliability for each of the scales as well as evidence of discriminant validity between the work interfering with family and family interfering with work scales.

Bohen and Viveros-Long (1981) developed a 19-item measure that assesses multiple aspects of role strain. It includes 11 work-interfering-with-family items, three family-interfering-with-work items, and three bidirectional items (e.g., 'I have a good balance between my job and my family time'). Most of the items were time-based, but some were strain-based. Some additional items did not appear to fit any of the Greenhaus and Beutell (1985) classification schemes (e.g., 'I feel more respected than I would if I didn't have a job').

The mean coefficient alpha for the overall measure was 0.76. When the family-interfering-with-work items were treated as a separate scale, the mean coefficient alpha was 0.65. The average intercorrelation between the scales, an indicator of discriminant validity, was 0.54.

Kopelman *et al.* (1983) developed an eight-item measure of interrole conflict in which the items actually reflect work interfering with family. As indicated in Table 4.1, this measure has been used more often than any other measure of work–family conflict. Some of this is due to its early appearance in the literature, but it has maintained its popularity in more

Table 4.2 Number of items for each scale categorized by direction and type

	Total	Work interferes with family			Family interferes with work		
		Time	Strain	Behavior	Time	Strain	Behavior
Bohen and Viveros-Long (1981)	19 (5)	9	2		1	2	
Carlson et al. (2000)	18	3	3	3	3	3	3
Frone et al. (1992)	4	2			2		
Gutek et al. (1991)	8	2	2		2	2	
Kopelman et al. (1983)	8 (1)	3	4				
Netemeyer et al. (1996)	5	4	1		4	1	
Stephens and Sommer (1996)	14	4	4	6			

Note: Numbers in parentheses indicate the number of items that did not fit into one of the categories. They are categorized as follows:
(a) Bohen and Viveros-Long: 3 were time-based and bidirectional, while 2 did not seem to fit anywhere ('I feel more respected than I would if I didn't have a job', 'I have as much patience with my children as I would like').
(b) Kopelman et al.: 1 item was more of a global measure of work to family conflict ('My job makes it difficult to be the kind of spouse or parent that I'd like to be').

Table 4.3 Coefficient alpha and correlations between work-interferes-with-family (WFC) and family-interferes-with-work (FWC) scales for each of the major work–family conflict measures

		Coefficient alpha		Correlation of WFC with FWC	
	Direction	Mean	Range	Mean	Range
Bohen and Viveros-Long	Bidirectional	0.76	0.62–0.92	N/A	N/A
Frone et al.	WFC	0.80	0.75–0.86	0.37	0.28–0.48
(2 items)	FWC	0.63	0.54–0.78		
Gutek et al.	WFC	0.84	0.70–0.88	0.28	0.23–0.39
	FWC	0.81	0.68–0.89		
Kopelman et al.	WFC	0.82	0.70–0.90	0.26	0.14–0.39
	FWC	0.78	0.56–0.83		
Netemeyer et al.	WFC	0.91	0.88–0.93	0.42 (1 study)	
	FWC	0.88	0.78–0.89		
Stephens and Summer	Time WFC	0.74		N/A	
	Strain WFC	0.77		N/A	
	Behav. WFC	0.80		N/A	
Carlson et al.	Time WFC	0.86	0.82–0.87	0.28, 0.21, 0.22[a]	0.14–0.31
	Strain WFC	0.87	0.85–0.90	0.36, 0.39, 0.43[a]	0.21–0.51
	Behav. WFC	0.81	0.78–0.85	0.30, 0.38, 0.79[a]	0.17–0.83
	Time FWC	0.81	0.79–0.86	0.28, 0.36, 0.30[a]	0.17–0.45
	Strain FWC	0.89	0.87–0.92	0.21, 0.39, 0.38[a]	0.19–0.48
	Behav. FWC	0.85	0.85–0.86	0.22, 0.43, 0.79[a]	0.14–0.83

[a] These correlations are, respectively, with time, strain and behavior-based measures in the opposite direction.

recent years as well. The items are a mix of both strain- and time-based conflict. The average coefficient alpha value for the measure is 0.82. Some researchers (e.g., Parasuraman *et al.*, 1996; Hammer *et al.*, 2003) have reworded the work-interfering-with-family items to reflect family interfering with work and a mean alpha for that scale is 0.78. Fields (2002) reports that a factor analysis of both types of items yielded two distinct factors with items loading appropriately on the separate factors. Further indication of the discriminant validity of the two scales is reflected in the mean correlation of only 0.26 between these two types of work–family conflict scales.

Gutek *et al.* (1991) modified and incorporated previous measures into scales that assessed both directions of conflict. For the work-interfering-with-family scale, they selected four items from Koppelman *et al.*'s (1983) scale, while for the family-interfering-with-work scale they took four items from Burley's (1989) unpublished dissertation. As evidenced by the citation counts in Table 4.1, other researchers have also used the items adapted by Gutek *et al.* (1991) and respective mean coefficient alphas for the two scales are quite good at 0.84 and 0.81. Evidence for discriminant validity is provided by the low mean correlation (0.28) between the scales. Additional strong evidence is provided by both factor analytic (Gutek *et al.*, 1991; Frone *et al.*, 1997) and structural equation modeling studies (Aryee *et al.*, 1999; Frone *et al.*, 1992b) reported in the literature verifying the empirical distinctiveness of the two scales.

Frone *et al.* (1992a, 1992b) developed two-item scales for both work interfering with family and for family interfering with work with all items time-based. The reference article indicates coefficient alphas of 0.76 and 0.56, respectively, for the two scales. These alphas are somewhat lower than those of the other measures cited, likely due to the brevity of the scales. Subsequent research indicates respective mean alphas of 0.83 and 0.77. However, these means include some studies where the Frone *et al.*'s items were combined with additional items, thus lengthening the scales. In studies that just used the two-item scales, mean coefficient alphas of 0.80 and 0.63 were obtained. In these latter studies, the two scales yielded mean correlations of 0.37. Additional evidence of discriminant validity is provided in the reference article in that each type of work–family conflict scale had unique predictors (job stressors for work interfering with family; family stressors and family involvement for family interfering with work).

It is worth noting that one study (Eagle *et al.*, 1997) used both the Frone *et al.* (1992a, 1992b) and the Gutek *et al.* (1991) measures, and demonstrated reasonable convergent validity for work interfering with family in two samples, with the respective scales correlating 0.65 and 0.74 with each other. However, the convergent validities for the family-interfering-with-work scales were somewhat weaker, with the respective scales correlating 0.49 and 0.60. Discriminant validity between the directions in that same study was demonstrated as Frone *et al.*'s work-interfering-with-family measure correlated 0.22 and 0.38 with Gutek *et al.*'s family-interfering-with-work scale, while Frone *et al.*'s family-interfering-with-work measure correlated 0.29 and 0.36 with Gutek *et al.*'s work-interfering-with-family scale.

Netemeyer *et al.* (1996) criticized previous measures of work–family conflict in that they were flawed in one or more of the following ways for using (a) a general one-item measure, (b) a mixture of items in both directions in a single scale, (c) items that reflect potential outcomes (e.g., somatic symptoms) due to work–family conflict or (d) measures that were not subjected to rigorous scale development. Consequently, they developed a pool of 110 items that included items (some reworded) from previous measures and 36 newly created items. Items reflected both directions of conflict and had roughly an equal number of time- and strain-based items for each direction. A panel of faculty judges evaluated the degree to which each item represented each of the two constructs. Items were retained only when all four judges classified the item at least as 'somewhat representative' of the construct, narrowing the list to 43 items.

This list of 43 items was administered to three different occupational groups along with measures of other related constructs. A confirmatory factor analysis sorted the items into a 22-item work-interfering-with-family scale and a 21-item family-interfering-with-work scale. Items were deleted based on number of heuristics suggested in the scale development literature (Bagozzi and Yi, 1988; DeVillis, 1991), leaving five items for each scale that reflect a combination of time and strain-based items. These items are shown in Appendix A.

Coefficient alphas reported in the reference article averaged 0.88 for work interfering with family and 0.86 for family interfering with work across the three samples. Across all studies that have used these measures, the alphas are very strong (0.91 and 0.88, respectively). Correlations between the two scales across all the studies are appropriately modest, with a mean correlation of 0.42. Additional evidence for discriminant validity is provided in the reference article, with the two scales showing different patterns of relationships with a number of variables (e.g., work interfering with family correlates more highly with burnout, job tension and number of hours worked than does family interfering with work).

Stephens and Sommer (1996) were the first to develop formally separate scales for time-, strain-, and behavior-based conflict, all involving work interfering with family. Based on the conceptual definitions of the three forms of conflict, subject matter experts categorized 28 items developed from the literature. The 16 items that survived this screening were then subjected to an exploratory factor analysis, which eliminated two additional items. This was followed by a confirmatory factor analysis on a separate sample, which supported a three-factor model.

Coefficient alphas on the scales were all above threshold, ranging from 0.74 to 0.80. Correlations among the three scales varied from 0.36 to 0.69, with the highest correlation between time- and strain-based conflict. Subsequent studies citing this measure have not actually used these specific scales other than to include the items in a larger pool of conflict items in developing additional measures (Carlson *et al.*, 2000).

Carlson *et al.* (2000), noting that Stephens and Sommer's (1996) measure only dealt with work interfering with family, proceeded to conduct a series of studies designed to develop and validate a scale that included all six unique dimensions (2 directions × 3 forms). Generating a list of 31 non-redundant items from many of the major scales previously mentioned (except Netemeyer *et al.*'s scale, which had not yet been published when the study began), a panel rated the degree to which each of the items represented each of the six dimensions. A retained item's highest mean ratings had to correspond to the intended work–family conflict dimension and be sufficiently different from the ratings obtained for the other categories. Twenty items survived this screening and were rated by a second group of public employees. An exploratory factor analysis on these data yielded only three factors; thus some dimensions were not represented.

Additional items (34) were developed so that each dimension contained a representative set of items. Another set of judges categorized all 54 of the items into one of the six dimensions. To be retained an item had to be categorized as reflecting its dimension by at least 70% of the judges. The five best items for each dimension were selected as the final scales.

An additional sample was obtained and a six-factor confirmatory model was estimated using structural equation modeling. Based on suggestions found in the scale development literature (Bagozzi and Yi, 1988; DeVillis, 1991), 12 of the items were removed, producing three items for each of the six dimensions. Of the 18 items used, five were from existing scales and 13 were newly developed. These items are shown in Appendix B.

A validation study was then conducted on a sample of 225 individuals employed full time. They completed the work–family conflict scales along with eight measures of a variety of hypothesized antecedents (e.g., role ambiguity, social support) and outcomes (e.g., job satisfaction, family satisfaction). A confirmatory factor analysis of these data indicated that a six-factor solution provided the best fit to the data. All coefficient alphas exceeded the conventional threshold of 0.70 and ranged from 0.78 to 0.87. Most of the correlations between the six dimensions were below 0.60, with two exceptions. Time- and strain-based family interfering with work correlated 0.76 with each other and the two behavior-based dimensions correlated 0.83 with each other. The relatively weak discriminant validity ($r = 0.74$) for the behavior-based dimensions is also found in subsequent research (Bruck *et al.*, 2003).

In addition, the six work–family conflict dimensions demonstrated different patterns of relationships with the antecedents and outcomes, thus providing other evidence of differential validity. One such example was that the strain-based conflict measures predicted three out of the four outcome variables (job satisfaction, family satisfaction and life satisfaction) that were not predicted by the other two forms of conflict. Somewhat curiously, the time-based measures, regardless of direction, failed to predict any of the outcomes.

Criticisms of work–family conflict measures

Although there are differences in the various measures of work–family conflict, nearly all have acceptable levels of internal consistency (alphas > 0.70) and discriminant validity. This is particularly true of the Netemeyer *et al.* (1996) measures, although they mix both time- and strain-based items. Owing to the comprehensiveness in developing the scales that represent all possible combinations of directionality and forms of work–family conflict, the Carlson *et al.* (2000) measure is quite appealing. However, their approach is not without criticism. Bellavia and Frone (2004) indicate that the construction of their strain-based items is not parallel for the two directions, with work interfering with family being more emotion-based and family interfering with work more cognitively based. This, they argue, makes it difficult to compare fairly the conflicts in the different directions. In addition, Bellavia and Frone (2004) state that, although there is solid empirical evidence for maintaining distinctions between the directions of conflict, there is much less support for distinctions between time-, strain- and behavior-based conflict. Rather, such distinctions are more appropriate to categorizing *causes* of work–family conflict, not the assessment of conflict itself. Indeed, they argue that developing separate scales based on these three forms of conflict (which particularly characterizes both the Stephens and Sommer, 1996, and the Carlson *et al.*, 2000, measures) risks conceptually confounding work–family conflict and its antecedents. Instead of using items that include wording that builds in causal attributions, Bellavia and Frone recommend the use of items that are as general as possible.

An additional general criticism of work–family measures is their occasional failure to distinguish between work–family conflict and work–non-work conflict. Although the former logically would be considered a subset of the latter, the two are not interchangeable. Huffman *et al.* (2004) point out that Carlson *et al.*'s (2000) strain-based work-interferes-with-family conflict measure includes an item 'Due to all the pressures at work, sometimes when I come home I am too stressed to do the things I enjoy', which clearly is more of a work–non-work conflict measure. Netemeyer *et al.*'s (1996) measures are also accused of this same drawback. Although the use of such items is understandable insofar as researchers and practitioners are often seeking items for organizational surveys intended to apply to a wide base of employees including single people, the distinction between work–family and such work–non-work conflicts as work–leisure is blurred. Hence, such scales are less pure assessments of work–family conflict, thus making any relationships more difficult to interpret. Indeed, in their study that included measures of both work–family and work–non-work conflict, Huffman *et al.* (2004) found that only work–family conflict predicted turnover intentions of employees with families, whereas work–non-work conflict predicted turnover intentions for those without families.

WORK–FAMILY FACILITATION

Recently, the nearly exclusive focus on work–family conflict in the literature has come under fire (Barnett, 1998; Barnett and Hyde, 2001). Bolstered by earlier work that indicated that multiple roles were beneficial to individual well-being (Baruch and Barnett, 1986), combined with renewed emphasis on studying 'Positive Psychology' (Seligman and Csikszentmihalyi, 2000), researchers have begun to explore the ways in which work and family roles enhance each other (Grzywacz and Marks, 2000). This work–family facilitation also is conceptualized as a bidirectional construct, paralleling the distinctions in work–family conflict measurement, in that there are both work-to-family and family-to-work components.

Although work on measuring work–family facilitation is just beginning to emerge (Frone, 2003), the Grzywacz and Marks (2000) research is particularly notable. They analyzed data from the National Survey of Midlife Development in the USA (MIDUS), which included 16 items that assessed four dimensions: negative spillover from work to family, positive spillover from work to family, negative spillover from family to work, and positive spillover from family to work. Factor analysis supported a four-factor solution with only two items (one each for the two positive spillover scales) failing to load on the proper dimension. Coefficient alphas for the modified scales are acceptable, ranging from 0.70 to 0.83. Discriminant validity of the measures is also demonstrated in the correlations among the factors, with the highest correlation between the two negative spillover measures ($r = 0.45$). Additional evidence for discriminant validity is provided by the findings that each of the four dimensions uniquely predict global measures of physical health, mental health and life satisfaction. Particularly pertinent to the context of the present discussion, resources within the workplace (e.g., high level of decision latitude and support from co-workers and supervisors) were related to positive spillover from work to family, whereas support from family members and spouses and a lower level of family criticism were associated with positive spillover from family to work. Thus, these measures appear to be a valid vehicle for investigating variables that are likely to provide work–family facilitation. More recently, Hanson (2003) indicates that the MIDUS scales may be more accurately depicted as a measure of work–family facilitation than of positive spillover, insofar as some of the items do not appear to assess spillover per se. Indeed some items seem to have a compensation flavor to them as they address social support from family helping at work.

Hammer and her colleagues (Hanson, Colton and Hammer, 2003; Hanson, 2003) are currently developing a measure of positive spillover as well, based on Edwards and Rothbard's (2000) theoretical model of types of spillover: mood, skills, behavior and values. Initial results indicate that skill and behavior form a single construct labeled instrumental positive spillover (Hanson, Colton and Hammer, 2003). Recent evidence from a confirmatory factor analysis (Hanson, Hammer and Colton, 2003) supports a six-factor model with three factors (affective, instrumental and values) for each of the two directions (work-to-family and family-to-work). Each of these six types has strong internal consistency (all coefficient alphas are 0.90 or above) and reasonable discriminant validity for most of the scales, although the work-to-family values scale correlates highly with the work-to-family instrumental scale.

WORK–FAMILY BALANCE AND FIT

There is some lack of clear agreement on the meaning of work–family balance and work–family fit. Pittman (1994) defined work–family fit as 'an assessment of the balance between the spheres and may be considered the acceptability of the multidimensional exchange between a family and work organization' (p. 186). Therefore, this definition appears to equate fit with balance and implies a satisfaction with the exchanges from the two role domains and not surprisingly, work–family balance or fit has been measured as satisfaction.

For example, Buffardi *et al.* (1999) analyzed a Survey of Federal Employees developed and conducted by the US Office of Personnel Management. Employees with childcare and/or eldercare concerns were identified and compared on a variety of work attitude measures. The work–family balance measure consisted of a single global item, 'I am satisfied with the balance I have achieved between my work and family life'. Although no coefficient alpha could be calculated, there was some evidence for discriminant validity, given that work–family balance correlated weakly to moderately with the other five multi-item work attitude measures, with the highest correlation being with perceived organizational support (0.30). In addition, many of the findings are consistent with expectations, as work–family balance scores were lower for those with eldercare and childcare responsibilities (especially for women) and lowest for those with both forms of dependant care.

Similarly, Berg *et al.* (2003) used a single item to measure work–family balance: 'All and all, to what extent would you say your company helps workers to achieve a balance between their work and family responsibilities?' One might argue that this item is not really assessing work–family balance but rather the perceptions of the employees as to how well the company is addressing the work and family needs of its employees.

Lee and Tremble (2003), in demonstrating that work–family balance partially mediated the organizational support–turnover intent relationship, derived a measure of work–family balance from a set of items included in a survey distributed to soldiers who joined the army during 1999. Data were collected at the end of training during year 1 and again approximately one year later from those who had a spouse, dependant, or both at time 2. Survey items relating to work–family balance and two other constructs (organizational support and comparison of job conditions in the army versus a civilian job) were identified. A confirmatory factor analysis supported a three-factor solution both at time 1 and time 2, although one of the eight items on the work–family balance scale was dropped owing to a weak factor loading. Coefficient alphas on the work–family balance scale were 0.79 and 0.83 on the two occasions. Most of the items imply balance from an absence of work-to-family conflict (e.g., 'Satisfaction with the time available to pursue your personal life goals' was the item with the highest loading). However, two other items describe positive spillover (e.g. 'The army will allow me to maintain the kind of balance I want between my work and personal life' was the item with the second highest loading on the measure on both occasions).

The item that was dropped due to a weak factor loading differed from the others in terms of direction. It described the influence of home life on work life, whereas the retained items referred to, or at least implied, the influence of work life on home life. Thus, this measure of work–family balance is constrained to the latter direction.

Others have conceptualized work–family fit to be distinct from work–family balance (Barnett, 1998; Barnett *et al.*, 1999; Voydanoff, 2002), with work–family fit reflecting a mediating process. According to Barnett (1998), work–family fit is the ability of employees to adapt their work–family strategies to meet their needs. Barnett *et al.* (1999) operationalized fit with respect to the number of hours worked by asking participants to indicate how well their schedules and the degree of flexibility in their schedules met their own needs, the needs of their spouses/partners and their children. This measure had a coefficient alpha estimate of internal consistency of 0.85 and a test–retest correlation over a one- to three-month period of 0.78. To our knowledge, this measure has not been used in other investigations, nor has it been modified to reflect fit on any other dimensions.

In examining the above measures of work–family conflict and the related literature, it would seem that measures of work–family fit and balance should incorporate both directions; that is, work to family and family to work, should be considered in assessing work–family balance. Based on the work–family conflict literature, which supports maintaining the directionality of the conflict from work to family and family to work, including items that represent both directions in the same measure would likely confound the resulting assessment and also likely lead to lower internal consistency estimates.

Interestingly, there is a small body of research that has maintained the separation of work to family and family to work in examining work–family balance and fit. Using this approach, rather than asking people to report a global, overall assessment of balance, people are asked to assess the components of balance: work-to-family conflict, work-to-family facilitation, family-to-work conflict, and family-to-work facilitation. This seems to be consistent with Edwards' (2002) position against asking people to make overall assessments of 'fit' when examining person–environment fit but rather to have them respond to the components of fit. The question is how these four components combine to reflect work–family balance.

In general, studies have taken the position that work–family balance includes both work–family facilitation and work–family conflict (see Chapter 5 for further discussion). According to Frone (2003), work–family balance includes both work–family facilitation and lack of work–family conflict. This definition would suggest that the polynomial regression approach (Edwards, 1995, 2002; Edwards and Parry, 2000) would be best for investigating work–family balance in order to be able to identify the form of the relation between facilitation and conflict.

Hammer *et al.* (2002) took this approach in one of the few longitudinal studies conducted in the work–family literature. They measured all four components of the work–family interface (e.g., conflict and positive spillover in each of the two directions for husbands and wives at two points in time one year apart. The work-to-family conflict measures (Netemeyer *et al.*, 1996) had acceptable coefficient alphas for both husbands and wives (0.90 and 0.91, respectively), as did the family-to-work conflict measures (0.88 for both husbands and wives). The correlations over the period of one year were 0.57 and 0.54 for wives' and husbands' work-to-family conflict, respectively, and 0.49 and 0.45 with respect to wives' and husbands' reported family-to-work conflict, respectively. Positive spillover was measured using items adapted from Stephens *et al.* (1997). Work-to-family positive spillover had coefficient alphas of 0.82 and 0.79 for wives and husbands, respectively, and the one-year test–retest correlations were similar for those of work–family conflict ($r = 0.43$ and 0.39 for work-to-family facilitation among wives and husbands, respectively; $r = 0.56$ and 0.40 for family-to-work facilitation among wives and husbands, respectively).

Hammer *et al.* (2002) used a compensatory model approach in examining the relations between work-to-family and family-to-work conflict as well as work-to-family and family-to-work positive spillover. That is, they analyzed the data separately for conflict and for positive spillover partly because of sample size constraints. Therefore, while this study provides us with important information on the stability of the four components, they did not actually assess work–family balance at least as conceptualized by Frone (2003), which would have required including work-to-family conflict and work-to-family facilitation in the same analyses and arguably family-to-work conflict and family-to-work facilitation.

Grzywacz and Bass (2003) recently tested three models of work–family fit consistent with the recommendations of Edwards and Rothbard (2000). The first model was similar to that of Hammer *et al.* (2002), which Grzywacz and Bass referred to as the independent effects model. Essentially, this model included work-to-family conflict work-to-family facilitation, family-to-work conflict and family-to-work facilitation as independent variables controlling for several demographic variables such as gender, marital status and age. All components except work-to-family facilitation significantly predicted depression and problem drinking and only work-to-family conflict and family-to-work conflict predicted anxiety disorder. The second model examined the interaction between work-to-family conflict and facilitation as well as the interaction between family-to-work conflict and facilitation reflecting a potential buffering effect of work-to-family and family-to-work facilitation. The data did not support the interaction effects except in predicting anxiety disorder in which both work–family facilitation moderates the effects of work–family conflict.

Lastly Grzywacz and Bass (2003) estimated what they referred to as the relative difference model. This model essentially was estimated by using difference scores to reflect the relation between family capabilities and demands; the individual components were not entered into the analysis. The data suggested that work-to-family balance, operationalized as a difference score, predicted depression but family-to-work balance, also operationalized as a difference score, did not predict depression. Alternatively, problem drinking was predicted by family-to-work balance but not work-to-family balance. Anxiety disorder was predicted by both work-to-family balance and family-to-work balance. Therefore, the results of this study supported a relative difference model most completely although the independent effects model received some support.

Two caveats must be noted regarding Grzywacz and Bass's (2003) study. First they used the MIDUS measures of work–family conflict and facilitation. These measures are not strictly commensurate; that is, they are not parallel in construction (Bellavia and Frone, 2004). Edwards (2002) explains: 'Commensurate measurement is required to ensure the conceptual relevance of the component measures to one another and is necessary to meaningfully interpret results in terms of congruence' (p. 361). It is unclear at this point whether work–family balance reflects 'congruence' per se so the impact of the lack of strictly commensurate measurement remains to be seen.

The other caveat about the Gryzwacz and Bass (2003) study is that while they did take a confirmatory approach by examining three a priori models it was disappointing that they did not also take an exploratory approach, perhaps on an ad hoc basis, to examine the full response surface between conflict and facilitation and the outcomes. This would have been an excellent opportunity to use a three-dimensional surface relating conflict and facilitation to the outcomes studied (Edwards, 1995, 2002), which could have explored quadratic and linear effects.

These studies, however, highlight an important need for further theoretical development of what is meant by work–family balance (Edwards and Rothbard, 2000). To assess work–family balance, is it necessary to maintain domain specificity or can work-to-family facilitation offset family-to-work conflict? Also, if conflict equals facilitation, is this a state of balance? Or does facilitation need to exceed conflict to achieve balance? This suggests that we do not yet have a clear conceptual definition of the construct.

Alternative approaches to assessing work–family balance

Although there appears to be emerging agreement on the idea that work–family balance is multidimensional, based on separate constructs of conflict and facilitation, other perspectives are possible. Clark (2000), taking a qualitative approach to understanding balance, suggests that part of work–family balance may be rather independent of spillover, either positive or negative. She suggests that people who segment their life domains (and thus minimize both negative *and* positive spillover) might still create a synergy between their various life domains because the domains are separate and different. Under this model of balance, Clark proposed that each domain provides for essential but different needs, mixing different activities stimulating involvement and engagement. Further, respites from a given domain such as work would allow one to renew their resources and energy. Indeed one of the family-to-work items from the MIDUS measure ('Your home life helps you relax and feel ready for the next days work') seems to tap facilitation from this segmentation approach. Clark's perspective is similar to Barnett *et al.*'s (1999) approach of defining work–family fit as need fulfillment.

Need for longitudinal research

A review of the work–family literature reveals a need for more longitudinal research. Much of the research has been cross-sectional, as is the case in other lines of research as well. There have been some longitudinal studies such as Hammer *et al.* (2002) and these are to be commended. However, in this section we would like to suggest more theoretical as well as empirical developments in understanding the process of work–family balance.

Time has been a much-neglected aspect of many of our theories (McGrath and Rotchford, 1983; Mitchell and James, 2001). We need to consider the timing of work–family conflict and facilitation. Many of the measures of work–family conflict and facilitation tend to capture rather chronic aspects of conflict and facilitation by asking respondents to indicate the extent to which they have experienced certain conflicts and facilitation or by asking respondents to indicate the degree to which they agree or disagree with a statement describing an aspect of conflict or facilitation.

Yet, much of the theorizing on work–family balance implies a much more dynamic perspective. How does an individual integrate the events of the day or week to assess whether there is adequate balance between work and family? Longitudinal designs may enhance our understanding of this process; however, we must consider carefully the time intervals used in our studies.

Some work has been done using a year as the interval (e.g., Hammer *et al.*, 2002; Lee and Tremble, 2003). While informative, we suggest that the work–family interface is dynamic and shorter time intervals need to be investigated. Although still rare in the work–family literature or the more global occupational stress literature, use of daily diaries or experience-sampling procedures appear to offer promise in advancing our understanding of the dynamics of work–family balance. (See Chapters 8 and 9 for examples of diary studies.)

Experience-sampling methodology has been in existence since the late 1970s (see Scollon *et al.*, 2003, and Smyth and Stone, 2003, for excellent reviews of the historical development of these procedures). Experience-sampling methodology, also referred to as ecological momentary assessment, involves collecting self-report data at multiple points in time. This method, therefore, takes a within-person perspective in understanding a phenomenon. Daily diaries reflect low-technology experience-sampling procedures with the drawbacks that data collection does not occur at random intervals and often participants do not complete the diaries at the times planned. Technological advancements such as personal data assistants (e.g., PalmPilots), hand-held computers and widespread Internet access have made it possible to collect data at random intervals and in multiple locations. Therefore, use of experience-sampling methodology allows researchers to collect data in 'real time', not having to rely on retrospective reports of emotions and cognitions or having to rely on the participants' integration of their experiences over a particular period of time to report their overall assessment of their emotions and cognitions (Scollon *et al.*, 2003; Schimmack, 2003; Smyth and Stone, 2003).

These procedures would thus allow researchers to examine both directions of work–family conflict and work–family facilitation over a period of days and measures could be taken both at work and at home. It should be noted that if one embarks on such a study and is planning on data collection at work, participants' employers must be agreeable (see Christensen *et al.*, 2003, for an excellent practical guide for conducting experience-sampling studies). Because of the versatility of these procedures, it is possible to collect open-ended responses as well as scaled responses to provide the researcher with useful contextual information in interpreting the quantitative information. In addition, use of ambulatory blood pressure monitors, for example, could link physiological responses with psychosocial factors. Therefore, these procedures provide data on the dynamic processes individuals experience in the natural work and home environments.

Like any research design, experience-sampling methodology is not without its challenges. Christensen *et al.* (2003) and Scollon *et al.* (2003) enumerate many of the challenges of this approach, including the high commitment required of participants and potential self-selection bias, the costs of equipment assuming the high-technology approach is taken, and reactivity. For example, if one asks participants repeatedly about work-to-family conflict, might this actually affect their responses, emotions and behaviors? Another challenge arises in analyzing the data. First, there is a large quantity of data to be analyzed. The nested structure of the data allows researchers to potentially analyze the data at the event, person and group levels. Multilevel modeling, such as hierarchical linear modeling and random coefficient modeling, allow researchers to examine within- and between-person effects, and spectral analysis may be useful in analyzing changes over time. However, these statistical procedures are relatively new and it is not clear how robust they may be to violations of the assumptions underlying the statistical analyses.

CONCLUSIONS AND FUTURE RESEARCH DIRECTIONS

Clearly, the main focus of most research on the dynamics between work and family domains has been on spillover (both positive and negative). However, it should be noted that spillover is only one of three interaction models generally proposed. Heretofore, with the exception of an occasional item dealing with facilitation, the compensatory and segmentation models have been largely overlooked. People may take very different paths in balancing their work and family lives. If one has a bad day at work, one person might react by segmenting the two domains ('I erase all the bad memories of the day from work as soon as I open the door to my house'), while another compensates for the bad day by doing something special with her family. Both approaches are adaptive ways of achieving balance. Separate scales based on these two models would likely lead to a more comprehensive approach. Some preliminary measures of these two approaches appear in McCarthy (1999) and Sumer and Knight (2001).

Before we can proceed with examining work–family balance and fit, it is clear that we need to be able to define what we mean by the construct (Cook and Campbell, 1979). The literature on work–family conflict and the emerging literature on work–family facilitation will guide our conceptualization of work–family balance. Interestingly, in preparing this chapter, we asked a group of undergraduates, who had not read the literature on work and family, what they though work–family balance was. The answers ranged from time equally spent between work and family at least in the long run, the degree of effort and dedication being equal across the two domains, the quality of the relationship between work and family, the satisfaction with the interaction between work and family, accomplishment of both work and family goals, and flexibility between the two domains. It is interesting that their definitions or at least indicators of work–family balance reflect all of the issues that have been considered in various operationalizations of work–family conflict as well as work–family balance. However, these various perspectives suggest a need for further refinement of the relevant dimensions in understanding the work–home interface, including the dynamic, give-and-take nature existent between the two domains.

Other recommendations for future research include the need to look at individual differences in disposition. Much of the research concerning work–family conflict is cross-sectional and often based on single source data (Allen *et al.*, 2000; Casper and Eby, 2000). Hence, the relationships found with conflict may be due to the employee's disposition. Individuals who are high on negative affect are likely to perceive stronger levels of work–family conflict and less satisfaction with both work and non-work outcomes, thus driving a negative correlation between conflict and the other variables (Burke *et al.*, 1993). Future research needs to assess the degree of the contribution of such dispositional attributes in the relationship between antecedents and consequences of work–family variables, recognizing that the potency of different dispositional attributes may vary across individuals' career and life span.

APPENDIX A

Source citation

Netemeyer, R. G., Boles, J. S., and McMurrian, R. (1996). Development and validation of work–family conflict and family–work conflict scales. *Journal of Applied Psychology, 81*, 400–410.

Work–family conflict scale

---

1. The demands of my work interfere with my home and family life.
2. The amount of time my job takes up makes it difficult to fulfill family responsibilities.
3. Things I want to do at home do not get done because of the demands my job puts on me.
4. My job produces strain that makes it difficult to fulfill family duties.
5. Due to work-related duties, I have to make changes to my plans for family activities.

Family–work conflict scale

---

1. The demands of my family or spouse/partner interfere with work-related activities.
2. I have to put off doing things at work because of demands on my time at home.

3. Things I want to do at work don't get done because of the demands of my family or spouse/partner.
4. My home life interferes with my responsibilities at work such as getting to work on time, accomplishing daily tasks, and working overtime.
5. Family-related strain interferes with my ability to perform job-related duties.

Anchors: strongly disagree to strongly agree, on a 7-point Likert-type scale.

APPENDIX B

Source citation

Carlson, D. S., Kacmar, K. M., and Williams, L. J. (2000). Construction and initial validation of a multi-dimensional measure of work–family conflict. *Journal of Vocational Behavior, 56*, 249–276.

Work–family Conflict Items

Time based work interference with family
1. My work keeps me from my family activities more than I would like.[a]
2. The time I must devote to my job keeps me from participating equally in household responsibilities and activities.[a]
3. I have to miss family activities due to the amount of time I must spend on work responsibilities.

Time based family interference with work
4. The time I spend on family responsibilities often interferes with my work responsibilities.
5. The time I spend with my family often causes me to not spend time in activities at work that could be helpful to my career.
6. I have to miss work activities due to the amount of time I must spend on family responsibilities.

Strain-based work interference with family
7. When I get home from work I am often too frazzled to participate in family activities/responsibilities.
8. I am often so emotionally drained when I get home from work that it prevents me from contributing to my family.
9. Due to all the pressures at work, sometimes when I come home I am too stressed to do the things I enjoy.

Strain-based family interference with work
10. Due to stress at home, I am often preoccupied with family matters at work.
11. Because I am often stressed from family responsibilities, I have a hard time concentrating on my work.
12. Tension and anxiety from my family life often weakens my ability to do my job.

Behavior-based work interference with family
13. The problem-solving behaviors I use in my job are not effective in resolving problems at home.[a]

14. Behavior that is effective and necessary for me at work would be counter-productive at home.[a]
15. The behaviors I perform that make me effective at work do not help me to be a better parent and spouse.[a]

Behavior-based family interference with work
16. The behaviors that work for me at home do not seem to be effective at work.
17. Behavior that is effective and necessary for me at home would be counter-productive at work.
18. The problem-solving behavior that works for me at home does not seem to be as useful at work.

---

[a] Items from Stephens and Sommer (1996).
Anchors: strongly agree to strongly disagree on a Likert-type 5-point scale.

REFERENCES

Allen, T. D., Herst, D. E., Bruck, C. S., and Sutton M. (2000). Consequences associated with work-to-family conflict: a review and agenda for future research. *Journal of Occupational Health Psychology*, 5, 278–308.

Aryee, S., Fields, D., and Luk, V. (1999). A cross-cultural test of a model of the work–family interface. *Journal of Management*, 25, 491–511.

Bagozzi, R. P., and Yi, Y. (1988). On the evaluation of structural equation models. *Journal of the Academy of Marketing Science*, 16, 74–94.

Barnett, R. C. (1998). Toward a review and reconceptualization of the work–family interace. *Genetic, Social, and General Psychology Monographs*, 124, 125–182.

Barnett, R. C., and Hyde, J. S. (2001). Women, men, work, and family: an expansionist theory. *American Psychologist*, 56, 781–796.

Barnett, R. C., Gareis, K. C., and Brennan, R. T. (1999). Fit as a mediator of the relationship between work hours and burnout. *Journal of Occupational Health Psychology*, 4, 307–317.

Baruch, G. K., and Barnett, R. C. (1986). Role quality, multiple role involvement and psychological well-being in midlife women. *Journal of Personality and Social Psychology*, 51, 578–585.

Bellavia, G., and Frone, M. R. (2004). Work–family conflict. In J. Barling, E. K. Kelloway and M. R. Frone (eds), *Handbook of work stress* (pp. 113–148). Thousand Oaks, CA: Sage.

Berg, P., Kalleberg, A. L., and Appelbaum, E. (2003). Balancing work and family: the role of high-commitment environments. *Industrial Relations*, 42, 168–188.

Bohen, H. H., and Viveros-Long, A. (1981). *Balancing jobs and family life: Do flexible schedules really help?* Philadelphia: Temple University Press.

Bruck, C. S., Allen, T. D., and Spector, P. E. (2002). The relation between work–family conflict and job satisfaction: a finer-grained analysis. *Journal of Vocational Behavior*, 60, 336–353.

Buffardi, L. C., Smith, J. L., O'Brien, A. S., and Erdwins, C. J. (1999). The impact of dependent-care responsibility and gender on work attitudes. *Journal of Occupational Health Psychology*, 4, 356–367.

Burke, M. J., Brief, A. P., and George, J. M. (1993). The role of negative affectivity in understanding relations between self-reports of stressors and strains: a comment on the applied psychology literature. *Journal of Applied Psychology*, *78*, 403–412.

Burley, K. (1989). Work–family conflict and marital adjustment in dual career couples: a comparison of three time models. Unpublished doctoral dissertation, Claremont Graduate School, Claremont, CA.

Carlson, D. S., Kacmar, K. M., and Williams, L. J. (2000). Construction and initial validation of a multidimensional measure of work–family conflict. *Journal of Vocational Behavior*, *56*, 249–276.

Casper, W. J., and Eby, L. (2000). Applying innovative research methodologies and data analysis techniques to work–family research. In L. T. Eby (Chair), *Examining Work and Family through a Methodological Lens*. Paper presented at the Society for Industrial–Organizational Psychology annual conference, New Orleans, LA.

Christensen, T. C., Barrett, L. F., Bliss-Moreau, E., Lebo, K., and Kaschub, C. (2003). A practical guide to experience-sampling procedures. *Journal of Happiness Studies*, *4*, 53–78.

Clark, S. C. (2000). Work/family border theory: a new theory of work/family balance. *Human Relations*, *53*, 747–770.

Cook, T. D., and Campbell, D. T. (1979). *Quasi-experimentation: Design and analysis issues for field settings*. Boston: Houghton Mifflin.

DeVillis, R. F. (1991). *Scale development: Theory and applications*. Newbury Park, CA: Sage.

Eagle, B. W., Miles, E. W., and Icenogle, M. L. (1997). Interrole conflicts and the permeability of work and family domains: are there gender differences? *Journal of Vocational Behavior*, *50*, 168–184.

Edwards, J. R. (1995). Alternatives to difference scores as dependent variables in the study of congruence in organizational research. *Organizational Behavior and Human Decision Processes*, *64*, 307–324.

Edwards, J. R. (2002). Alternatives to difference scores polynomial regression analysis and response surface methodology. In F. Drasgow and N. Schmitt (eds), *Measuring and analyzing behavior in organizations: Advances in measurement and data analysis* (pp. 350–400). San Francisco: Jossey-Bass.

Edwards, J. R., and Parry, M. E. (2000). On the use of polynomial regression equations as an alternative to difference scores in organizational research. *Academy of Management Journal*, *36*, 1577–1613.

Edwards, J. R., and Rothbard, N. P. (2000). Mechanisms linking work and family: clarifying the relationship between work and family construct. *Academy of Management Review*, *25*, 178–199.

Fields, D. L. (2002). *Taking the measure of work: A guide to validated scales for organizational research and diagnosis*. Thousand Oaks, CA: Sage.

Frone, M. R. (2003). Work–family balance. In J. C. Quick and L. E. Tetrick (eds), *Handbook of occupational health psychology* (pp. 143–162). Washington, DC: American Psychological Association.

Frone, M. R., Russell, M., and Cooper, M. L. (1992a). Prevalence of work family conflict: are work and family boundaries asymmetrically permeable? *Journal of Organizational Behavior*, *13*, 723–729.

Frone, M. R., Russell, M., and Cooper, M. L. (1992b). Antecedents and outcomes of work family conflict: testing a model of the work family interface. *Journal of Applied Psychology*, *77*, 65–78.

Frone, M. R., Russell, M., and Cooper, M. (1997). Relation of work–family conflict to health outcomes: a four-year longitudinal study of employed parents. *Journal of Occupational and Organizational Psychology*, *70*, 325–335.

Greenhaus, J. H., and Beutell, N. J. (1985). Sources of conflict between work and family roles. *Academy of Management Review*, *10*, 76–88.

Grzywacz, J. G., and Bass, B. L. (2003). Work, family, and mental health: testing different models of work–family fit. *Journal of Marriage and Family*, *65*, 248–262.

Grzywacz, J. G., and Marks, N. F. (2000). Reconceptualizing the work–family interface: an ecological perspective on the correlates of positive and negative spillover between work and family. *Journal of Occupational Health Psychology*, *5*, 111–126.

Gutek, B., Searle, S., and Klepa, L. (1991). Rational versus gender-role explanations for work family conflict. *Journal of Applied Psychology*, *76*, 560–568.

Hammer, L. B., Bauer, T. N., and Grandey, A. A. (2003). Work–family conflict and work-related withdrawal behaviors. *Journal of Business and Psychology*, *17*, 419–436.

Hammer, L. B., Cullen, J. C., Caubet, S., Johnson, J., Neal, M. B., and Sinclair, R. R. (2002). *The effects of work–family fit on depression: a longitudinal study*. Paper presented at *17th Annual SIOP Conference*, Toronto, Canada.

Huffman, A. H., Youngcourt, S. S., and Castro, C. A. (2004). Measuring role conflict in the work and nonwork domains. Paper presented at the *19th Annual Conference of the Society for Industrial and Organizational Psychology*, Chicago, IL.

Hanson, G. (2003). Development and validation of a multidimensional scale of work–family positive spillover. Unpublished manuscript. Portland State University.

Hanson, G. C., Colton, C. L., and Hammer, L. B. (2003). Work–family facilitation: an expansion of the work–family paradigm. Paper presented at *SIOP*, Orlando, FL.

Hanson, G. C., Hammer, L. B., and Colton, C. L. (2003). Multidimensional scale of work–family positive spillover. Unpublished manuscript. Portland State University.

Kopelman, R. E., Greenhaus, J. H., and Connolly, T. F. (1983). A model of work, family, and inter-role conflict: a construct-validation study. *Organizational Behavior and Human Performance*, *32*, 198–215.

Kossek, E. E., and Ozeki, C. (1998). Work–family conflict, policies, and the job–life satisfaction relationship: a review and directions for organizational behavior–human resources research. *Journal of Applied Psychology*, *83*(2), 139–149.

Lee, J. K., and Tremble, T. R. (2003). Work–family balance mediates organizational support and retention attitudes. Unpublished manuscript. George Mason University.

McCarthy, N. P. (1999). Relations between work–family interface modes and patterns of coping behavior. Unpublished doctoral dissertation, George Mason University, Fairfax, VA.

McGrath, J. E., and Rotchford, N. L. (1983). Time and behavior in organizations. *Research in Organizational Behavior*, *5*, 57–101.

Mitchell, T. R., and James, L. R. (2001). Building better theory: time and the specification of when things happen. *Academy of Management Review*, *26*, 530–547.

Netemeyer, R. G., Boles, J. S., and McMurrian, R. (1996). Development and validation of work–family conflict and work–family conflict scales. *Journal of Applied Psychology*, *81*, 400–410.

Parasuraman, S., Purohit, Y. S., Godshalk, V. M., and Beutell, N. J. (1996). Work and family variables, entrepreneurial career success, and psychological well-being. *Journal of Vocational Behavior*, *48*, 275–300.

Pittman, J. F. (1994). Work–family fit as a mediator of work factors on marital tension: evidence from the interface of greedy institutions. *Human Relations*, *47*, 183–209.

Schimmack, U. (2003). Affect measurement in experience sampling research. *Journal of Happiness Studies*, *4*, 79–106.

Scollon, C. N., Kim-Prieto, C., and Diener, E. (2003). Experience sampling: promises and pitfalls, strengths and weaknesses. *Journal of Happiness Studies*, *4*, 5–34.

Seligman, M. E. P., and Csikszentmihalyi, M. (2000). Positive psychology: an introduction. *American Psychologist*, *55*, 5–14.

Smyth, J. M., and Stone, A. A. (2003). Ecological momentary assessment research in behavioral medicine. *Journal of Happiness Studies*, *4*, 35–52.

Stephens, G. K., and Sommer, S. M. (1996). The measurement of work to family conflict. *Educational and Psychological Measurement*, *56*, 475–486.

Stephens, M. A. P., Franks, M. M., and Atienza, A. A. (1997). Where two roles intersect: spillover between parent care and employment. *Psychology and Aging*, *12*, 376–386.

Sumer, H. C., and Knight, P. A. (2001). How do people with different attachment styles balance work and family? A personality perspective on work–family linkage. *Journal of Applied Psychology*, *86*, 653–663.

Voydanoff, P. (2002). Linkages between the work–family interface and work, family, and individual outcomes. *Journal of Family Issues*, *23*, 138–164.

Part III

Relationships between work and home life

This part builds on the previous chapters to expand on the core approaches to examining relationships between work and family. In Chapter 3 Rothbard has introduced the related concepts of spillover and conflict. These are related concepts, but Rothbard has suggested that spillover is an approach used to explain observed relationships whereas role conflict is an outcome. Work within both these traditions is a key focus of chapters within this part, starting with Chapter 5, by Michael O'Driscoll, Paula Brough and Thomas Kalliath, which focuses on reviewing literature on work–family conflict, including its causes and consequences. This chapter further addresses the more recent and complementary approach of work–family facilitation (whereby work may have a positive impact or enrich home life).

One particular type of work which has the potential to impact either positively or negatively on family life is working at home (and by implication, flexible working). Conflicting evidence about these impacts is the focus of Chapter 6 by Cath Sullivan and Suzan Lewis.

Chapter 7 goes beyond looking at the effects of conflict between home and work on the individual employee to examine whether work factors may actually impact negatively (or indeed positively) on other family members, a phenomenon known as crossover. Mina Westman presents evidence indicating that this is indeed an important issue for work–life balance researchers.

The final chapter in this part, Chapter 8, by Fiona Jones, Gail Kinman and Nicola Payne, examines a further impact of work stress on life outside work, that of the impact of work factors on health behaviours, such as eating, exercise, smoking and alcohol consumption. This is a likely mechanism whereby work stressors may impact on both physical health of the individual and crossover to other family members. It is suggested that policies relating to health behaviors should be considered within the context of work–life balance initiatives.

5 Work–family conflict and facilitation

Michael O'Driscoll, Paula Brough and Thomas Kalliath

Since the late 1970s, when Rosabeth Kanter (1977) debunked the 'myth of separate worlds', there has been increasing interest (and concern) expressed by researchers, social commentators, the media, and people generally, in the interface between job-related activities and off-the-job life, especially family life. Numerous commentators (e.g., Burke and Greenglass, 1987; Edwards and Rothbard, 2000; Frone, 2003; Grzywacz and Marks, 2000; see also Chapters 1 and 3) have observed that changing demographics, conditions of work, family role expectations and other factors have contributed to a closer relationship between the domains of employment and family and to greater permeability between these domains. It is also apparent that increasingly sophisticated technologies (such as cell phones and laptop computers) have enabled greater flexibility in work patterns, and at the same time have contributed to a closer linkage between work and family lives, as the notion of 'work anytime, anywhere' becomes a reality for more and more people. Although these technologies do increase flexibility in terms of the capacity to fulfill job-related responsibilities, they also may create a blurring of boundaries between job and off-job roles. Consequently, as demonstrated in recent studies, conflict or interference between the two domains is increasingly likely for many individuals, as they endeavor to strike a balance between their work and family commitments. However, it is also the case that engagement in job roles and family roles can contribute positively to each other, and lead to an enhancement of people's lives (Grzywacz and Bass, 2003; Kirchmeyer, 1992a), although there has been less systematic research on this positive spillover effect than there has been on negative spillover between work and family roles.

Frone (2003) has noted that the literature has not presented a consistent definition of balance between job and family roles, and it would appear that sometimes work–family balance is conceived of simply as a lack of conflict between the two domains (for further definitions, see Chapter 4). He cogently argues that research on work–family balance needs to be expanded to include both positive spillover (facilitation) and negative spillover (conflict), as well as examining effects in both directions, that is, work-to-family and family-to-work. In the current chapter we discuss some of the studies that have investigated conflict and facilitation. Our aim is to highlight major themes and findings, and to discuss some critical issues that are salient in this field of research, rather than to provide a comprehensive research review; hence our inclusion of studies is selective rather than exhaustive.

We begin with a discussion of the literature on work–family conflict, which was defined by Greenhaus and Beutell (1985, p. 77) as 'a form of inter-role conflict in which the role pressures from the work and family domains are mutually incompatible in some respect.[1] That is, participation in the work (family) role is made more difficult by virtue of participation in the family (work) role.' This definition suggests that interference between the two domains can occur in both directions, that is, work-to-family interference (WFI) and family-to-work interference (FWI). Here we use the expressions WFI and FWI when referring to a specific direction of inter-ference, and work–family conflict when referring generically to conflict between the two role domains.

Greenhaus and Beutell's (1985) conceptualization of work–family con-flict also incorporated three different 'forms' of conflict: time-based, strain-based and behavior-based. Time-based conflict refers to the individual's inability to perform a task in one role, either physically or due to a cogni-tive preoccupation, as a result of time demands in another role. Time-based conflict builds upon the rational model (Gutek *et al.*, 1991) or the utilitarian model (Lobel, 1991) of work–family relations, which posit that time is a limited resource and devoting greater time to one area of life (such as one's job) inevitably reduces the amount of time available for another (e.g., the family). Hence, job and family impose demands on a person's time. For example, an approaching work deadline may result in more time spent at work, and thus less time with a partner/family. Similarly, personal/family responsibilities may produce high time demands, contributing to absentee-ism from the workplace.

Strain-based conflict is experienced when a preoccupation with the demands from one role interferes with the ability to perform adequately within a second role. Strain-based conflict is usually characterized by a spillover of negative emotions from one domain into the other. For instance, negative emotional reactions to workplace stressors can lead to expressions of irritability toward family members or withdrawal from family interaction in order to recuperate (O'Driscoll, 1996). Similarly, distress in one's family life might overflow into the job domain, affecting the individual's job satisfaction and ability to perform at expected levels.

Finally, behavior-based conflict refers to the display of specific behaviors in one domain that are incongruous with desired behaviors within the second domain, where norms and role expectations in one area of life are incom-patible with those required in the other domain. For example, at work an individual may be expected to be aggressive, ambitious, hard-driving and task-oriented. Successful job performance may be contingent upon the demonstration of these behaviors. In contrast, at home being loving, supportive and accommodating may be regarded as essential to developing and fostering a happy and healthy family life. Clearly these opposing expectations may create a tension between work and family behaviors, as well as impeding the transition from one environment to the other.

The same differentiations can be applied to work–family facilitation or enhancement, although there has been very little research on facilitation generally, and virtually none on the various forms of facilitation (see also Chapter 3). Work–family facilitation is defined as 'the extent to which participation at work (or home) is made easier by virtue of the experiences, skills, and opportunities gained or developed at home (or work)' (Frone, 2003, p. 145). Although the vast majority of studies on the work–family interface have focused on work–family conflict, the notion that experiences and activities in the two domains may enhance one another has been around for some time, having been outlined initially by Sieber (1974) and then Marks (1977). These sociologists noted that, contrary to the idea that work and family necessarily compete with each other for a person's time and energy, an individual can in fact be energized by their engagement in multiple roles, and that involvement in work and family can provide resources that may not develop from involvement in just one of these spheres.

We begin this chapter with an overview of research on work–family conflict, including antecedents and consequences of inter-domain conflict, along with a review of some variables that have been conceptualized as key moderators of the relationship between work–family conflict (as a stressor) and individuals' psychological states (strains). We then turn to the rather more limited literature on work–family facilitation, and discuss the potential importance of this issue, including a summary of some pertinent studies on this topic. Finally, we draw some conclusions on the state of play of research on the work–family nexus, and make some suggestions about future directions for research and practice.

WORK–FAMILY CONFLICT

The different expectations from roles in both work and family life can create conflict, leading to reduced participation, satisfaction and performance in either or both of these domains. Above we noted the different forms and directions of work–family conflict. Here we examine some of the major antecedents and outcomes of this stressor.

Few researchers have endeavored to develop measures of work–family conflict that encapsulate Greenhaus and Beutell's (1985) tripartite division of work–family conflict types (see Chapter 4). Instead a large proportion of work–family conflict research is largely based on the measurement of strain-based and/or time-based conflict. A notable exception is Stephens and Sommer's (1996) research on time-based, strain-based and behavior-based conflict, although their focus was solely on WFI. A more extensive exploration of the Greenhaus–Beutell conceptualization was reported by Carlson and Kacmar (2000). In addition to including separate assessments of time-based, strain-based and behavior-based conflict, they examined WFI and FWI as separate constructs. Similarly, Fu and Shaffer (2001) also tested the three forms of work–family conflict in both work-to-family and family-to-work directions. Fu and Shaffer (2001) found parental demands and the hours spent on household chores predicted time-based FWI, while role conflict, role overload and work hours predicted both time-based and strain-based WFI.

Directions of influence of work–family conflict

Based on any one or a combination of the above three forms of work–family conflict, theoretical models indicate that stressors from one role (e.g., work) have adverse 'strain' effects on the individual in their other role (e.g., family/non-work). Current thinking is that this spillover may occur in both directions (that is, work-to-family and family-to-work), although there is evidence that most people report greater levels of work-to-family than family-to-work interference (Aryee *et al.*, 1999; Netemeyer *et al.*, 1996). Methodologically this differentiation is important, because it acknowledges that WFI and FWI are distinct variables and should be assessed separately.

Figure 5.1 (derived from Carlson and Kacmar, 2000) provides a basic model of work–family conflict. This model distinguishes between WFI and FWI, while illustrating the positive reciprocal relationship between these two constructs. As WFI increases, so do levels of FWI. Figure 5.1 depicts common predictors and consequences of work–family conflict, and provides a valuable framework for the present discussion.

Antecedents of work–family conflict

Resources

Much work–family conflict research is based on the *role strain hypothesis* (Greenhaus and Beutell, 1985), which stipulates that individuals have finite amounts of psychological resources, time and physical energy. Each life role of an individual exerts demands on these finite resources (Kahn *et al.*, 1964). Strain occurs when the demands of multiple roles exceed the individual's resources, time and energy, resulting in a variety of negative consequences in both the home and work domains (Frone *et al.*, 1992; Frone, Russell and Cooper, 1997; Netemeyer *et al.*, 1996). The role strain hypothesis accounts for the suggestion that demands and strain from one

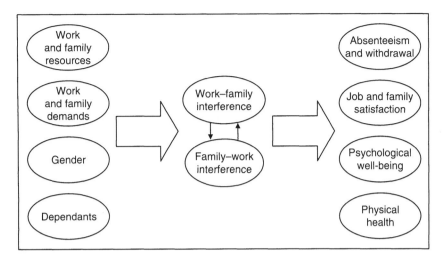

Figure 5.1 Predictors and consequences of work–family conflict

domain may spill over to affect health and performance in the second domain (Greenhaus and Beutell, 1985).

It is pertinent here to note that strain is commonly described as a *consequence* of work–family conflict. However, some researchers have also examined strain as an antecedent of conflict. Williams and Alliger (1994), for example, observed that family distress was predictive of FWI, but that work distress did not predict WFI. On the other hand, Kelloway *et al.* (1999) found that strain-based family-to-work interference positively predicted both psychological strain and turnover intentions, although no significant relationships existed with their strain-based WFI measure. The relationship between conflict and distress is therefore likely to be reciprocal; that is, conflict causes distress which in turn (and over time) results in more interrole conflict. However, few empirical investigations have actually tested this reciprocal relationship.

A principal characteristic of the role strain hypothesis is the salience or value of each role to an individual. A high value placed upon family life requires the devotion of time and energy to the family domain. If these preferences are blocked by, for example, job demands, then work–family conflict will occur (Carlson and Kacmar, 2000). The role of work and family stress as an antecedent of work–family conflict can also be explained by the *Conservation of Resources model* (COR; Hobfoll, 1989), as suggested by Grandey and Cropanzano (1999). The COR model proposes that individuals act to acquire and maintain a variety of resources, such as objects, energies, conditions and personal characteristics. Stress occurs when a loss of a resource is threatened or experienced. Work–family conflict occurs when attempts to balance work and home demands lead to the loss of resources from either (or both) domain(s) (Grandey and Cropanzano, 1999; Hobfoll, 1989). Individuals who have many resources will experience less stress and conflict, for some resources will act as buffers (moderators) against stress and conflict.

The COR model classifies variables such as gender, marital status, age, job tenure, job rank and status as resources. Employed women who may have a lower job rank, status and tenure, and thus fewer resources than their male colleagues, will experience higher levels of both stress and WFI. Grandey and Cropanzano (1999) suggested that this explains why some research has shown that employed women tend to experience higher levels of work–family conflict than employed men (Gutek *et al.*, 1991; Parasuraman *et al.*, 1996). In contrast to the more traditional role theory model (Kahn *et al.*, 1964), the COR model views having a spouse/partner positively – as an additional resource to be drawn upon. This perspective was supported by Grandey and Cropanzano (1999), who found that married/partnered individuals experienced lower self-reported family stress than individuals without a spouse or partner. Brough and Kelling (2002) also found positive associations between having a partner and reduced WFI and FWI. Similarly, the number of dependants an individual has at home is associated with a corresponding loss of the resources of time and energy, again resulting in stress and FWI. The COR model therefore also explains why research has identified the number of dependants as a source of work–family conflict (Brough and Kelling, 2002; Eagle *et al.*, 1997; Grandey and Cropanzano, 1999).

Work and family demands

Carlson and Frone (2003) suggest that work–family conflict is caused by two types of interference between the home and work domains: internal and external interference. Internal interference is created by self-inflicted demands, such as a preoccupation with work performance that hinders participation or performance in the home life, and vice versa. External interference occurs from a source external to the individual. For example, a work deadline may prevent or delay the individual's participation in his/her family life. Similarly, family responsibilities such as childcare demands may prevent attendance at work (Carlson and Frone, 2003). Thus internal and external sources may contribute to both work and family interference, producing four 'types' of interference (see Figure 5.2).

A major predictor of behavioral involvement in both the family and work domains is time demands (Greenhaus and Beutell, 1985). As time demands in a domain increase, the level of behavioral involvement in that domain also increases, resulting in less behavioral involvement in the second domain, thus producing work–family conflict (Gutek *et al.*, 1991). Carlson and Frone (2003) found that work hours were associated with external WFI: as the time spent at work increased, so too did the experience of WFI. Carlson and Frone (2003) also found that increased family

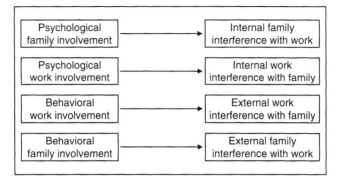

Figure 5.2 The four types of work and family interference. From Carlson and Frone (2003). Reproduced with permission of the authors and Kluwer Academic/Plenum Publishers

involvement was associated with internal FWI, such that thoughts about family life while in the work domain interfered with work performance.

A detailed examination of how time demands affect work–family conflict was conducted by Major *et al.* (2002). These authors found associations between the amount of time spent at work and WFI, career identity salience, work role overload, organizational work hour expectations, non-job responsibilities and financial need. Major *et al.* (2002) also found that long work hours per se were predictive of work–family conflict and that work time mediated the relationships between various work and family characteristics and WFI.

An interesting corollary of the above is the application of time management techniques. For instance, Adams and Jex (1999) observed that three time management techniques (setting goals and priorities, engaging in time management and general organization activities) predicted levels of work–family conflict (with some indirect pathways occurring through the perception of control). That is, engaging in (for instance) time management may induce a perception that one is in control over work and family demands, which in turn will reduce feelings of conflict between these domains. Adams and Jex (1999) suggested that these time management techniques are salient to the reduction of work–family conflict. However, as discussed later, Jex and Elacqua (1999) were unable to demonstrate significant moderating (buffering) effects of time management on conflict–strain relationships.

Grandey and Cropanzano (1999) concluded that role stress at work was related to WFI, while role stress at home was related to FWI (see also Aryee *et al.*, 1999; Frone, Yardley and Markel, 1997). Work demands (stressors) have been consistently found to be a source of WFI. For example, Parasuraman and Simmers (2001) found that work demands were stronger predictors of both work–family conflict and psychological well-being, compared with family-based demands. Finally, using structural equations analysis, Boyar *et al.* (2003) observed that work conflict, overload and ambiguity all positively predicted WFI, while family responsibilities (personal responsibilities and dependant characteristics) predicted FWI.

Gender

Numerous comparisons have been conducted of male and female experiences of work–family conflict. It is suggested that social pressures, including gender role socialization, remain a strong influence on the accepted 'normal' values and behaviors for both men and women and that 'deeply ingrained norms' (Major, 1993, p. 150) continue to emphasize a woman's family responsibilities and a man's income-generating responsibilities. Such reasoning is used to explain why WFI is often higher among men, while FWI is generally stronger for women (Aryee *et al.*, 1999; Frone *et al.*, 1996).

However, other research has begun to challenge this view, coinciding with the change in social expectations for achieving an improved quality of life for both women and men. For example, family roles and the quality of family life have been found to be equally as important to both men and women (Frone, 2003; Schwartzberg and Dytell, 1996; Thomas and Ganster, 1995). Carr (2002) has suggested that the strategies adopted by both men and women for dealing with work and family responsibilities are beginning to converge, with increasing family responsibilities adopted by each new male generation. Nevertheless, female workers continue to shoulder a greater proportion of family responsibilities, particularly through temporary withdrawal from paid employment.

Research evidence on male/female differences in levels of work–family conflict is inconsistent, and several recent studies have found little, if any, gender differences. In a recent review of the relationships between gender, work and family, Barnett and Hyde (2001, p. 784) suggested that 'psychological gender differences are not, in general, large or immutable'. Research supports this conclusion, with studies by Eagle *et al.* (1997), Frone *et al.* (1996), Grandey and Cropanzano (1999) and Schwartzberg and Dytell (1996) all demonstrating no significant differences between men and women in overall levels of work–family conflict.

It should be noted, however, that some studies have obtained gender differences in specific directions of work–family conflict. For example, Stephens and Sommer (1996) observed that women experienced a greater amount of WFI than did their male counterparts (these researchers did not, however, assess FWI, which has often been assumed to be greater for women). Wallace (1999) investigated work–family conflict in a sample of married lawyers and noted that males reported higher levels of time-based work–family conflict than did females. Wallace (1999) also found that female lawyers reported higher levels of work overload, but that male lawyers on average worked longer hours. Wallace concluded that while work hours do contribute to the experience of work–family conflict, the subjective feelings of an excessive workload make a more important contribution to levels of interrole conflict.

In addition to direct associations between gender and work–family conflict, the moderating effects of gender have also been explored and will be outlined later.

Dependants

The presence of dependants produces an increase in home demands and generally entails a reduction in paid employment time. Brough and Kelling (2002) compared the work hours of women with and without dependants and found the former group was employed for significantly longer hours (40 hours compared to 36 hours per week, respectively). Nordenmark (2002) also found that the number of children in a family was linearly associated with the desire for both parents to reduce their working hours and to spend more time with their children. However, it is the total number of hours worked in *both* paid employment and on household/family tasks which is pertinent to the conflict debate and is associated with decreased health outcomes. Noor (2002) suggested that the total hours worked each week for individuals in family groups (three or more dependants) were 90 hours for women and 70 hours for men – an average gender difference of about 2.5 hours per day.

The presence of dependants has been associated with increased levels of both work–family conflict and psychological strain (Tausig and Fenwick, 2001). Nordenmark (2002) concluded that employed fathers experienced higher levels of psychological strain compared with employed non-fathers. Similarly, Beatty (1996) observed that employed mothers had increased level of work–family conflict and negative health outcomes, compared with employed non-mothers. Additionally, mothers who received little spousal support also had higher levels of depression. Brough and Kelling (2002) found that single (female) parents experienced higher levels of psychological strain than did parents with a partner.

The number and ages of children, particularly the age of the youngest child, are also generally considered to increase parental demands. A child of infant or preschool age produces the greatest parental demands (Major *et al.*, 2002; Parasuraman and Simmers, 2001), but having adolescent children has also been linked with higher parental levels of work–family conflict (Kim and Ling, 2001).

Interestingly, Wallace (1999) found that having preschool children *reduced* strain-based WFI in a sample of female lawyers. Wallace suggested that it is not the presence of children per se which predicts work–family conflict, but rather the absence of effective external services providing childcare and household assistance. With adequate assistance, preschool children may contribute to employed mothers' perceptions of satisfaction and fulfillment in their multiple roles. Major *et al.* (2002) offer some support for this view by noting that the time spent at work was not directly associated with either the number or the ages of children in their sample of employed parents.

Consequences of work–family conflict

A meta-analysis of the consequences of work–family conflict by Allen *et al.* (2000) provides a viable starting point for examination of the consequences of work–family conflict. Allen *et al.* suggested that there are three groups of consequences: work-related outcomes (e.g., job satisfaction, commitment, turnover intentions, absenteeism, performance and success), non-work-related outcomes (e.g., marital, family, leisure and life satisfaction, family performance), and stress-related outcomes (e.g., psychological strain, physical health, depression, burnout, substance abuse and work and family stress). A selection of these consequences is discussed here.

Absenteeism and other withdrawal behaviors

In general, work–family conflict is positively related to work absenteeism (Thomas and Ganster, 1995) and to turnover intentions (Netemeyer *et al.*, 1996). Gignac *et al.* (1996) found that only WFI predicted workplace absenteeism, while FWI did not. Similarly, Greenhaus *et al.* (2001) found WFI had a greater impact on withdrawal behaviors than did FWI. Greenhaus *et al.* (2001) suggested that career involvement moderates the conflict–withdrawal relationship, such that high levels of work withdrawal behaviors are exhibited more by individuals who have low levels of career involvement.

Comparing the effects of both WFI and FWI on turnover intentions, Boyar *et al.* (2003) found that while both forms of conflict positively predicted turnover intentions, WFI produced a slightly stronger relationship. Similarly, MacEwen and Barling (1994) reported that both directions of work–family conflict predicted withdrawal behaviors from both the work and family domains. Furthermore, the influence of interrole conflict on withdrawal behaviors occurred *within* each domain and applied to both men and women (i.e., WFI positively predicted family withdrawal behaviors, and FWI positively predicted workplace withdrawal). Although some studies (e.g., Greenhaus *et al.*, 1997) have reported only a weak association between work–family conflict and *actual* turnover behaviors, in their meta-analysis Allen *et al.* (2000) reported a moderate relationship between work–family conflict and turnover intentions. Interestingly, this relationship was stronger than the association between job satisfaction and work–family conflict, which is more commonly investigated.

Satisfaction

Figure 5.1 suggests that a consequence of work–family conflict is reduction in both domain-specific and general life satisfaction. Numerous studies with a wide variety of occupational samples have demonstrated pathways between interrole conflict and satisfaction across domains (e.g., Allen *et al.*, 2000; Carlson and Kacmar, 2000; Kim and Ling, 2001; Thomas and Ganster, 1995). That is, WFI is linked with reduced family/marital satisfaction and FWI results in decreased job satisfaction. Life satisfaction is an amalgamation of both family and job satisfaction, and therefore spans both the work and family domains. Life satisfaction and work–family conflict have a strong negative relationship (Allen *et al.*, 2000). The relationship between FWI and job satisfaction appears to be more consistent than the relationship between WFI and family satisfaction (Aryee *et al.*, 1999; Frone, Yardley and Markel, 1997).

Psychological well-being

Associations between work–family conflict and psychological distress have been widely explored and suggest that increased conflict is associated with increased psychological distress (Major *et al.*, 2002; Stephens *et al.*, 2001). Relationships between work–family conflict and depression have also been demonstrated (MacEwen and Barling, 1994; Noor, 2002). Typically, experiences of both types of work–family conflict produce increased depression levels (Allen *et al.*, 2000) and this association is similar for both men and women (Frone *et al.*, 1996).

In a longitudinal investigation, Bacharach *et al.* (1991) found that work–family conflict predicted burnout to a similar extent within two samples of nurses and engineers. In their study, burnout was composed of strain from both the work and home domains. Kelloway *et al.* (1999), using cross-lagged analyses, demonstrated that the experience of stress at time 1 predicted subsequent (time 2) work–family conflict. Kelloway *et al.* concluded that as well as predicting strain, inter-domain conflict also appears to be caused by prior stress experiences.

Physical health

Early research suggested no association between work–family conflict and physical health outcomes (e.g., Klitzman *et al.*, 1990). However, recent research suggests a negative association does exist and that high levels of work–family conflict produce adverse physical health (Frone, Russell and Cooper, 1997). For example, Lee (1997) found that the dual demands of both paid employment and caregiving were associated with the classic physical stress–strain symptomatology: weight loss or gain, headaches, drowsiness and insomnia. The strain imposed by work–family conflict has also been linked to coronary heart disease (Haynes *et al.*, 1984), decreased appetite and energy levels, increased fatigue, nervous tension and anxiety (Allen *et al.*, 2000), as well as increased cholesterol levels and somatic complaints (Thomas and Ganster, 1995).

Additional consequences

Other consequences of work–family conflict include increased alcohol consumption (e.g., Frone *et al.*, 1996; Noor, 2002; see also Chapter 8), organizational commitment, work performance and career outcomes (Allen *et al.*, 2000; Netemeyer *et al.*, 1996; O'Driscoll, 1996). Consequences within the family domain have been examined less frequently, but include parental performance, destructive parenting and child behaviors (MacEwen and Barling, 1994). The effects of work–family conflict upon individual cognitive abilities have also received some attention, especially in terms of reduced concentration and attention levels (MacEwen and Barling, 1994).

MODERATORS OF WORK–FAMILY CONFLICT RELATIONSHIPS

In addition to research that has considered direct associations between work–family conflict and other variables, some studies have examined the moderating (or buffering) role of certain variables. A moderator effect is obtained when the relationship between the predictor and criterion variables varies for different levels of some third variable (referred to as the 'moderator' variable). For instance, it has been suggested that the relationship between work-related demands and WFI and that between family demands and FWI may vary for males and females. Specifically, as discussed in more detail below, it has been posited that women may experience greater FWI resulting from family demands, whereas men may report more WFI due to work demands. Hence, gender may be a possible moderator of the relationship between demands (work or family) and work–family conflict (WFI or FWI).

Figure 5.3 depicts two mechanisms by which moderators can affect relationships involving work–family conflict. In the first, labeled moderator A, the moderator is predicted to influence the association between stressors (e.g., work or family demands) and levels of work–family conflict. The example given above for gender illustrates this type of moderation effect. A second form of moderation (depicted as moderator B in Figure 5.3) occurs when the moderator variable affects the relationship between work–family conflict and various 'outcomes', such as job or family satisfaction, psychological strain or overall well-being. For instance, social support from either

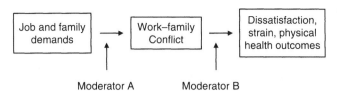

Figure 5.3 Moderation effects in relationships between job/family demands, work–family conflict, and 'outcomes'

work colleagues (e.g., supervisors) or family members may function to reduce the negative impact of work–family conflict on an individual. This would be an example of moderation B. Below we discuss examples of research that has been conducted on both forms of moderator effect.

Despite the intuitive logic and obvious salience of moderators, there has been surprisingly little assessment of moderator influences in research on work–family conflict, with the vast majority of studies focusing on direct relationships between work–family conflict and other variables rather than possible stress-buffering effects. Of the moderator variables that have been considered in work–family research, two that have received most attention are gender and social support, although a handful of studies have investigated some other possible moderators. As with the previous discussion of antecedents and consequences of work–family conflict, in this section we do not aim to provide an exhaustive review of this literature but rather to illustrate some overall trends with a selection of studies. We begin by considering research on social support.

Social support

Several researchers have investigated the potential moderating effects of social support from either work colleagues or family members. For example, Carlson and Perrewe (1999) examined social support as a moderator of the relationship between various stressors (antecedents) and levels of work–family conflict. They noted that previous studies have considered the direct, mediating and moderating effects of social support, both work-related and family-related. There is considerable evidence that social support is directly related to (reduced) levels of work–family conflict. Previous research on the moderating effects of support, however, has been far from conclusive, with some studies reporting a significant buffering role for this variable (Ganster *et al.*, 1986), but others finding either limited or no evidence of a buffering effect (e.g., Frone *et al.*, 1995; Parasuraman *et al.*, 1992). Carlson and Perrewe's research examined direct, mediating and moderating effects, but only the moderation effect will be discussed here. Consistent with Frone *et al.* (1995), they found no significant moderating effects of social support from work on the relationship between work demands/stressors and WFI nor of social support from family on the relationship between family demands/stressors and FWI. Instead, a model that positioned social support (from work and family) as an antecedent of reduced work–family conflict produced a better fit to the data, suggesting that higher levels of support may have a direct (rather than moderating) role in reducing work–family conflict.

Other studies have considered support from the person's partner or spouse as a critical moderator variable. For instance, Matsui *et al.* (1995) and Aryee *et al.* (1999) found that social support from one's spouse buffered the relationship between parental overload and FWI. When more support was felt from one's spouse, the association between overload and FWI diminished. However, Matsui *et al.* did not explore the relationship between work overload and WFI, and in the Aryee *et al.* study spouse support did not moderate the relationship of work overload and WFI.

By and large, although research findings have not been totally uniform, the literature indicates that support from others can function as a buffer between job or family demands (the stressors) and levels of work–family conflict. However, more exploration is needed of (a) the importance of social support for different individuals, (b) the types of support that are most beneficial, and (c) the frequency and intensity of support provided by family members, work colleagues and others.

Gender

Differences between males and females in both levels of work–family conflict and the relationship between this variable and others have been frequently researched. In a relatively early study of the antecedents and consequences of work–family conflict, Duxbury and Higgins (1991) explored possible gender differences in levels of (non-directional) work–family conflict, as well as considering the moderating role of gender in the relationships between work–family conflict and other variables. Based on gender role expectations, Duxbury and Higgins anticipated that among women work–family conflict would be more strongly linked with increased work involvement, whereas for men it might be expected that increased involvement in the family might contribute to greater work–family conflict. Duxbury and Higgins also examined whether gender moderated the relationship of work–family conflict with both quality of work life and quality of family life.

Of the six hypotheses involving work–family conflict in this study, four results were statistically significant. In particular, work and family involvement appeared to have different relationships with work–family conflict, confirming the notion that involvement in 'non-traditional' roles may be problematic for both men and women. Similarly, conflict between work and family had a more negative impact on women's quality of work life and on men's quality of family life, as might be expected from a gender roles perspective. We know of no other studies that have directly examined the same variables and hypotheses that Duxbury and Higgins investigated; hence it is not possible to comment on whether their findings would be replicated today, when the climate of gender role expectations may have evolved from what it was in the late 1980s.

Gutek *et al.* (1991) also examined the possible moderating effects of gender, in a study that compared two alternative standpoints: the gender role perspective and the 'rational' perspective. The latter posits that there will be no differences between males and females in their reported levels of work–family conflict, and in relationships between time demands (from the job and family) and work–family conflict. The gender role perspective, on the other hand, predicts differential relationships between work demands and WFI and between family demands and FWI for men and women. Specifically, for men, there should be no relationship between work hours and WFI, but a strong relationship between family hours and FWI. For women, the opposite pattern is predicted by this perspective. Gutek *et al.*'s findings offered greater support for the rational view than for the gender role perspective. Time devoted to a specific domain (whether work or family) was closely connected with the degree of interference between that domain and the other, and the relationships were uniformly stronger for women than for men. Hence there was no evidence that women are less affected by family demands and men are less affected by work-related demands, even though women did tend to report higher levels of WFI than did men. (Reported levels of FWI were similar for men and women.)

A contrasting finding was reported by Martins *et al.* (2002), who looked at the moderating role of gender, in terms of the relationship between WFI and career satisfaction. (Their study did not focus on FWI.) Consistent with the gender role perspective, WFI was found to be significantly negatively correlated with career satisfaction for women, but not for men. Martins *et al.* suggested that men and women may prioritize their work and family roles differently. Age also emerged as a significant moderator, with the career satisfaction of older workers (both genders) being most influenced by WFI. 'Whereas women's career satisfaction was negatively affected by work–family conflict throughout their lives, men showed such adverse effects only in later career, when they were 40 or older' (p. 406). Contrary to their expectations, however, no moderating effects were observed for marital and parental status.

It is critical to consider the direction of conflict (that is, WFI versus FWI) when exploring the moderating influence of gender. For example, contrary to the gender role perspective, Grzywacz and Marks (2000) observed no differences between men and women in the linkage between family demands and FWI, but low levels of work support were more closely linked with WFI for women than for men. It is possible that social support may operate in different ways for males and females, especially in respect of its influence on work–family conflict.

Other moderators

Some studies have examined individual difference variables (e.g. dispositions) as moderators of relationships between work–family conflict and affective reactions. For instance, Behson (2002) examined the stress-buffering effects of a form of coping which he referred to as 'informal work accommodations to family' (IWAF). He noted that, while the literature on stress has given prominence to coping mechanisms, little empirical research has been carried out on the informal strategies used by individuals to help balance their work and family lives, such as arranging leave from work to attend to family matters, taking care of household tasks while at work and working through lunch so that one can go home early. Behson constructed a set of 16 such 'accommodations'. He found that the total IWAF score was a significant moderator of the relationship between FWI and negative emotional reactions to work experiences. Among respondents who reported greater use of these coping behaviors, the association between FWI and negative emotions was reduced, suggesting that IWAF attenuated the positive relationship between this direction of work–family conflict and job-related psychological strain.

Jex and Elacqua (1999) also examined the moderating effects of coping behavior on the relationship between work–family conflict (both WFI and FWI) and psychological strain. They reasoned that work–family conflict often results from time pressures, and that the ability to manage one's time efficiently should therefore alleviate the negative impact of WFI and FWI. Jex and Elacqua tested this proposition with three dimensions of time management: goal setting/prioritization, mechanics of time management and preference for organization. Of the three, only mechanics of time management showed a statistically significant moderating effect, and the direction of the moderator effect was opposite to that anticipated, with a stronger WFI–strain association being reported by respondents who scored high on time management. Jex and Elacqua concluded that 'these effects are probably not substantively meaningful' (p. 189) and that time management did not serve to buffer conflict–strain relationships in this study.

Based upon a social identity perspective on work–family relations, Greenhaus *et al.* (2001) predicted that level of involvement in both family and career would moderate the relationships of WFI and withdrawal intentions and behaviors. Individuals who were highly involved in their family life were expected to display a stronger linkage between WFI interference and withdrawal than their less family-involved counterparts. In contrast, individuals with high levels of career involvement were expected to show a weaker linkage between WFI and withdrawal than those whose career involvement was lower. The results of their study illustrated a moderator effect only for career involvement. Greenhaus *et al.* suggested that these findings indicate that 'there is less of a reason to put up with extensive work-to-family conflict if work is not a highly salient part of one's life' (p. 96). On the other hand, where career is highly important to the person, interference of work with family life may be less of an issue. The hypothesized role of family involvement was not supported, however. Greenhaus *et al.* conjectured that WFI may be accepted as a necessary by-product of having to provide financial support for the family, even by individuals whose family involvement is quite high. Alternatively, although not suggested by Greenhaus and his colleagues, it may well be that the negative impact of work–family conflict on withdrawal intentions and behavior is resistant to moderation by family involvement.

Harvey *et al.* (2003) investigated employee level of trust in management as a moderator of relationships between work overload and three indicators of strain: burnout, psychological strain and WFI. It was predicted that greater overall trust in their managers would not only be directly associated with reduced negative outcomes, but would also attenuate the correlation between workload and the three criterion variables. Data from this study indicated that individuals with lower work overload reported lower work interference with family, and there was a significant interaction between work overload and trust in management. However, the difference between high- and low-trust individuals in terms of WFI was less pronounced at higher work overload levels than at lower levels of this variable, which on the surface would appear to be counter to the buffering hypothesis. Harvey *et al.* suggested that 'employees who have trust in their management may be less affected by more work' (p. 313), but additional research is needed to confirm this speculation. Nevertheless, this study is salient in that it identified a variable (trust in management) that may have important connotations for work–family policies and interventions.

Finally, in keeping with the more general literature on stressor–strain relations, there has been some investigation of negative affectivity as a moderator in the relationship between work–family conflict and strain variables. Individuals who score highly on negative affectivity are presumed to be more vulnerable and less resistant to stressors, and they may not adopt effective coping mechanisms. This expectation was confirmed by Stoeva *et al.* (2002), who found that family pressures were linked with greater FWI among individuals who were high on negative affectivity than among their low negative affectivity counterparts. However, there was no evidence in this study of a moderating effect for negative affectivity on the corresponding relationship between work pressures and WFI. Stoeva *et al.* suggested that work pressures may be more difficult to contend with than family pressures, and hence even respondents low on negative affectivity may experience detrimental effects from excessive work demands.

In summary, empirical research on moderator effects has not been totally systematic, nor have the findings been uniformly consistent. There is certainly evidence that social support (especially from family members such as one's partner/spouse) can function as a buffering variable, although its effects have not always been significant and we need to learn more about how the types and frequency of support play a role in mitigating the negative effects of both forms of work–family conflict. The moderating role of gender is less evident. Although many studies have illustrated that women typically experience higher levels of work–family conflict (in both directions), relationships between work–family conflict and other variables have not been consistently different between men and women. Finally, other moderators have not been so extensively researched, although it seems plausible that dispositional factors (such as positive and negative affectivity) and coping behaviors may be salient in this context.

WORK–FAMILY FACILITATION

So far we have discussed how work and family demands can be sources of conflict and stress, and how negative experiences in one domain can interfere with engagement in the other domain. It is recognized, however, that work and family can also be a source of strength to one another (Frone, 2003; see also Chapter 3). For instance, support from members of one's family can be a source of strength when faced with demanding job challenges (Crouter, 1984; Grzywacz and Marks, 2000; Kirchmeyer, 1992a). Similarly, family-supportive work environments have been shown to be associated with greater levels of benefit usage, family and job satisfaction and organizational commitment (Allen *et al.*, 2000). Thus, involvement in one domain (work or family) can facilitate enhanced engagement in the other domain (work or family).

Different terms have been used to refer to the facilitative process through which one domain positively influences the other. The term *work–family enhancement* has been used by a number of authors to refer to the positive influence process (Frone, 2003; Greenhaus and Parasuraman, 1999), although Grzywacz (2002) noted that 'enhancement' actually refers to an outcome rather than a process. Other authors have referred to positive spillover between work and family (Crouter, 1984; Grzywacz and Marks, 2000; Kirchmeyer, 1992a; Stephens *et al.*, 1994). There is also reference to 'work–family compensation' (Edwards and Rothbard, 2000), and 'work–family enrichment' (Rothbard, 2001). A close scrutiny of these terms reveals considerable content overlap, although subtle differences remain (Grzywacz, 2002). In this chapter we use the term 'work–family facilitation', which has been defined by Frone (2003, p. 145) as 'the extent to which participation at work (or home) is made easier by virtue of the experiences, skills, and opportunities gained or developed at home (or work)'.

An important methodological point concerns the distinct nature of the two constructs: conflict and facilitation. Grzywacz and Marks (2000) showed that work-to-family facilitation and family-to-work facilitation are distinct attributes, and are independent of WFI and FWI. Wayne *et al.* (2004) confirmed that conflict and facilitation were orthogonal, consistent with Grzywacz and Marks' (2000) finding. One implication of the orthogonal nature of conflict and facilitation is that their origins are distinct, and they may have different antecedents.

Most research has explored the negative side of the work–family interface (that is, work–family conflict), whereas work–family facilitation has received very little research attention (Frone, 2003; Grzywacz, 2002). The remainder of this section will review key concepts proposed by Grzywacz (2002), who has developed a preliminary theory of work–family facilitation to guide research in this area.

Antecedents of work–family facilitation

As noted, few empirical studies have been conducted on facilitation between work and family roles. Kirchmeyer (1992b) assessed the impact of off-the-job experiences on job-related attitudes and experiences, observing that high levels of off-job involvement were more associated with work–family facilitation (or enhancement) than with interrole conflict. The central constructs in the theoretical model of work–family facilitation proposed by Grzywacz (2002) are (a) individual dispositional characteristics, (b) exploitable family work-related resources, (c) selective permeability of family and workplace boundaries and (d) demand characteristics.

Individual dispositional characteristics

Grzywacz (2002) has argued that work–family facilitation can be initiated and sustained by 'developmentally generative disposition characteristics' (p. 9), such as innovativeness, openness and conscientiousness. This proposition was confirmed in Wayne *et al.*'s (2004) study of the role of personality in work–family experiences. Wayne *et al.* found that conscientiousness and agreeableness were positively related to work–family facilitation but not to work–family conflict, which suggests that facilitation and conflict have different origins. On the other hand, new skills and behaviors acquired on the job could be transferred to family, requiring a high degree of openness.

Exploitable family and work-related resources

According to Campbell Clark (2000), two contextual factors central to the link between work–family facilitation and attainment of valued ends are the availability of resources, which are materials, assets or commodities in the environment, and interpersonal activities. The salary paid to the employee is an economic resource, while social support is a by-product of family. The extent to which resources are exploitable increases the possibility of work–family facilitation. An example of this relationship would be the ability of skilled professionals to transfer some of their knowledge and skills to their children through informal family interactions.

Selective boundary permeability

Grzywacz (2002) has posited that selective boundary permeability is required for work–family facilitation to occur. Work–family facilitation is more likely to occur when resources in one domain (e.g., work) are exploitable and can be utilized in the other domain (e.g., family). An example would be decision making. Grzywacz and Marks (2000) found a strong correlation between high levels of decision latitude in the job and work-to-family facilitation, which illustrates positive spillover from work to family leading to higher levels of work–family facilitation.

Demand characteristics

Certain attributes of individuals elicit specific responses from the social environment that either promote or undermine work–family facilitation. Gender provides a good illustration of the impact of socially constructed demand characteristics. Owing to gender role expectations concerning family responsibilities, women are more likely than men to scale back their careers and working hours to accommodate family demands, and to balance work and family (Becker and Moen, 1999). Hence, demand characteristics such as gender role expectations may elicit differential opportunities for individuals to maintain work–family balance.

Consequences of work–family facilitation

Grzywacz (2002) suggested that consequences of work–family facilitation include improved individual-level outcomes such as physical health and well-being (Frone, 2003; Grzywacz, 2000), better marriages and parent–child interactions, along with greater occupational commitment, job satisfaction and productivity. However, to date there has been no systematic research on these potential outcomes of facilitation. Although she did not directly examine work–family facilitation, Kirchmeyer (1992a) obtained data indicating that time devoted to off-the-job roles such as parenting can actually increase, rather than detract from, job satisfaction and organizational commitment. In keeping with the facilitation hypothesis, involvement in parenting can enrich personal resources (e.g. competencies, self-esteem) that carry over into the job role and 'enhance the person's capacity to meet work demands and his or her importance to the organization' (Kirchmeyer, 1992a, p. 790). The only other published study to date (Grzywacz, 2000) found that work-to-family and family-to-work facilitation were linked with better mental health, in both men and women.

To summarize our discussion of work–family facilitation, it is evident that there needs to be considerably more empirical research on this dimension, focusing on the benefits (as well as the burdens) of multiple role involvement. As discussed by Grzywacz (2002), facilitation between work and family can function as a resource that enables individuals to function more effectively in both domains and enriches their lives. Grzywacz (2002) and Frone (2003) have both commented that work–family conflict and work–family facilitation may offset each other, and Frone's discussion of work–family balance clearly illustrates that balance is more than simply a lack of conflict between the two domains. To promote better balance, it is important for individuals and organizations to develop mechanisms that encourage and support the enhancement of both work and family life.

SUMMARY AND IMPLICATIONS

In this chapter we have discussed some key issues emerging from the literature on the work–family nexus, and have overviewed some of the main research findings on the two aspects of this interface: work–family conflict and work–family facilitation. These findings have several implications for individual and organizational endeavors to promote work–family 'balance'. It is clear that balance between these two major domains in people's lives can only be achieved via collaboration between workers and management in organizations, who share the responsibility for ensuring that individuals do not experience excessive work–family conflict and that all efforts are made to enhance people's work and family lives.

A first step in the process of achieving balance is to examine stressors (which cause conflict) and resources (which may result in facilitation). Some of the major contributors to both conflict and facilitation have been discussed here. Any intervention needs to be based upon an assessment of the extent to which these variables are present and affect the person's life. In particular, an audit of work life and family demands, along with the impact of these demands on the person, should form the starting point and will provide valuable information on areas to be addressed. Along with these antecedents, recognition of moderators (or buffers) is also important. For example, as illustrated here, the extent to which a person has access to appropriate forms and levels of social support (at both work and in the family) can play a critical role in alleviating the negative effects of work–family conflict.

Finally, along with others (e.g., Frone, 2003; Grzywacz, 2002) we suggest that greater effort needs to be expended on research exploring the ways in which work and family experiences contribute positively to each other. The overwhelming research focus to date has been on negative spillover between these two domains, with very few studies conducted on work–family facilitation. Although there is certainly a need for ongoing systematic exploration of the factors that contribute to interrole conflict, and the mechanisms by which such conflict can be reduced or alleviated, we believe that increased attention to positive work–family spillover would be fruitful in generating ideas about effective ways to achieve balance between work and family life.

NOTE

1 For a historical approach to the development of the literature on work–family conflict, see Chapter 3.

REFERENCES

Adams, G. A., and Jex, S. M. (1999). Relationships between time management, control, work–family conflict, and strain. *Journal of Occupational Health Psychology*, *4*, 72–77.

Allen, T. D., Herst, D. E. L., Bruck, C. S., and Sutton, M. (2000). Consequences associated with work-to-family conflict: a review and agenda for future research. *Journal of Occupational Health Psychology*, *5*, 278–308.

Aryee, S., Luk, V., Leung, A., and Lo, S. (1999). Role stressors, interrole conflict and wellbeing: the moderating influence of spousal support and coping behaviors among employed parents in Hong Kong. *Journal of Vocational Behavior*, *54*(2), 259–278.

Bacharach, S. B., Bamberger, P., and Conley, S. (1991). Work–home conflict among nurses and engineers: mediating the impact of role stress on burnout and satisfaction at work. *Journal of Organizational Behavior*, *12*, 39–53.

Barnett, R. C., and Hyde, J. S. (2001). Women, men, work, and family. *American Psychologist*, *56*, 781–796.

Beatty, C. A. (1996). The stress of managerial and professional women: is the price too high? *Journal of Organizational Behavior*, *17*, 233–251.

Becker, P., and Moen, P. (1999). Scaling back: dual-earner couples' work–family strategies. *Journal of Marriage and Family*, *61*(4), 995–1007.

Behson, S. J. (2002). Coping with work-to-family conflict: the role of informal work accommodations to family. *Journal of Occupational Health Psychology*, *7*(4), 324–341.

Boyar, S. L., Maertz, C. P., Pearson, A. W., and Keough, S. (2003). Work–family conflict: a model of linkages between work and family domain variables and turnover intentions. *Journal of Managerial Issues*, *15*, 175–190.

Brough, P., and Kelling, A. (2002). Women, work and well-being: an analysis of the work–family conflict. *New Zealand Journal of Psychology*, *31*, 29–38.

Burke, R. J., and Greenglass, E. (1987). Work and family. In C. L. Cooper and I. Robertson (eds), *Occupational stress and organizational effectiveness* (pp. 273–320). New York: Praeger.

Campbell Clark, S. (2000). Work/family border theory: a new theory of work/family balance. *Human Relations*, *53*, 747–770.

Carlson, D. S., and Frone, M. R. (2003). Relation of behavioral and psychological involvement to a new four-factor conceptualization of work–family interference. *Journal of Business and Psychology*, *17*, 515–535.

Carlson, D. S., and Kacmar, K. M. (2000). Work–family conflict in the organization: do life role values makes a difference? *Journal of Management*, *26*, 1031–1054.

Carlson, D. S., and Perrewe, P. L. (1999). The role of social support in the stressor–

strain relationship: an examination of work–family conflict. *Journal of Management*, *25*(4), 513–540.

Carr, D. (2002). The psychological consequences of work–family trade-offs for three cohorts of men and women. *Social Psychology Quarterly*, *65*, 103–124.

Crouter, A. C. (1984). Spillover from family to work: the neglected side of the work–family interface. *Human Relations*, *37*, 425–442.

Duxbury, L. E., and Higgins, C. A. (1991). Gender differences in work–family conflict. *Journal of Applied Psychology*, *76*(1), 60–74.

Eagle, B. W., Miles, E. W., and Icenogle, M. L. (1997). Interrole conflicts and the permeability of the work and family domains: are there gender differences? *Journal of Vocational Behavior*, *50*, 168–184.

Edwards, J. R., and Rothbard, N. P. (2000). Mechanisms linking work and family: clarifying the relationship between work and family constructs. *Academy of Management Review*, *25*(1), 178–199.

Frone, M. R. (2003). Work–family balance. In J. C. Quick and L. E. Tetrick (eds), *Handbook of occupational health psychology* (pp. 143–162). Washington, DC: American Psychological Association.

Frone, M. R., Russell, M., and Barnes, G. M. (1996). Work–family conflict to substance use among employed mothers: the role of negative affect. *Journal of Marriage and the Family*, *56*, 1019–1030.

Frone, M. R., Russell, M., and Cooper, M. (1992). Prevalence of work–family conflict: are work and family boundaries asymmetrically permeable? *Journal of Organizational Behavior*, *13*(7), 723–729.

Frone, M. R., Russell, M., and Cooper, M. L. (1995). Relationship of work and family stressors to psychological distress: the independent moderating influence of social support, mastery, active coping, and self-focused attention. In R. Crandall and P. L. Perrewe (eds), *Occupational stress: A handbook*. Washington, DC: Taylor & Francis.

Frone, M. R., Russell, M., and Cooper, M. L. (1997). Relation of work–family conflict to health outcomes: a four year longitudinal study of employed parents. *Journal of Occupational and Organizational Psychology*, *70*, 325–335.

Frone, M. R., Yardley, J. K., and Markel, K. S. (1997). Developing and testing an integrative model of the work–family interface. *Journal of Vocational Behavior*, *50*, 145–167.

Fu, C. K., and Shaffer, M. A. (2001). The tug of work and family: direct and indirect domain-specific determinants of work–family conflict. *Personnel Review*, *30*, 502–522.

Ganster, D., Fusilier, M., and Mayes, B. (1986). Role of social support in the experience of stress at work. *Journal of Applied Psychology*, *71*, 102–110.

Gignac, M. A. M., Kelloway, E. K., and Gottlieb, B. H. (1996). The impact of caregiving on employment: a mediational model of work–family conflict. *Canadian Journal on Aging*, *15*, 525–542.

Grandey, A. A., and Cropanzano, R. (1999). The Conservation of Resources model applied to work–family conflict and strain. *Journal of Vocational Behavior*, *54*, 350–370.

Greenhaus, J. H., and Beutell, N. (1985). Sources of conflict between work and family roles. *Academy of Management Review*, *10*, 76–88.

Greenhaus, J. H., Collins, K. M., Singh, R., and Parasuraman, S. (1997). Work and family influences on departure from public accounting. *Journal of Vocational Behavior*, *50*, 249–270.

Greenhaus, J. H., and Parasuraman, S. (1999). Research on work, family, and gender: current status and future directions. In G. N. Powell (ed.), *Handbook of gender and work* (pp. 391–412). Newbury Park, CA: Sage.

Greenhaus, J. H., Parasuraman, S., and Collins, K. M. (2001). Career involvement and family involvement as moderators of relationships between work–family conflict and withdrawal from a profession. *Journal of Occupational Health Psychology*, *6*(2), 91–100.

Grzywacz, J. G. (2000). Work–family spillover and health during midlife: is managing conflict everything? *American Journal of Health Promotion*, *14*, 236–243.

Grzywacz, J. G. (2002). Toward a theory of work–family facilitation. Paper presented at the *33rd Annual Theory Construction and Research Methodology Workshop*, Houston, TX.

Grzywacz, J. G., and Bass, B. L. (2003). Work, family and mental health: testing different models of work–family fit. *Journal of Marriage and Family*, *65*(1), 248–261.

Grzywacz, J. G., and Marks, N. F. (2000). Reconceptualizing the work–family interface: an ecological perspective on the correlates of positive and negative spillover between work and family. *Journal of Occupational Health Psychology*, *5*, 111–126.

Gutek, B. A., Searle, S., and Klepa, L. (1991). Rational versus gender role explanations for work–family conflict. *Journal of Applied Psychology*, *76*, 560–568.

Harvey, S., Kelloway, E. K., and Duncan-Leiper, L. (2003). Trust in management as a buffer of the relationship between overload and strain. *Journal of Occupational Health Psychology*, *8*(4), 306–315.

Haynes, S. G., Eaker, E. D., and Feinleib, M. (1984). The effects of unemployment, family, and job stress on coronary heart disease patterns in women. In E. B. Gold (ed.), *The changing risk of disease in women: An epidemiological approach* (pp. 37–48). Lexington, MA: Heath.

Hobfoll, S. E. (1989). Conservation of resources: a new attempt at conceptualizing stress. *American Psychologist*, *44*, 513–524.

Jex, S. M., and Elacqua, T. C. (1999). Time management as a moderator of relations between stressors and employee strain. *Work and Stress*, *13*(2), 182–191.

Kahn, R. L., Wolfe, D. M., Quinn, R., Snoek, J. D., and Rosenthal, R. A. (1964). *Organizational stress*. New York: Wiley.

Kanter, R. M. (1977). *Work and family in the United States: A critical review and agenda for research and policy*. New York: Russell Sage Foundation.

Kelloway, E. K., Gottlieb, B. H., and Barham, L. (1999). The source, nature, and direction of work and family conflict: a longitudinal investigation. *Journal of Occupational Health Psychology*, *4*, 337–346.

Kim, J. L. S., and Ling, C. S. (2001). Work–family conflict of women entrepreneurs in Singapore. *Women in Management Review*, *16*, 204–221.

Kirchmeyer, C. (1992a). Nonwork participation and work attitudes: a test of scarcity versus expansion models of personal resources. *Human Relations*, *45*(8), 775–796.

Kirchmeyer, C. (1992b). Perceptions of nonwork-to-work spillover: challenging the common view of conflict-ridden domain relationships. *Basic and Applied Social Psychology*, *13*(2), 231–249.

Klitzman, S., House, J., Israel, B. A., and Mero, R. P. (1990). Work stress, nonwork stress, and health. *Journal of Behavioral Medicine*, *13*, 221–243.

Lee, J. A. (1997). Balancing elder care responsibilities and work: two empirical studies. *Journal of Occupational Health Psychology*, *2*, 220–228.

Lobel, S. A. (1991). Allocation of investment in work and family roles: alternative theories and implications for research. *Academy of Management Review*, *16*, 507–521.

MacEwen, K. E., and Barling, J. (1994). Daily consequences of work interference with family and family interference with work. *Work and Stress*, *8*, 244–254.

Major, B. (1993). Gender, entitlement, and the distinction of family labor. *Journal of Social Issues*, *49*, 141–159.

Major, V. S., Klein, K. J., and Ehrhart, M. G. (2002). Work time, work interference with family, and psychological distress. *Journal of Applied Psychology*, *87*, 427–436.

Marks, S. (1977). Multiple roles and role strain: some notes on human energy, time and commitment. *American Sociological Review*, *42*, 921–936.

Martins, L., Eddleston, K., and Veiga, J. (2002). Moderators of the relationship between work–family conflict and career satisfaction. *Academy of Management Journal*, *45*(2), 399–409.

Matsui, T., Ohsawa, T., and Onglatco, M.-L. (1995). Work–family conflict and the stress-buffering effects of husband support and coping behaviour among Japanese married working women. *Journal of Vocational Behavior*, *47*, 178–192.

Netemeyer, R., Boles, J., and McMurrian, R. (1996). Development and validation of work–family conflict and family–work conflict scales. *Journal of Applied Psychology*, *81*(4), 400–410.

Noor, N. M. (2002). The moderating effect of spouse support on the relationship between work variables and women's work–family conflict. *Psychologia: An International Journal of Psychology in the Orient*, *45*, 12–23.

Nordenmark, M. (2002). Multiple social roles – a resource or a burden: is it possible for men and women to combine paid work with family life in a satisfactory way? *Gender, Work and Organization*, *9*, 125–145.

O'Driscoll, M. P. (1996). The interface between job and off-job roles: enhancement and conflict. In: C. L. Cooper and I. T. Robertson (eds), *International review of industrial and organizational psychology* (pp. 279–306). Chichester: Wiley.

Parasuraman, S., and Simmers, C. (2001). Type of employment, work–family conflict and well-being: a comparative study. *Journal of Organizational Behavior*, *22*(5), 551–568.

Parasuraman, S., Greenhaus, J., and Granrose, C. (1992). Role stressors, social support and well-being among two-career couples. *Journal of Organizational Behavior*, *13*(4), 339–356.

Parasuraman, S., Purohit, Y. S., and Godshalk, V. M. (1996). Work and family variables, entrepreneurial career success, and psychological well-being. *Journal of Vocational Behavior*, *48*(3), 275–300.

Rothbard, N. (2001). Enriching or depleting? The dynamics of engagement in work and family roles. *Administrative Science Quarterly*, *46*(4), 655–684.

Schwartzberg, N., and Dytell, R. (1996). Dual-earner families: the importance of work stress and family stress for psychological well-being. *Journal of Occupational Health Psychology, 1*, 211–223.

Sieber, S. (1974). Toward a theory of role accumulation. *American Sociological Review, 39*, 567–578.

Stephens, G. K., and Sommer, S. M. (1996). The measurement of work to family conflict. *Educational and Psychological Measurement, 56*, 475–486.

Stephens, M. A., Franks, M. M., and Townsend, A. L. (1994). Stress and rewards in women's multiple roles: the case of women in the middle. *Psychology and Aging, 9*, 45–52.

Stephens, M. A., Townsend, A. L., Martire, L. M., and Druley, J. A. (2001). Balancing parent care with other roles: interrole conflict of adult daughter caregivers. *Journal of Gerontology, 56B*, 24–34.

Stoeva, A. Z., Chiu, R. K., and Greenhaus, J. H. (2002). Negative affectivity, role stress and work–family conflict. *Journal of Vocational Behavior, 60*, 1–16.

Tausig, M., and Fenwick, R. (2001). Unbinding time: alternate work schedules and work–life balance. *Journal of Family and Economic Issues, 22*, 101–119.

Thomas, L. T., and Ganster, D. C. (1995). Impact of family-supportive work variables on work–family conflict and strain: a control perspective. *Journal of Applied Psychology, 80*, 6–15.

Wallace, J. E. (1999). Work-to-nonwork conflict among married male and female lawyers. *Journal of Organizational Behavior, 20*, 797–816.

Wayne, J., Musisca, N., and Fleeson, W. (2004). Considering the role of personality in the work–family experience: relationships of the big five to work–family conflict and facilitation. *Journal of Vocational Behavior, 64*, 108–130.

Williams, K. J., and Alliger, G. M. (1994). Role stressors, mood spillover and perceptions of work–family conflict in employed parents. *Academy of Management Journal, 37*, 837–868.

6   Work at home and the work–family interface

Cath Sullivan and Suzan Lewis

Most research on the work–family interface assumes that paid work and family takes place in different locations, creating potential for work–family conflict (Allen *et al.*, 2000; Major *et al.*, 2002) and the need to actively manage work and family (or other non-work) boundaries (Milkie and Peltola, 1999; Clarke, 2000). But what happens when both forms of activity occur in the same place; that is, in the home? Recent statistics show that just over one quarter of the UK workforce perform some of their work at home (Felstead *et al.*, 2000). Employees are increasingly expected to manage and motivate themselves (Lewis and Cooper, 1995), and work is increasingly characterized by flexibility and less clear boundaries between work and family (see Chapter 1), and therefore, arguably, working at home is likely to become both more attractive (Standen *et al.*, 1999) and more feasible (New Ways to Work, 1996).

Interest in paid work performed in the home is often focused on the concept of telework but debate over definitions of home-working, tele-working and related terms continues. A key aspect of this debate has been the distinction between teleworking and home-working (Sullivan, 2003). Definitions of teleworking have been varied and disputed, but there is a growing consensus that it involves working remotely with the use of information and communication technologies (ICTs) (Sullivan, 2003). However, there is evidence to suggest that many home-workers do not use ICTs extensively (Gillespie *et al.*, 1995; Wikström *et al.*, 1997). Consequently, telework should not be seen as a synonym for work at home. The focus of this chapter is on work at home (therefore including home-based telework) as this is likely to have greater practical, social and psychological implications for the work–family interface than other forms of remote or decentralized employment. This definition of work at home encompasses a wide variety of people in different social and occupational contexts and so next we present a brief overview of the nature of work at home in the UK workforce.

Traditionally, home-workers have been seen as predominantly female manual workers who are likely to be low paid and financially exploited. In contrast, a more modern perspective suggests that home-work spans the range from high-paid professional work to low-paid manual. People working at home may be involved in a wide range of occupations on an employed or self-employed basis. However, the amount of time spent working at home may be related to the type of occupation (Felstead *et al.*, 2000). The UK Labour Force Survey (LFS) data suggests that those working at home, either mainly or very occasionally, tend to be from higher occupational groups, whereas amongst those who work partly from home (at least one day a week but not mainly at home) the distribution of occupational groups tends to be similar to that in the workforce as a whole (Felstead *et al.*, 2000). Non-manual occupations are over-represented amongst people working at home, irrespective of the proportion of their working time that they spend at home (Felstead *et al.*, 2000). On average, the pay of people who work at home is greater than that of the workforce in general, although this differs for manual and non-manual workers and is influenced by gender. Men and women who are manual workers receive significantly less pay than their on-site equivalents, yet amongst non-manual workers women's pay is significantly greater than their on-site equivalents while non-manual men's pay is not significantly different from their on-site equivalents (Felstead *et al.*, 2000). LFS data show that, amongst those people who mainly work at home, women outnumber men, but for those working at home less frequently men outnumber women (Felstead *et al.*, 2000). Although these figures challenge the notion that work at home tends to be performed mainly by women who are financially exploited in comparison to other employees, the LFS also reveals that 91% of those who are poorly paid and work mainly at home are women (Felstead *et al.*, 2000).

The family and its relationship to, and boundaries with, paid work are central themes in the literature on home-based telework and other forms of work at home. Furthermore, work at home has often been seen as a response to a growing demand for flexibility and the reconciliation of work and family (Hinssen and ter Hofte, 1994; Scarpitti, 1994). It is promoted as a potential means of achieving what is often referred to as work–life balance (Huws, 1993; Telecottage Association, 1993; Schepp, 1995; Dooley, 1996), or what might more usefully be termed 'work–life integration', in acknowledgement that work and non-work are not inevitably competing (Rapoport *et al.*, 2002; Lewis *et al.*, 2003). For example, it is increasingly common to find work at home, or telework, included in lists of 'family-friendly policies' (see, for example, Kossek and Ozeki, 1999). This is based on the assumption that the flexibility associated with work at home and telework will increase family time (Carsky *et al.*, 1991) and improve the quality of relationships within the family (Schepp, 1995). However, evidence about the impact of work at home on work and non-work boundaries suggests that the real picture is rather more complex. In this chapter we review existing research on the potential impact of work at home on work–family boundaries, the management of family responsibilities and on family life. We will include literature from a number of areas: the work–family interface, temporal flexibility, gender roles, the management of domestic work and childcare and family functioning. In each of these areas we will initially outline the predictions that have been made in relation to the potential impact of work at home before moving on to consider the extent to which these have been supported by research to date. Throughout this, directions for future research will be identified. The implications of the research evidence will also be considered.

THE WORK–FAMILY INTERFACE

Many commentators have attempted to predict the potential impact of working at home and teleworking on the management of the work–home interface but there is little consensus about whether to expect this to be positive or negative (Ellison, 1999). Two main themes can be found in this literature.

First, it has been argued that work at home can facilitate the management of work and family (Conner *et al.*, 1993; Standen *et al.*, 1999). This assertion is largely based on the argument that work at home increases flexibility (Hill *et al.*, 1996; Standen *et al.*, 1999; see also Chapter 11) and also that it provides extra time by reducing time spent commuting (Olson and Primps, 1984). On the other hand, it has also been argued that work at home can make work and family more difficult to balance or integrate in satisfactory ways (Carsky *et al.*, 1991), increase the extent to which stress can spill over from work to family (Schepp, 1995) and possibly create greater interrole conflict (Gurstein, 1991; Ellison, 1999). There are a number of possible reasons for expecting these more negative consequences. These include the possibility that family may interfere more with work when working at home (Haddon, 1992), possibly because the structure and culture of the workplace are not there to limit family's impact on work (Standen *et al.*, 1999) and the possibility that the very flexibility afforded by telework will enable work to permeate into more and more of workers' time and space, crowding out family (Sullivan and Lewis, 2001). Some commentators argue that such negative effects, whatever their direction, could exacerbate family stress (Telecottage Association, 1993). Research with on-site workers highlights the potential of work–family conflict to reduce physical and psychological well-being (Burke and Greenglass, 1999; Frone *et al.*, 1996; Kirchmeyer and Cohen, 1999) and it is therefore important to assess the veracity of these concerns about the potential of work at home to influence work–family conflict.

Empirical research examining work and family dynamics in home-working households remains much more sparse than research with on-site workers. Studies that have been conducted to date yield mixed results and caution against simplistic generalizations about the impact of work at home.

There is some evidence supporting both views outlined above; that is, suggesting that work at home can have both negative and positive outcomes. Certainly work at home is often accompanied by blurred boundaries between work and family (Gurstein, 1991; Ahrentzen, 1992; Sullivan, 2000a; Sullivan and Lewis, 2001; Dimitrova, 2003), although there is a great deal of diversity in the way that these blurred boundaries are experienced. For some, blurring is experienced as generally negative, while for others a greater degree of synergy between work and family is experienced largely positively (Fothergill, 1994; Wikström *et al.*, 1997). Moreover, it seems that those working at home and their co-residents experience blurred boundaries as positive in some respects and negative in others (Sullivan and Lewis, 2001).

Several studies of those working at home have shown that there may be an increase in conflictual overlap between work and family roles (Shamir and Salomon, 1985; Pitt-Catsouphes and Marchetta, 1991; Venkatesh and Vitalari, 1992). There is also some evidence that people working at home may be seen as more available by their families than on-site workers (Haddon and Silverstone, 1993), and may be more susceptible to interruptions from family members or family tasks while working (Fothergill, 1994; Jurik, 1998; Sullivan, 2002). Such interruptions from family have been shown, in on-site workers, to be related to increased work–family conflict (Loerch *et al.*, 1989). There is also evidence that the lack of separation between the different domains that accompanies home work can be experienced as work intruding into the home by both the worker and their families (Wikström *et al.*, 1997; Sullivan, 2000a), highlighting the potential of work at home to impact negatively on the whole family.

Nevertheless, other research suggests that work at home may have the potential to facilitate the management of work and family (Hill *et al.*, 1996; Sullivan and Lewis, 2001; Perrons, 2003). Research from both the USA and the UK suggests that home-workers' work–family conflict is influenced by similar factors to those that influence work–family conflict in on-site workers (e.g., work hours) (Silver, 1993; Sullivan, 2002). However, there is also some evidence that work at home may have the capacity to reduce work–family conflict when these factors are controlled for (Silver, 1993).

In addition to these conflicting findings there is also some evidence that home-workers report similar levels of work–family conflict to those generally found in studies of on-site workers (Sullivan, 2000b) and, like on-site workers, home-workers report significantly more interference from work to family than from family to work (Sullivan, 2002). It is possible, especially given the range of different family and organizational contexts in which work at home occurs, that the range of mixed findings from studies to date is partly a result of varying samples. Studies that systematically compare those working at home with their on-site equivalents should illuminate this further. Until recently, there have been very few studies of this type although two comparative studies have been published recently finding predominantly positive effects.

Madsen (2003), using matched samples of home-workers and office workers, found that home-workers reported significantly less strain-based and behavior-based conflict from work to family and less time-based and strain-based conflict from family to work – although there were no significant differences between the samples on time-based conflict from work to family and behavior-based conflict from family to work. Similarly, another US study found that employees working at home reported significantly greater work–family balance than their on-site equivalents (Hill *et al.*, 2003). These studies provide fairly strong evidence that those working at home experience less conflict between work and family than those working on site. However, as work at home is such a broad phenomenon that includes a vast range of different occupational contexts, caution in generalizing from these studies must be exercised. Also, it is worth noting that the magnitude of difference between the mean scores for home-working and on-site groups is fairly small in both studies. Moreover, studies of this nature give little insight into the nuanced ways in which work and family are negotiated and made sense of in home-working households, and qualitative studies have shown that there is great diversity in people's ways of conceptualizing and experiencing work–family boundaries (Sullivan, 2000a; Nippert-Eng, 1996).

FLEXIBILITY

Many of the predictions that work at home will be beneficial for the work–home interface are based, explicitly or implicitly, on the premise that work at home will increase levels of flexibility that workers experience. Although there is some evidence to support this (Gillespie *et al.*, 1995; Hill *et al.*, 1996; Huws *et al.*, 1996) and home-workers and their partners tend to conceptualize home-based work as a flexible option (Sullivan, 2001), few studies have employed systematic comparisons between equivalent groups of home-workers and on-site workers. One comparative study, from the USA, did find that those working at home reported significantly more flexibility than their on-site equivalents (Hill *et al.*, 1996). However, other studies have found that increased work at home does not significantly predict increased reports of flexibility (Vitterso *et al.*, 2003). Also, perceived flexibility tends to be dependent upon the occupation of the home-worker (Silver, 1993), so results from such comparisons may not be generalizable to other occupational groups. More research is therefore needed before conclusions can be drawn. Evidence from the LFS (Felstead *et al.*, 2000) has been used to assess the flexibility associated with work at home and the large-scale nature of this survey should enable it to shed some light on this issue. Analysis of recent LFS data shows that approximately 70% of all types of home-workers reported having work hours that vary on a weekly basis, whereas in the workforce as a whole this is limited to 47% (Felstead *et al.*, 2000). While this could be seen as evidence that people working at home have greater flexibility, it could also indicate a higher incidence of contingent, sporadic work or episodes of overwork. Some studies have also found that work-related constraints on time management and the scheduling of work can inhibit work at home's potential to increase autonomy and flexibility and facilitate work and family management (Carsky *et al.*, 1991; Wikström *et al.*, 1997; Jurik, 1998; Dimitrova, 2003). If people working at home do not necessarily experience improved flexibility, this could explain why some studies have found negative effects, or no effects, on the relationship between work and family.

Furthermore, any potential flexibility gains will not necessarily be used for better integrating work and family (Olson and Primps, 1984). A study of UK home-workers found that home-workers' reports of flexibility were not related to their reports of work–family conflict (Sullivan, 2002), which is surprising in the light of evidence of the relationship between flexibility and work–family conflict that is commonly found amongst on-site workers (e.g., Berry and Rao, 1997). One possible reason why people working at home might not experience improved work–family integration or reduced work–family conflict is that flexibility is often used for overworking rather than for non-work. A study of mobile workers in the USA found that although they perceived telework as enhancing work–family management, their reports of work–family balance were not significantly different from those still working on site – possibly because the mobile workers' reports also suggested that they were less able to control overzealous work tendencies (Hill *et al.*, 1996). Studies from the UK, Canada and New Zealand have also found that, for some, work at home can increase tendencies to overwork (Armstrong, 1997; Sullivan and Lewis, 2001; Dimitrova, 2003). For these people, it seems that rather than making work and family lives more integrated and well balanced, work at home blurs boundaries and increases the dominance of work over family (Kompast and Wagner, 1998). Longer working hours predict less involvement with children (Biernat and Wortman, 1991), and this could inhibit parents' capacity to perform family roles and increase perceptions of interference between work and family roles (Greenhaus and Parasuraman, 1999). It is also worth noting, however, that some people seem less inclined to overwork when working at home and may be able to reduce their work hours by a reduction in overtime due to greater productivity and less time spent commuting (Mirchandani, 1998). Thus, while home-based work can increase flexibility and control in some circumstances, it remains unclear to what extent and in what contexts this enhances work–life integration or simply creates the opportunity to work more and perhaps increase time-based work–family conflict.

One factor that is likely to be relevant to understanding the impact of flexibility is gender. It is clear that the management of work–family boundaries is not gender neutral. Thus gender is a crucial factor in understanding how work and family roles are related (Lewis, 1994; Greenhaus and Parasuraman, 1999) and therefore is an important focus in the study of work and family in home-working households. In the next section, we consider the role of gender in relation to work at home and the work–family interface.

THE ROLE OF GENDER

It has been suggested that women working at home will be particularly likely to experience conflict between work and family (e.g., Ellison, 1999) and that this might be particularly the case for mothers who may feel especially concerned about being drawn away from their family responsibilities by their work (Gurstein, 1991). In a study of US home-workers, mothers were found to experience more conflict between work and family demands than either men or women home-workers without children (Jurik, 1998), although other research has found that men and women working at home do not report significantly different levels of family–work or work–family conflict (Madsen, 2003). There is currently insufficient evidence to determine whether there are any direct or indirect (e.g., via parental responsibilities) effects of gender upon home-workers' levels of work–family conflict.

When work at home facilitates work–family management, it generally does so without challenging gendered work and family roles (Mancorda, 1997; Mirchandani, 1998; Sullivan and Lewis, 2001; Perrons, 2003). Women are more likely than men to be motivated to work at home as a way of combining paid work and family responsibilities – particularly motherhood (Olson and Primps, 1984; Salmi, 1997; Sullivan and Lewis, 2001) and there is some evidence that women in particular value work at home specifically because it facilitates combining work and family (Haddon and Silverstone, 1993). However, women do not necessarily value home-based work more than men. For example, a US study of parents' importance ratings of a range of family-friendly policies suggested that women were no more likely than men to value work at home (Frone and Yardley, 1996). Similarly, in a recent UK survey men were more likely than women to want to work at home. The authors suggest that this may be because they are more likely than women to be uninterrupted at home (Hogarth *et al.*, 2000). This is supported by findings that the tendency to use flexibility to overwork is more common amongst men, whereas for women flexibility is more likely to be used to better accommodate work and family (Kompast and Wagner, 1998; Sullivan and Lewis, 2001). In general, these research findings suggest that gendered work and family roles tend not to be challenged by work at home and that men and women's motivations and preferences in relation to work at home are linked to these gendered roles. Evidence from the LFS further supports this by revealing that having children significantly increases women's likelihood of working at home, while significantly decreasing men's likelihood (Felstead *et al.*, 2000). It is likely that these gendered preferences and arrangements are rooted in women's tendency to retain major responsibility for domestic labour and childcare (Brannen, 2000) and the gendered nature of employment and family roles (Ferree, 1990; Sullivan and Lewis, 2001; Perrons, 2003).

Further research needs to focus more on the processes whereby home-based work reproduces or challenges gendered experiences. One such process may be through the management of unpaid work in home-working households.

THE MANAGEMENT OF DOMESTIC WORK AND CHILDCARE

Despite considerable changes in gender identities and relationships, women tend to retain the major responsibility for domestic labour and childcare (Brannen, 2000). When men do participate in childcare and housework, they tend to be involved in pre-planned and pleasurable tasks and activities rather than day-to-day care or dealing with childcare emergencies (Hochschild, 1989; Galinsky *et al.*, 1993; Milkie and Peltola, 1999). For example, Berry and Rao (1997) asked fathers to rate how likely they are to perform a number of childcare activities. Those activities that are pre-planned (for example, pre-arranged doctor's or school visit) were rated as likely by approximately 30% of fathers, whereas the unplanned interruption of work because of childcare demands was reported as likely to occur by less than 10% of fathers. Furthermore, men's domestic labour and childcare is still often constructed as 'help', thereby failing to question the assumption that women are fundamentally responsible for this work (Dempsey, 2000).

As work at home has the potential to blur boundaries between paid work and family it is interesting to examine whether it also has the capacity to blur distinctions that are made in relation to the allocation of unpaid domestic work and childcare that is performed in the home. There are two conflicting views on the potential for change in this respect.

Some commentators have identified a view of work at home, known as the 'new opportunities for flexibility' model (Huws *et al.*, 1996; Sullivan and Lewis, 2001). Proponents (e.g., Dooley, 1996) of this approach argue that work at home will facilitate the fulfillment of family role responsibilities and provide access to people whose participation in conventional on-site work is restricted (Ahrentzen, 1992). It has been argued that crises that occur within the family (e.g., changes to childcare arrangements, sick children) can be more easily managed when working at home (Schepp, 1995; Hill *et al.*, 1996). While some proponents of this model treat domestic work as gender neutral, others have specifically argued that work at home has the potential to facilitate the breakdown of these traditional gendered roles and increase men's domestic participation (see Sullivan and Lewis, 2001). This may be contrasted with the 'exploitation model' (Huws *et al.*, 1996; Sullivan and Lewis, 2001) that views work at home as perpetuating women's exploitation and reinforcing their domestic burden of responsibility (Ahrentzen, 1992; Haddon and Silverstone, 1993), leaving them exploited, socially isolated (Ahrentzen, 1992) and subject to demands from both family and employer (Felstead *et al.*, 2000).

A number of studies have examined the division of domestic work in home-working households in order to address claims that work at home may have the potential to increase men's participation and bring about greater role sharing. In the next section, these studies will be reviewed.

There is some evidence that men working at home may sometimes undertake substantial domestic work and even assume the role of 'house-husband' (Huws *et al.*, 1996). Caution must be exercised, however, in attributing change to the effects of home-based working, as it has been suggested (by Burgess, 1997, for example), that men's domestic participation is slowly increasing in the population generally. Furthermore, other research has found that work at home has the capacity to confirm women's domestic role (Gunnarsson, 1997; Sturesson, 1997) and that the domestic labour of home-working men is still constructed as 'help', rather than as the fulfillment of a primary role (Jurik, 1998; Sullivan and Lewis, 2001). Most evidence suggests that the distribution of domestic labour that existed before the commencement of telework, whether equitable or inequitable, tends to prevail (Haddon and Silverstone, 1993; Silver, 1993; Hill *et al.*, 1996; Salmi, 1997; Sullivan and Lewis, 2001).

A study of arrangements for domestic labour and childcare in UK home-working households suggests that women who work at home are taking on no more domestic labor and childcare than other women in the UK (Sullivan, 2002). The home-workers and partners included in this study were significantly more likely to report that domestic arrangements had stayed the same since home-working commenced than to report that they had changed (Sullivan, 2002). Work at home per se therefore appears to have little impact on the gendered allocation of household responsibilities.

Research on motivation for home-working also sheds some light on the relationship between this form of work and people's family role responsibilities. Although work at home may not always be voluntary, when it is voluntary it is often presented as a strategic response to occupational (Haddon and Silverstone, 1993) and family circumstances (Haddon, 1992). Some research suggests that women are more likely than men to report that they are motivated to work at home by family-related factors (Olson and Primps, 1984; Haddon and Silverstone, 1993; Aitken and Caroll, 1996; Sturesson, 1997; Kompast and Wagner, 1998), especially childcare (Sullivan and Lewis, 2001). An in-depth study of UK home-working households examined perceptions of the advantages of home-working and found that men and women were equally likely to report family-related advantages, but that the nature of these family-related advantages differed for men and women (Sullivan and Lewis, 2001). The home-working men in this study presented their family advantages as being about spending time with the family or about 'helping' with childcare or domestic tasks, while the women emphasized the importance of work at home in helping them to fulfill domestic responsibilities – especially parenting (Sullivan and Lewis, 2001). It is likely that this is related to a general tendency for men's caring and domestic work to be conceptualized as voluntary (Perkins and DeMeis, 1996), as 'help' (Dempsey, 2000) and to the tendency for men and women to conceptualize their family role differently from each other (Greenhaus and Parasuraman, 1999).

For some, combining work at home with childcare is the only feasible option in the face of childcare services that are expensive and difficult to obtain (Olson and Primps, 1984; Fothergill, 1994; Bryant, 1999). It has been argued that some poorly paid women home-workers in the UK are placed in a particularly exploitative relationship with their employer by a combination of their commitment to traditional roles and the scarcity and high cost of childcare and domestic services (Phizacklea and Wolkowitz, 1995). Nevertheless, while work at home may be perceived as very important in facilitating arrangements for childcare (Hill *et al.*, 1996; Sturesson, 1997; Sullivan and Lewis, 2001; Sullivan, 2001), attempting to combine childcare and work at home simultaneously is problematic and it is often pointed out that work at home should not be seen as a feasible alternative to childcare (Ahrentzen, 1990; Huws *et al.*, 1996; Pyöriä, 2003). Women attempting to combine work at home and childcare are especially likely to fit their work around their children's timetables and may tend to work only when their children are at school or asleep (Haddon and Silverstone, 1993; Sullivan and Lewis, 2001).

Gender may also influence the division of family work indirectly, for example in relation to the nature of the job, and especially the amount of autonomy and control it provides. A study of the impact of job characteristics on the allocation of childcare tasks in home-working households suggests that home-workers with jobs characterized by uncontrollable workflow, the need for immediate responses and less ability to determine when work will be carried out were less likely to perform childcare and fit their work around their children's timetables (Hardwick and Salaff, 1997). However, as the authors point out, the fact that men tend not to have major responsibility for childcare may lead to them being over-represented in those types of jobs, thereby perpetuating the unequal division of family roles. This is consistent with the tendency amongst some UK men and women in home-working households to conceptualize motherhood, particularly when children are young, as inevitably restricting women's on-site employment, and consequently to conceptualize mothers' work at home, especially when carried out part time, as a suitable alternative to not being in paid employment at all – rather than as an alternative to on-site work (Sullivan, 2002).

People working at home are sometimes expected to do more domestic labor simply because they are around the house more (Haddon, 1992) – although evidence suggests that this may not actually lead to any changes in the allocation of domestic labor (as discussed earlier). There is some evidence that co-residents are aware of their tendency to expect the home-worker with whom they live to do more domestic work and that they recognize this as unfair and try to challenge such expectations (Sullivan, 2001). Furthermore, some partners of home-workers perceive the home-worker as facilitating some aspects of household management simply by being present at home when they themselves are out at work – for example, by being there to take delivery of parcels or being available to deal with callers to the house (Sullivan, 2001). However, research on many aspects of work at home, including its impact on family life and the management of domestic tasks, has tended not to include the perspectives of co-residents and so the impact on co-residents is still not well understood.

The research evidence suggests that the gendered division of work and family responsibilities tends to remain unchallenged by work at home. There is little evidence to support the assertion that work at home will revolutionize gender roles and increase men's participation in childcare and domestic work – although there is some evidence that, where there is a specific commitment to role sharing, work at home may facilitate this (Sullivan and Lewis, 2001). This, especially in the light of evidence that the flexibility that may arise from work at home is conceptualized in traditionally gendered ways, casts some doubt on the 'new opportunities for flexibility model'. However, there is also evidence that women and men do perceive work at home as useful in balancing work and family and as facilitating childcare. Therefore, the 'exploitation model' also seems not to be supported by the available research evidence. It seems, as we have argued elsewhere (Sullivan and Lewis, 2001), that neither of these models is sufficiently complex to explain gendered work and family roles and responsibilities in home-working contexts. Another important area where work at home may have a substantial impact is in relation to family functioning and family satisfaction. This will be considered next.

FAMILY FUNCTIONING

Arguments about the impact of work at home on family life also vary with, once again, some being more negative than others. It has been argued that the flexibility given by working at home can increase opportunities for family activities and benefit children, bringing about a more harmonious family life (e.g., Carsky *et al.*, 1991; Schepp, 1995). However, as discussed above, the impact of flexibility is not clear cut. One view is that people working at home typically spend more time with their families because they interact with their families in place of the short social interaction breaks that usually occur in the office (Nilles, 1994). However, this has to be considered alongside predictions that working at home will lead to irregular working hours and overworking, which may increase the amount of conflict between partners (Telecottage Association, 1993) and have a negative impact on family life (Ellison, 1999). For example, it may reduce the amount of time available for family interaction.

Although relatively little attention has been paid to children's perspectives, it has also been suggested that children may have trouble understanding that, despite their presence in the home, parents are not available to spend time with them (Telecottage Association, 1993). In a similar vein, Aitken and Carroll (1996) argue that, despite the fact that men may be physically present in the house when home-working, and may even share family meals, they are not really interacting with other family members to any great extent. In the next section, these claims about family functioning and work at home will be evaluated in the light of available research evidence. Comparatively few studies have been conducted to investigate these anticipated effects of work at home on the family and, once again, findings are mixed. First, we will consider research evidence that relates to family time and then evidence relating to conflict and dissatisfaction within the family.

There is some evidence to support the view that work at home is perceived by home-workers and their families as increasing family time. A study of Swedish home-workers found that both men and women used working at home as a way of spending more time with their children and accomplishing childcare tasks – for example, transporting children to and from school or taking breaks from work to spend time together (Wikström *et al.*, 1997). Work at home may offer the flexibility to work in the evenings as a way of spending more time with, or caring for, children, but this can then reduce the amount of time available for time with partners (Wikström *et al.*, 1997). While time for partners may be increased by being able to spend breaks from work together (Sullivan, 2001), which would not be possible with on-site work, this may not be sufficient to significantly increase time together (Wikström *et al.*, 1997). A study of the cohabiting partners of UK home-workers also indicates that work at home may increase family time, although, for some partners, family interaction may not reach the level that was anticipated prior to the adoption of work at home (Sullivan, 2001).

Despite this evidence for the potential of work at home to increase family time, it is crucial to bear in mind, as noted above, that time gains (for example, resulting from reduced commuting time) can lead to overwork, rather than being channeled into more leisure or family time (Armstrong, 1997; Sullivan and Lewis, 2001). Clearly, work at home does not necessarily lead always to longer work hours or always to more family time. While some of the home-based teleworkers studied by Hill *et al.* (1996) reported increased opportunities for family time, others reported that increased work hours had taken them further away from their families. Further research is clearly needed to help understand the factors that might lead to these different outcomes in different family contexts.

Even if work at home does have the capacity to increase the amount of time that parents spend with children, it is also important to consider that co-residents are often faced with a situation where the home-worker is unavailable to them despite being physically present at home. As described above, it has been suggested that this may counteract gains in family time and may be particularly challenging for children. A study of the cohabiting partners of UK home-workers (Sullivan, 2001) provides some evidence that children may have difficulty accepting that their home-working parent is unavailable to them even if, as previous research (Sullivan, 2000) suggests, they understand what is happening when a parent works at home. However, research that examines children's perspectives on work at home is very rare, and this is an area where more research is urgently needed if the effects on the family are to be fully understood.

A number of studies also shed light upon conflict and satisfaction within the family in home-working contexts. Pitt-Catsouphes and Marchetta (1991) suggest that the blurred boundaries that accompany work at home lead to increased conflict within the family. There is also some evidence that the presence of work, and work-related visitors, can be a source of conflict and dissatisfaction for the families of people working at home (Sullivan, 2000; Baines and Gelder, 2003). The presence of workers at home can impinge on the freedom of co-residents to come and go as they please (Wikström *et al.*, 1997; Sullivan, 2000), which could provide another source of potential conflict and dissatisfaction, and challenge the very notion of home as a haven from the public sphere.

Satisfaction with family life may also be influenced by work at home. One study of home-based teleworkers found that satisfaction with work at home was negatively related to satisfaction with family relationships (Hartman *et al.*, 1991). It is possible that this is indicative of work at home impacting negatively on satisfaction with family relationships. However, the correlational nature of the evidence means that an alternative explanation is equally possible. That is, the association found in this study could also mean that those people who are more dissatisfied with their family relationships are more likely to devote more energy and resources to their work, a process known as 'compensation' (Greenhaus and Parasuraman, 1999), and therefore derive greater satisfaction from the work.

Other research has shown inconsistent findings. For example, Silver (1993) found no significant differences between on-site workers and home-workers with regard to satisfaction with marriage and family, and a study by Olson and Primps (1984) found that men working at home reported improved relationships with their children. In the few studies that have been conducted on the co-residents of home-workers, there is some evidence of a negative relationship between the amount of time spent working at home and partners' life satisfaction (Vitterso *et al.*, 2003), although other research suggests that co-residents are unlikely to perceive work at home as reducing their satisfaction with family life (Sullivan, 2001).

Clearly there are numerous unanswered questions about the impact of work at home on the family and family life and, as with studies in this area generally, there is a paucity of research that examines the perspectives of co-residents – especially children. It is particularly important to recognize that work at home operates within a dynamic family context. Spatial demands and priorities within home-working households change and fluctuate over time (Sullivan, 2000) and the changing context of family life (e.g., changes in childcare demands as children are born, grow and leave home) influence the way in which home-workers and co-residents experience the flexibility of work at home (Sullivan, 2002). The home as a workplace, like contemporary on-site workplaces, may be in a continual state of flux.

IMPLICATIONS

For some commentators, work at home has the potential to challenge gendered work and family roles in ways that enhance gender equity and facilitate the combination of work and family responsibilities (see above). Similarly, work at home is often presented uncritically as an example of a 'family-friendly' employment practice; that is, a practice designed to enable employees to integrate work and family (see, for example, Schepp, 1995). Research on other policies that tend to be designated as family friendly, for example, part-time work and career breaks, reveals that they are mainly utilized by women and, rather than challenging organizational culture or the allocation of domestic and paid work, they often marginalize those who use them (Lewis, 1997). Therefore, it is important to consider what research on work at home, gender and the work–family interface reveals about whether work at home is family friendly and gender equitable.

It can be argued that any potential impact of work at home on gender equity will be limited by men and women's different reasons for working at home and by the lack of impact on the distribution of family responsibilities. Women with young children are particularly likely to work at home in the UK (Felstead *et al.*, 2000). Taken together with growing evidence that work at home has little capacity to challenge gendered work and family roles and responsibilities or to increase men's participation in family roles (e.g., Gunnarsson, 1997; Sullivan and Lewis, 2001; Sullivan, 2002), it may be the case that work at home has potential to bolster traditional gendered family roles. Furthermore, concerns are raised about the potential impact of work at home on women's position within the labor market. Some argue that the career prospects of those working at home may suffer due to reduced workplace presence (Huws *et al.*, 1990). However, recent research from the USA suggests that this negative impact may not occur in organizations where work at home is well established and generally accepted (Hill *et al.*, 2003). However, for those not fortunate enough to be employed in such organizations, home-working may be a mixed blessing. It may be family friendly in as much as it enables women to combine work and family but evidence suggests that it is not gender equitable in its operation and effects.

The potential for work at home to enhance opportunities for integrating work and family is usually thought to be a function of greater flexibility, which allows rigid boundaries to become permeated. However, we have argued that this flexibility can be used in different ways: to provide more time for family, or to enable paid work to encroach more into family time and space. Furthermore, there is a tendency for these processes to be gendered. Women may more often use home-based work to multitask and manage boundaries, men to overwork and sustain segregated boundaries. Like all so-called work–family or 'family-friendly' policies, home-based work needs to be well managed at a number of different levels. It needs to be managed by workers themselves, who adopt a variety of boundary-crossing strategies (Clarke, 2000), and by families in the negotiation of paid and unpaid work. It also needs to be managed by line managers who need a high level of trust, when employees are not visible in the workplace, and a focus on outputs rather than input of time (Felstead *et al.*, 2003). Future research should focus on the negotiation processes that occur at each level.

Over all, the research we have reviewed suggests a high degree of diversity in people's experiences of working at home. This has important implications for people undertaking work at home and for the organizations that they are part of. Clearly, there is no single 'best way' of approaching work at home and we would be sceptical of any simplistic prescriptive guidelines that are presented as solutions for all home-workers in all contexts. This is not to suggest that guidance cannot be established on the basis of previous experiences and research, but that people and organizations must be encouraged to use this as a starting point for developing work at home that is tailored to individual organizations, employees and their families. For example, research suggests that the management of physical space is an important aspect of managing work–family boundaries, but the diversity of ways in which this is experienced and managed suggests that simplistic recommendations (e.g., 'all home-workers should have a separate, lockable workroom') are inappropriate (Sullivan, 2001). However, information can be given to potential home-workers about the kinds of issues that have arisen for other people working at home and suggestions can be made to help them and their families devise ways of tailoring solutions that suit them. Organizations and employees and their co-residents may find that tailored solutions that are flexible are most appropriate and that the dynamic context in which work at home operates may require these solutions to be changed from time to time.

CONCLUSIONS

Currently, both popular arguments about the likely effects of home-based work on workers and their families and empirical research examining these impacts are mixed. While there are some generic issues in the study of work at home and the work–family interface, there is also much diversity and it is important not to assume too much homogeneity among home-workers. At a generic level, boundaries between paid work and family are less clear cut for home-based workers. However, these unclear boundaries can be double edged; they provide flexibility to integrate work and family, but also opportunities for paid work to pervade all aspects of life. Future research should examine the impact of teleworking and work at home on more diverse populations, including, for example, single parents and workers with disabilities. This may help to identify more of the factors that influence the ways in which work–family boundaries are managed and the experiences of conflict and integration. More research is also needed on the processes whereby working from home can, under different circumstances, enhance positive work–family integration. Only then will it be possible to convert research into practice and provide evidence-based advice to home-based workers, their families and their managers.

REFERENCES

Ahrentzen, S. B. (1990). Managing conflict by managing boundaries: how professional homeworkers cope with multiple roles at home. *Environment and Behavior, 22*, 723–752.

Ahrentzen, S. B. (1992). Home as a workplace in the lives of women. In I. Altman and S. Low (eds), *Place attachment* (pp. 279–304). London: Plenum Press.

Aitken, S., and Carroll, M. (1996). Man's place in the home: telecommuting, identity and urban space. Retrieved 2 May 1997 from http://www.ncgia.ucsb.edu/conf/BALTIMORE/authors/aitken/paper.html

Allen, T., Herts, D., Bruck, C., and Sutton, M. (2000). Consequences associated with work to family conflict: a review and agenda for future research. *Journal of Occupational Health Psychology, 5*, 278–308.

Armstrong, N. (1997). Negotiating the boundaries between 'home' and 'work': a case study of teleworking in New Zealand. In E. Gunnarsson and U. Huws (eds), *Virtually free? Gender, work and spatial choice* (pp. 175–200). Stockholm: Nutek.

Baines, S., and Gelder, U. (2003). What is family friendly about the workplace in the home? The case of self-employed parents and their children. *New Technology, Work and Employment, 18*, 223–234.

Berry, J. O., and Rao, J. M. (1997). Balancing employment and fatherhood. *Journal of Family Issues, 18*(4), 386–402.

Biernat, M., and Wortman, C. (1991). Sharing of home responsibilities between professionally employed women and their husbands. *Journal of Personality and Social Psychology, 60*, 844–860.

Brannen, J. (2000). Mothers and fathers in the workplace. In L. L. Haas, P. Hwang and G. Russell (eds), *Organizational change and gender equity: International perspectives on fathers and mothers at the workplace* (pp. 29–42). London: Sage.

Bryant, S. (1999). At home on the electronic frontier: work, gender and the information highway. *New Technology, Work and Employment, 15*, 19–33.

Burgess, A. (1997). *Fatherhood reclaimed: The making of the modern father.* London: Vermilion.

Burke, R. J., and Greenglass, E. R. (1999). Work–family conflict, spouse support, and nursing staff well-being during organizational restructuring. *Journal of Occupational Health Psychology, 4*, 327–336.

Carsky, M. L., Dolan, E. M., and Free, R. K. (1991). An integrated model of homebased work effects of family quality of life. *Journal of Business Research, 23*, 37–49.

Clarke, S. C. (2000). Work/family border theory: a new theory of work–family balance. *Human Relations, 53*, 747–770.

Conner, M., Fletcher, W., Firth-Cozens, J., and Collins, S. (1993). Teleworking, stress and health. In H. Schroder, K. Reschke, M. Johnston and S. Maes (eds), *Health psychology: Potential in diversity* (pp. 309–313). Roderer Verlag: Regensbery, Germany.

Dempsey, K. C. (2000). Men's share of child care: a rural and urban comparison. *Australian Journal of Marriage and Family, 6*, 245–266.

Dimitrova, D. (2003). Controlling teleworkers: supervision and flexibility revisited. *New Technology, Work and Employment, 18*(3), 181–195.

Dooley, B. (1996). At work away from work. *The Psychologist, 9*, 155–158.

Ellison, N. B. (1999). Social impacts: new perspectives on telework. *Social Science Computer Review, 17*, 338–356.

Felstead, A., Jewson, N., Phizacklea, A., and Walters, S. (2000). *A statistical portrait of working at home in the UK: Evidence from the LFS.* Leicester: ESRC.

Felstead, A., Jewson, N., and Walters, S. (2003). Managerial control of employees working at home. *British Journal of Industrial Relations, 41*(2), 241–264.

Ferree, M. M. (1990). Beyond separate spheres: feminism and family research. *Journal of Marriage and the Family, 52*, 866–884.

Fothergill, A. (1994). Telework: women's experiences and utilization of information technology in the home. In A. Adam, E. Green and J. Owen (eds), *Women, work and computerisation* (pp. 333–347). Amsterdam: Elsevier Science.

Frone, M. R., and Yardley, J. K. (1996). Workplace family-supportive programmes: predictors of employed parents' importance ratings. *Journal of Occupational and Organizational Psychology, 69*, 351–366.

Frone, M. R., Russell, M., and Barnes, G. M. (1996). Work–family conflict, gender and health-related outcomes: a study of employed parents in two community samples. *Journal of Occupational Health Psychology, 1*, 57–69.

Galinsky, E., Bond, J. T., and Friedman, D. E. (1993). *The changing workforce: Highlights of the national study.* New York: Families and Work Institute.

Gillespie, A., Richardson, R., and Cornford, J. (1995). *Review of telework in Britain: Implications for public policy.* Report prepared for the Parliamentary Office of Science and Technology. Centre for Urban and Regional Development Studies, University of Newcastle upon Tyne.

Greenhaus, J. H., and Parasuraman, S. (1999). Research on work, family and gender: current status and future directions. In G. N. Powell (ed.), *Handbook of gender in organizations* (pp. 391–412). Newbury Park, CA: Sage.

Gunnarsson, E. (1997). Gendered faces? Teleworking from a Swedish perspective. In E. Gunnarsson and U. Huws (eds), *Virtually free? Gender, work and spatial choice* (pp. 57–78). Stockholm: Nutek.

Gurstein, P. (1991). Working at home and living at home: emerging scenarios. *Journal of Architectural and Planning Research, 8*(2), 164–180.

Haddon, L. (1992). *Clerical teleworking and family life.* Martlesham, UK: British Telecom.

Haddon, L., and Silverstone, R. (1993). *Teleworking in the 1990s: A view from the home.* SPRU CICT Report No. 10, CICT, SPRU, University of Sussex.

Hardwick, D., and Salaff, J. W. (1997). Teleworking mothers and fathers: how control over time and place of paid work determines the ways in which they do child care work. Paper presented at the *New Forms of Work and Employment ASA meetings*, Toronto, Canada.

Hartman, R. I., Stoner, C. R., and Arora, R. (1991). An investigation of selected variables affecting telecommuting productivity and satisfaction. *Journal of Business and Psychology, 6*, 207–225.

Hill, E. J., Hawkins, A. J., and Miller, B. C. (1996). Work and family in the virtual office: perceived influences of mobile telework, *Family Relations, 45*, 293–301.

Hill, E. J., Ferris, M., and Märtinson, V. (2003). Does it matter where you work? A comparison of how three work venues (traditional office, virtual office, and home office) influence aspects of work and personal/family life. *Journal of Vocational Behavior, 63*, 220–241.

Hinssen, P. J. H., and ter Hofte, G. H. (1994). Two discussion scenarios on the future of telework. Paper presented to the *European Assembly on Teleworking and New Ways of Working.* Berlin, November 1994.

Hochschild, A. R. (1989). *The second shift: Working parents and the revolution at home.* New York: Viking

Hogarth, T., Hasluck, C., Pierre, G., Winterbotham, M., and Vivian, D. (2000). *Work–life balance 2000: Baseline study of work–life balance practices in Great Britain.* London: Department for Education and Employment.

Huws, U. (1993). *Teleworking in Britain.* Sheffield: Department of Employment.

Huws, U., Korte, W., and Robinson, S. (1990). *Telework: Towards the elusive office.* Chichester: Wiley.

Huws, U., Podro, S., Gunnarsson, E., Weijers, T., Arvanitaki, K., and Trova, V. (1996). *Teleworking and gender.* Brighton: Institute of Employment Studies.

Jurik, N. C. (1998). Getting away and getting by: the experiences of self-employed homeworkers. *Work and Occupations, 25*(1), 7–35.

Kirchmeyer, C., and Cohen, A. (1999). Different strategies for managing the work/non-work interface: a test for unique pathways to work outcomes. *Work and Stress, 13*, 59–73.

Kompast, M., and Wagner, I. (1998). Telework: managing spatial, temporal and cultural boundaries. In P. Jackson and J. Van der Wielen (eds), *Teleworking: International perspectives from telecommuting to the virtual office* (pp. 95–117). London: Routledge.

Kossek, E., and Ozeki, C. (1999). Bridging the work–family policy and productivity gap. *Community, Work and Family, 2*, 7–32.

Lewis, S. (1994). Role tensions and dual career families. In M. Davidson and

R. Burke (eds), *Women in management: Current research issues* (pp. 230–241). London: Paul Chapman.

Lewis, S. (1997). Family friendly employment policies: a route to changing organisational culture or playing about at the margins? *Gender, Work and Organizations, 4*, 13–23.

Lewis, S., and Cooper, C. L. (1995). Balancing the work/home interface: a European perspective. *Human Resource Management Review, 5*, 289–305.

Lewis, S., Rapoport, R., and Gambles, R. (2003). Reflections on the integration of paid work and the rest of life. *Journal of Managerial Psychology, 18*, 824–841.

Loerch, K. H., Russell, J. E. A., and Rush, M. C. (1989). The relationships among family domain variables and work–family conflict for men and women. *Journal of Vocational Behavior, 35*, 288–308.

Madsen, S. R. (2003). The effects of home-based teleworking on work–family conflict. *Human Resource Development Quarterly, 14*, 35–58.

Major, V., Klein, K., and Ehrhart, M. (2002). Work time, work interference with family and psychological distress. *Journal of Applied Psycholoy, 87*, 427–436.

Mancorda, P. M. (1997). Telework and women: some remarks on the Italian case. In E. Gunnarsson and U. Huws (eds), *Virtually free? Gender, work and spatial choice* (pp. 229–234). Stockholm: Nutek.

Milkie, M. A., and Peltola, P. (1999). Playing all the roles: gender and the work–family balancing act. *Journal of Marriage and the Family, 61*, 476–490.

Mirchandani, K. (1998). No longer a struggle? Teleworkers' reconstruction of the work–non-work boundary. In P. J. Jackson and J. M. Van der Wielen (eds), *Teleworking: International perspectives from telecommuting to the virtual organisation* (pp. 118–135). London: Routledge.

New Ways to Work (1996). *Changing places: A managers' guide to working from home*. London: New Ways to Work.

Nilles, J. M. (1994). *Making telecommuting happen: A guide for telemanagers and telecommuters*. New York: Van Nostrand Reinhold.

Nippert-Eng, C. (1996). *Home and work: Negotiating boundaries through everyday life*. Chicago: University of Chicago Press.

Olson, M. H., and Primps, S. (1984). Working at home with computers: work and non-work issues. *Journal of Social Issues, 40*, 97.

Perkins, H. W., and DeMeis, D. K. (1996). Gender and family effects on the 'second-shift' domestic activity of college-educated young adults. *Gender and Society, 10*(1), 78–93.

Perrons, D. (2003). The new economy and the work–life balance: conceptual explorations and a case study of new media. *Gender, Work and Organization, 10*(1), 65–93.

Phizacklea, A., and Wolkowitz, C. (1995). *Homeworking women: Gender, racism and class at work*. London: Sage.

Pitt-Catsouphes, M., and Marchetta, A. (1991). *A coming of age: Telework*. Boston: Boston University, Centre on Work and Family.

Pyöriä, P. (2003). Knowledge work in distributed environments: issues and illusions. *New Technology, Work and Employment, 18*(3): 166–180.

Rapoport, R., Bailyn, L., Fletcher, J., and Pruitt, B. (2002). *Beyond work–family balance: Advancing gender equity and work performance*. London: Wiley.

Salmi, M. (1997). Home-based work, gender and everyday life. In E. Gunnarsson and U. Huws (eds), *Virtually free? Gender, work and spatial choice* (pp. 131–150). Stockholm: Nutek.

Scarpitti, G. (1994). New ways to work. Paper presented to the *European Assembly on Teleworking and New Ways of Working*. Berlin, November 1994.

Schepp, D. (1995). *The telecommuter's handbook*. New York: McGraw Hill.

Shamir, B., and Salomon, M. (1985). Work at home and the quality of working life. *Academy of Management Review*, *10*, 455–464.

Silver, H. (1993). Homework and domestic work. *Sociological Forum*, *8*, 181–204.

Standen, P., Daniels, K., and Lamond, D. (1999). The home as a workplace: work–family integration and psychological well-being in telework. *Journal of Occupational Health Psychology*, *4*, 368–381.

Sturesson, L. (1997). Telework: symbol of the Information Society. In E. Gunnarsson and U. Huws (eds), *Virtually free? Gender, work and spatial choice* (pp. 79–90). Stockholm: Nutek.

Sullivan, C. (2000a). Space and the intersection of work and family in homeworking households. *Community, Work and Family*, *3*, 185–204.

Sullivan, C. (2000b). Gender, perceived flexibility and work–family conflict amongst homeworkers. Paper presented to the *British Academy of Management Annual Conference*. Edinburgh University Management School, September 2000.

Sullivan, C. (2001). Living with a homeworker: female and male partners' experiences of the management of work and family and family satisfaction. Paper presented at the *ESRC Seminar Series 'Impact of a changing labour market on families, children and mental health: Building research-user alliances'*. University of Aberdeen, 31 May 2001.

Sullivan, C. (2002). Work at home, gender and the intersection of work and family. Unpublished PhD thesis, Department of Psychology, Manchester Metropolitan University.

Sullivan, C. (2003). What's in a name? Definitions and conceptualizations of teleworking and homeworking. *New Technology, Work and Employment*, *18*(3), 158–165.

Sullivan, C., and Lewis, S. (2001). Home-based telework, gender, and the synchronization of work and family: perspectives of teleworkers and their co-residents. *Gender, Work and Organization*, *8*, 123–145.

Telecottage Association (1993). *What is teleworking?* Kenilworth, UK: Telecottage Association.

Venkatesh, A., and Vitalari, N. (1992). An emerging distributed work arrangement: an investigation of computer-based supplemental work at home. *Management Sciences*, *12*, 1687–1706.

Vittersø, J., Akselsen, S., Evjemo, B., Julsrud, T. E., Yttri, B., and Bergvik, S. (2003). Impacts of home-based telework on quality of life for employees and their partners: quantitative and qualitative results from a European study. *Journal of Happiness Studies*, *4*, 201–233.

Wikström, T., Lindén, K. P., and Michelson, W. (1997). *Hub of events or splendid isolation: The home as a context for teleworking*. Lund, Sweden: Lund University, School of Architecture.

7 Crossover of stress and strain in the work–family context

Mina Westman

CROSSOVER AND CONTAGION OF STRESS AND STRAIN

The literature contains ample evidence of the impact of job stress on workers' mental and physical well-being (Kahn and Byosiere, 1992). However, it is only recently that researchers have turned their attention to the phenomenon of stress contagion that has been labeled crossover, namely, the reaction of individuals to the job stress experienced by those with whom they interact regularly. In this chapter, the differentiation of Bolger *et al.* (1989) between two situations in which stress is contagious is followed: *spillover* – stress experienced in one domain of life results in stress in the other domain for the same individual; and *crossover* – stress experienced in the workplace by the individual leads to stress being experienced by the individual's spouse at home. Whereas spillover is an intra-individual, inter-domain contagion of stress (see Chapter 3), crossover is a dyadic, inter-individual, inter-domain contagion, generating similar reactions in another individual. In other words, spillover occurs from home to work and from work to home, for the same individual, whereas crossover is conceptualized as a process occurring from one individual at the workplace to his/her spouse at home. This indicates that whereas spillover affects only the individual, crossover can affect the dyad and the group.

The objectives of this chapter are: to integrate prior research and stimulate additional inquiry into the phenomenon of crossover; to propose a comprehensive theoretical framework relating to the crossover process that extends our understanding of work and family life; and to suggest new topics for crossover research such as the role of gender in the crossover process, and positive crossover.

This chapter integrates crossover research into a job-stress model. It begins with a discussion of current models of the work–family interface, emphasizing the development of crossover. The theoretical perspective for studying crossover is then introduced, and the core mechanisms of the model are proposed and discussed.

CURRENT MODELS OF WORK–FAMILY INTERACTION

Scholars in the work–family domain rely on models such as segmentation, compensation and spillover to characterize the process by which work and family are linked. These three models have received extensive attention in the work–family literature (Piotrkowski, 1979; Zedeck, 1992) and are discussed in further detail in Chapter 3. In summary, Segmentation theory postulates that the two domains are distinct, serve different functions and exist side by side, a separation that allows compartmentalization of one's life (Dubin, 1973). Compensation theory postulates an inverse relationship between work and family such that work and family experiences are incompatible. Compensation is achieved by decreasing involvement in a dissatisfying domain and increasing involvement in a potentially satisfying one (Lambert, 1990). Spillover theory conceives of a process by which attitudes and behavior carry over from one role to another for the same individual (Crouter, 1984; Piotrkovski, 1979). It assumes a similarity between what occurs in the work and family domains (Staines, 1980).

SPILLOVER AND CROSSOVER OF STRESS AND STRAIN

All the above models relate to the impact of work on the family domain or the impact of family in the work domain for the same individual. Positive and negative spillover research has been conducted at the individual level of analysis, under the assumption that the role behavior of one spouse in the two spheres is unaffected by that of the other. Crossover research is based upon the propositions of the spillover model, recognizing the fluid boundaries between work and family life, and noting that spillover is a necessary, but not sufficient condition for crossover. The crossover model adds another level of analysis to previous approaches by considering the inter-individual level and the dyad as an additional focus of research.

With the accumulated findings of crossover research, it is reasonable to posit that variables reflecting job and family demands are antecedents of the crossover process. The focus of the present chapter is therefore on the individual's job and family demands that trigger this process, thus defining the boundaries of the model. Important as they are, other non-work domains such as social network and the community are beyond its scope but suggest opportunities for future research. The proposed framework sets out to guide research and formulate explanations that clarify how the crossover process is initiated and maintained.

A THEORETICAL PERSPECTIVE

Several experts in the field of work–family research have criticized the 'state of the art' work–family models. Barnett (1998) and Zedeck (1992) criticized their atheoretical basis and Lambert (1990) found work–family theories inadequately conceptualized, neither delineating well-specified causal models nor capturing all the processes that link work and home.

Using a system theory, Bronfenbrenner (1977) asserted that no systematic work–family research incorporated the dynamic, interpersonal, social system perspectives. He made the point that components within the system tend to interrelate and affect each other such that processes operating in different settings are not independent of each other. Nevertheless, most researchers in the work–family arena focus on individual outcomes, even though it is recognized that what happens to one member of the family in the workplace affects other members of the family. The proposed model starts with the individual level and moves to the dyadic level, thereby benefiting from the incorporation of multiple levels of the work–family systems. Examining the crossover effects of stress and strain using the couple as the unit of analysis may increase our understanding of the complexities of multiple roles in different domains. It also enables the investigation of the possible ripple effect of stress starting at the workplace, crossing over to the spouse, who in turn might in extreme circumstances convey the consequences to his/her co-workers, who transmit it to their spouses at home.

The proposed model integrates crossover research into a job-stress model and anchors it in role theory (Kahn *et al.*, 1964). The usefulness of role theory as a basis for crossover research is that it underscores the interrelations between a focal person and his/her role senders in the work and family settings. Furthermore, role theory is a sound basis for crossover research because it focuses on a wider role stress paradigm than the work–family interface models.

According to role theory, the work and family settings are involved in elaborate interchanges over time with their social environments. Kahn *et al.* (1964) referred to members of a role set as role senders and to their communicated expectation as a sent role. They described such interactions using the term 'role episode', that is, a complete cycle of role sending of the individuals taking part in this episode, responses by the focal person and the effects of that response on the role senders. Furthermore, interpersonal and personal factors may affect the role episode by influencing the focal person, the role senders and the relationship between them.

The model delineated in Figure 7.1 uses role theory as an anchor for theoretical development in the work–family domain and can guide research to determine how experiences and processes in the work and family domain are linked

CORE CONSTRUCTS OF THE CROSSOVER MODEL

The conceptual model classifies a selected array of stresses and strains as antecedent influences of the crossover process. Furthermore, it posits

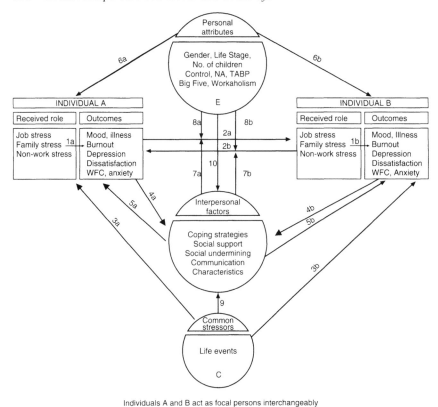

Figure 7.1 The crossover process (adapted from Westman, 2001). With permission from Sage Publications

personal attributes and interpersonal variables as possible moderators. The core assumption of the model is that one's stress has an impact on others in different settings, indicating a complex causal relationship between stress and strain in the individual arena and between stress and strain of the dyads. Job stress arises when demands exceed abilities, while job-related strains are reactions or outcomes resulting from the experience of stress (Jex and Beehr, 1991). Figure 7.1 distinguishes between six dimensions of the crossover process: role stress, life events, strain, personal attributes, coping and the interpersonal interaction process. The model shows that the received role may lead to strain (boxes A and B). The stress of one individual may cause stress and strain directly in the other individual (arrows 2a and 2b). The model also suggests that common stressors (e.g., life events) also impact the individual's strain. Some of the linkages in the model are very well supported empirically (stress, strain), whereas others (the interpersonal interaction process) require further support, and several of the variables have seldom been investigated in crossover research (coping, personal attributes).

Stress and strain (boxes A and B)

Studies have focused on different variables in the crossover process. Some have focused on the crossover of job stress from the individual to the spouse (e.g., Burke *et al.*, 1980), some have examined the process whereby job stress of the individual affects the strain of the spouse (Jones and Fletcher, 1993a, 1996; Long and Voges, 1987) and others have studied how psychological strain of one partner affects the strain of the other (Mitchell *et al.*, 1983; Westman and Etzion, 1995; Westman *et al.*, 2001; Westman, Etzion and Horovitz, 2004; Westman, Vinokur, Hamilton and Roziner, 2004). Crossover research has focused mostly on five major strains: physical health, burnout, depression, work–family conflict, anxiety and dissatisfaction.

Some crossover studies have examined heterogeneous samples (e.g., Barnett *et al.*, 1995; Rook *et al.*, 1991), though most of them have examined specific groups. Samples cover the range of police officers (Jackson and Maslach, 1982; Beehr *et al.*, 1995), prison officers (Long and Voges, 1987), administrators of correctional institutes (Burke *et al.*, 1980), career officers (Westman and Etzion, 1995, Westman, Vinokur, Hamilton and Roziner, 2004), plant operators (Jackson *et al.*, 1985) and bank employees (Hammer *et al.*, 1997). To illustrate, Burke *et al.* (1980) found that specific occupational demands experienced by male administrators of 'correctional institutions' were correlated with greater levels of dissatisfaction and distress in their spouses. Long and Voges (1987) found that wives of prison officers could accurately perceive the sources of their husbands' stress and that both husband and wife had reduced psychological well-being compared to norms. Westman and Etzion (1995) have examined the crossover of burnout between career officers and their spouses. Their findings suggest a bidirectional crossover of burnout between male and female partners (i.e., burnout in one partner was positively related to burnout in the other), after controlling for their own job stress and resistance resources. Hammer *et al.* (1997), who were the first to look at the crossover of work–family conflict, found a bidirectional crossover of work–family conflict from husbands to wives and vice versa in a sample of bank employees. Replicating the findings in various occupational groups augments external validity and extends the generalizability of these findings.

HYPOTHETICAL MECHANISMS FOR THE CROSSOVER PROCESS

Most crossover research does not rely on a systematic theoretical approach that distinguishes between the possible explanations of crossover effects. Without an understanding of these mechanisms, a model that accurately captures the complexities of the work–family nexus cannot be specified and tested. Furthermore, a better understanding of these processes will enable identification of effective strategies for coping with the stress cross-over effectively.

Westman and Vinokur (1998) specified three main mechanisms that can account for the crossover process: (1) direct crossover through empathic reactions; (2) common stressors; and (3) an indirect mediating interaction process.

Direct empathetic crossover (arrows 2a and 2b)

The first view expressed in the model is a direct transmission of stress and strain from one partner to the other as a result of empathic reactions. The basis for this view is the finding that crossover effects appear between closely related partners who share the greater part of their lives together. Empathy, which literally means 'feeling into', has been variously defined by different researchers. Starcevic and Piontek (1997) define it as a predominantly emotional form of interpersonal communication, involving the ability to be affected by the other's affective state as well as to be able to read in oneself what that affect has been. According to Lazarus (1991, p. 287), empathy is 'sharing another's feelings by placing oneself psychologically in that person's circumstances'. Whatever the definition, the core aspect of empathy involves an understanding and recognition of a partner's thoughts and feelings (Levenson and Ruef, 1992).

This view is supported by social learning theorists (e.g., Bandura, 1969; Stotland, 1969) who have explained the transmission of emotions as a conscious processing of information. Similarly, Riley and Eckenrode (1986) suggested that the effect of the undesirable events one experiences on the significant other's distress may be the result of empathy expressed in reports like 'We feel their pain is our own' (p. 771).

The role of common stressors in crossover research (arrows 3a and 3b)

The second type of crossover proposed by Westman and Vinokur (1998) is generated by common stressors affecting both partners. They have, however, suggested that the effect of common stressors in simultaneously increasing both partners' strain should be viewed as a case of spurious crossover. In their opinion, the common stressors in a shared environment merely constitute a third variable that independently but simultaneously increases the strain of each spouse, producing a positive correlation between partners' strain that may be erroneously interpreted as a genuine crossover effect.

Hobfoll and London (1986) suggested that many stressors make simultaneous demands on both individuals in a dyad. On the basis of their findings that the number of stressful events undergone by others co-varied with the reported distress over those events, Riley and Eckenrode (1986) argued that stressful life events influence the entire network of close ties. Only three of the reviewed crossover studies measured common stressors. Vinokur *et al.* (1996) found that family financial strain had an impact on the crossover process and on the supportive and undermining transactions between the partners. Westman, Vinokur, Hamilton and Roziner (2004), studying officers in the Russian army and their spouses, found that financial strain was related to both spouses' distress. Westman and Vinokur (1998) found that common life events affected the crossover process by increasing each partner's depression. The common stressors may also influence the interpersonal factors, social undermining and social support (arrow 9).

Crossover as an indirect process (circles D and E)

The third crossover mechanism specified by Westman and Vinokur (1998) was the *indirect crossover of strain*, moderated by personal attributes (circle E) and the interaction between the partners (circle D). The explanation of crossover as an indirect process focuses on specific coping strategies and interpersonal transactions, such as social support, social undermining and communication style.

There is no systematic empirical evidence on the contribution of *personal attributes* to the crossover process. The most frequently investigated characteristics include gender and number of children, and they have generally been weakly related to crossover.

Researchers have rarely looked into other personality attributes that might help explain the crossover process. This lack is noteworthy, considering the importance of personality in stress research (Spector and O'Connell (1994). Future crossover research should include personal attributes such as the Big Five trait dimensions (Digman, 1990), type A behavior pattern (TABP) (Edwards and Baglioni, 1991) and workaholism (Burke, 2004) and their role in moderating the crossover relationship. This would help to fill an important gap in crossover research.

A personal trait relevant to crossover research is negative affectivity (NA), defined by Watson and Clark (1984) as a stable tendency to experience negative emotions across time and situations. Watson *et al.* (1986) suggested that the tendency of high-NA individuals to report negative emotions biases self-report measures of job demands and affective reactions. Though many studies have concluded that NA may be associated with over-reporting of job stress and strain (Burke *et al.*, 1993), none has examined the impact of NA in explaining the crossover process. The NA of one partner may affect his/her report on stress and strain, and the 'crossover' detected may be spurious. Furthermore, couples may influence each other's perceptions of their social environment. Thus, what we consider stress crossover may be crossover of NA. By not controlling NA, crossover research may have overestimated the effect of one's job stress on the spouse's well-being.

Coping strategies represent efforts to prevent or reduce the negative effects of stress. Most studies that have investigated coping strategies have examined the direct effect of an individual's coping on his/her well-being or the moderating effects of coping on the relationship between stress and strain/outcomes (Edwards *et al.*, 1990). However, only a few studies have examined the relationship between one person's coping and the other's well-being. Coping can be viewed as a predictor (arrows 5a and 5b) of the other's strain (Beehr *et al.*, 1995) or as a mediator (arrows 4a and 5b) or moderator (arrows 7a and 7b) of the relationship between one's stress and the other's strain/outcomes (Jackson and Maslach, 1982). Researchers have suggested two main directions of the relationships between one's coping and the significant other's well-being. Monier and Hobfoll (1997) demonstrated the impact of one's coping on the well-being of the significant other. They found that active coping by the other was negatively related to the individual's depression and that active, prosocial coping was inversely related to future depression, demonstrating that it may have some long-term ameliorative crossover effects. The other view, proposed by Burke *et al.* (1980) and Kahn *et al.* (1985), is that the individual's strain may determine the spouse's coping strategies (arrows 4a and 4b). Burke *et al.* found that wives whose husbands reported high occupational demands used more emotion-focused coping strategies, such as distraction, explosive outbursts and talking to others. However, they used problem-focused coping strategies when their husbands reported lower occupational demands. Kahn *et al.*'s (1985) findings that spouses of depressed persons used more aggressive strategies support this direction. The results supporting the second perspective may imply that women who use less constructive coping experience greater crossover of stress from their husbands than women using problem-focused strategies. The possibility that one's stress may exhaust the spouse's coping capacity, thereby increasing the spouse's vulnerability to stress and thus affecting the crossover process, has not been investigated.

The two main views of whether depression affects the spouse's coping or whether coping affects his/her depression are not contradictory and may even be reciprocal, suggesting a feedback loop. The process may commence at either points with one person's coping or depression. The important issue is the spiral that starts where one role sender's state and actions affect the role receiver and vice versa. Only experimentation and longitudinal studies can unravel the initiation of the process. Another area that merits further research is the impact of coping strategy on the focal respondent's partner, that is, whether certain patterns of the partners' coping strategies attenuate or strengthen (i.e., moderate) the crossover process. Certain coping strategies may simultaneously enhance the well-being of the coper and result in worse outcomes for partners. To illustrate, withdrawal from stressful episodes may be functional for the individual adopting such a strategy, but it may involve delegating communal responsibilities to a partner who may not be prepared to assume the added burdens. In the long run, such coping strategies may also result in negative psychological outcomes for the coper. The possibility that problem-focused coping may negatively affect those close to the focal respondent has been considered only by Hobfoll *et al.* (1994). Therefore, it is important to investigate how the interaction process affects both of the partners. It will require longitudinal designs to detect changes in coping and their effects over time.

The social interaction process

Communication characteristics refer to what people say to each other or how they react to events in which they are involved. The intensity and openness of the information exchange between spouses are also a specific kind of coping that affects the crossover process. The literature supporting this explanation implies the need to focus on the couple's communication pattern in terms of the kinds of interaction likely to enhance the partners' experience of stress or strain. Jones and Fletcher (1993b) have addressed the nature of information communicated between the partners as mediating the crossover process, suggesting that the communication may mediate the relationship between the partners' mood. They found that the woman's mood was affected by her partner's communication pattern: it was more positive when her husband offloaded worries and frustrations, but more negative when he became withdrawn or distracted. Jones and Fletcher (1996) observed that women's moods were related to their perception of their partners' communication patterns. They suggested that the frequency and nature of couples' work-related discussion is likely to be a mediator in the transmission process. Crossfield *et al.* (2005) analyzed the impact of frequency of discussion and communication on the crossover process. They found that, for men, frequent discussion was related to reduced well-being and higher levels of anxiety about their partner's jobs, whereas the quality of the communication made little difference. However, for women, frequency of discussion made little difference, but the perception that communication with their partner is based on mutual understanding and helpfulness was related to higher levels of psychological well-being.

Accurate knowledge of the spouse's job stress may be an important mechanism in the crossover process. Partners can talk about their job stress, or one can learn about the other's job stress through his/her behavior. The amount and kind of discussion are not a necessary condition for crossover, as partners can learn about their spouses' stress and strain from other sources. Pearlin and Turner (1987) found that many interviewees, husbands and wives alike, tried to segregate stress arising in the workplace from the family domain, explaining their distress would only anguish the spouse, the spouse would blame them for the problems or the spouse would give them unwanted or inappropriate advice. Whatever the reason, people rarely succeeded in barricading distress generated in the work domain. Focal respondents indicated they could tell when their partners were stressed, regardless of whether the partner discussed the problems. Mood changes, shifts in activities and other clues aroused awareness to the distress of their partners, even when they did not know the reason for it. Attempts to screen stresses from the family and the uncertainty created by such attempts were additional sources of strain. These findings show that attempts at segmentation are rarely successful and may even intensify the crossover process.

Social support refers to transactions with others that provide emotional, appraisal, informational and instrumental support (House, 1981). Antonovsky (1979) found that inadequate social support in stressful situations may increase the vulnerability to psychological distress, emotional problems and somatic illness. Therefore, an interaction style that does not provide enough support, or demands support from a spouse unable to provide it, can affect the crossover process. Jones and Fletcher (1993a) suggested that lack of social support might lead to a greater tendency to transmit stress to the other, though they did not investigate social support in this context.

Many of the researchers who have demonstrated the beneficial effects of social support (e.g., Beehr, 1995) have focused on the recipient, overlooking the impact on the donors (Hobfoll *et al.*, 1994). The role of the donor in the interaction may be one of the keys to the crossover process. Kessler and McLeod (1984) found that caring for a wide network of people was an additional burden for women, translating into contagion of stress from their network to themselves. Similarly, Riley and Ekenrode (1986) found that significant others are influenced by each other's distress indirectly, via reduced social support, noting that demand for social support by one caused a drain of resources in the other in the dyad. They underscored diminishing of resources experienced by the providers of social support, both by sharing them and by empathetically experiencing the demands of the needy. These findings may also indicate that the stress experienced by one partner creates demands upon the other to provide support and, when unable to meet these expectations, the other is apt to feel anxious or guilty. Conversely, a crisis experienced by one partner may diminish the social support available to the other. Riley and Eckenrode also found that network events such as divorce and unemployment were particularly distressing to women who had limited social support resources due to the 'cost of helping'. In accordance with role theory, this may lead to role overload, which in this case is excessive demands for supplying support, with its consequent effect on the donor's well-being.

Similarly, Hobfoll and London (1986) studying Israeli women whose relatives were mobilized to serve during wartime found two distinct effects. Social support aided the recipients but depleted the resources of the donors at a time they too needed their stress resistance resources. The indications are that social support is a finite resource and that people compete for in a zero-sum game. Therefore, the expected donors experience strain either because of their inability to provide support or because of their depleted resources.

A recent study of unemployed individuals and their employed spouses (Westman, Etzion and Horovitz, 2004) found that at the first wave of data collection immediately after the axe fell, the employed spouses, family members and friends provided a high level of support to the newly unemployed. However, after two months the amount of social support from all these sources decreased significantly. This might have occurred because the donors themselves lost resources or felt that their resources were being threatened and they could no longer provide the amount of support they had in the past.

Social undermining is referred to in the literature as social hindrance, social conflict and negative social support. According to Vinokur and van Ryn (1993), social undermining consists of behaviors directed toward the target person that express negative affect, convey negative evaluation or criticism or hinder the attainment of instrumental goals. Researchers have shown that social conflict is symptomatic of the stress and strain of cohabiting partners (Abbey *et al.*, 1985; Kahn *et al.*, 1985; Vinokur and van Ryn, 1993). The explanation that the crossover process is mediated by negative social interactions is supported by empirical findings from two lines of research. First, research documents that frustration is often an outcome of stressful conditions that trigger aggression (Berkowitz, 1989). Second, the literature on family processes also reports that stressed couples exhibit high levels of negative conflictual interactions (Schaefer *et al.*, 1981). The increased distress and its accompanying frustration lead to aggressive behavior (Berkowitz, 1989) or alternatively lead an individual to initiate or exacerbate a negative interaction sequence with the partner, as shown in studies on social undermining (Duffy *et al.*, 2002; Vinokur and van Ryn, 1993).

There are two main views on the relationship between social undermining and depression concerning the initiation of the crossover process. Some researchers (Coyne and Downey, 1991; Rook, 1984; Russell and Cutrona, 1991; Vinokur and van Ryn, 1993) have shown that social undermining increases the stress and strain of partners (arrows 5a and 5b). Vinokur and van Ryn (1993), for example, found in a longitudinal study of recently unemployed respondents that increase in social undermining produced a change for the worse in their mental health. The rival hypothesis that mental health affected social undermining was not supported in this study.

There are, however, also advocates of the inverse view (arrows 4a and 4b) that depression precedes conflicting interactions (Nelson and Beach, 1990; Schmaling and Jacobson, 1990). Empirical support for the effects of distress on social undermining can ·be found in a host of studies that describe the stress process leading to conflictual interactions (Conger *et al.*, 1993; MacEwen *et al.*, 1992). For example, MacEwen *et al.* (1992) found that overload resulted in anxiety and depression, which in turn resulted in more negative marital interactions. Similarly, Crouter *et al.* (1989) found that high levels of stress at work were related to increased negative marital interactions at home. Other studies went further and showed how distress increases conflictual interactions (Schaefer *et al.*, 1981), which, in turn, augments depression and marital dissatisfaction (Coyne and Downey, 1991; Vinokur *et al.*, 1996). The cross-sectional design of most of the studies precludes any conclusions as to whether social conflict is an antecedent or consequence of changes in well-being. To illustrate, Abbey *et al.* (1985), studying young students, found positive correlations between social conflict and anxiety and depression. They concluded: 'The greater the amount of social conflict respondents reported receiving from the person closest to them, the greater their anxiety' (p. 119). However, they note in their discussion that, though for theoretical reasons they interpret these relations in terms of causal pathways, neither their research design nor research evidence precludes the rival hypothesis: the greater the depression and anxiety, the higher the degree of social conflict. This causal inconclusiveness is typical of crossover research.

Westman and Vinokur (1998) supported the mediating role of undermining in the crossover process. They showed that the crossover of women's depression at both waves of their longitudinal study increased their undermining behaviors toward their husbands, which in turn increased the husbands' depressive symptoms. In sum, some studies have found that depression precedes conflictual interactions and others have found that conflictual interactions precede depression. Westman and Vinokur's (1998) findings suggest recursive relationships of social undermining acting as an antecedent of strain for one person and as a consequence of depression for the other. Feedback loops may occur between undermining and depression, triggering a vicious circle in which one amplifies the other.

The three mechanisms of crossover can operate independently of one another and are not mutually exclusive. Therefore, it is quite possible that some of the proposed mechanisms operate jointly. Vinokur *et al.* (1996) found that financial strain, representing common stressors, increased depression in the job seeker and in the spouse. These depressive symptoms increased the partner's undermining behavior, which increased depressive symptoms in the job seeker, indicating an indirect crossover effect via social interaction. Similarly, Westman and Vinokur (1998) found both direct and indirect crossover between spouses as well as effects due to common stressors. Westman, Vinokur, Hamilton and Roziner (2004) found both direct crossover and indirect crossover operating together, but only for males. The possibility that several mechanisms may operate simultaneously requires an analytical model that takes into account all the potential contributors to crossover.

THE ROLE OF GENDER IN THE CROSSOVER PROCESS

A review of crossover research demonstrates that crossover may be unidirectional (arrow 2a or 2b) or bidirectional (arrows 2a and 2b). The first stress crossover studies were unidirectional and examined and found effects of husbands' job stress on the well-being of their wives (Burke *et al.*, 1980; Jackson and Maslach, 1982; Long and Voges, 1987; Pavett, 1986; Rook *et al.*, 1991). These studies related to the wives as the passive recipients of stress and strain from their husbands, neither assessing nor controlling wives' job and life stress, and in some cases had mixed samples of working and non-working wives. Therefore, we cannot rule out the possibility that what appears as direct crossover of stress from husbands to wives is an outcome of wives' job or life stress or of common family stressors or life events affecting both partners.

Reviewing the directionality of crossover of stress and strain raises the issue of the role of gender in the crossover process. Gender is certainly a potential moderator of the impact of one's stress on the spouse's strain, because of differences in the traditional role demands and expectations for men and women (Lambert, 1990). There is some indication that women are more susceptible than men to the impact of stressors affecting their partners (Kessler, 1979). Kessler and McLeod (1984) showed that events happening to significant others are more distressing for women than for men. They suggested that because of their greater involvement in family affairs, women become more sensitive not only to the stressful events that they themselves experience but also to those that affect other family members. Johnson and Jackson (1998) demonstrated that whereas men's levels of stress dropped after re-entering the workforce after redundancy, their wives' strain remained high. They suggest that women may act as 'shock absorbers', taking on the men's stress. Although the notion that women may be more vulnerable to stress than men is not well established, it does appear that the relevance of the family as a direct source of stress is stronger for women than for men. There is also evidence that people differ in the way they can read others. Haviland and Malatesta (1981) found that women were more vulnerable to emotional contagion than men.

Recent studies of dual-career families found bidirectional crossover effects of stress or strain of similar magnitude from husbands to wives and from wives to husbands (Barnett *et al.*, 1995; Hammer *et al.*, 1997, 2003; Mauno and Kinnunen, 2002; Westman and Etzion, 1995; Westman and Vinokur, 1998; Westman and Etzion, in press). To illustrate, Westman and Etzion (1995) demonstrated a crossover of burnout from career officers to their spouses and vice versa, after controlling husband's and wife's own job stress. Hammer *et al.* (1997) also found a bidirectional crossover of work–family conflict from husbands to wives and vice versa. Similarly, Westman and Etzion (in press) found a bidirectional crossover of work–family conflict between air force women and their spouses. These were cross-sectional studies, but the bidirectional nature of the crossover effect has also been demonstrated in studies using longitudinal designs. Barnett *et al.* (1995), Westman and Vinokur (1998) and Westman, Etzion and Horovitz (2004) found bidirectional crossover of distress, depression and anxiety from husbands to wives and from wives to husbands using longitudinal designs.

At the same time, some researchers detected only unidirectional crossover from husbands to wives. To illustrate, Jones and Fletcher (1993a) found transmission of husbands' job demands on wives' anxiety and depression after controlling wives' job stress. However, they did not find such an effect from wives to husbands, perhaps because the women in their sample did not experience high levels of stress and there was therefore no transmission to their husbands. Similarly, Westman *et al.* (2001) and Westman, Vinokur, Hamilton and Roziner (2004) found crossover of burnout and marital dissatisfaction from husbands to wives but not from wives to husbands.

Evidence concerning gender differences in the crossover process is mixed. Considering the inconsistency of the results concerning the role of gender in the crossover process, and bearing in mind that gender is often confounded with occupation, status and culture, the role of gender needs to be re-examined in the context of single- versus dual-career earners as well as in terms of traditional versus modern gender role ideology. The study of Russian officers and their wives (Westman, Vinokur, Hamilton and Roziner 2004) demonstrating a strong crossover of marital dissatisfaction from husband to wives but no crossover from wives to husbands exemplifies the dual-career family with a relatively traditional gender role ideology (Olson and Matskovsky, 1994). Conversely, Mauno and Kinnunen (1999) found no gender differences in their study of couples and relate this finding to the fact that in Finland the roles of women and men are relatively equal compared to other countries. This among other findings indicates that culture should be considered in research on cohabiting couples.

POSITIVE CROSSOVER

Westman (2001) has suggested broadening the definition of crossover into contagion of positive as well as negative events. All the reviewed studies investigated negative crossover, such as when job stress of one spouse affects the stress or strain of the other. Crossover studies to date have investigated crossover of negative emotions and states, including job stress, depression, dissatisfaction, burnout, anxiety and work–family conflict (for a review see Westman, 2001). One possible reason for the neglect of the possibility of positive crossover is that stress research relies heavily on medical models, with their emphasis on negative effects, just as negative affectivity was investigated for many years before researchers broadened their interest to positive affectivity.

The empathy definitions mentioned before allow for the sharing of both positive and negative emotions. If the crossover process operates via empathy, one would expect to find not only negative crossover but positive crossover as well. Thus, empathy could just as easily involve the sharing of another's positive emotions and the conditions that bring them about. Positive experiences and feelings are not merely the absence of stress; they are qualitatively different experiences (Fredrickson, 2001; Fredrickson and Joiner, 2002). Thus, positive events and emotions may also cross over to the partner and have a positive impact on his or her well-being.

Investigating the issue of positive crossover, Etzion and Westman (2001) examined the effect of a two-week organized tour abroad on crossover of burnout between spouses. Though they did not detect positive crossover, they did find an ameliorating impact of the vacation on the crossover of burnout. Whereas they demonstrated a crossover of burnout before vacation, no significant crossover effect was found after the vacation. These findings indicate that positive events such as vacations, or a change from a stressful environment to a tranquil one, may stop the vicious circle of crossover of strain from one spouse to another.

Only one study (Bakker *et al.*, 2005) detected crossover of work engagement (vigor and dedication) among partners in a study of 323 couples working in a variety of occupations. The crossover relationships were significant, also after controlling for characteristics of the work and home environment of both partners. These findings expand previous crossover research, particularly by showing that positive experiences at work may be transferred to the home domain.

One can think of many instances of positive crossover, such as enjoyable experiences at one's job leading to the crossover of job satisfaction and engagement, eliciting a good mood in the partner at home. Similarly, supportive family relationships and attitudes can create positive crossover to the work setting. Altogether, positive crossover appears to be a fertile field for enhancing theoretical thinking and making practical contributions to the literature.

THEORETICAL IMPLICATIONS

The literature reviewed supports the theoretical and practical relevance of the proposed model. Overall, it seems feasible based on the existing evidence, though additional research is needed to test it more directly, particularly with regard to certain moderators and suggested additional underlying mechanisms. To investigate the crossover process thoroughly we have to examine three phases of relationships in the causal chain: the relationships between the individual's stress and strain; the work–family links – the level of spillover, compensation or segmentation for the same individual; and the crossover of one's stress to his/her partner. Each phase is a necessary but not sufficient condition for the next, because of the mediating variables that may intervene in each relationship. As our model and findings show, the social interaction has a strong impact on the crossover process. Though investigating all these relationships sequentially within one study is an ambitious undertaking, it will shed light on the crossover process, eliciting ample opportunities to buffer this chain of influence, whether in the two intra-individual phases or at the inter-individual level.

This model is proposed as an exploratory tool that can help to close the gap in our knowledge of the ways in which work influences family life and vice versa. The effect of a job demand and or life events may be multiple, affecting the individual, a spouse, family members, friends, managers and co-workers. Furthermore, findings of crossover reinforce the idea that a more complete understanding of the relationship between family and work stress may be achieved by changing the unit of study from the individual to the family and the work team.

The role theory model has interesting methodological implications for studying the crossover of a stressful event that starts at work, is transferred from the employee to spouse and to other employees, then from the spouse to others in the family. This is a study of a 'network crossover effect' of a stressful event through various direct and indirect layers of the workgroup and family. The full scenario includes reciprocal effects recurring over time.

Furthermore, whereas crossover is usually defined and studied as a transmission of stress, it is suggested that the scope of its definition and investigation should be broadened to include the transmission of positive events or feelings as well. Future crossover studies should incorporate the crossover processes of positive affect and related experiences.

In the past few years there has been growing interest in the field of positive psychology, which includes topics such as optimism, happiness, love and support. The investigation of positive crossover can add to theoretical thinking and broaden the current boundaries of crossover models. It also carries many practical implications, as suggested by Westman (2001): for example, positive actions taken by management may contribute to additional positive outcomes that have not been originally planned, including eliciting good mood and satisfaction in the employee's team members and spouse.

The focus of crossover research should be extended in the family from the spouse to also include children, emphasizing the serious implications crossover has on children (e.g., Repetti, 1994; Repetti and Wood, 1997; Barling *et al.*, 1998). Furthermore, it should also be extended from the family milieu, where the vast majority of crossover studies have been conducted, to the workplace. As suggested by Westman (2001), the work team is a venue eminently conducive to the development of relations characterized by crossover, and the identification of both positive and negative crossover in the workplace has crucial theoretical and practical implications. So far, only three studies have examined crossover in the work setting (Bakker *et al.*, 2001; Bakker and Schaufeli, 2000; Westman and Etzion, 1999) and this new research domain needs further investigation.

Information about the couple as a dyad adds to our understanding of well-being in husbands and wives above and beyond that provided by information about the individual. Thompson and Walker (1982) pointed out that for research to be dyadic the problem must be conceptualized at the level of the relationship and the analysis must be interpersonal. The focus must be on the pattern of the responses between the two individuals. Crossover research suffers from a paucity of findings specifying the relationship between one person's stress and strain and the partner's stress and strain. There is a need for systematic research of the individual and societal conditions under which one or another form of crossover is more likely to emerge.

PRACTICAL IMPLICATIONS

Sandler *et al.* (1997) suggest that the first step in developing interventions for preventing the adverse consequences of stress is to evaluate conceptual models of the explanatory pathways. The findings of some crossover studies are based on a conceptual model with explicit pathways and therefore offer an important direction for the design of future interventions for couples experiencing stress and strain. Some of these findings suggest that such interventions should focus on the reduction of social undermining as it is found to be a powerful mediator of the adverse impact of stress on strain.

From the organizational perspective, the ripple effect of stress and strain has far-reaching implications. Because of the important role of coping in the crossover process, special attention should be paid to the appropriate coping strategies to buffer crossover. The result of such attention might be more effective employees and happier families.

Findings also suggest that efforts to reduce the stress and strain of employees should target their spouses too. It would be advisable for management to provide assistance programs to individuals working in stressful conditions and their spouses. Some of the findings demonstrate that a distressed wife is likely to generate a process of social undermining that will have an adverse effect on the husband and then later, through the husband, on herself. It appears that if a distressed spouse is not part of the solution, he or she is likely to become a big part of the problem. Thus, what is needed are programs that train and counsel couples in developing skills for reducing negative interactions and enhancing their relationships (Markman *et al.*, 1994). The primary objective of such programs is prevention and ongoing improved functioning, achieved by focusing on techniques designed to help couples manage negative affect and handle conflict situations constructively.

REFERENCES

Abbey, A., Abramis, D. J., and Caplan, R. D. (1985). Effects of different sources of social support and social conflict on well-being. *Basic and Applied Social Psychology*, 6, 111–129.

Antonovsky, A. (1979). *Health, stress and coping*. San Francisco: Jossey-Bass.

Bakker, A. B., and Schaufeli, W. B. (2000). Burnout contagion processes among teachers. *Journal of Applied Social Psychology*, *30*, 2289–2308.

Bakker, A. B., Schaufeli, W. B., Sixma, H. J., and Bosweld, D. (2001). Burnout contagion among general practitioners. *Journal of Social and Clinical Psychology*, *20*, 82–98.

Bakker, A. B., Demerouti, E., and Schaufeli, W. B. (2005). The crossover of burnout and work engagement among working couples. *Human Relations*, *58*, 661–689.

Bandura, A. (1969). *Principles of behavior modification*. New York: Holt, Rinehart, & Winston.

Barling, J., DuPre, K., and Hepburn, C. (1998). Effects of parents' job insecurity on children's work beliefs and attitudes. *Journal of Applied Psychology*, *83*, 112–118.

Barnett, R. C. (1998). Toward a review and reconceptualization of the work/family literature. *Genetic, Social, and General Psychology Monographs*, *124*, 125–182.

Barnett, R, C., Raudenbush, S. W., Brennan, R. T., Pleck, J. H., and Marshall, N. L. (1995). Changes in job and marital experience and change in psychological distress: a longitudinal study of dual-earner couples. *Journal of Personality and Social Psychology*, *69*, 839–850.

Beehr, T. A. (1995). *Psychological stress in the workplace*. London: Routledge.

Beehr, T. A., Johnson, L. B., and Nieva, R. (1995). Occupational stress: coping of police and their spouses. *Journal of Organizational Psychology*, *16*, 3–25.

Berkowitz, L. (1989). Frustration–aggression hypothesis: examination and reformulation. *Psychological Bulletin*, *106*, 59–73.

Bolger, N., DeLongis, A., Kessler, R., and Wethington, E. (1989). The contagion of stress across multiple roles. *Journal of Marriage and the Family*, *51*, 175–183.

Bronfenbrenner, U. (1977). Toward an experimental ecology of human development. *American Psychologist*, *32*, 513–531.

Burke, R., J. (2004). Workaholism, self-esteem, and motives for money. *Psychological Reports*, *94*, 457–463.

Burke, R. J., Weir, T., and DuWors, R. E. (1980). Work demands on administrators and spouse well-being. *Human Relations*, *33*, 253–278.

Burke, R. J., Brief, A. P., and George, J. M. (1993). The role of negative affectivity in understanding relations between self-report of stressors and strains: a comment on the applied psychology literature. *Journal of Applied Psychology*, *78*, 402–412.

Conger, R. D., Lorenz, R. O., Edler, G. H., Simons, R. L., and Xiaojia, G. E. (1993). Husband and wife differences in response to undesirable life events. *Journal of Health and Social Behavior*, *34*, 71–88.

Coyne, J. C., and Downey, G. (1991). Social factors and psychopathology: stress, social support, and coping processes. *Annual Review of Psychology*, *42*, 401–425.

Crossfield, S., Kinman, G., and Jones, F. (2005). Crossover of occupational stress in dual-career couples: the role of work demands, supports, job commitment and marital communication. *Community, Work, and Family*, *8*, 211–232.

Crouter, A. (1984). Spillover from family to work: the neglected side of work–family interface. *Human Relations*, *37*, 425–442.

Crouter, A. C., Perry-Jenkins, M., Huston, T. L., and Crawford, D. W. (1989). The influence of work-induced psychological states on behavior at home. *Basic and Applied Social Psychology*, *10*, 273–292.

Digman, J. M. (1990). Personality structure: emergence of the five-factor model. *Psychological Assessment*, *41*, 417–440.

Dubin, R. (1973). Work and nonwork: institutional perspectives. In M. D. Dunnette (ed.), *Work and nonwork in the year 2001* (pp. 53–68). Belmont, CA: Wadsworth.

Duffy, M., Ganster, D., and Pagon, M. (2002). Social undermining in the workplace. *Academy of Management Journal*, *45*, 331–351.

Edwards, J. R., and Baglioni, A. J. (1991). Relationship between type A behavior pattern and mental and physical symptoms: a comparison of global and component measures. *Journal of Applied Psychology*, *76*, 276–290.

Edwards, J. R., Baglioni, A. J., and Cooper, C. L. (1990). Stress, type-A, coping, and psychological and physical symptoms: a multi-sample test of alternative models. *Human Relations*, *43*, 919–956.

Etzion, D., and Westman, M. (2001). Vacation and the crossover of strain between spouses: stopping the vicious cycle. *Man and Work*, *11*, 106–118.

Fredrickson, B. (2001). The role of positive emotions in the positive psychology: the broaden-and-build theory of positive emotions. *American Psychologist*, *56*, 218–226.

Fredrickson, B., and Joiner, T. (2002). Positive emotions trigger upward spirals toward emotional well-being. *Psychology Science*, *13*, 172–175.

Hammer, L. B., Allen, E., and Grigsby, T. D. (1997). Work–family conflict in dual-earner couples: within individual and crossover effects of work and family. *Journal of Vocational Behavior*, *50*, 185–203.

Hammer, L. B., Bauer, T., and Grandey, A. (2003). Work–family conflict and work-related withdrawal behaviors. *Journal of Business and Psychology*, *17*, 419–436.

Haviland, J. M., and Malatesta, C. Z. (1981). The development of sex differences in nonverbal signals: fallacies, facts and fantasies. In C. Mayo and N. M. Henley (eds), *Gender and nonverbal behavior* (pp. 183–208). New York: Springer-Verlag.

Hobfoll, S. E., and London, P. (1986). The relationship of self concept and social support to emotional distress among women during war. *Journal of Social Clinical Psychology*, *12*, 87–100.

Hobfoll, S. E., Dunahoo, C. L., Ben-Porat, Y., and Monnier (1994). Gender and coping: the dual-axis model of coping. *American Journal of Community Psychology*, *22*, 49–82.

House, J. S. (1981). *Job stress and social support*. Reading, MA: Addison-Wesley.

Jackson, S. E., and Maslach, C. (1982). After-effects of job-related stress: families as victims. *Journal of Occupational Behavior*, *3*, 63–77.

Jackson, S. E., Zedeck, S., and Summers, E. (1985). Family life disruptions: effects of job-induced structural and emotional interference. *Academy of Management Journal*, *28*, 574–586.

Jex, S. M., and Beehr, T. A. (1991). Emerging theoretical and methodological issues in the study of work-related stress. *Research in Personnel and Human Resources Management*, *9*, 311–365.

Johnson, A., and Jackson, P. (1998). A longitudinal investigation into the experience of male managers who have re-entered the workforce after redundancy, and their families. In *Proceedings of the International Work Psychology Conference*, Sheffield, July.

Jones, E., and Fletcher, B. (1993a). An empirical study of occupational stress transmission in working couples. *Human Relations*, *46*, 881–902.

Jones, E., and Fletcher, B. (1993b). Transmission of occupational stress: a study of daily fluctuations in work stress and strain and their impact on marital partners. In H. Schroder, K. Rescke, M. Johnston and S. Maes (eds), *Health psychology: Potential diversity* (pp. 328–338). Regensburg: Roderer Verlag.

Jones, E., and Fletcher, B. (1996). Taking work home: a study of daily fluctuations in work stressors, effects on mood and impact on marital partners. *Journal of Occupational and Organizational Psychology*, *69*, 89–106.

Kahn, R. L., and Byosiere, P. (1992). Stress in organizations. In D. Dunnette and L. M. Hough (eds), *Handbook of industrial and organizational psychology* (pp. 571–651). Palo Alto, CA: Consulting Psychology Press.

Kahn, J. P., Coyne, J. C., and Margolin, G. (1985). Depression and marital disagreement: the social construction of despair. *Journal of Social and Personal Relationships*, *2*, 447–461.

Kahn, R. L., Wolfe, D. M., Quinn, R. P., Snoek, J. D., and Rosenthal, R. A. (1964). *Organizational Stress*. New York: Wiley.

Kessler, R. C. (1979). A strategy for studying differential vulnerability to the psychological consequences of stress. *Journal of Health and Social Behavior*, *20*, 100–108.

Kessler, R. C., and McLeod, J. D. (1984). Sex differences in vulnerability to undesirable life events. *American Sociological Review*, *49*, 620–631.

Lambert, S. J. (1990). Processing linking work and family: a critical review and research agenda. *Human Relations*, *43*, 239–257.

Lazarus, R. S. (1991). *Emotion and adaptation*. New York: Oxford University Press.

Levenson, R., and Ruef, A. (1992). Empathy: a physiological substrate. *Journal of Personality and Social Psychology*, *63*, 234–246.

Long, N. R., and Voges, K. E. (1987). Can wives perceive the source of their husbands' occupational stress? *Journal of Occupational Psychology*, *60*, 235–242.

MacEwen, K., Barling, J., and Kelloway, K. (1992). Effects of short-term role overload on marital interactions. *Work and Stress*, *6*, 117–126.

Markman, H. J., Renick, M. J., Floyd, F., and Stanley, S. M. (1994). Preventing marital distress through effective communication and conflict management: a four- and five-year follow-up. *Journal of Consulting and Clinical Psychology*, *61*, 70–77.

Mauno, S., and Kinnunen, U. (1999). The effects of job stressors on marital satisfaction among Finnish dual-earner couples. *Journal of Organizational Behavior*, *20*, 879–895.

Mitchell, R., Cronkite, R., and Moos, R. (1983). Stress, coping and depression among married couples. *Journal of Abnormal Psychology*, *92*, 433–448.

Monier, J., and Hobfoll. S. (1997). Crossover effects of communal coping. *Journal of Social and Personal Relations*, *14*, 263–270.

Nelson, G., and Beach, S. (1990). Sequential interaction in depression: effects of depressive behavior on spousal aggression. *Behavior Therapy*, *21*, 167–182.

Olson, D. H., and Matskovsky, M. S. (1994). Soviet and American families: a comparative overview. In J. W. Maddock, M. J. Hogan, A. I. Anatolyi and M. S. Matskovsky (eds), *Families before and after perestroika: Russian and U.S. perspectives* (pp. 9–35). New York: Guilford.

Pavett, C. M. (1986). High-stress professions: satisfaction, stress, and well-being of spouses of professionals. *Human Relations*, *39*, 1141–1154.

Pearlin, L., and Turner, H. A. (1987). The family as a context of the stress process.

In S. Kasl and C. Cooper (eds), *Stress and health: Issues in research methodology.* New York: Wiley.

Piotrkowski, C. (1979). *Work and the family system: A naturalistic study of the working-class and lower-middle-class families.* New York: Free Press.

Repetti, R. L. (1994). Short-term and long-term processes linking job stressors to father–child interaction. *Social Development, 3*(1), 1–15.

Repetti, R. L., and Wood, J. (1997). Effects of daily stress at work on mother's interactions with preschoolers. *Journal of Family Psychology, 11*(1), 90–108.

Riley, D., and Eckenrode, J. (1986). Social ties: costs and benefits within different subgroups. *Journal of Personality and Social Psychology, 51,* 770–778.

Rook, S. K. (1984). The negative side of social interaction: impact on psychological well-being. *Journal of Personality and Social Psychology, 46,* 1097–1108.

Rook, S. K., Dooley, D., and Catalano, R. (1991). Stress transmission: the effects of husbands' job stressors on emotional health of their wives. *Journal of Marriage and the Family, 53,* 165–177.

Russell, D. W., and Cutrona, C. E. (1991). Social support, stress, and depressive symptoms among the elderly: test of a process model. *Psychology and Aging, 6,* 190–201.

Sandler, I. N., Wolchik, S. A., MacKinnon, D., Ayers, T. S., and Roosa, M. W. (1997). Developing linkages between theory and intervention in stress and coping processes. In S. A. Wolchik and I. N. Sandler (eds), *Handbook of children's coping: Linking theory and intervention* (pp. 3–40). New York: Plenum.

Schaefer, C., Coyne, J. C., and Lazarus, R. S. (1981). The health-related functions of social support. *Journal of Behavioral Medicine, 4,* 381–406.

Schmaling, K., and Jacobson, N. (1990). Marital interaction and depression. *Journal of Abnormal Psychology, 99,* 229–236.

Spector, P. E., and O'Connell, B. J. (1994). The contribution of personality traits, negative affectivity, locus of control and type A to the subsequent reports of job stressors and job strains. *Journal of Occupational and Organizational Psychology, 67,* 1–12.

Staines, G. L. (1980). Spillover versus compensation: a review of the literature on the relationship between work and nonwork. *Human Relations, 33,* 111–129.

Starcevic, V., and Piontek, C. M. (1997). Empathic understanding revisited: conceptualization, controversies and limitations. *American Journal of Psychotherapy, 51,* 317–328.

Stotland, E. (1969). Exploratory investigations of empathy. In L. Berkowitz (ed.), *Advances in experimental social psychology* (Vol. 4, pp. 271–314). New York: Academic Press.

Thompson, L., and Walker, A. J. (1982). The dyad as a unit of analysis: conceptual and methodological issues. *Journal of Marriage and the Family, 44,* 889–900.

Vinokur, A., and van Ryn, M. (1993). Social support and undermining in close relationships: their independent effects on mental health of unemployed persons. *Journal of Personality and Social Psychology, 65,* 350–359.

Vinokur, A., Price, R. H., and Caplan, R. D. (1996). Hard times and hurtful partners: how financial strain affects depression and relationship satisfaction of unemployed persons and their spouses. *Journal of Personality and Social Psychology, 71,* 166–179.

Watson, D., and Clark, L. E. (1984). Negative affectivity: the disposition to experience aversive emotional states. *Psychological Bulletin, 96,* 465–498.

Watson, D., Pennbaker, J. E., and Folger, R. (1986). Beyond negative affectivity: measuring stress and satisfaction in the work place. *Journal of Organizational Behavior Management, 8,* 141–157.

Westman, M. (2001). Stress and strain crossover. *Human Relations, 54,* 557–591.

Westman, M., and Etzion, D. (1995). Crossover of stress, strain and resources from one spouse to another. *Journal of Organizational Behavior, 16,* 169–181.

Westman, M., and Etzion, D. (1999) The crossover of strain from school principals to teachers and vice versa. *Journal of Occupational Health Psychology, 4,* 269–278.

Westman, M., and Etzion, D. (in press). The crossover of work–family conflict from one spouse to another. *Journal of Applied Social Pychology.*

Westman, M., and Vinokur, A. (1998). Unraveling the relationship of distress levels within couples: common stressors, emphatic reactions, or crossover via social interactions? *Human Relations, 51,* 137–156.

Westman, M, Etzion, D., and Danon, E. (2001). Job insecurity and crossover of burnout in married couples. *Journal of Organizational Behavior, 22,* 467–481.

Westman, M., Etzion, D., and Horovitz, S. (2004). The toll of unemployment does not stop with the unemployed. *Human Relations, 57,* 823–844.

Westman, M., Vinokur, A., Hamilton, L., and Roziner, I. (2004). Crossover of marital dissatisfaction during downsizing: a study of Russian army officers and their spouses. *Journal of Applied Psychology, 89,* 769–779.

Zedeck, S. (1992). Introduction: exploring the domain of work and family concerns. In S. Zedeck (ed.), *Work, families and organizations* (pp. 1–32). San Francisco: Jossey-Bass.

8 Work stress and health behaviors: a work–life balance issue

Fiona Jones, Gail Kinman and Nicola Payne

Early work on spillover (discussed in Chapter 3) suggested that work may impact on the non-work domain in terms of time, strain and behavior (Staines, 1980). For example, it may affect the *time* people have available for family and friends, it may lead them to experience *strain* even when they are not at work or it may influence their *behavior* when at home. All of these aspects of spillover have the potential to affect the extent to which individuals engage in healthy and unhealthy behaviors (such as physical activity, healthy eating, smoking and drinking alcohol). Inactive employees may be physically inactive in their private lives, overworked employees may have less time to exercise or cook healthy meals or may place less priority on health practices when under stress (Griffin *et al.*, 1993). Alternatively, health behaviors may be used as methods of coping (Ingledew *et al.*, 1996). For example, people may drink alcohol or smoke in order to regulate their feelings of arousal as a result of the strains of work. These possibilities were seldom considered in the early spillover research. However, in recent years, with the expansion in health psychology research, there has been growing interest in the role of health behavior as a potential mechanism whereby stressors may impact on health outcomes such as cardiovascular disease (Steptoe, 1991).

Although studies have increasingly examined the impact of work stress on health behavior, this area of research is typically not seen as relevant to the work–life balance debate. Employers have generally only concerned themselves with those aspects of health behaviors of employees which directly affect either the work environment or work performance, such as alcohol consumption, smoking and drug use. However, this chapter will present the argument that, given the increasing erosion of boundaries between work and home life, it is in the interests of both employer and employee to ensure that the design of work and of work environments facilitates healthy rather than health-damaging behavior.

This chapter will briefly present the ways in which health behaviors may play a role in coping with work stress. It will then discuss evidence drawn from studies that have looked at multiple health behaviors and their relationships with work stressors. The impacts of work stress on a number of specific health behaviors, including drinking, smoking, exercise and healthy eating, will then be considered. The possible mechanisms for these relationships will be discussed. Finally, workplace health promotion interventions to improve health behaviors will be considered.

HEALTH BEHAVIOR AND COPING

Lazarus and Folkman (1984) have suggested that the kind of coping employed by individuals in any situation is dependent on their appraisal of the threat of the situation. They distinguish between two types of appraisal: *primary and secondary appraisal. Primary appraisal* is the process by which the person evaluates the potential threat imposed by the stressor. *Secondary appraisal* is the process by which the individual evaluates what can be done to prevent or reduce harm. Thus, health behaviors may be important during the secondary appraisal process as they may be included in an individual's repertoire of coping strategies. Coping theorists have identified two main types of coping strategy: problem focused and emotion focused (Carver *et al.*, 1989; Lazarus and Folkman, 1984). Problem-focused coping consists of strategies designed to address a specific stressor, such as action planning or seeking advice. Emotion-focused coping is designed to deal with the emotion aroused by the stressor and may include strategies such as denial, seeking distraction or use of drugs and alcohol, smoking or comfort eating. The latter are regarded as escapist or avoidant forms of coping (Folkman and Lazarus, 1988). While it is easy to view problem-focused coping as a more adaptive form of coping and much research has supported this view (Holahan *et al.*, 1996), there are situations in which emotion-focused coping may be useful in dealing with acute stressors (Lazarus, 1993).

One of the most commonly used measures of coping, the COPE scale (Carver *et al.*, 1989), includes measures of alcohol and drug disengagement, but other health behaviors such as eating and exercise are not considered. However, work by Ingledew *et al.* (1996) has highlighted the role of these additional health behaviors as coping strategies in their own right. They have suggested that exercise, eating and self-care behaviors are distinct dimensions with coping functions that may differ from those of emotion and problem-focused coping.

Typically, measures such as the COPE deal with reactive coping, i.e., coping strategies used after a stressful event to alleviate tension. They therefore neglect the potentially important role of proactive or preventive coping (Aspinwall and Taylor, 1997). This may function by influencing primary appraisal of a stressor (i.e., an individual's evaluation of the potential harm or benefit of a stressor). Ingledew *et al.* suggest that health-enhancing behaviors may also be seen as a form of preventive coping whereby the individual builds up resources (i.e., stamina and good health) that will enable them to cope better with future demands. Someone taking on a particularly stressful work role may, for example, try to make time for increased physical activity to ensure that they have the energy and stamina to cope with the demands they are about to face. These effects have, however, seldom been explored.

EFFECTS OF WORK STRESS ON HEALTH BEHAVIORS

In many studies that examine relationships between stressors and health outcomes, such as cardiovascular disease, the role of health behaviors in causing disease is recognized and taken into account. Typically, however, health behaviors are viewed as risk factors in their own right that are unrelated to work. Thus health behaviors are controlled for rather than examined as variables which may themselves be the result of work stressors and which may be part of the coping response. However, in recent years a range of studies have begun to examine the extent to which work stress predicts health behavior. A number of major studies focusing on a range of health behaviors will be considered below, followed by a discussion of literature that has focused in more depth on specific health behaviors.

Some studies have focused on the impact of general perceived stress on health behaviors. In such studies it is not possible to distinguish the effects of work stressors as opposed to other life stressors. Nevertheless, where employee samples are used it is likely that stress perceptions encompass work issues. These studies typically show that stress has a negative effect on a range of health behaviors. Ng and Jeffery (2003), for example, drew on surveys of 12,110 working people (based in 26 US worksites) and found that high perceptions of stress were associated with higher-fat diet, less frequent exercise and more cigarette smoking. They found no association between perceived stress and alcohol consumption. A UK-based workplace study of perceived stress (Heslop *et al.*, 2001) found similar results to Ng and Jeffrey in relation to smoking and exercise for men, but stress was not related to exercise behavior in women. Unlike Ng and Jeffrey, however, this study also found that stress was linked to higher alcohol consumption.

Research specifically focusing on the effects of work stress on health behavior has frequently drawn on one particular theoretical framework: the job strain model (Karasek, 1979). This suggests that strain is predicted by a combination of job demands and job control. The model suggests four types of job, based on different combinations of demand and control. A 'high-strain' job, likely to predispose the employee to poor physical and psychological well-being, is one which is low in control but high in demand. The opposite combination, a job that is high in control and low in demand, is thought to be 'low strain'. Two alternative types of job are the 'active job', which is high in both demand and control, and the 'passive job', which is low in both demand and control. While the active job may lead the individual to develop new behaviors (both at work and outside of work), the passive job may lead to learned helplessness and reduced activity. This model suggests clear hypotheses in terms of job strain and health behaviors. Thus high-strain jobs might be expected to lead to increases in the stress-relieving health behaviors of drinking and smoking; they may also reduce more positive, but time-consuming and energy-demanding, health behaviors of healthy eating and exercise. Active jobs may lead to similarly active lifestyles, while passive jobs may lead to passive lifestyles. This latter link has been demonstrated in a study by Karasek *et al.* (1987), in which workers whose jobs were enriched increased their participation in non-work pursuits, including study and political activities.

Since the early 1990s a number of large community studies based on the job strain framework have shown that these work characteristics were related to a range of health behaviors (e.g., Hellerstedt and Jeffery, 1997; Johannson *et al.*, 1991; Lallukka *et al.*, 2004). The nature of the relationships found, however, was often complex and differed for men and women. Johannson *et al.* (1991), for example, used the model to predict smoking and exercise/sedentary behavior using data obtained from telephone interviews with over 7000 people in Sweden. The study found that job demands (such as shift work, physical demands and unpleasant working conditions) tended to be related to increased smoking and sedentary behavior, whereas control (over timing and methods of work) was related to increased exercise. Relationships were slightly different for men and women, with psychological demands increasing the likelihood of both smoking and sedentary behavior amongst women only.

Hellerstedt and Jeffery (1997) also found different relationships for men and women in a study of smoking, exercise and fat intake in 4000 employees at US worksites. In terms of the job types given above, male smokers in high-strain jobs smoked more than those in other jobs. Women in high-strain jobs tended to have higher body mass indices than women in other job types. Also consistent with the job strain model, men in passive jobs took less exercise than other men, while women in active jobs engaged in more exercise than other women; however, if they were smokers, they also tended to smoke more. When the specific job characteristics were examined, other significant relationships were found. High levels of control were linked to higher levels of exercise for men and women, whereas high levels of demand were linked to a number of smoking-related variables for both genders and a high fat intake for women only.

Weidner *et al.* (1997) also found gender differences using a combined measure of health behaviors. Specifically, overall much stronger relationships were found between job demands and control and for men than for women. The authors suggested this is because most of the women were married and had families. Hence work factors were only one of several potential stressors for women. In contrast, Lallukka *et al.* (2004) found that job strain was associated with eating, smoking and physical activity for women only. Low-strain jobs were associated with healthier behavior on all these variables. Associations were, however, typically weak. They also found that active jobs were related to positive effects in terms of healthier eating for women. Overall, while the findings in the studies discussed in this section are often somewhat inconsistent and varied between studies and across genders and health behaviors, they do give a general picture of high-strain jobs being associated with various damaging health behaviors.

The above research has focused on stressful work characteristics that are likely to be relatively stable. It is also likely that other more acute features of the work environment may have a negative impact on health behaviors. Major disturbances in routine such as changes in working conditions or change in job responsibilities may also be stressful and lead to disrupted health behaviors. Furthermore, on a day-to-day basis, minor hassles are likely to be distressing and disrupt routines.

The impact of major events on health behaviors is demonstrated in a number of studies (e.g. Melamed *et al.*, 1997; Rose *et al.*, 1998). For example, Rose *et al.* looked at 1000 Swedish male employees in the motor industry. They found that negative life events, particularly work events, were associated with mental strain and depressed mood, which, in turn, was associated with increased alcohol consumption in white-collar workers and increased smoking in blue-collar workers. In general, there was more evidence of work-related life events affecting white-collar than blue-collar workers.

The effects of daily hassles on health behaviors were demonstrated in a daily diary study conducted in the UK by Steptoe *et al.* (1998). This drew on the hassles and uplifts approach of (Lazarus and Folkman, 1989) and looked at relationships between daily hassles, exercise, alcohol and food consumption. The hassles measured included 10 work-related and 10 home-related hassles. During the course of the study, 44 nurses and teachers completed daily questionnaires for eight weeks. Findings revealed that work hassles were greater than home hassles. The two highest and two lowest stress weeks were identified for each participant based on their perceptions of stress. The authors found that, compared to low-stress weeks, consumption of 'fast foods' increased during high-stress weeks. Cheese consumption also increased, but only for those who used foods to regulate their mood. Sweet foods were eaten at a relatively high level by individuals who chose foods to regulate mood, irrespective of stress. However, other people increased their intake only when feeling under pressure. In addition, alcohol consumption increased in high-stress weeks but only for individuals who drank alcohol as a way of coping with stress. Stress did not affect exercise behavior in general, but people who used exercise to regulate mood engaged in more exercise overall. This study sheds light on the ways health behaviors may be used as a form of emotion-focused coping.

Few studies have examined how work–life balance issues impact on health behaviors. However, a study by Metcalfe *et al.* (2003) does consider the effects of frequent job changes: a factor which they consider to be a consequence of the changing patterns of work and the increased flexibility of the workplace. They found that men and women who had changed jobs more frequently were more likely to smoke, consume more alcohol and exercise less.

These studies provide evidence that a range of aspects of work do indeed impact on health behaviors; they also highlight ways in which different health behaviors respond to job stressors and the complexity of relationships found. Interrelationships between different types of health behavior are also indicated in these studies; for example, the relationship between smoking and sedentary behavior (Johansson *et al.*, 1991). Nevertheless, in order to highlight specific risk factors and consider potential interventions, it is useful to consider evidence related to each behavior independently. In the following sections four key types of health behaviors – drinking, smoking, eating and exercise – will be considered in more detail. Concluding sections will then consider the mechanisms for these relationships and the implications for managers, professionals and researchers.

ALCOHOL CONSUMPTION

Studies conducted in the UK, Australia, Canada and the USA over the last decade have highlighted the prevalence, severity and cost of alcohol abuse (Alcohol Concern, 2003; Collins and Lapsley, 1996; Harwood, 2000; Single *et al.*, 1998). The majority of adults who are at risk for alcohol problems are employed (Roman and Blum, 2002); consequently the misuse of alcohol is a serious problem for organizations. Alcohol abuse can lead to, for example, employee ill health, absenteeism, premature retirement, high turnover rates, reduced productivity, poor interpersonal relations with co-workers and customers, increased levels of error-making and workplace accidents and impaired customer safety (Bertera, 1991; Bhattacherjee *et al.*, 2004; Blum, *et al.*, 1993; Bush and Autry, 2002; Rodgers, 1998). Clearly, the impact of problem drinking is not confined to the workplace; it has been associated with financial problems, homelessness and housing difficulties (Alcohol Concern, 2003) and impaired marital satisfaction, quality and stability (Leonard and Rothbard, 1999; Marshall, 2003).

Some occupations are thought to be at higher than average risk of alcohol abuse: for example, offshore oil and fishing workers (Aiken and McCance, 1982; Sutherland and Flin, 1989); military personnel (Bray *et al.*, 1999); police (Alexander and Walker, 1994; Richmond *et al.*, 1999) and physicians and nurses (BMA, 1993; Plant *et al.*, 1991). The *physical and social availability* of alcohol at the workplace also appears to influence its consumption (Frone, 2000). *Physical availability* refers to the ease with which workers can consume alcohol during working time or during their breaks. Research findings suggest that individuals working in occupations where alcohol is readily available, such as those employed in the hospitality industry, are at particular risk of developing alcohol-related problems (Corsun and Young, 1998; Loughlin and Kayson, 1990; Nusbaumer and Reiling, 2002). *Social availability* relates to the beliefs, values and behaviors about alcohol that are developed and maintained by organizational culture. Some occupations (often those that are male dominated) have 'heavy drinking' cultural norms in which employees use alcohol to reduce boredom and dissatisfaction and maintain solidarity with colleagues (Janes and Ames, 1989). The importance of the social availability of alcohol is highlighted in several studies: for example, Macdonald *et al.* (1999) found that perceptions of a 'drinking' subculture and social pressure to drink were amongst the most significant predictors of problematic alcohol consumption amongst 2468 employed Canadians.

Work stress and alcohol

There is evidence to suggest that characteristics of the work environment are more likely to predict problematic drinking behavior than occupational status or the physical and social availability of alcohol at work. As discussed earlier, drinking alcohol may be used as a form of emotion-focused coping because of its perceived tension-reducing properties (Greeley and Oei, 1999). Perceptions of frequency and severity of work stress have been related to frequency and severity of alcohol consumption (e.g., Ragland *et al.*, 2000). Research discussed earlier also suggests that stressors such as major life events, minor hassles and frequent job changes are related to increased drinking (Metcalfe *et al.*, 2003; Rose *et al.*, 1998; Steptoe *et al.*, 1998). Problem drinking has also been associated with more specific stressors such as low levels of skill discretion and lack of job control (Ames and Janes, 1992; Hemmingsson and Lundberg, 1998; Leigh and Jiang, 1993; Macdonald *et al.*, 1999; Neale, 1993; Roxburgh, 1998). Utilizing the job strain model, prospective studies conducted by Bromet *et al.* (1988) and Crum *et al.* (1995) found that men (but not women) who were working in jobs characterized by high demands and low control were more at risk of alcohol abuse than those in low-strain jobs.

Employee alcohol consumption is not only related to jobs that are unenriched, demanding and lacking in control, but has also been associated with other stressors such as dangerous and/or noxious working conditions, work overload, workplace harassment, interpersonal conflict with supervisors and co-workers, job insecurity, role conflict and frequent working away from home (Frone, 1999; Grieger *et al.*, 2003; Hagihara *et al.*, 2001; Havlovic and Keenan, 1991; Macdonald *et al.*, 1999; Rospenda, 2002).

While many studies have examined direct relationships between job stressors and alcohol, some have failed to produce convincing evidence of such a relationship (e.g., Cooper *et al.*, 1992; Lallukka *et al.*, 2004; Moore *et al.*, 2000). A relationship between work stressors and alcohol abuse may only be found amongst individuals who have particular vulnerabilities and behavioral tendencies: for example, those with fewer personal and social resources (such as social support) and those who hold more favorable beliefs about the effects of drinking alcohol (e.g., Cooper *et al.*, 1992; Harris and Heft, 1992). Furthermore, as discussed above, associations between stressors and alcohol use may only be found amongst individuals who use these behaviors as a way of coping with tension or negative mood engendered by stressors (Steptoe *et al.*, 1998). There is also evidence that employees who report higher frequencies of alcohol use are more likely to use avoidance coping strategies in response to stressors (Nowack and Pentkowski, 1994).

In terms of the work–home interface, research suggests that the combination of workplace and family stressors can contribute to alcohol abuse (e.g., Cohen *et al.*, 1991). A growing body of evidence also indicates that perceived conflict between the work and family domains can directly and indirectly promote alcohol consumption (Bromet *et al.*, 1990; Frone *et al.*, 1993). Conflict between work and family is not unidirectional and it is important to make a conceptual distinction between work interfering with family life and family interfering with work (Barling, 1989). Research that has examined the bidirectional nature of work and family conflict and substance use is scarce, and findings are mixed. Frone *et al.* (1997) followed employed parents over a four-year period and found that conflict between family and work reported in 1989 predicted psychological and physical symptomatology experienced four years later, whereas perceived conflict between work and family was a predictor of heavy drinking. A subsequent survey of 2700 working adults conducted by Frone (2000), however, found that both work-to-family and family-to-work conflict predicted substance dependence.

Utilizing social ecological theory, Grzywacz and Marks (2000) examined relationships between work demands, work–home conflict and problem drinking in a large sample of employed adults. Drawing on the enhancement hypothesis (which indicates that work and family roles are not necessarily in conflict, but can have a salutogenic as well as a pathogenic influence on the employee), the impact of positive as well as negative 'spill-over' was also investigated. Findings indicated that negative person–environment interactions, namely work-related strain and marital disagreements, were associated with problem drinking. Perhaps more interestingly, however, positive spill-over from family to work was related to lower odds of problem drinking, but positive spill-over from work to family was associated with higher odds of problem drinking. The authors suggest that individuals who hold expectations that alcohol is an appropriate way to demonstrate a satisfying job may be more prone to alcohol abuse.

Clearly, evidence suggests that work stressors and work–family conflict are related to increased alcohol consumption. Given the potential of excess alcohol consumption to impact on performance both at home and at work, more specific work–life balance interventions may be important in order to counteract these effects.

SMOKING

Smoking rates have dropped substantially in the USA, Australia and UK since the 1970s nevertheless they remain a cause for concern (Australian Bureau of Statistics, 2000; Centers for Disease Control, 2004; Rickards *et al.*, 2004). For example, around 26% of the UK population smoke and rates have remained relatively stable since the 1990s. US levels are only slightly lower, having reduced from 24% in 1998 to 22.5% in 2002. One in five deaths in the UK is caused by smoking and it is estimated that around one half of smokers will die from a smoking-related disease. The most common smoking-related causes of death are cardiovascular disease, lung cancer and chronic obstructive lung disease. Passive smoking also increases the risk of lung cancer and cardiovascular disease by 25% and around one in five non-smokers are exposed to passive smoking at work (Rickards *et al.*, 2004; Petersen and Peto, 2004).

A large body of research has examined relationships between general life stress and smoking. Since excess smoking does not pose the same problem for performance at work as alcohol abuse, there is far less focus on the work situation or work stressors as a specific cause of smoking behavior. Studies frequently do not differentiate between work and other types of stressors. A comprehensive review of the relationship between stress and smoking was carried out by Kassel *et al.* (2003) and the conclusions are summarized here.

There are a number of possible ways that stress may be associated with smoking. First, it may increase the likelihood of taking up smoking in the first place; second, stress may increase the amount of smoking in those who already smoke; and third, it may affect those trying to stop smoking by causing them to lapse. Kassel *et al.* examine the evidence in relation to each of these stages in the smoking career. In considering the first stage, they suggest that there is strong evidence that taking up smoking, which typically occurs in adolescence, is associated with various indices of stress, including negative life events (e.g., Koval and Pederson, 1999) and perceived stress (Dugan *et al.*, 1999). However, the authors point out that many studies are cross-sectional; therefore smoking may also increase the risk of stress via a tendency for smokers to experience increased depression and negative affect over time. Longitudinal studies offer mixed evidence as to whether symptoms of anxiety and depression pre-date the initiation of smoking.

In relation to the later stages of smoking, where work stress is more likely to be implicated, the review suggests that smokers not only report more stress than non-smokers, but also that smokers smoke more when experiencing stress. This has been found when using relatively objective indicators of work stress (e.g., Hellerstedt and Jeffery, 1997) in addition to laboratory stressors (e.g., Rose *et al.*, 1983). Kassel *et al.* conclude that the studies they reviewed make 'a compelling case that stress increases – that is cues – smoking amongst smokers' (p. 278). They acknowledge, however, that some studies provide conflicting findings. For example, one study by (Shiffman *et al.*, 2002) using ecological momentary assessments (i.e., recording cigarettes smoked and moods throughout the day on a handheld computer) found smoking to be unrelated to mood.

There is stronger evidence for the relationship between stress and lapsing, though much of this is drawn from retrospective studies. Summarizing a number of studies, Kassel *et al.* conclude that between 35% and 100% of smokers say they lapsed while experiencing stress or negative affect. These findings have also been supported using momentary assessments in which participants were asked to make ratings of mood after any lapse (Shiffman *et al.*, 1996). However, Shiffman *et al.* suggest that such findings may not be a result of any stress-reducing properties of smoking, but an outcome of the disrupting effect of stress on self-control (Muraven and Baumeister, 2000).

Overall, Kassel *et al.* conclude that the relationship between stress and smoking is extremely complex. They state that almost all smokers attribute smoking to its calming effects. However, the authors suggest that it remains unclear whether it actually does have such effects. Parrott, for example, has controversially claimed that over time cigarette smoking causes *increased rather than decreased* levels of negative affect and stress (Parrott, 1999). Given the lack of clarity in findings, Kassel *et al.* suggest that mediating and moderating variables (including the environmental situation or the specific emotional state) need to be given more consideration, as it is likely that such factors may influence the relationship between stress and smoking.

Work stress and smoking

A number of the studies discussed earlier have examined the relationship between work stress and smoking alongside other health behaviors. For example, perceptions of high stress in employed samples seem to be related to an increase in smoking (e.g., Heslop *et al.*, 2001; Ng and Jeffery, 2003). High level of job strain was also linked to increased smoking in men (Hellerstedt and Jeffery, 1997). This was consistent with an earlier study of male employees of a chemical plant (Green and Johnson, 1990). However, Lallukka *et al.* (2004) found such relationships for women only and two other studies have also failed to find such relationships for men (Alterman *et al.*, 1994; Reed *et al.*, 1989). Where studies have looked at the independent effects of demands and controls, relationships have also been found between high levels of job demands and smoking (Hellerstedt and Jeffery, 1997; Johannson *et al.*, 1991). One prospective study has followed up men over a three year period and found that an increase in control over that time was associated with reduced smoking (Landsbergis *et al.*, 1998). No such associations were found for alcohol consumption or weight.

While most studies of work stress have used the job strain variables, some have used other approaches. Westman *et al.* (1985), for example, found links between a range of work stressors and increased smoking intensity among smokers. Long hours and lack of peer support were particularly important. Those with long hours, conflict, lack of influence and harsh working conditions were also less likely to give up smoking.

Overall, therefore, despite some inconsistent findings, these studies seem to indicate that there may be clearer links between work stress and smoking than other behaviors. This is perhaps not surprising given that it is a behavior that is easy to engage in, is often associated with relaxation and can often be engaged in during work time. However, Shiffman *et al.* (2002) found that people were less likely to smoke while they were working than at other times. They were most likely to smoke when inactive or engaged in leisure activities, or when at home. This was only partially explained by smoking restrictions that often exist at work. This would seem to suggest that working may help reduce smoking. However, given the volume of studies indicating that work characteristics are related to increased smoking, it is perhaps more likely that work stressors may spill over to lead to more smoking outside of work and in the home environment. This then is likely to be another way in which work impacts on the family (see also Chapter 7). Finally, as in the case of alcohol consumption, conflict between work and family may be an additional stressor that may lead some people to smoke. While research here is limited, Frone *et al.* (1994), found that work–family conflict in a sample of working mothers of adolescents was related to increased cigarette use as well as heavy drinking. Once again this evidence suggests that work–life balance policies may be needed in order to improve health behavior.

EXERCISE

There is increasing evidence of low levels of physical activity in western countries. A study in the UK found that 70% of those surveyed were below an acceptable level of activity that might provide significant health benefits such as protection from cardiovascular disease (HEA, 1992). Other countries have similar concerns; for example, a recent report from Canada found that 56% of Canadian adults are inactive and the numbers who were inactive had increased over the previous six-year period (Craig and Cameron, 2004). Poor physical fitness has been clearly linked to a range of negative physical outcomes including increased mortality (Blair *et al.*, 1989). The benefits of activity include improved cardiovascular health (Whelton *et al.*, 2002) and reduced risk of obesity (US Department of Health and Human Services, 1996) and osteoporosis (Bonaiuti *et al.*, 2002).

Work stress and exercise

There is now strong evidence that exercise also reduces stress, anxiety and depression (for reviews see Mutrie, 2000; Taylor, 2000). In the work context, therefore, exercise is frequently seen as a stress-reducing intervention.

For example, Bruning and Frew (1987) gave employees a 13-week course of stress management, relaxation or exercise. The authors found that exercise had the same effect as the more conventional stress reduction techniques in reducing physiological indicators of stress such as blood pressure and pulse rate. The provision of workplace gyms or other sports facilities is a popular way to encourage exercise and improve employee cardiovascular health. However, currently only a minority of companies provide such facilities. For example, research in Canada found that only 15% of firms offer exercise programs on site (Cameron *et al.*, 2002).

As discussed earlier, any relationship between work stress and exercise may be viewed as due to people using exercise as a coping strategy. Long and Flood (1993) propose that exercise may influence primary appraisal of a stressor. It may be a resource for preventive coping by changing general self-efficacy and self-schemata, as well as by increasing energy and stamina. Alternatively, exercise may influence secondary appraisal and be used as a stressor. Exercise may be used as an emotion-focused coping strategy, which may function by being relaxing, psychologically distracting or mood enhancing. The implication of this is that employees experiencing work stress may respond by exercising more as a form of coping. Some evidence in support of this has been found; e.g., Davis *et al.* (1987) found that, in the context of a health promotion scheme, more work stress was associated with increased participation in exercise programs.

However, while exercise may be beneficial in reducing work stress, it should be emphasized that work itself may impact on people's ability to exercise. The demands and stresses of work may make it more difficult for people to exercise. Work factors may present barriers by physically preventing attendance at sports and exercise activities (e.g., because of overtime working) or by causing tiredness and fatigue, which reduce motivation to exercise.

Research based on Karasek's job strain model supporting the existence of a negative relationship between work stress and exercise was discussed earlier in this chapter. As we saw, the model predicts that both high strain and passive jobs are likely to be related to low levels of physical activity. What these two job types have in common is low levels of job control. For example, Hellerstedt and Jeffery (1997) found that active jobs were associated with more exercise in women and passive jobs were associated with more inactive lifestyles in men. Both these patterns are consistent with the model's prediction. However, Johansson *et al.* (1991) found that work demands alone were also related to increased sedentary behavior.

Other studies focusing on exercise have further supported the link between work stress and exercise. For example, Payne *et al.* (2002) conducted a study in which over 200 employees were asked about their work stressors and exercise intentions for the following week. They were then followed up in order to investigate their actual behavior over this period of time. The study found that people in high-strain jobs did significantly less exercise than those in low-strain jobs, although their intentions were similar. This primarily seemed to be due to the effect of job demands, as people who failed to carry out their intentions to exercise had significantly higher work demands (as well as lower exercise self-efficacy) than those who succeeded.

Minor stressors have also been associated with exercise in a study by Stetson *et al.* (1997). Eighty-two women kept exercise diaries and weekly stress inventories over a period of eight weeks. While the stressors were not exclusively work focused, the most frequently reported stressful events were associated with time pressure to complete ongoing tasks. The results are consistent with those of Payne *et al.* described above in that, during weeks of high perceived stress, participants exercised less, missed more planned exercise sessions and had lower self-efficacy for meeting exercise goals. Stetson *et al.* further suggested that stress may have its impact through hindering performance of positive health behaviors such as exercise, increasing perception of exercise as a stressor (i.e., exercise is just 'one more thing' to do) or increasing engagement in unhealthy coping behaviors (e.g., smoking and alcohol abuse).

A significant association between job stress and exercise has not always been found. Kirkcaldy and Cooper (1993) found no difference in the stress profiles of UK and German managers who exercised regularly and those who did not. Furthermore, (Landsbergis *et al.*, 1998) failed to find a relationship between job strain and exercise behavior. The study by Steptoe *et al.* (1998) described earlier in this chapter also found no effects of work hassles on exercise. In addition, a daily diary study by Payne (2002) found no direct link between job demands and implementation of intentions to exercise. They did find, however, that on work days people were less likely to implement their intentions than on non-work days.

One explanation for the lack of consistency in the results of studies looking at the relationship between work stress and exercise is that the presence of different individuals manifesting the two alternative reactions to work stressors (i.e., exercising more in times of stress versus exercising less in times of stress) may lead to null results in some studies. Overall, therefore, there is a need for further research into what it is about work that may restrict exercise and what individual differences may be important. Despite the current uncertainty concerning the impact of work on physical activity, given the benefits of exercise for both psychological and physical health, interventions to facilitate exercise and to reduce the barriers posed by work should undoubtedly be an important element of workplace health interventions.

HEALTHY EATING

Across western countries there is increased concern about obesity. A report produced by the International Obesity Task Force claims the prevalence of obesity has increased by between 10% and 25% in most European countries (Brown, 2004). Currently rates stand at 10–20% for men and 10–25% for women (Brown, 2004). A recent study from Canada reported that 33% of Canadians were classified as overweight (body mass index 25–29.9) and a further 15% were obese, based on a body mass index of 30 or over (Craig and Cameron, 2004). Concerns about obesity in the USA are still greater, with the prevalence of obesity reported to have risen from 19.8% to 20.9% between 2001 and 2002 (Mokdad *et al.*, 2001). Furthermore, obesity has been linked with a wide range of health risks including diabetes, cardio-vascular disease, certain forms of cancer and a range of other conditions (National Task Force on the Prevention and Treatment of Obesity, 2000).

While links between occupational stress and eating have been largely overlooked by research, there is a wealth of literature examining general stress-induced or emotion-induced eating. A comprehensive review of this literature is beyond the scope of this chapter; however, a brief overview of some relevant research findings is presented here.

Greeno and Wing (1994) and Conner and Armitage (2002) suggest that most research looking at the general effects of stress suggests that it leads to an increase in food intake. However, this research has traditionally relied heavily upon animal studies, laboratory studies and studies investigating exam stress. In addition there is some conflicting evidence. For example, Stone and Brownell (1994) found stress led to reduced eating amongst those of normal weight and Willenbring *et al.* (1986) found that 48% of their sample decreased eating when stressed, compared to 44% who increased eating. Individual differences in reactions to stress are a likely explanation for such conflicting findings. The focus of research into individual differences has centered around three key types of eating reactions to stress: 'external eating', 'restrained eating' and 'emotional eating' (Conner and Armitage, 2002).

'External eaters' eat in response to external stimuli rather than in response to internal hunger cues (Schachter *et al.*, 1968). 'Restrained eaters' are people perpetually trying to restrict their food intake through exercising self-control (Herman and Polivy, 1975). 'Emotional eaters' have difficulty distinguishing between hunger and anxiety and thus tend to 'comfort eat' when anxious (van Strien *et al.*, 1986). These different types of eating patterns have been found to play a moderating role in a number of studies in this area.

In a review by Greeno and Wing (1994), restrained eating was con-sistently found to moderate the relationship between stress and eating, such that restrained eaters tend to increase eating under stress. In a daily diary study of snack consumption in students, Conner *et al.* (1999) found that on days when people reported greater numbers of hassles they reported eating more snacks than on days with fewer hassles. However, this relationship was moderated by external eating such that external eaters were responsible for the positive relationship between hassles and snacking. Restrained eating and emotional eating did not affect the relationship between hassles and snacking. This picture is further complicated by the role of gender, as women seem more prone to stress-induced eating. There was some evidence that the effects of stress on snacking were greater for women in the study by Conner *et al.* but there is contradictory evidence as to whether they eat more or less (Conner and Armitage, 2002).

It is likely that certain types of stressor may be more likely to impact on health behaviors. Greeno and Wing (1994) suggest that stressors that cause a general feeling of anxiety may be more likely to lead to increased food consumption than stressors that disrupt time schedules. They also posit that acute stressors may lead to decreased eating.

There is also evidence that stress may affect the types of food selected. Willenbring *et al.* (1986) have suggested that stress-eating adults tend to prefer foods high in caloric density. More specifically, Laitinen *et al.* (2002) found that people who were stress-driven eaters (based on scores on a single item 'I tried to make myself feel better by eating, drinking, using medication etc', p. 30). tended to consume more sausages, hamburgers, pizza and chocolate than others. They further found that stress-related eating and drinking was associated with obesity, particularly in women.

The impact of these individual difference variables has further been considered in research focusing on work stress, which is discussed below.

Work stress and healthy eating

Research described at the start of this chapter provides some insights into the role of work stress in eating. Hellerstedt and Jeffery (1997) found that men in low-strain jobs reported consuming fewer calories from high-fat foods (based on an 18-item Food Frequency Questionnaire) than did men in high-strain and active jobs. The diary study by Steptoe *et al.* (1998) also found increased food consumption in high-stress weeks compared to low-stress.

A subsequent study by Wardle *et al.* (2000) compared high work-stress weeks (in which department store employees worked longer hours, reported more work–home interference and reported greater perceived stress) to low work-stress weeks, in terms of food intake. The authors found that during weeks where high levels of work stress were experienced employees reported increased consumption of calories, fat and sugar (based on reported food intake over the previous 24-hour period). This relationship was moderated by restrained eating, such that restrained eaters were responsible for the positive relationship between stress and eating.

The picture is far from straightforward, however: for example, Payne *et al.* (2005) found that people in passive jobs (i.e., low-demand and low-control jobs) intended to consume more sweets and snack foods. This is likely to be because people in passive jobs anticipate having more time in which to consume such foods. However, people in low-strain jobs (i.e., low-demand and high-control jobs) were more likely to implement their intentions to consume sweets and snack foods. This may be because people in high-strain jobs are too busy to stop for snacks, or that people in low-strain jobs are bored because they don't have enough to do and so eat more. Thus, it may be important to ensure that there is a balance at work, such that employees are under a moderate level of job demand. Payne *et al.* found no relationship between job strain and consumption of fruit and vegetables. However, since stress is thought to be related primarily to consumption of foods high in caloric density, this finding may not be surprising (Willenbring *et al.*, 1986).

That there is no clear link between job demands and eating is confirmed by a recent review by Overgaard *et al.* (2004). The authors examined 10 studies looking at the relationship between psychological workload and body weight and found no evidence for a consistent association. This further suggests the importance of investigating individual differences in this area.

Thus, overall, evidence for the impact of work stress on eating behavior is unclear but it seems likely that, at least for some, work stressors may damage their diet. Given the importance of diet for overall health, employers have some responsibility to consider such issues and facilitate healthy eating where possible. There is also a need for work cultures that encourage work–life balance, which may include encouraging employees to take proper meal breaks and not eat 'fast food' at their desks.

WHY DOES WORK AFFECT HEALTH BEHAVIOR? MODELS AND MECHANISMS

Many studies that report relationships between work stressors and health behaviors are cross-sectional and correlational in design; consequently the direction of causality is unclear. For example, negative work characteristics might be a result, rather than a cause, of alcohol problems experienced by employees. Alternatively, a self-selection process may occur where workers who drink heavily may choose occupations where such behavior is accepted, encouraged or facilitated (Plant, 1979). For example, working away from home on a frequent basis may be a highly desirable feature for an individual who wishes to hide his or her alcohol consumption from employers and/or family. Unfit and overweight individuals may similarly be selected into unenriched jobs or may choose jobs that support unhealthy behaviors. However, most research looking at the mechanisms linking work stressors with health behaviors is based on an assumption that, for the most part, stressors lead to health behavior rather than the reverse. Hence the emphasis has been placed on the role of intervening variables and individual differences in this relationship. A number of frameworks have been set out and these are discussed below.

Mediation and moderation

Two main mechanisms have been suggested by which intervening variables such as coping or individual differences may impact on the relationship between other variables such as stressors and health behaviors. These are mediation and moderation (Baron and Kenny, 1986):

- *The mediation model* – where an intervening variable 'transmits' the effects of one variable to another. Potential mediators of the relationship between work stressors and health behaviors include job dissatisfaction, negative affect, fatigue and coping. For example, job demands might lead to low mood which, in turn, could result in increased alcohol consumption. Frone (1999), in reviewing the evidence in relation to alcohol use, supports this model. For example, Greenberg and Grunberg (1995) found that job dissatisfaction and the use of alcohol as a way of coping with stress mediated the relationship between job stressors and problem drinking. In terms of work–family conflict, Vasse *et al.* (1998) report that a range of work stressors (including negative impact of work on private life) led to negative affect which, in turn, predicted alcohol consumption in a sample of Dutch white- and blue-collar workers.
- *The moderation model* – where work stressors interact with other variables (such as the potential mediators outlined above) to either place an individual at *increased* risk of unhealthy behaviors, or act as a *protective* factor. Frone (1999) in his review of the alcohol literature finds that this mechanism operates in addition to the mediation mechanism. For example, in a sample of 645 white- and blue-collar workers, Grunberg *et al.* (1999) found that job stress was positively associated with alcohol consumption only in those who endorsed 'escapist' reasons for drinking alcohol (i.e., individuals who indicated that alcohol 'helped them relax', 'made them feel more in control' and 'made them forget about their jobs'). For participants who did not endorse these reasons for drinking, work stress was unrelated to alcohol consumption. Support has also been found for the moderation mechanism for eating behavior. For example, Steptoe *et al.* (1998) found that the consumption of certain foods increased during high-stress weeks only for people who use foods to regulate their mood. In terms of work–family conflict, a positive relationship between work–family conflict and drinking to cope and problem drinking was only found for employees who believed that alcohol aids relaxation and relieves negative mood (Frone *et al.*, 1993).

A mediational model for coronary heart disease risk factors

Landsbergis *et al.* (1998) have suggested a model (adapted from Karasek and Theorell, 1990, and Johannson *et al.*, 1991) that identifies specific variables which mediate the relationships between job stressors and a number of health behaviors implicated in coronary heart disease risk (sedentary behavior, weight, alcohol overuse and smoking). This model is shown in Figure 8.1. Pathway A (based on Karasek and Theorell, 1990, and Johannson *et al.*, 1991) suggests that jobs which are high in demand and low in control (i.e., high-strain jobs) lead to fatigue and the need for long recovery periods after work (especially when the job involves long hours or repetitive work). This fatigue in turn may lead to sedentary behavior at home. Pathway A also suggests that smoking and excess alcohol may be used to try to regulate arousal and reduce distress associated with high-strain jobs, supporting the approach of health behaviors as coping. Pathway B suggests an alternative whereby jobs that are both low in control and low in demand (i.e., passive jobs) may lead to poor health behavior. It is suggested that passive jobs may lead to a passive and sedentary lifestyle (via spillover mechanisms; see Chapters 3 and 7), low self-efficacy and depression. These in turn may lead to poor health beliefs and correspondingly poor health behaviors. However, the authors also propose that some jobs may lead to more adaptive health behaviors, in that active jobs (high demand, high control) may result in a wider range of coping strategies that may include better health behaviors. Tests of these pathways may be useful in helping to improve understanding of how work might be designed to improve health rather than damage it.

Barriers to performing health behavior

Fatigue and need for recovery may also mean that people find it difficult to overcome the potential barriers that stand in the way of healthy behaviors. This is likely to be problematic in the case of behaviors that actively promote health (e.g., healthy eating and physical activity), which typically require more effort, organization and planning than the more negative health behaviors of smoking and drinking alcohol. A number of studies have examined the potential barriers to adaptive health behaviors. Both time- and strain-based spillover might be expected to impact on these barriers. For example, working long hours may affect an individual's ability to perform activities such as shopping for fresh food, cooking and going to the gym. However, strain-based spillover in terms of fatigue or preoccupation with work may also mean the effort of exercising or cooking, for example, becomes too great. Thus work stress may lead to the person experiencing and perceiving a number of barriers to more healthy behaviors.

Brownson *et al.* (2001) found that the four most commonly reported barriers to exercise in a sample of 1818 US adults were lack of time, feeling too tired, already getting enough exercise at work and having no motivation to exercise; these findings suggest that both types of spillover may be operating.

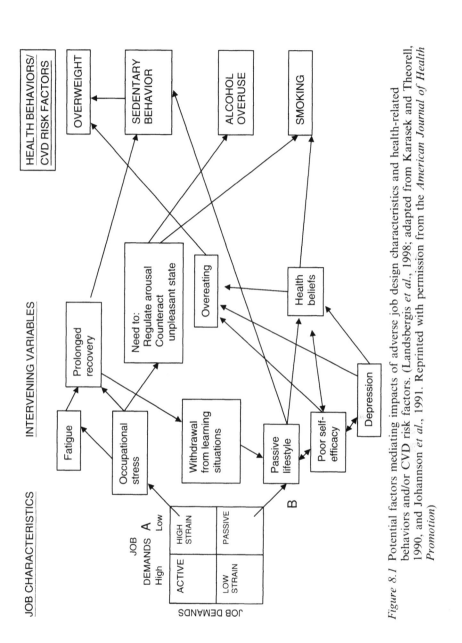

Figure 8.1 Potential factors mediating impacts of adverse job design characteristics and health-related behaviors and/or CVD risk factors. (Landsbergis *et al.*, 1998; adapted from Karasek and Theorell, 1990, and Johannson *et al.*, 1991. Reprinted with permission from the *American Journal of Health Promotion*)

Two studies have examined barriers specifically in working women. Jaffee *et al.* (1999) found that, in a sample of 393 women, lack of time due to work was seen as a greater disincentive to exercise than lack of time due to family. Even though the participants' workplace provided a gym, the majority of the women reported lack of time in the working day as a major barrier to exercise; further reasons were self-consciousness in front of co-workers and concern about appearance. In addition, Jaffee *et al.* suggested that women with a long commute, those who travelled or those who worked long hours may have found exercise low on their list or priorities. Tessaro *et al.* (1998) interviewed 121 blue-collar working women in the USA and found that they reported lacking the skills and information necessary to make changes in exercise, diet and smoking. Again, this study found that lack of time and lack of willpower were barriers. However, social support in the workplace was considered a facilitator. Overall, time, tiredness and willpower seem to be recurring themes across these studies. These variables all seem to be highly related to work stress and need for recovery, suggesting that barriers might usefully be incorporated within the mediational model discussed above.

Overall, the mechanisms considered here suggest ways in which work stressors impact on health behaviors. Further research and theoretical development are still required to identify the moderators and mediators. This can be useful to help develop targeted interventions; for example, focusing on those who use unhealthy eating as a way of coping with work stress.

WORKPLACE HEALTH PROMOTION INTERVENTIONS

If work organizations create conditions for unhealthy work, they also hold a responsibility for reducing that risk (Cox, 1997). Additionally, organizations are likely to benefit, in terms of lower levels of absenteeism and turnover and higher levels of productivity, if they improve the health of the workforce. Such interventions are also likely to contribute to improvements in work–life balance for employees. Furthermore, since we spend much of our waking lives at work, the workplace provides a particularly convenient forum for health behavior change interventions. Indeed, workplace health promotion schemes have grown dramatically in the past few decades (Schreurs *et al.*, 1996) and there is now a considerable research literature on their efficacy. For example, Wilson *et al.* (1996) in their systematic review found 288 articles relating to work health promotions on exercise, health risk appraisal, weight control, nutrition and cholesterol.

There is considerable variability in the types of intervention used in the workplace. They may focus on specific health and safety issues at work (e.g., wearing protective clothing or hand washing in medical staff), or may cover a range of more general health behaviors. These schemes may also vary greatly in terms of content and scope. O'Donnell (1986) describes three levels of intervention. At the most basic level (level one) they may consist of simple awareness programs, which may include posters, newsletters and screening sessions. O'Donnell suggests that these are not usually successful in changing behaviors, but are likely to be a useful first step in increasing awareness amongst employees. At level two, the focus is on actual lifestyle change. These may involve specific programs such as fitness training aimed at encouraging people to change a particular behavior, or they may have a wider focus. Level two programs may involve a number of steps, including education, assessment, goal setting and support. O'Donnell suggests that these are more likely to be successful than simple awareness programs. Level three interventions aim to provide work environments that support behavior change in employees. This involves organizational change to develop supportive *physical environments*, organizational *policies*, *structures* and *cultures*. As an example of an improvement in the *physical environment*, O'Donnell proposes that organizations stock vending machines with healthy foods. A supportive *policy* might, for example, involve establishing work schedules that are flexible enough to allow employees to have time to exercise before, during or after the work day. Supportive *structures* include Employee Advisory Programs or Occupational Health Departments. Supportive *cultures* might involve group norms that deem it is acceptable to ask a co-worker not to smoke in their working environment.

Most interventions have focused on levels one and two and a range of interesting and innovative schemes have been described in the literature, particularly focusing on alcohol use. For example, an interactive web-based self-assessment program, 'Coping Matters', has been developed by Matano *et al.* (2000). This allows employees to assess their personal stress levels and coping styles and the extent to which they are at risk of developing alcohol-related problems. From this information, personalized feedback is provided together with links to relevant online educational resources and an interactive forum. The website also offers advice for employees who may be concerned about the drinking patterns of colleagues and families of problem drinkers. A considerable strength of this medium is that it is anonymous and, therefore, free from stigma. Preliminary data suggest that this program reaches employees who are at higher risk of harmful or hazardous drinking.

Another example of an innovative level two alcohol intervention, the Yale Work and Family Stress Project (Snow *et al.*, 2002), is unusual in its equal focus on both work and family issues. This aims to identify and modify risk factors and protective influences that impact on problem drinking. The intervention used is based on Pearlin and Schooler's (1978) hierarchy of coping mechanisms that involve changing stressful situations at source. It focuses on identifying stressors and personal resources, developing skills (including problem solving and stress management skills) and enhancing social support networks. It also aims to increase understanding of eating patterns and exercise and to encourage people to use self-monitoring, goal setting and social support to change habits and behaviors. Some support for this intervention has been found with employees in a range of work settings and occupational groups (reported in Snow *et al.*, 2002).

Neither of the above interventions seek to change the organizations in which participants work. However, O'Donnell suggests that comprehensive health promotion programs can combine all three levels to address the needs of people at different stages of health behavior change. Thus, they can encompass employees who lack the basic knowledge about health behaviors and need education, those who are ready to change who would be helped by the programs described above, and those who are trying to maintain already established behaviors who need supportive environments. Writing 10 years later than O'Donnell, Wilson *et al.* (1996), in their review of existing studies, find that most research in the area is based on individual or group interventions and few studies included organization-wide strategies. Furthermore, as few of the studies reviewed were theory based, it could not easily be established why they worked or how they could be transferred to other organizations.

A number of reviews have considered the effectiveness of workplace health promotion schemes (e.g., Peersman *et al.*, 1998; Wilson *et al.*, 1996). Wilson *et al.* do generally support the effectiveness of worksite health promotion, although findings are often indicative rather than conclusive. This review does not include smoking or alcohol interventions. However, a subsequent review by Eriksen and Gottlieb (1998) considered 52 workplace smoking cessation interventions and supports their effectiveness. Perhaps unsurprisingly, they found that smoking cessation group programs were more effective than more minimal interventions (e.g., short videos or provision of a telephone help line). A note of caution is, however, sounded in a review (by Peersman *et al.*, 1998) which finds that few studies use rigorous methodology and that evidence about effectiveness of interventions was therefore inconclusive. Furthermore they suggest that there is a need for greater participation of employees in planning and implementation of programs.

The way forward

As we have seen, most worksite health promotion interventions have focused on encouraging the employee to change his or her health behaviors. This is despite the fact that, for many years, academic writers have been calling for the need for organization-level intervention (e.g., Erben *et al.*, 1992; Heaney, 2003; Schreurs *et al.*, 1996). For example, Heaney (2002) argues that, since evidence indicates that organizations constrain employee behaviors, change efforts need to encompass organizational change. As with stress management programs, health promotion interventions focusing purely on the individual are likely to be ineffective. Similarly, Schreurs *et al.* offer a vision of workplace health promotion that is based on a total package at both individual and organizational levels.

However, it may well be that such interventions are more difficult to implement. For example, Elo and Leppänen (1999) used worksite health promotion teams in a highly participative attempt to improve the psychosocial work environment in a metal factory. Despite the use of surveys and the identification of problems with work content and design, the teams had more success in establishing activities to increase individual levels of physical fitness than in making more fundamental organizational changes. Perhaps due to such difficulties, there is a dearth of evidence concerning the effectiveness of organizational level of interventions. However, one study by Erfurt *et al.* (1991) found that workplace approaches that included an organizational component were more successful than those that did not. There is a need for further research to find practical and effective organizational interventions.

It seems likely that in many cases fairly simple organizational changes could be made with limited disruption. For example, providing more convenient facilities for exercising (e.g., a worksite gym), coupled with allowing more flexibility in working hours in order to use these facilities, may help promote exercise participation. To improve diets, it would be helpful to provide easy access to healthy and tempting convenience foods, rather than high-sugar and high-fat foods. The provision of healthier foods would have to be applied to the worksite shop, canteen and vending machines, both in and out of normal working hours. No-smoking policies that operate in many workplaces also help to encourage healthy behavior. However, such interventions are likely to be ineffective if they do not fit the needs of both the organization and the employees (Heaney, 2003). Heaney argues that 'it is important that the intervention design process blend social science theory and evidence with local preferences, experiences and needs' (p. 319). This suggests the importance of a participative approach involving an ongoing dialogue with employees.

Furthermore, participation will also be required at the highest levels in order to change the culture of organizations to support lifestyle changes. For example, changes involving reducing levels of stress or long hours may require strategic initiatives. Too often programs for health promotion are seen as a fringe activity, run by Occupational Health departments. They are not integrated either with occupational safety or work–life balance initiatives. Work–life balance policies need to encompass recognition of the importance of enabling employees to invest time and energy in their own positive health behaviors and leisure activities as well as their family needs.

REFERENCES

Aiken, G. J., and McCance, C. (1982). Alcohol consumption in offshore rig workers. *British Journal of Addiction*, 77(3), 305–310.

Alcohol Concern (2003). *Alcohol and the work place: A European comparative study on preventive and supporting measures for problem drinkers in their working environment.* London: Alcohol Concern.

Alexander, D. A., and Walker, L. G. (1994). A study of methods used by Scottish police officers to cope with work-induced stress. *Stress Medicine, 10*(2), 131–138.

Alterman, T., Shekelle, R. B., Vernon, S. W., and Burau, K. D. (1994). Decision latitude, psychologic demand, job strain, and coronary heart disease in the Western Electric Study. *American Journal of Epidemiology, 139*(6), 620–627.

Ames, G. M., and Janes, C. R. (1992). A cultural approach to conceptualising alcohol and the workplace. *Alcohol Health Research World, 16*(2), 112–119.

Aspinwall, L. G., and Taylor, S. E. (1997). A stitch in time: self-regulation and proactive coping. *Psychological Bulletin, 121*, 417–436.

Australian Bureau of Statistics (2000). *Australian social trends 2000: health risk factors: trends in smoking.* Retrieved 26 October 2004 from http://www.abs. gov.au/ausstats/abs@.nsf/0/7EB80C48627DD3B1CA256A7100188A5D?Open.

Barling, J. (1989). *Employment, stress and family functioning.* London: Wiley

Baron, R. M., and Kenny, D. A. (1986). The moderator–mediator variable distinction in social psychological research: conceptual, strategic and statistical considerations. *Journal of Personality and Social Psychology, 51*(6), 1173–1182.

Bertera, R. L. (1991). The effects of behavioral risks on absenteeism and health-care costs in the workplace. *Journal of Occupational Medicine, 33*(11), 1119–1124.

Bhattacherjee, A., Chau, N., Sierra, C. O., Legras, B., Benamghar, L., Michaely, J. P., Ghosh, A. K., Guillemin, F., Ravaud, J. F., and Mur, J. M. (2003). Relationships of job and some individual characteristics to occupational injuries in employed people: a community-based study. *Journal of Occupational Health, 45*(6), 382–391.

Blair, S. N., Kohl, H. W., Paffenbarger, R. S., Clark, D. G., Cooper, K. H., and Gibbons, L. W. (1989). Physical fitness and all cause mortality: a prospective study of healthy men and women. *Journal of the American Medical Association, 262*(17), 2395–2401.

Blum, T. C., Roman, P. M., and Martin, J. K. (1993). Alcohol consumption and work performance. *Journal of Studies on Alcohol, 54*(1), 61–70.

BMA (1993). *The morbidity and mortality of the medical profession.* London: BMA.

Bonaiuti, D., Shea, B., Iovine, R., Negrini, S., Robinson, V., Kemper, H. C., Wells, G., Tugwell, P., and Cranney, A. (2002). Exercise for preventing and treating osteoporosis in postmenopausal women. *Cochrane Database of Systematic Reviews,* (3), CD000333.

Bray, R. M., Fairbank, J. A., and Marsden, M. E. (1999). Stress and substance use among military women and men. *American Journal of Drug and Alcohol Abuse, 25*(2), 239–256.

Bromet, E. J., Dew, M. A., Parkinson, D., and Schulberg, H. (1988). Predictive effects of occupational and marital stress on the mental health of a male workforce. *Journal of Organizational Behavior, 9*(1), 1–13.

Bromet, E. J., Dew, M. A., and Parkinson, D. K. (1990). Spillover between work and family: a study of blue collar working women. In J. Eckenrode and S. Gore (eds), *Stress Between Work and Family* (pp. 133–152). New York: Plenum Press.

Brown, D. (2004). *About obesity: incidence, prevalence and co-morbidity.* Retrieved 11 October 2004 from http://www.obesity.chair.ulaval.ca/IOTF.htm

Brownson, R. C., Baker, E. A., Housemann, R. A., Brennan, L. K., and Bacak, S. J.

(2001). Environmental and policy determinants of physical activity in the United States. *American Journal of Public Health*, *91*(12), 1995–2003.

Bruning, N. S., and Frew, D. R. (1987). Effects of exercise, relaxation, and management skills training on physiological stress indicators: a field experiment. *Journal of Applied Psychology*, *72*(4), 515–521.

Bush, D. M., and Autry, J. H. (2002). Substance abuse in the workplace: epidemiology, effects, and industry response. *Occupational Medicine*, *17*(1), 13–25.

Cameron, C., Craig, C. L., Stephens, T., and Ready, T. A. (2002). *Increasing physical activity: Supporting an active workforce*. Ottawa: Canadian Fitness and Lifestyle Institute.

Carver, C. S., Scheier, M. F., and Weintraub, J. K. (1989). Assessing coping strategies: a theoretically based approach. *Journal of Personality and Social Psychology*, *56*(2), 267–283.

Centers for Disease Control (2004). Smoking prevalence among U.S. adults. Retrieved 26 October 2004 from http://www.cdc.gov/tobacco/research_data/adults_prev/prevali.htm

Cohen, S., Schwartz, J. E., Bromet, E. J., and Parkinson, D. K. (1991). Mental health, stress, and poor health behaviors in two community samples. *Preventative Medicine*, *20*(2), 306–315.

Collins, D. J., and Lapsley, H. M. (1996). *The social costs of drug abuse in Australia in 1988 and 1992*. Commonwealth Department of Human Services and Health.

Conner, M., and Armitage, C. J. (2002). *The social psychology of food*. Buckingham, UK: Open University Press.

Conner, M., Fitter, M., and Fletcher, W. (1999). Stress and snacking: a diary study of daily hassles and between-meal snacking. *Psychology and Health*, *14*, 51–63.

Cooper, M. L., Russell, M., Skinner, J. B., Frone. M. R., and Mudar, P. (1992). Stress and alcohol use: moderating effects of gender, coping, and alcohol expectancies. *Journal of Abnormal Psychology*, *101*(1), 139–152.

Corsun, D. L., and Young, C. A. (1998). An occupational hazard: alcohol consumption among hospitality managers. *Marriage and Family Review*, *28*(1/2), 187–212.

Cox, T. (1997). Work place health promotion. *Work and Stress*, *11*(1), 1–5.

Craig, C. L., and Cameron, C. (2004). Increasing physical activity: assessing trends from 1998–2004. Ottawa: Canadian Fitness and Lifestyle Institute.

Crum, R. M., Muntaner, C., Eaton, W. W., and Anthony, J. C. (1995). Occupational stress and the risk of alcohol abuse and dependence. *Alcoholism: Clinical and Experimental Research*, *19*(3), 647–655.

Davis, K. E., Jackson, K. L., Kronenfeld, J. J., and Blair, S. N. (1987). Determinants of participation in worksite health promotion activities. *Health Education Quarterly*, *14*(2), 195–205.

Dugan, S., Lloyd, B., and Lucas, K. (1999). Stress and coping as determinants of adolescent smoking behavior. *Journal of Applied Social Psychology*, *29*(4), 870–888.

Elo, A.-L., and Leppänen, A. (1999). Efforts of health promotion teams to improve the psychosocial work environment. *Journal of Occupational Health Psychology*, *4*(2), 87–94.

Erben, R., Franzkowiak, P., and Wenzel, E. (1992). Assessment of the outcomes of health intervention. *Social Science and Medicine*, *35*(4), 359–365.

Erfurt, J. C., Foote, A., and Heirich, M. A. (1991). Worksite wellness programs:

incremental comparison of screening and referral alone, health education, follow-up counseling, and plant organization. *American Journal of Health Promotion*, *5*(6), 438–448.

Eriksen, M. P., and Gottlieb, N. H. (1998). A review of the health impact of smoking control in the workplace. *American Journal of Health Promotion*, *13*(2), 83–104.

Folkman, S., and Lazarus, R. (1988). *Manual for the ways of coping questionnaire*. Palo Alto, CA: Consulting Psychologists Press.

Frone, M. R. (1999). Work stress and alcohol use. *Alcohol Research and Health*, *23*(4), 284–291.

Frone, M. R. (2000). Work–family conflict and employee psychiatric disorders: the national comorbidity survey. *Journal of Applied Psychology*, *85*(6), 888–895.

Frone, M. R., Russell, M., and Cooper, M. L. (1993). Relationship of work–family conflict, gender, and alcohol expectancies to alcohol use/abuse. *Journal of Organizational Behavior*, *14*(6), 545–558.

Frone, M. R., Barnes, G. M., and Farrell, M. P. (1994). Relationship of work–family conflict to substance use among employed mothers: the role of negative affect. *Journal of Marriage and the Family*, *56*(4), 1019–1030.

Frone, M. R., Russell, M., and Cooper, M. L. (1997) Relation of work–family conflict to health outcomes: a four-year longitudinal study of employed parents. *Journal of Occupational and Organizational Psychology*, *70*, 325–336.

Greeley, J., and Oei, T. (1999). Alcohol and tension reduction. In K. E. Leonard and H. T. Blane (eds), *Psychological theories of drinking and alcoholism* (2nd edn). London: Guilford Press.

Green, K. L., and Johnson, J. V. (1990). The effects of psychosocial work organization on patterns of cigarette smoking among male chemical plant employees. *American Journal of Public Health*, *80*(11), 1368–1371.

Greenberg, E. S., and Grunberg, L. (1995). Work alienation and problem alcohol behavior. *Journal of Health and Social Behavior*, *36*, 83–102.

Greeno, C. G., and Wing, R. R. (1994). Stress-induced eating. *Psychological Bulletin*, *115*(3), 444–464.

Grieger, T. A., Fullerton, C. S., Ursano, R. J., and Reeves, J. J. (2003). Acute stress disorder, alcohol use, and perception of safety among hospital staff after the sniper attacks. *Psychiatric Services*, *54*(10), 1383–1387.

Griffin, K. W., Friend, R., Eitel, P., and Lobel, M. (1993). Effects of environmental demands, stress and mood on health practices. *Journal of Behavioral Medicine*, *16*(6), 643–661.

Grunberg, L., Moore, S., Anderson-Connolly, R., and Greenberg, E. (1999). Work stress and self-reported alcohol use: the moderating role of escapist reasons for drinking. *Journal of Occupational Health Psychology*, *4*(1), 29–36.

Grzywacz, J. G., and Marks, N. F. (2000). Family, work, work–family spillover and problem drinking during midlife. *Journal of Marriage and the Family*, *62*(2), 336–348.

Hagihara, A. K., Tarumi, K., and Nobutomo, K. (2001). A signal detection approach to the combined effects of work stressors on alcohol consumption. *Journal of Studies on Alcohol*, *62*(6), 798–805.

Harris, M., and Heft, L. (1992). Alcohol and drug use in the workplace: issues, controversies and directions for future research. *Journal of Management*, *18*(2), 239–266.

Harwood, H. (2000). *Updating estimates of the economic costs of alcohol and drug abuse in the United States: Estimates, update methods and data.* Rockville, MD: National Institute of Alcohol Abuse and Alcoholism.

Havlovic, S. J., and Keenan J. P. (1991). Coping with work stress: the influence of individual differences. *Journal of Social Behavior and Personality*, 6(7), 199–212.

HEA (1992). *Allied Dunbar national fitness survey.* London: Sports Council and Health Education Authority.

Heaney, C. A. (2003). Worksite health promotion interventions: targets for change and strategies for attaining them. In J. C. Quick and T. L. E. (eds), *Handbook of occupational health psychology* (pp. 305–323). Washington, DC: American Psychological Association.

Hellerstedt, W. L., and Jeffery, R. W. (1997). The association of job strain and health behaviors in men and women. *International Journal of Epidemiology*, 26(3), 575–583.

Hemmingsson, T., and Lundberg, I. (1998). Work control, work demands, and work social support in relation to alcoholism among young men. *Alcoholism: Clinical and Experimental Research*, 22, 921–927.

Herman, C. P., and Polivy, J. (1975). Anxiety, restraint and eating behavior. *Journal of Abnormal Psychology*, 84(6), 666–672.

Heslop, P., Davey-Smith, G., Carroll, D., Macleod, J., Hyland, F., and Hart, C. (2001). Perceived stress and coronary heart disease risk factors: the contribution of socio-economic position. *British Journal of Health Psychology*, 6, 167–178.

Holahan, C. J., Moos, R. H., and Schaefer, J. A. (1996). Coping, stress resistance and growth: conceptualizing adaptive functioning. In M. Zeidner and N. S. Endler (eds), *Handbook of coping: Theory, research, applications* (pp. 24–43). New York: Wiley.

Ingledew, D. K., Hardy, L., Cooper, C. L., and Jemal, H. (1996). Health behaviors reported as coping strategies: a factor analytic study. *British Journal of Health Psychology*, 1(3), 263–281.

Jaffee, L., Lutter, J. M., Rex, J., Hawkes, C., and Bucaccio, P. (1999). Incentives and barriers to physical activity for working women. *American Journal of Health Promotion*, 13(4), 215–218.

Janes, C. R., and Ames, G. (1989). Men, blue collar work and drinking: alcohol use in an industrial subculture. *Culture, Medicine and Psychiatry*, 13(3), 245–274.

Johansson, G., Johnson, J. V., and Hall, E. M. (1991). Smoking and sedentary behavior as related to work organization. *Social Science and Medicine*, (7), 837–846.

Karasek, R. (1979). Job demands, job decision latitude and mental strain: implications for job design. *Administrative Science Quarterly*, 24, 285–308.

Karasek, R., and Theorell, T. (1990). *Healthy work: Stress, productivity and the reconstruction of working life.* New York: Basic Books.

Karasek, R., Gardell, B., and Lindell, J. (1987). Work and non-work correlates of illness and behavior in male and female Swedish white collar workers. *Journal of Occupational Behavior*, 8, 187–207.

Kassel, J. A., Stroud, L. R., and Paronis, C. A. (2003). Smoking, stress, and negative affect: correlation, causation, and context across stages of smoking. *Psychological Bulletin*, 129(2), 270–304.

Kirkcaldy, B. D., and Cooper, C. L. (1993). The relationship between work stress and leisure style: British and German managers. *Human Relations*, *46*(5), 669–680.

Koval, J. J., and Pederson, L. L. (1999). Stress-coping and other psychosocial risk factors: a model for smoking in grade 6 students. *Addictive Behaviors*, *24*(2), 207–218.

Laitinen, J., Ek, E., and Sovio, U. (2002). Stress-related eating and drinking behavior and body mass index and predictors of this behavior. *Preventive Medicine*, *34*, 29–39.

Lallukka, T., Sarlio-Lähteenkorva, S., Roos, E., Laaksonen, M., Rahkonen, O., and Lahelma, E. (2004). Working conditions and health behaviors among employed women and men: the Helsinki Health Study. *Preventive Medicine*, *38*(1), 48–56.

Landsbergis, P. A., Schnall, P. L., Deitz, D. K., Warren, K., Pickering, T. G., and Schwarz, J. E. (1998). Job strain and health behaviors: results of a prospective study. *American Journal of Health Promotion*, *12*(4), 237–245.

Lazarus, R. S. (1993). Coping theory and research: past, present and future. *Psychosomatic Medicine*, *55*, 234–247.

Lazarus, R. S., and Folkman, S. (1984). *Stress, appraisal and coping*. New York: Springer.

Lazarus, R. S., and Folkman, S. (1989). *Manual for the hassles and uplifts scale*. Palo Alto, CA: Consulting Psychologists Press.

Leigh, J. P., and Jiang, W. Y. (1993). Liver cirrhosis deaths within occupations and industries in the California occupational mortality study. *Addiction*, *88*, 767–779.

Leonard, K. E., and Rothbard, J. C. (1999). Alcohol and the marriage effect. *Journal of Studies in Alcohol Supplement*, *13*, 139–146.

Long, B. C., and Flood, K. R. (1993). Coping with work stress: psychological benefits of exercise. *Work and Stress*, *7*(2), 109–119.

Loughlin, K. A., and Kayson, W. A. (1990). Alcohol consumption and self-reported drinking-related problem behaviors as related to sex, work environment, and level of education. *Psychological Reports*, *67*(3), 1323–1328.

Macdonald, S., Wells, S., and Wild, C. T. (1999). Occupational risk factors associated with alcohol and drug problems. *American Journal of Drug and Alcohol Abuse*, *25*(4), 351–369.

Marshall, M. P. (2003). For better or for worse? The effects of alcohol use on marital functioning. *Clinical Psychology Review*, *23*(7), 959–997.

Matano, R. A., Futa, K. T., Wanat, S. F., Mussman, L. M., and Leung, C. W. (2000). The employee stress and alcohol project: the development of a computer-based alcohol abuse prevention program for employees. *Journal of Behavioral Health Services and Research*, *27*(20), 152–165.

Melamed, S., Kushnir, T., Strauss, E., and Vigiser, D. (1997). Negative association between reported life events and cardiovascular disease risk factors in employed men: the Cordis study. *Journal of Psychosomatic Research*, *43*(3), 247–258.

Metcalfe, C., Davey-Smith, G., Sterne, J. A. C., Heslop, P., Macleod, J., and Hart, C. (2003). Frequent job change and associated health. *Social Science and Medicine*, *56*(1), 1–15.

Mokdad, A. H., Bowman, B. A., Ford, E. S., Vinicor, F., Marks, J. S., and Koplan, J. P. (2001). The continuing epidemics of obesity and diabetes in the United States. *Journal of the American Medical Association*, *286*(10), 1195–1200.

Moore, S., Grunberg, L., and Greenberg, E. (2000). The relationships between alcohol problems and well-being, work attitudes, and performance: are they monotonic? *Journal of Substance Abuse*, *11*(2), 183–204.

Muraven, M., and Baumeister, R. F. (2000). Self-regulation and depletion of limited resources: does self-control resemble a muscle? *Psychological Bulletin*, *2000*(126), 247–259.

Mutrie, N. (2000). The relationship between physical activity and clinically defined depression. In S. J. H. Biddle, K. R. Fox and S. H. Boutcher (eds), *Physical activity and psychological well-being* (pp. 42–62). London: Routledge.

National Task Force on the Prevention and Treatment of Obesity (2000). Overweight, obesity and health risk. *Archives of Internal Medicine*, *160*(7), 898–904.

Neale, D. J. (1993). *Work-based alcohol risks in Alberta: an assessment.* Alberta: Alberta Alcohol and Drug Abuse Commission.

Ng, D. M., and Jeffery, R. W. (2003). Relationships between perceived stress and health behaviors in a sample of working adults. *Health Psychology*, *22*(6), 638–642.

Nowack, K. M., and Pentkowski, A. M. (1994). Lifestyle habits, substance use and predictors of job burnout in professional working women. *Work and Stress*, *8*(1), 19–35.

Nusbaumer, M. R., and Reiling, D. M. (2002). Environmental influences on alcohol consumption practices of alcoholic beverage servers. *American Journal of Drug and Alcohol Abuse*, *28*(4), 733–742.

O'Donnell, M. (1986). Definition of health promotion. Part II: Levels of programs. *American Journal of Health Promotion*, *1*(2), 6–9.

Overgaard, D., Gyntelberg, F., and Heitmann, B. L. (2004). Psychological workload and body weight: is there an association? A review of the literature. *Occupational Medicine – Oxford*, *54*(1), 35–41.

Parrott, A. C. (1999). Does cigarette smoking cause stress? *American Psychologist*, *54*(10), 817–820.

Payne, N. (2002). The determinants of health behaviours in employees: the impact of work stressors and other predictors. Unpublished thesis, University of Hertfordshire.

Payne, N., Jones, F., and Harris, P. (2002). The impact of working life on health behavior: the effect of job strain on the cognitive predictors of exercise. *Journal of Occupational Health Psychology*, *7*(4), 342–353.

Payne, N., Jones, F., and Harris, P. R. (2005). The impact of job strain on the predictive validity of the theory of planned behaviour: An investigation of exercise and healthy eating. *British Journal of Health Psychology*, *10*, 115–131.

Pearlin, L., and Schooler, C. (1978). The structure of coping. *Journal of Health and Social Behavior*, *19*, 2–21.

Peersman, G., Harden, A., and Oliver, S. (1998). *Effectiveness of health promotion interventions in the workplace: A review.* London. Health Educational Authority.

Petersen S., and Peto, V. (2004). Smoking statistics. London: British Heart Foundation. Retrieved 26 October 2004 from http://www.heartstats.org/datapage. asp?id=3916

Plant, M. A. (1979). Occupations and alcohol related problems. *British Journal of Alcohol and Alcoholism*, *14*(3), 119–120.

Plant, M. L., Plant, M. A., and Foster, J. (1991). Alcohol, tobacco and illicit drug use amongst nurses: a Scottish study. *Drug and Alcohol Dependency*, *28*(2), 195–202.

Ragland, D. R., Greiner, B. A., Yen, I., and Fisher, J. (2000). Occupational stress factors and alcohol-related behavior in urban-transit operators. *Alcoholism: Clinical and Experimental Research, 24*(7), 1011–1019.

Reed, D. M., LaCroix, A. Z., Karasek, R. A., Miller, D., and MacLean, C. E. (1989). Occupational strain and the incidence of coronary heart disease. *American Journal of Epidemiology, 129*, 495–502.

Richmond, R. L., Kehoe, L., Hailstone, S., Wodak, A., and Uebel-Yan, M. (1999). Quantitative and qualitative evaluations of brief interventions to change excessive drinking, smoking and stress in the police force. *Addiction, 94*(10), 1509–1521.

Rickards, L., Fox, K., Roberts, C., Fletcher, L., and Goddard, E. (2004). *Living in Britain: Results from the 2002 General Household Survey*. Norwich: HMSO.

Rodgers, L. M. (1998). A five year study comparing early retirements on medical grounds in ambulance personnel with those in other groups of health service staff. Part II: Causes of retirements. *Occupational Medicine, 48*(2), 119–132.

Roman, P. M., and Blum, T. C. (2002) The workplace and alcohol problem prevention. *Alcohol Research and Health, 26*(1), 49–57.

Rose, G., Bengtsson, C., Dimberg, L., Kumlin, L., Eriksson, B., and Group, C. P. (1998). Life events, mood, mental strain and cardiovascular risk factors in Swedish middle aged men. Data from the Swedish part of the Renault/Volvo Coeur Study. *Occupational Medicine, 48*, 329–336.

Rose, J. E., Ananda, S., and Jarvik, M. E. (1983). Cigarette smoking during anxiety-provoking and monotonous tasks. *Addictive Behaviors, 8*(4), 353–359.

Rospenda, K. M. (2002). Workplace harassment, services utilization, and drinking outcomes. *Journal of Occupational Health Psychology, 7*(2), 141–155.

Roxburgh, S. (1998). Gender differences in the effect of job stressors on alcohol consumption. *Addictive Behaviors, 23*, 101–107.

Schachter, S., Goldman, R., and Gordon, A. (1968). Effects of fear, food deprivation and obesity on eating. *Journal of Personality and Social Psychology, 10*, 91–97.

Schreurs, P. J. G., Winnubst, J. A. M., and Cooper, A. (1996). Workplace health programmes. In M. J. Schabracq, J. A. M. Winnubst and A. Cooper (eds), *Handbook of work and health psychology* (pp. 463–481). Chichester: Wiley.

Shiffman, S., Paty, J. A., Gnys, M., Kassel, J. A., and Hickcox, M. (1996). First lapses to smoking: within-subjects analysis of real-time reports. *Journal of Consulting and Clinical Psychology, 64*(2), 366–379.

Shiffman, S., Gwaltney, C. J., Balabanis, M. H., Liu, K. S., Paty, J. A., Kassel, J. D., Hickcox, M., and Gnys, M. (2002). Immediate antecedents of cigarette smoking: an analysis from ecological momentary assessment. *Journal of Abnormal Psychology, 111*, 531–545.

Single, E., Robson, L., Xie, X., and Rehm, J. (1998). The economic costs of alcohol, tobacco and drugs in Canada, 1992. *Addiction, 93*, 991–1006.

Snow, D. L., Swan, S. C., and Wilton, L. (2002) A workplace coping skills intervention to prevent alcohol abuse. In J. Bennett and W. E. K. Lehman (eds), *Preventing workplace substance abuse: Beyond drug testing to wellness* (pp. 57–96). Washington, DC: APA.

Staines, G. L. (1980). Spillover versus compensation: a review of the literature on the relationship between work and non-work. *Human Relations, 33*, 111–129.

Stetson, B. A., Rahn, J. M., Dubbert, P. M., Wilner, B. I., and Mercury, M. G.

(1997). Prospective evaluation of the effects of stress on exercise adherence in community-residing women. *Health Psychology*, *16*(6), 515–520.

Steptoe, A. (1991). The links between stress and illness. *Journal of Psychosomatic Research*, *35*(6), 633–644.

Steptoe, A., Lipsey, Z., and Wardle, J. (1998). Stress, hassles and variations in alcohol consumption, food choice and physical exercise: a diary study. *British Journal of Health Psychology*, *3*, 51–63.

Stone, D. N., and Brownell, K. D. (1994). The stress eating paradox: multiple daily measurements in adult males and females. *Psychology and Health*, *9*, 425–436.

Sutherland, K. M., and Flin, R. H. (1989). Stress at sea: a review of working conditions in the offshore oil and fishing industries. *Work and Stress*, *3*(3), 269–285.

Taylor, A. H. (2000). Physical activity, anxiety, and stress. In S. J. H. Biddle, K. R. Fox and S. H. Boutcher (eds), *Physical activity and psychological well-being* (pp. 10–46). London: Routledge.

Tessaro, I., Campbell, M., Benedict, S., Kelsey, K., Heisler-MacKinnon, J., Belton, L., and DeVellis, B. (1998). Developing a worksite health promotion intervention: health works for women. *American Journal of Health Behavior*, *22*(6), 434–442.

US Department of Health and Human Services (1996). *Physical activity and health: A report of the Surgeon General*. Atlanta, GA: Centers for Disease Control and Prevention (CDC), National Center for Chronic Disease Prevention and Health Promotion. Retrieved 29 October 2004 from www.cdc.gov/nccdphp/sgr/sgr.htm

van Strien, T., Frijters, J. E. R., Bergers, G. P. A., and Defares, P. B. (1986). The Dutch Eating Behavior Questionnaire for assessment of restrained, emotional and external eating behavior. *International Journal of Eating Behavior*, *5*, 295–315.

Vasse, R. M., Nijhuis, J. N., and Kok, F. (1998). Associations between work stress, alcohol consumption and sickness absence. *Addiction*, *93*(2), 231–241.

Wardle, J., Steptoe, A., Oliver, G., and Lipsey, Z. (2000). Stress, dietary restraint and food intake. *Journal of Psychosomatic Research*, *48*, 195–202.

Weidner, G., Boughal, T., Pieper, C., Connor, S. L., and Mendell, N. R. (1997). Relationship of job strain to standard coronary risk factors and psychological characteristics in women and men of the family heart study. *Health Psychology*, *3*, 239–247.

Westman, M., Eden, D., and Shirom, A. (1985). Job stress, cigarette smoking and cessation: the conditioning effects of peer support. *Social Science and Medicine*, *20*(6), 637–644.

Whelton, S. P., Chin, A., Xin, X., and He, J. (2002). Effect of aerobic exercise on blood pressure: a meta-analysis of randomized, controlled trials. *Annals of Internal Medicine*, *137*(7), 493–503.

Willenbring, M. L., Levine, A. S., and Morley, J. (1986). Stress induced eating and food preference in humans: a pilot study. *International Journal of Eating Disorders*, *5*(5), 855–864.

Wilson, M. G., Holman, P. B., and Hammock, A. (1996). A comprehensive review of the effects of worksite health promotion on health-related outcomes. *American Journal of Health Promotion*, *10*(6), 429–435.

Part IV

Managing the work–home interface

From the chapters in Part III it is clear that work moods and affect spill over into home life in potentially damaging ways, affecting the individual in terms of their well-being and that of other family members. This suggests there is clear need for action to improve work–life balance. Unfortunately, we have limited information about the strategies individuals and organizations can best employ to reduce conflict and spillover between work and home life. There are likely to be wide individual differences in people's preferences for working practices and the coping strategies they prefer. As yet few studies have investigated these issues. However, research is starting to provide information on how the individual employee can recover from the strains of the working day. This is outlined in Chapter 9 by Fred Zijlstra and Mark Cropley.

While the individual may be able to improve their own work–life balance by the strategies and activities they adopt outside of work, much of the responsibility also rests with employer. For organizational attempts to be successful, it is fundamental that organizational cultures support work–life balance. The ways in which organizations can facilitate work–life balance initiatives are the focus of Chapter 10 by Ronald Burke.

In Chapter 11 Leslie Hammer, Jennifer Cullen and Jennifer Shafiro provide valuable information on a wide range of innovative work–life balance initiatives that have been documented to be successful within organizations. Finally, while both individual and organizational strategies are vital, Paulette Gerkovich (in Chapter 12) suggests there is also a need for radical change in organizations and, by implication, in society as a whole, so that work–family and work–life issues are no longer seen as predominantly women's issues.

9   Recovery after work

Fred Zijlstra and Mark Cropley

INTRODUCTION

Strain and fatigue are the most common short-term effects of a workday. These are the consequences of our effort investments throughout the day in order to meet the demands of work. During the day our energetic (and emotional) resources are depleted, and need to be replenished from time to time. This process is referred to as 'recuperation' or 'recovery'. Recovery is important because it allows us to prepare and be ready for the challenges of a new (work)day. We can think about the working day as consisting of three separate domains: working and traveling to work time, non-work time and sleep. Non-work time can be further divided into leisure time, referring to the time spent solely on activities one wishes to pursue, and other non-paid work time activities such as doing domestic chores. The way our society is currently organized implies that when at work we have to work, and the time after work is meant for resting and recovering from the daily hassles. However, people (need to) engage in various activities after work: i.e., domestic duties, (child)care, social activities, sports, etc. These activities might also impose demands on our resources. A relevant question, therefore, is to what extent do these activities facilitate or prohibit recovery? Sleep plays an important role in the recovery process, although the exact role of sleep in the process of recovery is not yet completely understood. The aim of this chapter is to review some of the perspectives in this domain, by reviewing the concept of recovery and discussing the role of various activities in relation to recovery.

LEISURE AND RECOVERY

Work plays a very prominent role in the life of most people between 18 and 65 years of age. For most people working times are important because they specify when they have to be at work, and therefore also determine what time is left for other activities, such as household, caring activities, other family activities and leisure. Therefore it can be said that working times structure the day, and thus are an important determinant of the cycle of work and rest. However, it hasn't always been like that. Over time the role and place of work in life have changed. In medieval times people lived in small communities that were mostly self-supporting. This implied that people usually worked for themselves (i.e., as craftsman, farmers, etc.) and their workplace was around their house. As a consequence work and domestic life were integrated and all family members took part in providing a living. People were relatively autonomous with respect to decisions concerning their work; they could decide themselves when they would start to work, or when they would like to stop, but also whether they wanted to work hard or not. This gradually changed when people started thinking about optimizing the ordering of society in the Age of Enlightenment. This period was characterized by developing new ideas and philosophies that were strongly based on reasoning. Also the religious orientation changed in this period. The Protestant Church gained influence, and a Puritan (or Protestant) work ethic emerged, in which work was given a very central place in life.

Furthermore, people started to think more rationally about all kind of phenomena, and these ideas also extended to how to organize society. Various cultural changes began in this era and many of our current political, economic and religious ideas and values can be traced back to this period. For instance, the ideas of Adam Smith on the economic ordering of society (published in his *Treatise on the Wealth of Nations*, 1772) were influential. He suggested that people and also communities should specialize. The rationale behind this idea was that when people specialize they can produce more effectively and efficiently, and thus produce more goods and of better quality. Instead of being self-supporting, individuals and communities would have to trade with each other. These ideas changed economic life.

Economic life became now less centered around the small communities, but people went to specific places (factories) to work. This led to a segregation of work and domestic life; as a consequence a stronger emphasis on organization and regulation of work was required. Working times are one of the first, and most important, aspects to be regulated; it synchronizes people's presence and therefore facilitates any form of organizing. One of the consequences of regulated working times was that people could no longer decide for themselves when they would start and/or finish working or take a break. Hence the time *after* work was the time that people had to rest and recover from work. This was the first step towards our modern industrial society and coincided with the beginning of the Industrial Revolution.

It is clear that in this line of reasoning leisure can be seen as a by-product of our industrial society (Marrus, 1974), where work is strictly regulated, very demanding and, most of all, primarily seen as an obligatory duty. The essence of leisure, according Iso-Ahola (1980), is perceived freedom and intrinsic motivation. This is believed to be in strong contrast to most work situations, where people's activities are regulated and prescribed. Also, it should be clear that leisure is not synonymous with non-work time, since people may have to fulfill other obligations, like household or childcare, after work. These activities are not always intrinsically motivated, and people do not always perceive freedom when engaging in these types of activities.

The role and function of leisure are dependent on one's view in this matter. In most western countries, where the Puritan work ethic prevails, work is glorified and leisure is devalued. It is possible, however, to see the merits of leisure in its own right, such as promoting mental health and developing one's personality (Iso-Ahola, 1997). In societies that do not value leisure, people are not able to reconcile work and family, have little time for cultivating hobbies and find it difficult to engage in civic activities that would nourish a democratic society. In these situations leisure becomes a derivative of work, solely used for recuperation from it (Hunnicut, 1988). Work is dominant in a 'work–spend–work–spend' mentality and leisure becomes trivial (Schor, 1991), and might even lead to escapism in leisure. Escapism refers to the fact that people do not seek meaningful leisure activities for their own growth and development but, instead, resort to passive activities to escape their everyday problems. Escapism in leisure leads to a passive lifestyle and to boredom, which in turn might feed into apathy and depression. From this perspective, is the fact that watching television is seemingly the most popular activity for many people in their free time rather troublesome. From a psychological perspective it would be better if people would engage in activities in which they seek challenges and would try to match them with their skills. Such optimal experiences correlate positively with mental health (Csikszentmihalyi, 1990). This clearly illustrates the importance of leisure for mental health and well-being. In western countries the Puritan (or Protestant) work ethic is dominant, and consequently leisure has primarily been seen as an opportunity for recovering from fatigue, but also to allow for distraction to prevent boredom (Friedman, 1946). This has particularly been the view on leisure in the 1950s and 1960s when a lot of rather monotonous industrial manufacturing work could still be found. Despite various cultural and economic changes over time, work ethics have not changed. Actually one might say that work has become more central in our lives (De Keyzer *et al.*, 1988).

It is assumed that leisure contributes to recovering from the demands of work; however, people have certain obligations and duties to fulfill after work, like household activities and looking after children. These activities are not always perceived as 'freedom', and are not always regarded as 'intrinsically motivated', and therefore are not 'leisure' (Iso-Ahola, 1980). Furthermore, non-work activities also impose demands upon people and may therefore have an effect on the recovery process. Several authors hold the opinion that household activities should be seen as 'another duty or responsibility', like work, which imposes considerable demands upon people (Hochchild, 1989). And implicitly it is assumed that these responsibilities prohibit recovery. Apart from household and (child)care people do engage in numerous other activities as well.

THE CYCLE OF WORK AND REST

Although it is intuitively evident that after a period of work people need some rest to recover, the topic of recovery has not received much scientific attention. Only recently have theoretical models been developed in which the concept of recovery has been specified. The Effort–Recovery model (Meijman and Mulder, 1998) specifies a particular role for recovery. This model was originally developed to describe the impact of workload. According to this model people will have to mobilize their capacities and resources to meet the demands of work. It is assumed that people decide for themselves how much of their resources will be invested and how they will deal with the demands. Depending on the complexity of the demands, and people's capacities and decision to mobilize resources, people will experience a certain level of fatigue at the end of the work period. The model assumes that people are not passively exposed to demands, but, instead, are actively mobilizing their resources and capacities to deal with the demands. Hence the importance of the notion of 'strategy' in this model. Strategy implies some level of autonomy and, therefore, for instance, having freedom to take breaks at one's own discretion. Fatigue is seen as a reversible consequence of workload and is regarded primarily as having a motivational effect. People may lose the motivation to continue working on a particular task, or may even feel some resistance to further mobilizing their resources. In order to reverse these consequences recovery is needed. Recovery is conceived as a rest period in which people are (temporarily) relieved of the demands that are being imposed upon them. The absence of demands allows the resources to be replenished. If there is no recovery, or if recovery is insufficient, fatigue will accumulate and ultimately may lead to irreversible consequences, which could imply structural 'damage' to the individual's capacities or resources. In practice, this means that lack of recovery could lead to health effects that might not easily be reversed. Although the model does not specify or give any indications as to how the process of recovery works, it is one of the few models that suggests a cycle of work and rest.

Most early studies in occupational health tended to concentrate on factors associated with work stressors and considered the absolute magnitude and intensity of the stress exposure to be the critical factor for health. It is now thought, however, that speed of recovery may be as important in the aetiology of disease and illness as the acute reactivity in response to the stress (Linden *et al.*, 1997; McEwen, 2003). Recovery can be defined as 'the post-stress rest period that provides information about the degree to which the reactivity in the physiological and psychological parameters measured persists after the stressor has ended' (Linden *et al.*, 1997, p. 117). In a more general sense recovery can also refer to the work–rest ratio (Sluiter *et al.*, 1999), or to the feeling that one is sufficiently rested and capable of commencing work at a specified or optimum level.

Another theoretical approach that should be mentioned in the light of recovery is the Conservation of Resources theory (COR) by Hobfoll (1998; see also Chapter 5). This approach claims that people strive to minimize the loss of resources when they mobilize their resources in order to face the challenges that confront them. Resource loss is seen as the primary operating mechanism driving stress reactions. Thus limiting resource loss is key to survival, because resources are essential to individuals' abilities to offset stress, improve their conditions and deter future stressful experiences. If resources are conceived in terms of energy resources this model perfectly fits into a recovery model. People want to preserve their energy in order to be able to deal with future demands or problems. This then implies that people need to rest in order to preserve, or rather restore their energy resources.

A logical conclusion from this perspective is that a relaxation period between periods of stress allows regrouping of resources. In line with this, Westman and Eden (1997) have explored the effects of a short holiday. They found that burnout scores were lower during and after a two-week vacation, although the relief was found to be short lived. Other studies have confirmed these temporary salutary effects of vacation (Westman and Etzion, 2001; Eden, 2001). Etzion *et al.* (1998) extended the scope of this type of research to suggest that non-work time of any sort (not just holidays) could help to manage stress and relieve the symptoms of burnout. Thus the daily recovery that occurs in the evenings after normal working days or during the weekend respite is important to maintain a particular level of well-being. From an energetic perspective this seems to make perfect sense.

In the last couple of decades various societal changes have had an effect on work times. These changes are of demographic, social and technological nature (Roe *et al.*, 1994). Without pretending to be exhaustive, it is relevant to mention a few of these developments (see Chapter 1 for more detailed discussion). First of all, due to cultural and social developments, the labour force has changed. Increasingly women have entered the labour market, resulting in an increase of the number of dual-earner families, and making it socially acceptable that modern couples renegotiate their domestic duties with the intention to share these duties (Blair, 1998). One of the side effects of this development is that organizations have started to realize that it is important to maintain a healthy balance in life, and that for optimal performance at work it is necessary that private life can be combined with working life. For this reason many organizations do acknowledge that a work–life balance policy is an important aspect of an organizational Human Resources policy. One of the elements of such a policy could be the introduction of flexible working times in order to allow for childcare arrangements.

Another development with a huge impact on working times concerns the introduction of information technology. Technological developments such as mobile telecommunication and the Internet have disentangled the concepts of 'time' and place' in relation to work. No longer is it strictly necessary to be at a certain location at a specified time in order to perform particular activities. People can actually communicate or work from virtually all kinds of locations at a time of their convenience. This development has stimulated new forms of work such as tele-home work, working at a distance and virtual teams. This allows people to do their work from home and yet be in contact with their organization. When people work from home, there is no need for a physical relocation (commute). Hence this option may be attractive, to women in particular, because it facilitates the combination of active pursuit of a professional career with managing responsibility for domestic duties (e.g., looking after children). Although these developments are relatively new and the number of 'teleworkers' not very high, initial evaluation studies suggest that people's expectations in this respect are only partly fulfilled (see Chapter 6). It appears that, in particular, people who had opted for such an arrangement in order to be able to combine childcare with being able to work experience higher levels of frustration, conflict and stress (Ahrentzen, 1990). The primary beneficiaries of such arrangements seem to be people without children. The implication of most sorts of tele-home work arrangements is that the dividing line between working life and private life becomes fluid and unclear. The psychological implication is that many people are left with the feeling of never being finished with either work or domestic duties. When people continue with their work in the evening this effectively means an extension of their working day.

Working late in the evening necessarily reduces the opportunity for recovery. Rau and Triemer (2004) found that people who regularly worked overtime had more sleep problems than those who worked regular hours. However, the people in this study did not work at home, but worked in their official workplace. Information is lacking concerning the association between working at home and sleep. As more people are taking work home or are working from home (see above), it is important to know whether these job-related activities affect recovery. This evidently has an impact on the daily work–rest cycle, as there is now more time allocated to work and thus less time for leisure or recovery.

Furthermore, work itself has changed considerably over the past decades. Most western societies have changed from an industrial orientation into economies that are primarily service oriented (see also Chapter 1). Most people work nowadays in professions that can be labeled as 'white-collar', i.e., work in offices, with their heads rather than with their hands. In terms of work demands, this means that the emphasis in work now has shifted from primarily physical demands to mental or cognitive demands (Zijlstra *et al.*, 1996). The use of information technology has stimulated this development. Also, owing to ongoing rationalization and various efficiency operations in organizations in the 1990s, work has become more intense and intensive, resulting in an increase in the number of people complaining about work pressure (Paoli and Merllié, 2001). More than half of the working population complained about having to work under pressure. Occupationally induced fatigue is the short-term effect of a working day and is primarily experienced *after* a day of work (Sluiter, 1999). Current indications are that fatigue is a common complaint in the working population, which affects about 25–33% of the working population (Bultmann *et al.*, 2002). This implies that the fatigue people experience may have an effect on what kind of activities they are willing to undertake after work. People may decide that they are just too tired for certain activities, like social activities, and stay home instead of going out, or resort to a passive type of leisure (e.g., watching television). In the late 1970s, Piotrkowski (1978) reported that, in addition to the impacts of positive and negative experiences at work on the family, some workers were just too drained by physical tiredness or by working in boring jobs that they developed apathy for family life.

These developments have clearly not been without consequences for the health and well-being of working people. Work-related stress is now a leading cause of sickness absence and lost productivity. People with mental health problems (e.g., psychological complaints such as burnout, depression and stress-related complaints) are currently the fastest-growing category among people receiving Incapacity Benefit in western European countries.

SLEEP AND RECOVERY

Sleep is considered to be the most important recovery mechanism available to humans, and therefore a prerequisite for optimal daily functioning and health. It is assumed that sleep must be continuous for it to be restorative (Walsh and Lindblom, 2000). Sleep loss and sleep disturbance can lead to performance decrements, fatigue, mood changes and in extreme cases even to immune function impairment (Harrison and Horne, 1999). Even moderate sleep loss is associated with deficits in alertness and performance (Dinges *et al.*, 1997; Akerstedt *et al.*, 2002a). Lack of sleep or poor quality of sleep is also associated with absenteeism, reduced productivity and an increased risk of fatigue-related accidents (Stoller, 1994; Akerstedt *et al.*, 2002b). However, most studies on recovery, and actually in general in the domain of work and health, have neglected to include measures of sleep. This is surprising considering the association between high work demands and sleep disturbance (Akerstedt *et al.*, 2002a; Cropley *et al.*, 1999).

The mechanisms by which occupational stress is associated with sleep disturbance are not known. One possibility may be that people in stressful jobs are very active during the evening and therefore are physiologically aroused at bedtime. Thus far, no empirical evidence has supported this interpretation: studies that have examined physical activity have found no difference in variations in job stress and energy expenditure over the working day or evening (Steptoe and Cropley, 2000). Another possibility is that people have difficulty 'switching off' from work-related issues and thoughts at bedtime, and therefore have difficulties falling asleep. Harvey (2000) showed that pre-sleep cognition affects sleep quality, and manipulations of cognitive arousal before sleep leads to longer sleep latencies (Gross and Borkovec, 1982). In particular, when people have problems to deal with at work, or when there have been conflicts at work, people may have ruminative thoughts, which make it difficult to switch off from work. We do not know the number of workers who have difficulty 'switching off' from work-related thoughts. However, a recent survey on sleep behavior found that about 17% of a representative sample of the working population in the UK reported having sleeping problems caused by worrying about their work (Groeger *et al.*, 2004). Recent studies have shown that a failure to unwind after work leads to sleep complaints and consequently makes people feel unrefreshed the next morning (Meijman *et al.*, 1992; Sluiter *et al.*, 1999). The failure to unwind is associated with particular job characteristics, working in a demanding environment, working long hours and accompanied by a lack of perceived control at work and home (Cropley and Millward-Purvis, 2003).

Zijlstra and de Vries (2000) showed that, in particular, people who scored high on the burnout dimension 'emotional exhaustion' slept fewer hours per night and were not feeling refreshed when getting up. Furthermore, it was found that these exhausted people rate their effort expenditure at work in the morning as much higher than people who were not feeling exhausted. In other words, exhausted people apparently do not feel up to the demands that are imposed upon them in the morning. The study was based upon a cross-sectional survey; therefore we cannot draw any causal inferences, but the relation between feeling unrefreshed in the morning and having to exert high levels of effort suggests that there may be cumulative effects of lack of recovery, as suggested by the Effort-Recovery model (Meijman and Mulder, 1998). It certainly indicates that sleep is important in the process of recovery.

AFTER-WORK EXPERIENCES

Individuals respond to a stressful workday with specific behavior during leisure time that helps alleviate the negative impact of the strain experienced during work (Repetti, 1993).

This means that people will have a preference for certain types of activities; for instance, when tired the choice for a passive activity may seem logical. The implication is that people are evading the demands being placed upon them, which allows them to replenish their resources again. However, as noted before, not all non-work time can be regarded as leisure. Although leisure activities can also be demanding, the nature of their demands is assumed to be different from work demands, primarily because people engage in these activities voluntarily (Iso-Ahola, 1997; Haworth, 1997). This is in contrast with work, where people have an obligation to show up and to expose themselves to the demands of work, while their level of control or autonomy is often limited by organizational constraints.

Since all activities, including non-work activities, impose demands, it is relevant to question whether activities do actually facilitate or inhibit recovery. This leads to further questions: Is there enough time/opportunity for recovery? What is the role of domestic duties (household and childcare activities) in relation to recovery? Do we need to differentiate between types of leisure activities that are beneficial for recovery and others that are not? More specifically, what activities contribute to recovery?

Recently a few diary studies have tried to shed some light on the question concerning the extent to which various activities contribute to recovery (Sonnentag, 2001; Zijlstra and Rook, 2003). After-work activities have been categorized into five groups (see Sonnentag, 2001). A first group of activities consists of 'job-related activities'. These activities can include regular work activities that many people do in the evening but can also include filling out tax forms. These activities were predicted to inhibit recovery since it is assumed recovery can only occur when demands are absent. Secondly, a group of activities were labeled as household activities; these include domestic duties like cleaning, cooking and caring. These activities also have an obligatory character and place demands upon people; i.e., people cannot (easily) withdraw from these demands. In the perspective of Iso-Ahola (1980) these activities are not intrinsically motivated and thus should not be considered as leisure. Therefore these activities are also predicted to inhibit or prevent recovery. A third group of activities are so-called 'low-effort activities'. These activities are primarily passive in nature and place very few demands on people's resources (like watching television), and are therefore assumed to enable recovery, or at least not to inhibit recovery. A fourth category consists of 'social activities', like going out or visiting friends. Since work demands are absent in these situations, and these activities are generally believed to be intrinsically motivated and thus not having an obligatory character (and thus enjoyable), they are predicted to facilitate recovery. Finally, a fifth category consists of 'physical activities' (sports, working out, etc.), which are believed to be beneficial for recovery since these activities require different resources to be used from those that are typically used at work. Also, physical activities have been extolled as beneficial in their own right because they seem to alleviate feelings of depression, and therefore becoming an 'antidote' to anxiety, stress and burnout (Hull, 1990; Iso-Ahola, 1997; Iwasaki, 2001). For example, Bultmann *et al.* (2002) have been able to demonstrate in a longitudinal study that people who exercise less are more likely to be fatigued.

Sonnentag's study revealed that the amount of time spent during non-work time on job-related activities had a deleterious effect on recovery, and the amount of time spent on low-effort, physical and social activities was conducive to recovery. In this study recovery was operationalized as an increase in situational well-being at bedtime. Zijlstra and Rook (2003) have asked people to keep a diary of their activities during a week (inclusive of the weekend) and to indicate what category of activities (see above) they have engaged in and for how long. Furthermore people had to indicate their level of fatigue at the end of the day (i.e., just before going to bed) and to complete a sleep questionnaire on the following morning. This included questions on sleep quantity (i.e., at what times they went to bed and got up, for how long they had slept) and sleep quality (i.e., whether their sleep was disturbed or they had sleeping problems) and whether they felt refreshed on waking up.

Fatigue and recovery are related concepts: fatigue is the state that results from having been exposed to work demands, and recovery is the process of replenishing the depleted resources or rebalancing suboptimal systems. Fatigue can therefore be seen as a proxy for recovery. The results of this study for the most part confirmed the findings by Sonnentag: the more time that was spent on job-related activities after official working hours (i.e., in the evening) the higher the level of fatigue. Interestingly enough, it appeared that domestic duties did not contribute to predicting fatigue before bedtime. Apparently household activities have no detrimental effect on recovery. It may well be that engagement in household activities, and in particular looking after (and playing with) children, means that people are distracted from the daily hassles and concerns with work, and therefore this does not contribute to elevated levels of fatigue. Alternatively, the fact that people generally have more autonomy and control over their own domestic duties than over their work activities may play a significant role. Autonomy and control imply that people can work at their own pace and can take breaks whenever they want. This prevents them from getting fatigued (Karasek and Theorell, 1990).

Furthermore, it appeared that low-effort activities played no significant role in predicting recovery (i.e., reducing levels of fatigue), while social activities were just marginally related. On the other hand, physical activities appeared to have a significant contribution in predicting recovery. An explanation offered by Haworth (1997) and Iso-Ahola (1997) is that active engagement and involvement in (leisure) activities has a much greater restorative effect than being passive. Being actively involved in activities implies that people have to concentrate and divert attention to that activity, which helps to disengage from the previous activities. This explanation could also apply to domestic duties, in particular looking after children. It helps people to disengage from the daily hassles at work and therefore helps them to 'switch off' from work. Steptoe *et al.* (2000), who investigated the effects of family structure and physiological recovery, demonstrated this in their study, in which physiological parameters were monitored to assess tension over the working day and evening (from 9 a.m. to 10.30 p.m.). The influence of family structure was assessed by dividing the sample into parents, married non-parents (or cohabiting couples) and single individuals without children. There were no significant differences across these three groups over the working day; however, day/evening differences (adjusted for age and body mass index) were significant. Greatest recovery (reduction in tension) was observed for parents, then married/cohabiting non-parents and, finally, singles. There were no gender differences, and the findings could not be attributed to variation across groups in subjective feelings of job stress, physical activity or location during measurement. Thus, recovery appeared also to be facilitated by social support, as those parents who reported higher levels of social support also showed the greatest decline in tension in the evening after the working day. This study suggests that attention to familial issues and being in a cohesive relationship can distract someone away from work-related thoughts. The implication is that being actively involved in activities has a greater contribution to recovery than passive activities. Also, sleep quality emerged as a significant predictor for recovery. When people had slept well the night before, and thus felt refreshed in the morning, this resulted in lower levels of fatigue at bedtime.

Zijlstra and Rook showed a weekly pattern of sleep and fatigue. First of all, as expected, the general level of fatigue during the week was significantly higher than at the weekend. However, the highest levels of fatigue could be found in the first half of the week: Monday to Wednesday. Furthermore, level of fatigue during the first half of the week significantly predicted levels of fatigue over the weekend (explaining 46% of the variance of weekend fatigue). Interestingly, according to people's assessment of the quality of their sleep, people generally seem to sleep worst during the night from Sunday to Monday. An explanation for this phenomenon might be that people shift their sleep–wake pattern during the weekend by getting up late on Sunday and therefore also going to bed late on Sunday evening, thus feeling less well rested on Monday morning. However, this interpretation doesn't seem likely since fatigue scores remain high for a few days and then drop again. It is not likely that a shift in sleep–wake rhythm for one day should have an effect lasting three days. Alternatively, this finding could also be interpreted as an anticipation effect: on Sunday evening people start to anticipate the demands of work, as though they dread the coming working week. Many people will actually take a look into their diary in order to see what they should expect in the coming week. This does not necessarily imply that people dread their work as such; it may very well be the general set-up they are dreading: the commute; the fact that on weekdays the pace is generally higher than at the weekend. This interpretation seems to be consistent with the fatigue scores being higher on Monday to Wednesday; after Wednesday people are looking forward to the weekend again and they anticipate being able to live a more easy-going life for two days.

Interestingly enough demographic variables (age, gender and presence of children) did not play a role in predicting fatigue. This means that the above findings did not only apply to families with (young) children, but also rather seem to reflect general perceptions of working people.

Sleep problems are also associated with fatigue and recovery. Lack of sleep or disrupted sleep results in not feeling refreshed in the morning. Zijlstra and Rook (2003) demonstrated that people who have higher levels of fatigue sleep fewer hours per night, rate their sleep as poorer and feel less refreshed in the morning, while also being significantly less physically active.

The mechanisms by which occupational stress is associated with sleep disturbance are not exactly known. An explanation could be that some people may have difficulties 'switching off' from work-related issues and therefore still have all kinds of thoughts about work at bedtime. This may be particularly true when people are experiencing difficulties or are having problems and conflicts at work (which are typically associated with stressful conditions). In those situations people cannot ban the thoughts about these problems from their mind, a situation which in the clinical literature is called 'ruminating'. These thoughts are intrinsically generated and unavoidable; i.e., people cannot stop them. Ruminating might be a strategy whereby people are trying to solve the problem; that is, continuously thinking of the problem might be seen as an attempt to simulate all kinds of alternative solutions. However, it is a strategy that may have negative effects on sleep and recovery.

CONCLUSION

Work has a very central place in our lives; this is referred as a 'Puritan work ethic'. Work has also become very demanding, which has led to an increase in pressures on the working population over the past decades. The effects of the working day affect the time after work. Working patterns have also changed, with more flexibility and more people working from home. We are beginning to understand how emotional strains spill over, but this question has not yet been considered from the perspective of 'recovery'. Also family roles have changed, making people aware of the fact that a healthy work–life balance is necessary to ensure sufficient recovery from the daily strains. A healthy work–life balance not only refers to the combination of working life and family life, but also implies sufficient time for leisure. Leisure has benefits not only for the individual in terms of personal growth and quality of life, but also for society in general.

The studies referred to in the previous sections make clear that various activities contribute differently to recovery of daily strains of work. Sleep is evidently important for recovery. However, the exact processes and mechanisms involved are not yet completely understood. Physical activity (sports) has been found to be beneficial for recovery (Thorlindsson, Vilhjalmsson and Valgeirsson, 1990), but also domestic duties appeared not to hinder recovery from work. In general, the more passively oriented activities seemed to have the least impact on recovery. As far as recovery from work is concerned it seems that actively engaging in activities is important, because it might help people 'switch off' from work. Worries and concerns about work will make the mind constantly wander to these work-related issues and prevent people from relaxing from the daily strains. Ruminating about work should probably be conceived as trying to think of solutions for various issues/problems that have arisen at work. By simulating mentally the various options that are available people may try to find out what solution(s) might work.

A practical recommendation with respect to recovery is to make sure that work schedules are installed that offer people the opportunity to engage in various activities and to allow them to combine their various duties and roles. Have adequate work–rest cycles during the working day (i.e., allow for a substantive lunch break). Part of these recommendations should also be to make sure that people have manageable portions of (daily) work. Allowing people to finish a substantive piece of work will facilitate 'switching off' from work and prevent people from ruminating about work. The fatigue of work well accomplished gets people ready for sleep.

Recovery after work is an important topic, with major implications for people's health and well-being. We are just beginning to research those activities that facilitate the recovery process and these findings will have important implications for how we conceptualize and investigate recovery after work.

This also illustrates that as far as work and health are concerned we should not limit ourselves to looking only at work-related factors, but should adopt a much wider perspective including non-work aspects as well, such as the activities people engage in after work.

REFERENCES

Ahrentzen, S. B. (1990). Managing conflict by managing boundaries: how professional homeworkers cope with multiple roles at home. *Environment and Behavior, 22,* 723–752.

Akerstedt, T., Knutsson, A., Westerholm, P., Theorell, T., Alfredsson, L., and

Kecklund, G. (2002a). Sleep disturbances, work stress and work hours: a cross-sectional study. *Journal of Psychosomatic Research, 53*, 741–748.

Akerstedt, T., Fredlund, P., Gillberg, M., and Jansson, B. (2002b). A prospective study of fatal occupational accidents: relationship to sleeping difficulties and occupational factors. *Journal of Sleep Research, 11*, 69–71.

Blair, S L. (1998). Work roles, domestic roles and marital quality: perceptions of fairness among dual-earner couples. *Social Justice Research, 11*, 313–335.

Bultmann, U., Kant, I., Kasl, S. V., Schroer, K. A. P., Swaen, G. M. H., and van den Brandt, P. A. (2002). Lifestyle factors as risk factors for fatigue and psychological distress in the working population: prospective results from the Maastricht Cohort Study. *Journal of Occupational and Environmental Medicine, 44*, 116–124.

Cropley, M., Steptoe, A., and Joekes, K. (1999). Job strain and psychiatric morbidity. *Psychological Medicine, 29*, 1411–1416.

Cropley, M., and Millward-Purvis, L. (2003). Job strain and rumination about work issues during leisure time: a diary study. *European Journal of Work and Organizational Psychology, 12*, 195–207.

Csikszentmihalyi, M. (1990). *Flow*. New York: Harper & Row.

De Keyser, V., Qvale., T., Wilpert, B., and Ruiz-Quintanilla, S. A. (eds) (1988). *The Meaning of Work and Technological Options*. Chichester: Wiley.

Dinges, D. F., Pack, F., Williams, K., Gillen, K. A., Powell, J. W., Ott, G. E., Aptowicz., C., and Pack, A. I. (1997). Cumulative sleepiness, mood disturbance, and psychomotor vigilance performance decrements during a week of sleep restricted to 4–5 hours per night. *Sleep, 20*, 267–277.

Eden, D. (2001). Vacations and other respites: studying stress on and off the job. In C. Cooper and I. Robertson (eds), *Well-being in organizations: A Reader for Students and Practitioners* (Chapter 10). Chichester: Wiley.

Etzion, D., Eden, D., and Lapidot, Y. (1998). Relief from job stressors and burnout: reserve service as a respite. *Journal of Applied Psychology, 83*, 577–585.

Friedman, G. (1946). *Problemes humains du machinisme industriel*. Paris: Gaillimard.

Groeger, J., Zijlstra, F. R. H., and Dijk, D. J. (2004). Sleep quantity, sleep difficulties and their perceived consequences in a representative sample of some two thousand British adults. *Journal of Sleep Research, 13*, 359–371.

Gross, R. T., and Borkovec, T. D. (1982). The effects of a cognitive intrusion manipulation on the sleep-onset latency of good sleepers. *Behaviour Therapy, 13*, 112–116.

Harrison, Y., and Horne, J. A. (1999). One night of sleep loss impairs innovative thinking and flexible decision making. *Organizational Behavior and Human Decision Processes, 78*, 128–145.

Harvey, A. G. (2000). Pre-sleep cognitive activity: a comparison of sleep-onset insomniacs and good sleepers. *British Journal of Clinical Psychology, 39*, 275–286.

Haworth, J. T. (1997). *Work, leisure and well-being*. London: Routledge.

Hobfoll, S. E. (1998). *Stress, culture, and community: the psychology and physiology of stress*. New York: Plenum.

Hochschild, A. (1989). *The second shift*. New York: Avon.

Hull, R. (1990). Mood as a product of leisure: causes and consequences. *Journal of Leisure Research, 22*, 99–111.

Hunnicut, B. (1988). *Work without end: Abandoning of shorter hours for the right to work*. Philadelphia, PA: Temple University Press.

Iso-Ahola, S. (1980). *The social psychology of leisure and recreation.* Dubuque, IA: W.C. Brown.

Iso-Ahola, S. (1997). A psychological analysis of leisure and health. In J. T. Haworth (ed.), *Work, leisure and well-being* (pp. 131–144). London: Routledge.

Iwasaki, Y. (2001). Contributions of leisure to coping with daily hassles in university students' lives. *Canadian Journal of Behavioral Science, 33,* 128–141.

Karasek, R. A., and Theorell, T. (1990). *Healthy work: stress and productivity in working life.* New York: Basic Books.

Linden, W., Earle, T. L., Gerin, W., and Christenfeld, N. (1997). Physiological stress reactivity and recovery: conceptual siblings separated at birth? *Journal of Psychosomatic Research, 42,* 117–135.

Marrus, M. (1974). *The emergence of leisure.* San Francisco: Harper & Row.

McEwen, B. S. (2003). Interacting mediators of allostasis and allostatic load: towards an understanding of resilience in aging. *Metabolism: Clinical and Experimental, 52,* 10–16.

Meijman, T. F., and Mulder, G. (1998). Psychological aspects of workload. In P. J. D. Drenth, H. Thierry and C. J. deWolff (eds), *Handbook of work and organizational psychology* (2nd edn). *Work Psychology* (Vol. 2., pp. 5–33). Hove: Psychology Press.

Meijman, T. F., Mulder, G., and Van Dormolen, M. (1992). Workload of driving examiners: a psychophysiological field study. In H. Kragt (ed.), *Enhancing industrial performances* (pp. 245–260). London: Taylor & Francis.

Paoli, P., and Merllié, D. (2001). *Third European survey on working conditions 2000.* Dublin: European Foundation for the Improvement of Working and Living Conditions. Retrieved from http://www.eurofound.eu.int/publications/files/EF9721EN.pdf

Piotrkowski, C. S. (1978). *Work and the family system.* New York: Free Press.

Rau, R., and Triemer, A. (2004). Overtime in relation to blood pressure and mood during work, leisure, and night time. *Social Indicators Research, 67,* 51–73.

Repetti, R. L. (1993). Short-term effects of occupational stressors on daily mood and health complaints. *Health Psychology, 12,* 125–131.

Roe, R. A., Berg, P. T. van den, Zijlstra, F. R. H., Schalk, M. J. D., Taillieu, T. C. B., and van der Wielen J. M. M. (1994). New concepts for a new age: information service organizations and mental information work. *European Work and Organizational Psychologist, 3,* 177–192.

Schor, J. (1991). *The overworked American: The unexpected decline of leisure.* New York: Basic Books.

Sluiter, J. K. (1999). *How about work demands, recovery and health? A neuroendocrine field study during and after work.* PhD thesis. Amsterdam: AMC.

Sluiter, J. K., van-der-Beek, A. J., and Frings-Dresen, M. H. V. (1999). The influences of work characteristics on the need for recovery and experienced health: a study on coach drivers. *Ergonomics, 42,* 573–583.

Sonnentag, S. (2001). Work, recovery activities, and individual well-being: a diary study. *Journal of Occupational Health Psychology, 6,* 196–210.

Steptoe, A., and Cropley, M. (2000). Persistent high job demands and reactivity to mental stress predict future ambulatory blood pressure. *Journal of Hypertension, 18,* 581–586.

Steptoe, A., Lundwall, K., and Cropley, M. (2000). Gender, family structure and cardiovascular activity during the working day and evening. *Social Science and Medicine*, *50*, 531–539.

Stoller, M. K. (1994). Economic effects of insomnia. *Clinical Therapy*, *16*, 873–897.

Thorlindsson, T., Vilhjalmsson, R., and Valgeirsson, G. (1990). Sport participation and perceived health status: a study of adolescents. *Social Science and Medicine*, *31*, 551–556.

Walsh, J. K., and Lindblom, S. S. (2000). Psychophysiology of sleep deprivation and disruption. In M. R. Pressman and W. C. Orr (eds), *Understanding sleep, the evaluation and treatment of sleep disorders* (pp. 73–110). Washington, DC: APA.

Westman, M., and Eden, D. (1997). Effects of a respite from work on burnout: vacation relief and fade-out. *Journal of Applied Psychology*, *82*, 516–527.

Westman, M., and Etzion, D. (2001). The impact of vacation and job stress on burnout and absenteeism. *Psychology and Health*, *16*, 595–606.

Zijlstra, F. R. H., and de Vries, J. (2000). Burnout en de bijdrage van socio-demografische en werkgebonden variabelen. [Burnout and the contribution of socio-demographic and work-related variables.] In I. L. D. Houtman, W. B. Schaufeli and T. Taris (eds), *Psychische Vermoeidheid en Werk: Cijfers, trends en analyses* (pp. 83–95). Alphen a/d Rijn: Samsom.

Zijlstra, F. R. H., and Rook, J. (2003). The contribution of various types of activities to recovery. Paper presented at the *11th European conference on work and organizational psychology*, Lisbon, 14–17 May.

Zijlstra, F. R. H., Schalk, M. J. D., and Roe, R. A. (1996). Veranderingen in de Arbeid. Conse-quenties voor Werkenden. [Changes in Work: Consequences for working people.] *Tijdschrift voor Arbeidsvraagstukken*, *12*, 251–263.

10 Organizational culture: a key to the success of work–life integration*

Ronald J. Burke

As discussed in Chapter 1, the increasing number of women entering the workforce has led to concerns about the need for balanced commitment to work and personal life (Schwartz, 1992; Davidson and Burke, 1994). In addition, these concerns are not only women's concerns; as societal values change, men have expressed interest in a more balanced work commitment as well (Burke and Nelson, 1998; Friedman and Galinsky, 1992; Parasuraman and Greenhaus, 1997).

Kofodimos (1993) proposes that the root causes of imbalance are deeply imbedded in the social character of many in the industrialized world. It stems from the importance of work and the perceived benefits of a mastery-oriented approach to both working and living. As a result, individuals seeking integration will have to make basic changes in their approach to life and in the workings of their organizations.

This chapter reviews research findings on the role of organizational culture on the success of initiatives to facilitate work–life integration and characteristics of those cultures that help in this process. Beginning with an examination of the family-friendly workplace, barriers to implementing work–life programs are noted. The notion of a work–family culture is then introduced. We then present research findings from some of our own studies that examine the role of organizational culture. Features of supportive organizational cultures are identified. The chapter concludes with suggestions about future research needs.

The phrase 'family-friendly' was coined to describe those firms attempting to support work–personal life balance (Rodgers and Rodgers, 1989; Konrad, 1990). Many of these early efforts involved the creation of workplace policies more conducive to balanced investments in work and personal life. The efforts of these innovative organizations have been chronicled in lists of 'best places to work' as well as described in the more

* This research was supported in part by the School of Business, York University. Zena Burgess, Fay Oberklaid, Graeme Macdermid and Cobi Wolpin assisted with data collection and analysis, and Fiona Jones provided constructive feedback.

mainstream professional and academic journals (see *Women in Management Review*, 1995; *Equal Opportunities International*, 1997; *Women in Management Review*, 1999). Unfortunately some of these efforts have not made much difference or have not had staying power (Bailyn, 1994; Higgins *et al.*, 2000). More promising are attempts to fundamentally address workplace norms that reduce both work–personal life balance and organizational performance (Bailyn *et al.*, 1997; Fletcher and Bailyn, 1996; Fletcher and Rapoport, 1996).

The term 'family-friendly' is an umbrella term describing a variety of policies and programs having the goal of facilitating the ability of employees to fulfill their family responsibilities (e.g., on-site day care, flexible working hours). However, Scheibl and Dex (1998) believe that the term 'family-friendly' is vague, lacking a concise definition. In addition, it is also important to broaden the term to include employees without children who are striving for work–personal life balance. An increasing number of organizations have developed such policies and programs over the past 20 years in response to both demographic changes in the workforce and competitive pressures to attract and retain quality staff (Friedman and Galinsky, 1992).

Thompson *et al.* (1992) note that the most popular family-responsive programs and policies fall under four major categories: (1) dependent care; (2) parental leave programs; (3) spouse relocation and job locator programs; and (4) alternative work schedules (e.g., flexible work hours, job sharing, part-time work and reduced workload arrangements). While many of these policies focus on families with children, others may benefit childless couples or individuals simply wanting to balance work and leisure activities.

It is believed that the provision of such programs will have benefits for both employees and employing firms. Unfortunately relatively little research has examined this belief (Kossek and Ozeki, 1998). Most evaluations are anecdotal; the more substantial research studies present mixed findings (Gonyea and Googins, 1992; Lobel, 1999).

DO WORK–FAMILY PROGRAMS AND POLICIES WORK?

Rosin and Korabik (2001) found that it is satisfaction with family-friendly policies rather than mere access to or utilization of them that produces a reduction in work–family conflict and positive work and personal outcomes. It is critical that these policies and programs meet employee needs (i.e., they must work) and are implemented in a supportive environment, if companies are to benefit from the development of such initiatives. Otherwise, family-friendly policies and programs will be underutilized and not achieve their objectives (Lewis, 1997).

Thus the presence of these policies and programs does not guarantee that they will be used or will work effectively. Finkel *et al.* (1994), in a study of university staff, found that 77% of women faculty thought that taking a maternity leave would have negative career consequences, and only 30% who gave birth took the full leave provided by their universities. Others (Hammonds, 1997; Perlow, 1995; Schwartz, 1995) have found that similar concerns exist among various groups of women employees. And these concerns are warranted. Judiesch and Lyness (1999) found that taking family leave was negatively associated with subsequent promotions and salary increases.

Thompson *et al.* (1992) identify four barriers to the successful implementation of work–family programs. These were: (1) prevailing assumptions about gender roles and their relation to work and family, primarily the masculinization of work and the feminization of the family; (2) the lack of consensus and national leadership on national policy regarding work–family issues; (3) the difficulty of managing flexibility; and (4) the clash of work–family programs and company cultures.

Thompson and Beauvais (2000) noted six barriers to implementing work–life programs in organizations: (1) ingrained cultural assumptions and values regarding work and non-work domains; (2) structural difficulties in implementing programs; (3) lack of support from managers and supervisors; (4) the perception that family issues are women's issues; (5) maintaining equity among all employees; and (6) lack of evaluation data on work–life programs. Thompson and Beauvais (2000) believe that the values and assumptions in the culture about work and non-work domains are the most significant.

CLASHES OF CORPORATE CULTURE AND CORPORATE POLICIES

Thompson and Beauvais (2000) report the results of a survey by RHI Managerial Resources of 1400 chief financial officers on the importance of organizational support in helping employees balance work and other aspects of their lives. They found that 55% said this was 'very important' and 39% said it was 'somewhat important' (p. 172). The most frequently offered benefit was flexible hours (45% said they offered it), followed by part-time work (40%), job sharing (27%) and telecommuting (13%). But offering a variety of work–family programs does not guarantee that a company will be seen as family-friendly by its employees. A key factor is whether the company's informal culture supports work–family balance (Smith, 1992).

A company may develop a wide range of innovative work–family programs only to have them resisted by line managers. Managers may continue to hold traditional views on what is important to business success (Bowen, 1998). The corporate culture can thwart the use of particular programs. Some corporate values work against the use of flexibility. Employees may not use particular programs because of the potential impact they believe using them will have on their careers (Allen and Russell, 1999).

Unfortunately, the most commonly used work–family programs (e.g., flexible hours, part-time work) do nothing to challenge the underlying structure of organizations or the culture that supports the masculinization of work. Instead, these programs blend into existing structures and organizational values. What is needed? At a minimum, organizations need to look at their corporate culture, the norms that define commitment, success and appropriate behaviors (Friedman and Johnson, 1996). Top management support is critical in this regard.

Although there has been considerable writing on specific work–family policies and programs and their effects, little attention has been devoted to the overall climate (e.g., cultural values) of organizational work–family support. However, one study by Jahn *et al.* (2003) looks at perceived organizational family support (POFS) involving 310 employees from 96 organizations. They advocate a more subjective approach based on employee perceptions of organizational support for balancing work and family. They do so because policies and practices espoused by a firm may not reflect reality. They distinguish between organization family support and perceived organizational family support. The former encompasses all the policies and programs offered by an organization; the latter is the employee's perception of the assistance available from the organization in terms of instrumental support, informational support and emotional support. Jahn and her colleagues found significant positive relationships between scores on the POFS and two more objective measures of organizational support. Interestingly, as predicted, POFS scores were independent of measures of lateness and absenteeism. They also found evidence of high interrater agreement (people working for the same firm tended to report similar POFS scores).

Allen (2001) developed a measure of global employee perceptions of the extent to which their organization was family supportive. Data were collected from 522 women and men in a variety of jobs and organizations. Perceptions of family supportiveness were related to the number of family-friendly benefits offered by the organization, benefit usage and perceived family support from supervisors. These global perceptions explained significant amounts of variance measures of work–family conflict, job satisfaction, organizational commitment and turnover intentions beyond the variance explained by the number of family-friendly benefits offered or level of supervision support. This global perception of employees of the overall work environment pertaining to family supportiveness impacts their views and reactions to specific family-friendly policies and practices.

Thompson and Beauvais (2000) suggest that we can discover how barriers to successful implementation of work–life programs have been overcome by studying companies known for their successful work–life policies and programs. They offer three common themes of successful company efforts: (1) work–life integration is considered a strategic initiative of the business (a bottom-line issue); (2) research is conducted on the behavioral and organizational effects of work–life policies and programs; and (3) cultural assumptions about the link between work and other life domains are examined and changed.

Lyness *et al.* (1999) examined individual and organizational factors associated with organizational commitment and planned timing of maternity leaves and return to work after childbirth in a sample of 86 pregnant women. Women who perceived supportive work–family cultures were more committed to their organizations and planned to return more quickly after childbirth than women who perceived less supportive cultures.

Thompson *et al.* (1999) considered work–family culture as 'the shared assumptions, beliefs and values regarding the extent to which an organization supports and values the integration of employee's work and family lives'. They proposed three dimensions of work–family culture: managerial support for work–family balance, fewer negative career consequences associated with using work–family benefits and fewer organizational time demands that might interfere with family responsibilities. They found that employees' perceptions of a supportive organizational work–family culture were positively related to affective commitment and negatively related to intention to quit.

Similar observations were made by Thompson *et al.* (1999), who suggested that employees were more likely to use work–family programs when they perceived a more supportive work–family culture. In addition, experiencing a more supportive work–family culture was related to greater organizational commitment, lower intention to quit and less work–family conflict.

A national study of about 3000 employees found that individuals reported less conflict and stress and developed better coping strategies when their supervisors and workplace cultures were supportive (Galinsky *et al.*, 1996). These employees also were more committed to their employers, had greater job satisfaction and were more willing to work harder to help their firms succeed. The way the policies and programs were implemented and managed by line managers and given credibility by the organization's culture seemed to be more important than the actual policies per se. They conclude that to get bottom-line business results from work–life policies and programs both corporate cultural values and managers' attitudes towards these policies and programs (and work–life integration more broadly) must be taken into account.

Kolb and Merrill-Sands (1999) describe collaborative action research projects with organizations having a dual aim: promoting gender equity and increasing organizational effectiveness. Running through these are the connections between work and family life. Policies and programs exist in many workplaces that keep people accommodated, but do not integrate their work and family lives. Families are accommodated (on-site childcare) or individuals accommodated (part-time work). These policies and programs failed to question work policies and organizational cultures that made using these family-friendly policies and programs problematic. Kolb and

Merrill-Sands believe that it is critical to focus on work practices and organizational cultures by challenging the assumptions (values) on which they are based and making efforts to change these if real progress is to be made.

They ask questions such as the following: 'To what degree do informal work practices and cultural assumptions reinforce certain work processes and outputs and narrow definitions of what it means to be a committed and competent worker?' 'How do current work practices make it difficult for people to integrate their work and personal lives and what repercussions does this have for women and men in the workplace and in the family?' The goal of their approach is to have people identify and question these cultural assumptions and develop a collaborative strategy to deal with the dysfunctional aspects of these cultural assumptions. There really is a connection between how a firm deals with gender and work–personal life issues and how effective its performance is.

While balance has been proposed as the ideal, Rapoport *et al.* (2002) argue that the image of work and personal life balance is outmoded, and propose work–personal life integration as a more useful image. The separation of work and personal life implied in the term 'balance' had made it difficult to deal successfully with the conflict between them. Balance implies giving equal weight to work and personal life – but not everyone wants to give equal weight to work and personal life. One should not have to give priority to one while sacrificing the other. They suggest that work and personal life should be integrated, not balanced. Individuals should be able to find satisfaction in both regardless of the amount of time they spend in each.

Although Kofodimos titled her book *Balancing act*, the subtitle (*How managers can integrate successful careers and fulfilling personal lives*) emphasizes the integration of work and personal life. Her insights into the factors that lead to imbalance come from a long-term action research project dealing with executive character and development. She, along with colleagues, conducted intensive clinical studies of individual executives, interviewing not only these executives but co-workers' families and friends. In addition, executives completed measures of their managerial profiles and personality.

NEW RESEARCH FINDINGS

We recently conducted two research studies to examine the role of organizational culture on work and family issues and the usefulness of work–family policies and programs.

Organizational values and work–personal life balance of managers

Questionnaires were mailed in late 1996 to about 1000 male and 1000 female MBA graduates of a single university in Canada. Names were randomly selected from a listing of graduates from 1970 to 1994. Responses were received from 591 individuals, a response rate of about 35%, when questionnaires that were returned because the respondent had moved were excluded. The sample became 530 when individuals who indicated they were no longer working full time were excluded.

A fairly wide range of responses was present on most demographic items. Respondent ages ranged from under 35 to over 50, with about half falling between 36 and 45. Almost 80% of respondents were married and 70% had children. MBA degrees were obtained over a range of years, most (almost 60%) before 1985. Almost 40% had also achieved one or more professional designations (CA, CFA, etc.). Almost one-third worked 46–50 hours per week. About half had incomes between $50,000 and $100,000 (Canadian dollars). About 80% placed themselves into middle or senior management levels. Almost three-quarters had been with their present employers 10 years or less and in their present jobs five years or less. Employing organizations ranged in size from 1 to 85,000, with about 33% in firms of fewer than 100 employees. The sample contained slightly more men ($N = 278$) than women ($N = 252$).

Organizational values encouraging work–personal life balance or imbalance were measured by scales proposed by Kofodimos (1993). (For alternative measures see Chapter 4.) Organizational values encouraging balance was measured by nine items ($\alpha = 0.86$) (e.g., setting limits on hours spent at work). Organizational values supporting imbalance ($\alpha = 0.83$) were measured by eight items (e.g., traveling to and from work destinations on weekends). Respondents indicated how positively valued each item was in their organization or represented desired qualities in managers (1 = very negatively valued, 3 = neither positively or negatively valued, 5 = very positively valued). A total balance score was obtained by combining both scales, reversing the imbalance scores.

Respondents indicated a mean of 26.5, SD = 5.73 ($N = 497$) on the nine-item Balance scale, the mean item value of 2.9 falling at the 'neither positively or negatively valued' point (3.0). The mean obtained on the eight-item Imbalance scale was 29.4, SD = 4.52 ($N = 496$), with an item mean of 3.7, which approached 'somewhat positively valued' (4.0). The mean on the Total Balance scale was 45.1, SD = 9.18 ($N = 492$), with an item mean of 2.6, falling between the 'somewhat negatively valued' (2) and 'neither positively or negatively valued' label (3). These data showed that managers described their organizations as not particularly supportive of work–personal life balance.

Sex differences

As hypothesized, females scored significantly lower on balance values and significantly higher on imbalance values. These differences were no longer statistically significant, however, when four demographic characteristics (age, marital status, number of children and year of MBA) were controlled. These data showed that although women reported less organizational support for work–personal life balance than did men, when statistical controls of demographic characteristics likely to influence work–personal life balance were introduced, women and men indicated similar levels of support for work–personal life balance. Organizational support for both women and men was only moderate.

Organizational values, work experiences and satisfaction

Women indicating organizational values more supportive of balance also reported less job stress, greater satisfaction with their jobs, careers and family, less intent to quit, fewer psychosomatic symptoms and higher levels of emotional well-being. Among these women, organizational support for work–personal life balance values had no relationship with hours worked, extra hours worked, job involvement, future career prospects, levels of satisfaction with friends and community involvement, and physical well-being (positive lifestyle behaviors).

Men indicating organizational values more supportive of work–personal life balance also reported working fewer hours per week and fewer extra hours, less job stress, greater satisfaction with their jobs, their careers and their career prospects, less intent to quit, greater satisfaction with friends and community, fewer psychosomatic symptoms, more positive lifestyle behaviors and higher levels of emotional well-being. Among these men, organizational values supporting balance had no relationship with levels of job involvement and family satisfaction.

Regression analyses

These data showed a greater number of statistically significant correlations between the measure of organizational values supporting work–personal life balance and the other measures used in the study for men than for women. It was unlikely that this pattern resulted from the larger sample size of the men's versus the women's groups. These findings suggested that men appeared to benefit more (i.e., a greater number of statistically significant correlations) from organizational values supporting work–personal life balance.

Regression analyses were undertaken to examine this possibility further. Multiple regression analysis takes into account the modest intercorrelations among the predictors in identifying those that have significant and independent relationships with a given criterion measure.

The regression findings showed a similar pattern for women and men when work and well-being outcomes were regressed on the organizational values measure. Women reporting organizational values supportive of work–personal life balance also indicated lower levels of psychosomatic symptoms and less intention to quit. Men reporting organizational values supportive of work–personal life balance indicated greater job satisfaction in addition to lower levels of psychosomatic symptoms and less intention to quit. Similar levels of variance were accounted for in both analyses.

A somewhat different pattern of findings was observed for women and men when the job experiences measures were regressed on the organizational values measure. While both men and women who reported values more supportive of work–personal life balance indicated less job stress, men reporting values more supportive of work–personal life balance also indicated more joy in work, working fewer hours per week and less feeling driven to work. The job experiences explained more variance on the organizational values measure for men than women (adjusted $R^2 = 0.25$ and 0.10, respectively).

Why should men benefit more than women from organizational values supportive of work–personal life balance? Several speculations are possible. Men in the sample worked more hours per week and were more work involved than were women. More men than women were married or living with a partner and more men had children. Men reported higher levels of organizational support for work–personal life balance than did women. Women still shoulder greater responsibility than men for 'second shift' duties such that the combination of work and extra work demands might be a greater burden for women than for men. Future research is needed to examine these and other possible explanations.

These results may also be consistent with findings from research examining models of career advancement for women and for men. Several of these studies (e.g., Tharenou *et al.*, 1994; Stroh *et al.*, 1992) have found that men, more than women, show greater career advancement benefits from identical characteristics (e.g., education) and experiences (job tenure, mobility). Our findings may show that an organizational characteristic, believed to be very important for women (personal life friendliness), may in fact be of greater benefit to men than women.

Organizational values and work–personal life balance of psychologists

This research project examines the relationship of female and male psychologists' perceptions of values in their organizational environment supporting an integrated commitment to work and personal life and their job experiences and work satisfaction, extra work satisfaction and levels of psychological and physical well-being. The general hypothesis underlying the study was that female and male psychologists reporting values supporting an integrated commitment to work and personal life would be more satisfied and psychologically healthier. It is not clear, however, how values supporting work–personal life integration would influence hours worked and job commitment. It also aimed to shed some light on how supportive a large sample of female and male psychologists and men perceive their workplaces to be.

The variables chosen to be studied reflected a variety of both work and personal life experiences. These included work outcomes such as job and career satisfaction and personal life outcomes such as family and community satisfaction. In addition, the ways in which work was experienced (stress, involvement) was also considered. Finally, indicators of psychological and physical well-being were included since a lack of work–personal life integration may, over time, have adverse well-being consequences. Previous studies of work and personal life integration have considered variables such as these (see Friedman and Greenhaus, 2000).

Questionnaires were mailed to 3561 members of the Australian Psychological Society in the state of Victoria. This produced 658 respondents, a response rate of 18%. The response rate obtained in this study is typical of those reported in other research. The present study includes only those psychologists working full time at the time of the research (324 women and 134 men). The total sample of respondents ($N = 658$) was similar to the total membership of the Australian Psychological Society in terms of age and gender. The psychologists in the sample worked in a range of settings (academic, clinical, organizational and educational).

Concerns about work–personal life integration are more likely to be observed in managerial and professional jobs where the employment contract is vague as to expected working hours. MA- and PhD-level psychologists seemed to fulfill this requirement. Psychology is also a female-dominated profession. Thus the question of whether working in a female-dominated profession has an effect on perceived organizational values supporting work and personal life integration could be explored.

About two-thirds of the sample were women (71%); a majority were married (70%) and had children (56%). They typically worked between 36 and 40 hours per week (35%), were between 41 and 50 years old (32%), had been in their present jobs less than 3 years (55%), with their present employer less than 5 years (55%) and worked in organizations having 100 or fewer employees (54%).

Integration values were again measured by the nine-item scale ($\alpha = 0.86$) developed by Kofodimos (1993). Respondents indicated the extent to which each item was positively valued in their organization or represented desirable qualities in employees. *Non-integration values* ($\alpha = 0.82$) were also measured by the same eight-item scale (Kofodimos, 1993). Respondents indicated the extent to which each item was positively valued in their organization or represented desirable qualities in employees.

The sample ($N = 492$) had a mean value of 51.9 on the 17th item measure of organizational values, supporting work–personal life integration (SD = 10.00). The mean item value was 3.0, indicating that items were ranked at 'neither positively nor negatively valued' = 3. Items on the integration scale averaged 3.3 (neither positively nor negatively valued = 3) while items on the non-integration scale also averaged 3.3 (neither positively nor negatively valued = 3).

Demographic differences

It is important first to examine gender differences on personal and situational characteristics before considering gender differences on the workaholism measures to put the latter into a larger context. Females and males were similar on a minority of the items: marital status and organizational size. However, there were considerably more statistically significant female–male differences on demographic items. Males were older, more likely to be in longer marriages, to have children, to have more children and were less likely to have gaps in their careers. They earned higher incomes in 1999 and 2000 and had been in their present jobs and with their present employers a longer period of time than women. It should be noted that many of these demographic characteristics were themselves significantly correlated and the sample sizes of both females and males were large.

Gender differences in job experiences

First, women and men were significantly different on five of the eight job experience measures, men scoring higher on four of the five (hours worked, extra hours worked, feeling driven to work and job stress). Women indicated significantly higher levels of work involvement than did men. The two groups were similar on job involvement and work enjoyment. Second, the two groups were similar on the four indicators of work satisfaction (job and career satisfaction, future career prospects, intent to quit). Third, women and men were significantly different on two of the three measures of extra work satisfaction. Women reported significantly higher levels of friends' satisfaction and significantly lower levels of community satisfaction than did men. Men and women reported similar levels of family satisfaction. Fourth, women indicated significantly higher levels of psychological symptoms than did men, but the two groups reported similar emotional and physical health. Finally, women and men reported similar levels of organizational support for work–personal life integration.

Organizational values, work experiences and satisfaction

Women indicating organizational values more supportive of integration also reported greater well-being, working fewer hours and extra hours per week, less time to job, less job stress, greater satisfaction with their jobs, careers and friends, more optimistic future career prospects and higher levels of emotional and physical well-being. Among these women, organizational support of work–personal life integration values had no relationship with job involvement, joy in work, intent to quit, levels of satisfaction with family and community involvement, and psychosomatic symptoms.

Men indicating organizational values more supportive of work–personal life integration also reported greater joy in work, less job stress, greater satisfaction with their jobs, careers and career prospects, less intent to quit, fewer psychosomatic symptoms, more positive lifestyle behaviors and higher levels of emotional well-being. Among these men, organizational values supporting integration had no relationship with hours and extra hours worked per week, levels of job involvement and time to job, or family, friends and community satisfaction.

These data showed a similar number of statistically significant correlations between the measure of organizational values supporting work–personal life integration and the other measures used in the study for men and for women. The pattern of significant relationships was slightly different for women and men, particularly in terms of hours worked and time to job. Women seemed to benefit from supportive values on these measures more than men did.

Regression analyses

The regression findings showed a slightly different pattern for women and men when work experiences were regressed on the organizational values measure. Women reporting organizational values supportive of work–personal life integration also indicated lower levels of job stress, job involvement and feeling driven to work. Men reporting organizational values supportive of work–personal life integration indicated lower levels of job stress. Similar amounts of variance were accounted for in both analyses.

A somewhat similar pattern of findings was observed for women and men when the work and well-being outcomes were regressed on the organizational values measure. Women reporting values more supportive of work–personal life integration also indicated more community satisfaction. None of the outcome measures had a significant and independent relationship with organizational values among men. The organizational values measure explained similar amounts of variance on the job experiences measures for men and women.

How supportive of work–personal life integration did these women and men find their employing organizations? The answer is only moderately supportive. It should be noted that the profession of psychology is a female-dominated profession with the betterment of the human condition as its core. Although more women now occupy managerial and professional jobs and more organizations pay at least lip service to work–family integration concerns, the women and men participating in this study did not describe their employing organizations as family or personal life friendly.

This research examined the relationship of perceptions of organizational values supporting work–personal life integration, work and job experiences and satisfaction, extra work satisfaction and aspects of psychological and physical well-being. The data, obtained from large samples of female and male psychologists, provided considerable support for the general hypothesis linking work–personal life integration values with more positive job experiences, satisfying work consequences and more favorable well-being outcomes. More specifically, female and male psychologists indicating organizational values more supportive of work–personal life integration also reported greater job and career satisfaction, less job stress, more optimistic future career prospects and higher levels of emotional and physical well-being.

Interestingly, the presence of these integration values had no relationship with a measure of job involvement. In addition, these values were independent of family and community satisfaction. These latter measures are undoubtedly influenced by a number of other factors, organizational values being only one. We conclude that organizational values supporting work–personal life integration have important work and personal consequences.

The findings reported here support two conclusions: one expected and one unexpected. First, women and men indicate benefits in working in organizations having values supportive of work–personal life integration. This conclusion is consistent with other research (Friedman and Greenhaus, 2000). Second, women appeared to benefit more from organizational values supportive of work–personal life integration than did men. This finding was unexpected; the Canadian study of managers showed no such differences.

Why should women benefit more than men from organizational values supportive of work–personal life integration? Several speculations are possible. Men in the sample worked more hours per week, were at higher organizational levels and were more work involved than were women. It may have been more difficult for men to take advantage of supportive organizational values. Women still shoulder greater responsibility than men for 'second shift' duties such that the combination of work and extra work demands might be a greater burden for women than for men. As a result, women more than men would be motivated to take advantage of supportive organizational values. Future research is needed to examine these and other possible explanations.

Organizational values, performance and family-friendliness

There has been considerable interest shown in the past decade in the influence of organizational culture, particularly cultural values, on work performance, productivity, learning and adaptability and, ultimately, organizational effectiveness (Deal and Kennedy, 1982; Peters, 1987; Schein, 1992). An increasing number of studies, both qualitative and quantitative, have examined the ways in which cultural values influence important work outcomes (Denison, 1990; Kotter and Heskett, 1992; Schneider, 1990); and although it has been suggested that cultural values have an influence on the work experiences of women in organizations (Bailyn, 1994; Schwartz, 1992; Konrad, 1990), little research has been devoted to this topic.

The absence of research findings here may be important since many firms believe that being family-friendly conflicts with being productive (Fierman, 1994). This raises the question of whether cultural values that support productivity and quality of service are different from, and at odds with, cultural values that support a level playing field and family-friendliness.

We examined the relationship between existing values in a professional services firm and a range of equal opportunity and family-friendly measures (Burke, 1997). There has generally been very little effort to study management and organizational processes in professional service organizations. This has resulted, in part, from the priority attached to technical skills and professional expertise in explaining the success of such firms. It is only fairly recently that issues of leadership and management, teamwork, the utilization and development of talents of an increasingly diverse workforce (Schwartz, 1992), and mission and values have been considered.

The following general questions were considered. Are cultural values related to family-friendliness, and in what way? Are cultural values related to equal opportunity measures, and in what way? Do the same cultural values predict both family-friendliness and perceptions of equal opportunity? Are cultural values related to productivity also related to family-friendliness?

This study represented a secondary analysis of attitude survey data collected within a single large professional services firm. The firm had about 2150 employees at the time of the survey. About three-quarters were university graduates, many having also obtained professional designations in their areas of special expertise. The survey was distributed via internal organization mail. It was accompanied by a covering letter explaining the purposes of the survey and guaranteeing anonymity. Conducting the study within a single organization controls context variables such as industry structure, technology, policies and procedures. The downside of such a strategy is that it limits the generalizability of the results to similar kinds of organizations in similar industries.

The sample ($N = 1608$) represented a 70% response rate. There were slightly more women than men, but men were at significantly higher organizational levels than were women. About 60% of respondents were married and about 40% of respondents had children. About 65% of the respondents had been with the firm six years or less and about 40% were under 30 years of age. Four organizational levels were present: partners, managers, professional field staff and clerical/support staff.

Cultural values

Respondents indicated both the importance of and the current existence of 10 values in the organization (rated on a scale where 1 = 'not at all', 5 = 'to a great extent'). These items included: people in this organization are dedicated to outstanding service to clients; maintain the highest standards of professionalism; will not compromise integrity, objectivity or independence; have respect for each other; and are committed to making the firm a better place.

Importance, presence and gaps in cultural values

The most prevalent cultural values were: dedicated to outstanding service to clients; high standards of professionalism; and will not compromise integrity. The least prevalent cultural values were: balancing responsibilities to themselves, families, communities and the firm; committed to making the firm a better place; having respect for each other; supporting the worldwide organization; and placing a high value on staff development.

For each of the 10 organizational values the presence in the firm was always lower than their rated importance, the average difference being 1.0, a full scale point on the five-point scale. The largest gaps existed on balance responsibilities towards families (1.6), respect for each other (1.4), committed to making firm better (1.3), high value for staff development (1.2), work as a team for clients (1.1) and dedicated to continuous improvement (1.0).

Three conclusions follow from these data. First, the organizational values in practice in this firm generally fell short when compared to their espoused importance. Second, the largest discrepancies were directly or indirectly related to work–family issues (e.g., balance, respect). Third, discrepancies in these organizational values were likely to reduce organizational performance as well (e.g., teamwork, continuous improvement, staff development).

Regression analyses

Hierarchical regression analyses were undertaken in which measures of family-friendliness and the presence of a level playing field were regressed, one at a time, on the 10 organizational values.

The following comments are offered in summary. First, a considerable number of organizational values, ranging from two to six, had significant and independent relationships with the criterion measures. On average, four organizational values showed such relationships. These ranged from two significant predictors for Sexual Harassment and six significant predictors for Biased Decisions.

Second, these predictors accounted for modest levels of explained variance (R^2) in the criterion measures, ranging from a low of 0.04 for Sexual Harassment to a high of 0.27 for Supportive Work–Family policies.

Third, three of the organizational values (dedicated to continuous improvement, support for the worldwide organization, and not willing to compromise integrity) had negative consequences for family-friendliness and level playing field concerns. That is, women and men reporting higher levels of these organizational values also described their work setting as less family-friendly and more biased.

Fourth, although nine of the 10 organizational values had at least one significant and independent relationship with the criterion variables (maintaining the highest standards of professionalism did not), a few had a disproportionate number of significant relationships with the criterion measures. Thus, respect for each other had significant relationships with six of the eight criterion measures. This was followed by not compromising integrity, objectivity or independence, five of eight; balanced responsibilities to themselves, their families, their communities as well as to the firm, four of eight; a high value on staff development, four of eight; making the firm a better place, four of eight; and dedication to continuous improvement, four of eight.

Fifth, four of the six most significant organizational values (respect, staff development, a better place, balance) emphasize human resources – personal balance, respect and development – rather than technical concerns. In addition, these particular organizational values were ones that were less commonly observed. That is, these four organizational values appeared in the bottom five rankings.

The findings obtained in this single large professional services firm reveal an association between particular organizational values present in the firm and measures of both family-friendliness and woman-friendliness. Not surprisingly, these particular values were human resource oriented as opposed to being technical or performance driven. In fact, particular organizational values were associated with less woman- and family-friendliness. Fierman (1994) suggests that companies may be becoming less family-friendly because they need greater contributions from their employees. Bailyn (1994) raises the same concerns. That is, values associated with high performance, high-involvement workplaces, while exciting and associated with both personal and career development, may make it more difficult for employees to achieve (or even want) balance in their work lives. This raises the possibility that, for some firms, the values that are being espoused may be creating conflict for particular employees.

The most important organizational value related to level playing field measures was respect for each other. It is useful to begin to define what this value entails more specifically. The following come to mind. It includes supporting and encouraging all staff, acknowledging staff and their value, treating staff as equals, spending time with staff, listening to staff, getting to know staff, appreciating and valuing staff, and responding to the unique needs of staff.

The most important organizational value related to family-friendliness was the endorsement of balance. This value, while significant to staff, was not being realized in the firm for reasons suggested by Bailyn (1994) and Fierman (1994). That is, this firm required increasing levels of performance in a more competitive market-place, requirements that may be at odds with the realization of balance. The firm had created work–family policies to support greater balance but these had been embraced half-heartedly and were not having the desired effect. Balance involves the provision of flexibility, the recognition and rewarding of performance, not face-time (putting in long hours), and acknowledging legitimate needs of staff to nourish themselves, their families and their communities.

An interesting issue is whether organizational values related to family-friendliness and the presence of a level playing field were different from, and perhaps opposed to, organizational values more supportive of a business or a bottom-line orientation. We examined these relationships in this firm, using the same measure of organizational values but different outcome indicators (Burke, 1997). For these analyses, measures of basic performance indicators and work outcomes were used. They included employee perceptions of the firm's quality of services and products compared to its competitors, barriers to service observed in the firm, support for service excellence, job satisfaction and intention to quit. The results showed that essentially the same organizational values predicted both work and organizational outcomes (e.g., performance) *and* family-friendliness and presence of a level playing field. It does not appear to be an either/or situation; that is, particular organizational values were antecedents of both firm effectiveness and family- and woman-friendliness. It should be remembered, however, that some organizational values had a negative relationship with family-friendliness and presence of a level playing field, as well as with one or more work outcomes. Thus a sensitive balancing act among organizational values may be necessary under the best of circumstances. Considerably more research must be undertaken to shed light on these conclusions and their implications.

Regression analyses were also undertaken in which the 10 discrepancies in organizational values were regressed on both family-friendly measures and indicators of organizational performance. The following comments are offered in summary. First, balanced responsibilities had a significant and independent relationship with each of the four family friendly policies and work–family conflict measures. In all cases, respondents indicating smaller discrepancies on this value also reported more favorable perceptions of the work–family policies (opportunities, not having to sacrifice one's career, less work–family conflict, less sexual harassment). Second, the gap in balanced responsibilities also had significant and independent relationships with the three organizational performance measures (job satisfaction, office morale, intent to quit). Respondents indicating larger discrepancies in balance to self and family also reported less job satisfaction, greater intent to quit and lower office morale.

Implications for organizations

What can organizations do to develop such work–personal life balance values? The most common approach is to create workplace policies that promote them. Unfortunately, accumulating evidence suggests that the presence of such policies has produced at best inconsistent benefits (Bailyn, 1994). In some cases such policies have brought about value, attitude and behavior changes; in other cases, such policies have existed only on paper. These latter organizations have only paid token lip service to the existence of such policies (Hochschild, 1997).

These findings have interesting implications if borne out in other samples. It has been suggested that women who work in demanding jobs experience work–personal life concerns (Hochschild, 1989). Our data indicated that those concerns are also shared by their male colleagues. As a consequence, organizations may come under increasing pressure to be more 'family-friendly'.

Work and personal life concerns tend to be pitted against each other with the organization all too often, not surprisingly, giving priority to work. The more viable approach would be to link work and personal life in an integrative way (Lewis and Lewis, 1996). That is, satisfying work and personal life concerns simultaneously, while challenging and requiring the investment of some organizational resources, may achieve work and personal life objectives (Rayman et al., 1999).

More recently, several researchers have begun to describe and evaluate more intensive collaborative projects with organizations interested in addressing work–personal life concerns. These projects make an explicit link between employees' personal needs (e.g., family responsibilities) and business objectives with the intention of changing work practices so that both the organization and its employees benefit (Rapoport et al., 1998).

The work of Bailyn and her colleagues describes several collaborative action research projects in which researchers work jointly with companies to bring about change in the work culture and the organization of work that would facilitate work–personal life integration in a meaningful way (Bailyn, 1997, 2002; Bailyn et al., 1997; Fletcher and Bailyn, 1996; Fletcher and Rapoport, 1996). Other compelling evaluations of additional organizational initiatives show that changes in organization values and practice can be accomplished. These efforts require considerable commitment to be successful, however. The benefits to employees may be far reaching.

Perlow (1997) has shown that the way work gets done in organizations (individual heroics) and the way work is rewarded perpetuate crises and continuous interruptions while discouraging cooperation. These practices reduce organizational productivity and the quality of people's lives outside of work. Working with a group of employees, she helped them develop times during the workweek that would be quiet times (no interruptions) and times during the week that would be interaction times.

One of the major barriers standing in the way of meaningful workplace changes that address the work–personal life balance question is the tendency to see work and personal life (or family) as either/or concepts (Rapoport *et al.*, 1998). That is, organizations can have a work-committed employee, a personal life- or family-committed employee, but not employees who are both work-committed and family-committed. Given this way of framing the problem it is no wonder that work–family programs are grudgingly implemented and usually fall short. Having a family continues to be a career liability for many women.

The real challenge for organizations is to identify ways that work is being undertaken that interferes with both performance and productivity goals and personal life needs. Only when personal life needs and job performance are linked, and both related to the bottom line, will lasting and significant progress be made. Examining organizational culture is a promising place to start (Lewis and Taylor, 1996).

The development of work–family policies has been described as the first stage in fostering work–family integration (Friedman and Johnson, 1996; Lewis, 2002, 2003). Unfortunately a gap often existed between policy and practice and policies were frequently implemented half-heartedly. Would work–family policies change organizational culture values and assumptions that define the ideal employee, determine whether work–family programs are successful and how men and women who take advantage of these programs are viewed? The evidence indicates that organizational culture values are too often a major barrier to the success of work–family programs (Burke, 2002; Lewis, 2001; Thompson *et al.*, 1999).

Several researchers have begun to describe and evaluate more intensive collaborative projects with organizations interested in addressing work–personal life concerns. These projects make an explicit link between employees' personal needs (e.g., family responsibilities) and business objectives with the intention of changing work practices so that both the organization and its employees benefit (Rapoport *et al.*, 1998). Bailyn (1994) observes that for successful work and personal life integration to occur organizations must include the personal needs of their employees when redesigning their work.

WHAT MAKES AN ORGANIZATION SUPPORTIVE?

Recent research has identified a number of aspects of the workplace environment that have been shown to help employees achieve work–personal life integration.

Control

Control – the ability to influence one's personal environment so that the environment becomes more rewarding and less threatening – has been found to play an important role in moderation of work–family conflict (Thomas and Ganster, 1995). Policies such as flexitime, job sharing and participation in decisions that affect their jobs – all offering greater control – should reduce the strains of work–family and family–work conflict.

Williams and Alliger (1994) found that greater control lowered levels of distress and increased feelings of calmness in both work and family domains. Thomas and Ganster (1995) observed that work arrangements that provided greater control to employees over work and family requirements helped them manage conflicting demands. Other researchers (Duxbury *et al.*, 1994; Pleck *et al.*, 1980) have similarly shown that greater control over scheduling, personal time off and hours of overtime reduces the likelihood of work–family conflict.

Thus, the ability of employees to plan, structure and control their work schedules and influence how they perform their jobs helps them balance and integrate work and family (Judge *et al.*, 1994).

Social support

A considerable body of research has suggested that social support at work and in the family can reduce levels of work–family conflict. Two types of support have been considered: instrumental and emotional. Instrumental support is the tangible support one receives directly from others. Emotional support is the individual's perception of the presence of caring others with whom they can discuss their experiences and feelings.

Social support has been found to reduce perceived work stressors, time demands and work–family conflict (Carlson and Perrewe, 1999; Perrewe and Carlson, 2002). Frone *et al.* (1997) have suggested that the effects of social support may be domain-specific. That is, social support at work has its greatest effect in reducing work strain while social support in the family has its greatest effect in reducing family strain.

Supportive supervision

Supportive supervisors play a key role in the implantation of family-supportive policies: supervisors embody and reflect the organizational culture (Powell and Mainiero, 1999; Scandura and Lankau, 1997). Research has shown that employees who receive social support from supervisors report less work–family conflict (Frone *et al.*, 1997; Thomas and Ganster, 1995).

Supportive supervisors work with employees who are struggling to integrate their work and family responsibilities. They permit flexibility in the scheduling of work, they serve as a sympathetic sounding board, they rearrange priorities to accommodate a family crisis (Duxbury and Higgins, 1997). Employees receiving this type of supervisor support experience less work–family conflict (Goff *et al.*, 1990). Kossek *et al.* (1999) reported that when managers provide an example of the success of flexible work arrangements and encourage their use, employees are more likely to take advantage of this option.

FUTURE RESEARCH DIRECTIONS

Unfortunately research examining the impact of family-friendly policies on work–family integration, employee well-being and organizational effectiveness is limited. Key questions still remain unanswered (Frone, 2003):

1 How important is top management support (Friedman *et al.*, 1998)?
2 What role does executive leadership and organizational culture play in the effectiveness of family-supportive programs (Morrison, 1992)?
3 What policies and practices best support work–family integration and for whom (Casper *et al.*, 2002)?
4 How do employees decide whether or not to use programs that are available to them (Powell and Mainiero, 1999)?
5 What role, if any, do family friendly policies and practices have in the current emphasis on strategic human resources management?
6 What type and pattern of family-friendly policies and practices have the greatest benefit to employees and their organizations?
7 Do family-friendly policies and practices contribute to an organization's competitive advantage (Grover and Crooker, 1995; Lambert, 2000)?
8 Do family-friendly polices and practices contribute to positive psychological outcomes such as flow, engagement, enthusiasm and strength (Perrewe *et al.*, 2003)?
9 Do work–personal life issues change in importance as women and men get older and occupy different career and life stages (Ruderman and Ohlott, 2002)?
10 What evidence is needed to convince organizations that work–personal life issues matter (Lobel and Faught, 1996; Lobel *et al.*, 1999; Morrison, 1992)?

In conclusion, women and men seem to benefit from participating in multiple roles. In addition, for an organization to be successful in an increasingly competitive global market-place, it needs to simultaneously meet the needs of its bottom line and the needs of its employees. It doesn't seem unreasonable for women and men also to find satisfaction in both their work and personal life either.

REFERENCES

Allen, T. D. (2001). Family-supportive work environments: the role of organizational perceptions. *Journal of Vocational Behavior, 58*, 414–435.

Allen, T. D., and Russell, J. E. A. (1999). Parental leave of absence: some not so family-friendly implications. *Journal of Applied Social Psychology, 29*, 166–191.

Bailyn, L. (1994). *Breaking the mold.* New York: Free Press.

Bailyn, L. (1997). The impact of corporate culture on work–family integration. In S. Parasuraman and J. H. Greenhaus (eds), *Integrating work and family: Challenges and choices for a changing world* (pp. 299–219). Westport, CT: Quorum.

Bailyn, L. (2002). Time in organizations: constraints on, and possibilities for, gender equity in the workplace. In R. J. Burke and D. L. Nelson (eds), *Advancing women's careers* (pp. 262–272). Oxford: Blackwell.

Bailyn, L., Fletcher, J. K., and Kolb, D. (1997). Unexpected connections: considering employees' personal lives can revitalize your business. *Sloan Management Review, 38*, 11–19.

Bowen, G. L. (1998). Efforts of leaders support in the work unit on the relationship between work spillover and family adaptation. *Journal of Family and Economics Issues, 19*, 25–52.

Burke, R. J. (2002). Organizational culture: a key to the success of work and family programs. In R. J. Burke and D. L. Nelson (eds), *Advancing women's careers* (pp. 287–309). Oxford: Blackwell.

Burke, R. J. (1997). Organizational values, work–family issues and the 'bottom line'. *Equal Opportunities International, 16*, 34–40.

Burke, R. J., and Nelson, D. L. (1998). Organizational men: masculinity and its discontents. In C. L. Cooper and I. T. Robertson (eds), *International review of industrial and organizational psychology* (pp. 225–272). New York: Wiley.

Carlson, D. S., and Perrewe, P. L. (1999). The role of social support in the stressor–strain relationship: an examination of work–family conflict. *Journal of Management, 25*, 513–540.

Casper, W. J., Martin, J. A., Buffardi, L. C., and Erdwins, C. J. (2002). Work–family conflict, perceived organizational support, and organizational commitment among employed mothers. *Journal of Occupational Health Psychology, 7*, 99–108.

Davidson, M. J., and Burke, R. J. (1994). *Women in management: Current research issues.* London: Paul Chapman.

Deal, T. E., and Kennedy, A. A. (1982). *Corporate cultures.* Reading, MA: Addison-Wesley.

Denison, D. (1990). *Corporate culture and organizational effectiveness.* New York: Wiley.

Duxbury, L., and Higgins, C. (1997). Supportive managers: what are they? Why do they matter? *HRM Research Quarterly, 1*, 1–4.

Duxbury, L., Higgins, C., and Lee, C. (1994). Work–family conflict: a comparison by gender, family type, and perceived control. *Journal of Family Issues, 15*, 449–466.

Equal Opportunities International (1997). The sounds of shattering glass: corporate initiatives for advancing managerial women. *Equal Opportunities International, 16*, 1–40.

Fierman, J. (1994). Are companies less family-friendly? *Fortune, 130*(3), 64–67.

Finkel, S. K., Oswang, S., and She, N. (1994). Childbirth, tenure and promotion for women faculty. *Review of Higher Education, 17,* 259–270.

Fletcher, J. K., and Bailyn, L. (1996). Challenging the last boundary: re-connecting work and family. In M. B. Arthur and D. M. Rousseau (eds), *The Boundaryless Careers* (pp. 256–267). Oxford: Oxford University Press.

Fletcher, J. K., and Rapoport, R. (1996). Work–family linkages as a catalyst for change. In S. Lewis and J. Lewis (eds), *Rethinking employment: The work family challenge* (pp. 137–156). London: Sage.

Friedman, D. E., and Galinsky, E. (1992). Work–family issues: a legitimate business concern. In S. Zedeck (ed.), *Work, families and organizations* (pp. 168–207). San Francisco: Jossey-Bass.

Friedman, S. D., and Greenhaus, J. H. (2000). *Work and family: Allies or enemies? What happens when business professionals confront life choices?* New York: Oxford University Press.

Friedman, D. E., and Johnson, A. A. (1996). Moving from programs to culture change: the next stage for the corporate work/family agenda. In S. Parasuraman and J. H. Greenhaus (eds), *Integrating work and family: Challenges and choices for a changing world* (pp. 192–208). Westport, CT: Quorum.

Friedman, S. D., DeGroot, J., and Christensen, P. (1998). *Integrating work and family: The Wharton resource guide.* San Francisco: Jossey-Bass.

Frone, M. R. (2003). Work–family balance. In J. C. Quick and L. Tetrick (eds), *Handbook of occupational health psychology* (pp. 143–162). Washington, DC: American Psychological Association.

Frone, M. R., Yardley, J. K., and Markel, K. S. (1997). Developing and testing an integrative model of the work–family interface. *Journal of Vocational Behavior, 50,* 145–167.

Galinsky, E., Bond, J. T., and Friedman, D. E. (1996). The role of employers in addressing the needs of employed parents. *Journal of Social Issues, 52,* 111–136.

Goff, S. J., Mount, M. K., and Jamison, R. L. (1990). Employer supported child-care, work–family conflict and absenteeism: a field study. *Personal Psychology, 43,* 793–809.

Gonyea, J. G., and Googins, B. K. (1992). Linking the worlds of work and family: beyond the productivity trap. *Human Resource Management, 31,* 209–226.

Grover, S. L., and Crooker, K. J. (1995). Who appreciates family-responsive human resource policies? The impact of family-friendly policies on organizational attachment of parents and non-parents. *Personnel Psychology, 48,* 271–288.

Hammonds, K. H. (1997). Work and family. Business Week's second survey of family-friendly corporate policies. *Business Week,* 15 September, 96–99, 102–104.

Higgins, C., Duxbury, L., and Johnson, K. L. (2000). Part-time work for women: does it really help balance work and family? *Human Resource Management, 39,* 17–32.

Hochschild, A. R. (1989). *The second shift.* New York: Avon.

Hochschild, A. R. (1997). *The time bind.* New York: Metropolitan.

Jahn, E. W., Thompson, C. A., and Kopelman, R. E. (2003). Rationale and construct validity evidence for a measure of perceived organizational family support (POFS): because purported practices may not reflect reality. *Community, Work and Family, 6*(2), 123–140.

Judge, T. A., Boudreau, J. W., and Bretz, R. D. (1994). Job and life attitudes of male executives. *Journal of Applied Psychology, 79*, 767–782.

Judiesch, M. K., and Lyness, K. S. (1999). Left behind? The impact of leaves of absence on managers' career success. *Academy of Management Journal, 42*(6), 641–651.

Kofodimos, J. (1993). *Balancing act.* San Francisco: Jossey-Bass.

Kolb, D. M., and Merrill-Sands, D. (1999). Waiting for outcomes: anchoring a dual agenda for change to cultural assumptions. *Women in Management Review, 14*, 194–202.

Konrad, W. (1990). Welcome to the women-friendly company. *Business Week*, 6 August, 48–53.

Kossek, E. E., and Ozeki, C. (1998). Work–family conflict, policies and the job-life satisfaction relationship: a review and direction for organizational behavior–human resources research. *Journal of Applied Psychology, 83*, 139–149.

Kossek, E. E., Barber, A. E., and Winters, D. (1999). Using flexible schedules in the managerial world: the power of peers. *Human Resource Management, 38*, 33–46.

Kotter, J. P., and Heskett, J. L. (1992) *Corporate culture and performance.* New York: Free Press.

Lambert, S. J. (2000). Added benefits: the link between work–life benefits and organizational citizenship behavior. *Academy of Management Journal, 43*, 801–815.

Lewis, S. (1997). Family friendly organizational policies: a route to organizational change or playing about at the margins. *Gender, Work and Organizations, 45*, 13–23.

Lewis, S. (2001). Restructuring workplace cultures: the ultimate work–family challenge? *Women in Management Review, 16*, 21–29.

Lewis, S. (2002). Work and family issues: old and new. In R. J. Burke and D. L. Nelson (eds), *Advancing women's careers* (pp. 67–82). Oxford: Blackwell.

Lewis, S. (2003). Integrating work and personal life: leadership past, present and future. In R. J. Burke and C. L. Cooper (eds), *Leading in turbulent times.* Oxford: Blackwell.

Lewis, S., and Lewis, K. (1996). *The work–family challenge: Rethinking employment.* London: Sage.

Lewis, S., and Taylor, K. (1996). Evaluating the impact of family-friendly employer policies: a case study. In S. Lewis and J. Lewis (eds), *The work–family challenge: Rethinking employment* (pp. 112–127). London: Sage.

Lobel, S. A. (1999). Impacts of diversity and work–life initiatives in organizations. In G. N. Powell (ed.), *Handbook of gender and work* (pp. 453–476). Thousand Oaks, CA: Sage.

Lobel, S. A., and Faught, L. (1996). Four methods for proving the value of work life interventions. *Compensation and Benefits Review*, November/December, 50–57.

Lobel, S. A., Googins, B., and Bankert, E. (1999). The future of work and family: critical trends for policy, practice and research. *Human Resource Management, 38*, 191–202.

Lyness, K. S., Thompson, C. A., Francesco, A. M., and Judiesch, M. K. (1999). Work and pregnancy: individual and organizational actors influencing organizational commitment, timing of maternity leave, and return to work. *Sex Roles, 41*, 485–508.

Morrison, A. M. (1992). *The new leaders.* San Francisco: Jossey-Bass.

Parasuraman, S., and Greenhaus, J. H. (1997). *Integrating, work and family: Challenges and choices for a changing world.* Westport, CT: Quorum.

Perlow, L. A. (1995). Putting the work back into work/family. *Group and Organization Management, 20,* 227–239.

Perlow, L. A. (1997). *Finding time: How corporations, individuals and families can benefit from new work practices.* Ithaca, NY: Cornell University Press.

Perrewe, P. L., and Carlson, D. (2002) Do men and women benefit from social support equally? A field examination within the work and family context. In D. L. Nelson and R. J. Burke (eds), *Gender, work stress, and health* (pp. 101–114). Washington, DC: American Psychological Association.

Perrewe, P. L., Treadway, D. C., and Hall, A. T. (2003). The work and family interface: conflict, family-friendly policies and employee well-being. In D. A. Hofmann and L. E. Tetrick (eds), *Health and safety in organizations: A multilevel perspective* (pp. 285–315). San Francisco: Jossey-Bass.

Peters, T. (1987). *Thriving on chaos.* New York: Alfred A. Knopf.

Pleck, J., Staines, G., and Lang, L. (1980). Conflicts between work and family life. *Monthly Labor Review, 103,* 29–32.

Powell, G. N., and Mainiero, L. A. (1999). Managerial decision making regarding alternative work arrangements. *Journal of Occupational and Organizational Psychology, 72,* 41–56.

Rapoport, R., Bailyn, L., Kolb, D., and Fletcher, J. K. (1998). *Relinking life and work: Toward a better future.* Waltham, MA: Pegasus Communications.

Rapoport, R., Bailyn, L. Fletcher, J. K., and Pruett, B. H. (2002). *Beyond work–family balance.* San Francisco: Jossey-Bass.

Rayman, P., Bailyn, L., Dickert, J., Carre, F., Harvey, M., Krim, R., and Read, R. (1999). Designing organizational solutions to integrate work and life. *Women in Management Review, 14,* 164–176.

Rodgers, F. S., and Rodgers, C. (1989). Business and the facts of family life. *Harvard Business Review, 67,* 121–129.

Rosin, H. M., and Korabik, K. (2001). Do family-friendly policies fulfill their promises? An investigation of their impact on work–family conflict and work and personal outcomes. In D. L. Nelson and R. J. Burke (eds), *Gender, work stress and health* (pp. 211–226). Washington, DC: American Psychological Association (in press).

Ruderman, M. N., and Ohlott, P. J. (2002). *Standing at the crossroads.* San Francisco: Jossey-Bass.

Scandura, T. A., and Lankau, M. J. (1997). Relationships of gender, family responsibility, and flexible work hours to organizational commitment and job satisfaction. *Journal of Organizational Behavior, 18,* 377–391.

Scheibl, F., and Dex, S. (1998). Should we have more family-friendly policies? *European Management Journal, 16,* 585–599.

Schein, E. H. (1992). *Organizational culture and leadership.* San Francisco: Jossey-Bass.

Schneider, B. (1990). *Organizational climate and culture.* San Francisco: Jossey-Bass.

Schwartz, D. B. (1995). The impact of work–family policies on women's career development: boon or bust? *Women in Management Review, 7,* 31–45.

Schwartz, F. N. (1992). *Breaking with tradition: Women and work, the new facts of life.* New York: Warner Books.

Smith, D. (1992). Corporate benefits only a start for family friendliness. *Employee Benefit Plan Review*, *3*, 46–52.

Stroh, L. K., Brett, J. M., and Reilly, A. H. (1992). All the right stuff: a comparison of male and female managers. *Journal of Applied Psychology*, *77*, 251–260.

Tharenou, P., Latimer, S., and Conroy, D. (1994). How do you make it to the top? An examination of influences on women's and men's managerial advancement. *Academy of Management Journal*, *37*, 899–931.

Thomas, L., and Ganster, D. (1995). Impact of family-supportive work variables on work–family conflict and strain: a control perspective. *Journal of Applied Psychology*, *80*, 6–15.

Thompson, C. A., and Beauvais, L. L. (2000). Balancing work/life. In D. Smith (ed.), *Women at work: Leadership for the next century* (pp. 162–189). Upper Saddle River, NJ: Prentice-Hall.

Thompson, C. A., Thomas, C. C., and Maier, M. (1992). Work–family conflict: reassessing corporate policies and initiatives. In U. Sekaran and F. Leong (eds), *Woman power: managing in times of demographic turbulence* (pp. 59–84). Newbury Park, CA: Sage.

Thompson, C. A., Beauvais, L. L., and Lyness, K. S. (1999). When work–family benefits are not enough: the influence of work–family culture on benefit utilization, organizational attachment, and work–family conflict. *Journal of Vocational Behavior*, *54*, 392–415.

Williams, J., and Alliger, M. (1994). Role stressors, mood spillover and perceptions of work–family conflict in employed partners. *Academy of Management Journal*, *37*, 837–868.

Women in Management Review (1995). The sounds of shattering glass: corporate initiatives for advancing managerial women. *Women in Management Review*, *10*, 3–53.

Women in Management Review (1999). Work–family initiatives: from policies to practices. *Women in Management Review*, *14*, 157–202.

11 Work–family best practices

Leslie B. Hammer, Jennifer C. Cullen and Margarita V. Shafiro

WHAT IS A WORK–FAMILY BEST PRACTICE?

There is no consistent use of the term 'work–family best practice' except that it typically relates to a documented strategy an organization uses to help manage the work and family demands of its workforce. In addition, the fact that something is categorized as a best practice means that in some way the documented strategy has revealed successes, ideally both for the organization and its employees. Thus, in the present chapter, the term 'work–family best practice' refers to *documented successful strategies employed by organizations in an effort to assist employees with effective management of work and family demands.* These successful strategies result in beneficial outcomes for both the organization and the employees.

Types of work–family best practices can be further clarified using the distinction between three general types of family-friendly workplace supports (Neal *et al.*, 1993). These include *policies*, such as flexible work arrangements, *services*, such as resource and referral information about dependent care options, and *benefits*, such as childcare subsidies. Thus, work–family best practices may include just one or even all three types of the family-friendly workplace supports noted by Neal *et al.* (1993). Furthermore, we argue that, ideally, work–family best practices are those policies, services and benefits that are not merely being provided by organizations, but are those that are actually being used by employees. Data documenting employee utilization of workplace-based family-friendly supports are more difficult to obtain than just availability data.

This chapter begins with a review of two primary factors contributing to the development of work–family best practices: global variations in state-supported programs and organizational size. We then discuss the difference between mere availability of supports and actual utilization of supports (see Chapter 10 for further discussion of these issues). This is followed by a description of several specific organizations that provide work–family best practices. These best practices represent various prototypes of what is available among today's corporations.

GLOBAL VARIATIONS AND THE US PARADOX

Interestingly, in researching case studies to present as part of this chapter, most available examples were from US companies. This may be the result of the general lack of national-level policies related to work–family support in the USA, as compared to that available in other countries. As a result, there is a heavier reliance on workplace-based family-friendly human resource policies in the USA than in other countries. For example, the USA is the only industrialized nation without a formal paid family leave program. What does exist in the USA, however, is the Family and Medical Leave Act (FMLA). The FMLA ensures up to 12 weeks of *unpaid* leave upon the birth of a child, adoption of a child and/or need to care for an ailing parent, spouse or other family member for employees working in companies with 50 or more employees. Although this 1993 Act was a landmark, it pales in comparison to the typical minimum three to nine months, partly or fully paid leave provided to employees living in most of the other industrialized nations across the globe.

According to Stebbins (2001), 119 countries currently meet the standard for providing at least 12 weeks of maternity leave, most of which offer some pay and many cover a full 100% of the leave time. For example, in countries such as Austria, France, Germany, Greece, Luxembourg, Netherlands, Portugal and Poland, full salary during maternity leave is provided (Lanquestin *et al.*, 2000). The USA is one of just 13 other countries that do not provide any pay for maternity leave (Stebbins, 2001). In addition to paid leave, support for childcare is much more widely provided in other western countries outside of the USA. In fact, most European countries have family allowance benefits and an income supplement to assist families with the cost of raising children (Fredrikson-Goldsen and Scharlach, 2001). Thus, a paradox exists where the lack of US federal government support for working families has led to US employers taking on greater responsibility in this area, leading to the finding that many of the reported work–family best practices are among US employers.

ORGANIZATIONAL SIZE AND THE LOW-WAGE PARADOX

In addition to global differences in the level of government support for family-friendly programs, there are also differences in organizational characteristics that limit the ability to provide such best practices. The most compelling indicator is company size. While most of the US workforce is employed in small companies with fewer than 50 employees, these are the very companies that are typically characterized as family-owned businesses with limited resources to provide comprehensive services and benefits to employees. Thus, the lack of government policies at the national level, coupled with the predominance of small family-owned businesses with limited resources, means that the majority of the US workforce has neither the opportunity nor the option to engage in work–family best practices. Moreover, these jobs are typically characterized as low-wage positions, and as such include employees who are most in need of family-related supports. Thus, a paradox exists among US workers who are not afforded the national policy coverage offered to their counterparts in other countries and the fact that many low-wage jobs are in smaller organizations where FMLA does not protect them.

BEST PRACTICE: DISTINGUISHING USE AND AVAILABILITY

The work–family supports being offered by organizations are designed to decrease the conflict employees experience between work and family demands, leading to improved attitudes and behaviors on the job, and to organizations' improved ability to recruit and retain qualified employees (Allen, 2001; Kossek and Ozeki, 1998). Furthermore, recent research suggests that the mere existence of work–family human resource policies is related to higher perceived organizational performance (Perry-Smith and Blum, 2000) and higher market values for such companies (Arthur, 2003). However, empirical research on employees' actual use of workplace supports that characterize work–family best practices is limited. In fact, the little research that is available on utilization has led to conflicting results (e.g., Hammer *et al.*, 2005), indicating that there are probably many moderator and mediator variables that impact the actual effectiveness of such supports. As Hill and Weiner (2003) note, the evaluation of work–life practices is rare, and most of what we know about their effectiveness is provided by anecdotal evidence. They offer a five-step process to the evaluation of work–life programs in corporate settings. This process involves identification of objectives, determination of methods for collecting data, gathering and analyzing data, linking the data to the bottom line and recommending actions (Hill and Weiner, 2003).

BEST PRACTICE CASE STUDIES

The best way to highlight premium practices is via global awards and recognition programs identifying companies that show a significant commitment to work–family services, policies and benefits. Some of these programs and their associated award recipients are described below. As was previously mentioned, owing to the scarcity of resources and opportunities available for small companies to offer work–family support the majority of case studies include larger US organizations.

The Psychologically Healthy Workplace Award: best practices honors

In 1999 the American Psychological Association (APA) started the Psychologically Healthy Workplace Award program. This program is designed for employers who recognize the 'critical links between employee health, well-being, productivity and the financial bottom line . . . [as a way] to take action to protect their most valuable asset – their employees' (APA, 2003, p. 1). This annual award program honors companies for innovative policies and programs that foster psychologically healthy work environments. The organizations vary in size and industry and can be either not-for-profit or for-profit companies. The applicants are judged according to four criteria: employee involvement, family support, employee growth and development, and health and safety (APA, 2003).

A recent publication highlighting the 2003 honorees made special note of Computer Associates International for making childcare carefree for employees (APA, 2003). Computer Associates International is a worldwide provider of solutions and services for the management of IT infrastructure, business information and application development, and is based out of New York with approximately 16,000 employees (APA, 2003). After Charles Wang, company founder and single father, requested that one of his top executives research the best childcare in the country, Computer Associates International opened eight Child Development Centers using the Montessori Method as a basis for guiding the development of the children, infant to kindergarten, enrolled at the centers. The staff at these centers consists of masters-level teachers and one consulting psychologist, who is used as a resource for the teachers, parents and children. Allowing parents to visit anytime they choose throughout the day, pick their children up for lunch in the company cafeteria, and fostering close relationships between parents and teachers, are all positive facets of the childcare centers and the company policy which alleviates the stress traditional employed parents have with respect to childcare (APA, 2003, p. 2). Thus, defined rather broadly, the Psychologically Healthy Workplace Award identifies companies that employ work–family best practices.

100 Best companies for working mothers

For the last 18 years, *Working Mother* magazine has put out a call to private and public firms of any size and in any US industry to apply to be on the list of the 100 top companies for working mothers ('Making It', October 2003). The application asks about the company family-friendly culture, the advancement of women within the company, childcare services, benefits and polices, flexibility in the way work is completed, leave policies for new parents, benefits for parents looking to adopt, etc. Although the application is a self-nomination, the companies are required to provide supporting documentation (e.g., benefits handbooks, results of employee surveys) to verify their self-reports of the family-friendly policies, benefits and services offered at their company. These companies are then rated on a point system, with heavier weight placed on three specific criteria: 'flexible scheduling, because it is essential for working mothers; advancement of women, because it is critical for women in the workplace; and childcare options, because without them, parents can't work' ('Making It', October 2003, p. 56).

The top 10 companies identified for 2003 (actual data from 2002) were (in alphabetical order): Abbott Laboratories; Booz, Allen, and Hamilton; Bristol-Meyers Squibb Co.; Eli Lilly & Co.; Fannie Mae; General Mills; International Business Machines Corporation (IBM); Prudential Financial Inc.; S. C. Johnson and Son, Inc.; and Wachovia Corporation. Below we highlight four of the top 10 companies on the list. Two of the representatives had the least number of employees (i.e., under 5000) when compared to the other companies on the list: Fannie Mae and S. C. Johnson and Son, Inc.; the other two companies had the greatest number of employees (i.e., greater than 80,000) when compared to others on the list: Wachovia Corporation and IBM. Although nearly 95% of all businesses in the USA are actually those under 100 employees, we clearly see that company size is one of the more important factors contributing to resource allocation of work–family policies, benefits and services, as mentioned earlier. Thus, we believe that size is a good criterion on which to base the company highlights. While it is desirable to present empirical findings on the outcomes associated with the work–family supports offered by these companies, the only company with extensive published research on its work–family programs is IBM. Hence, later in this chapter we present a detailed analysis of the published research on IBM.

Fannie Mae

Fannie Mae was one of the smallest companies recognized in the top 10 of the 100 best companies for working mothers, with just under 5000 employees. Fannie Mae is a secondary market investor with the critical role of providing mortgage funds to lenders across the country. Half of the entire Fannie Mae workforce is women, and nearly half of the executives, managers and top earning employees are women ('Making It', October 2003). In terms of childcare assistance, Fannie Mae offers backup childcare arrangements, before/after school care and summer programs. Approximately one-quarter of Fannie Mae employees have the option of setting aside pretax dollars to aid them with costs associated with childcare. Fannie Mae offers female employees a full 16 weeks of leave for childbirth, at full pay, and access to a lactation program if desired. The breastfeeding/lactation program for new mothers offers a lactation room at the workplace for pumping milk as well as optional consultations with a trained lactation specialist. Moreover, they also offer fathers four weeks of leave, at full pay, for the birth of a child. There is also adoption assistance for employees. Employees looking to adopt a child are offered a $10,000 stipend to help pay for the costs as well as four weeks of paid leave during the process. Fannie Mae was also noted as having eldercare resources available to employees who need them.

Some additional benefits, services and policies available to Fannie Mae employees that were not covered by the *Working Mother* magazine survey include five paid days per year given to employees to care for sick dependants (Fannie Mae, no date). In addition, many employees use flexitime work schedules, work on a regular part-time status, engage in job sharing, and use the 'Phase Back Program' after going on leave for child birth and/or adopting a child. For these benefits, Fannie Mae deserves to be recognized as a socially responsible company in its striving to be a family-friendly place to work.

S. C. Johnson & Son, Inc.

S. C. Johnson & Son, Inc. was the smallest company (in terms of number of employees) to be on the list of top 10 of the 100 best companies for working mothers ('Making It', October 2003). S. C. Johnson & Son, Inc. is a family-owned company that is known for the development of many widely used innovative household and personal care products. This 'small' company, at just under 4000 employees, manages to offer one company-sponsored on-site childcare center, with approximately 500 children enrolled (Johnson, no date). Specifically, the childcare center is a 20,000-square-foot complex located within the company's private park. This center is one of the few corporate childcare centers accredited by the national Association for Education of Young Children. In terms of help with older children, employees at S. C. Johnson & Son, Inc. have access to backup childcare arrangements, sick childcare arrangements, before/after school care and summer programs, all offered through the on-site childcare center.

S. C. Johnson & Son, Inc. was listed as best in class by *Working Mother* magazine for the flexibility options afforded to their employees. Specifically, the company was recognized for the high number of employees utilizing these programs. Approximately 55% of S. C. Johnson & Son employees reported using flexitime schedules, 64% work compressed workweeks in which 40 hours of work are accomplished in less than five work days, 37% work at home or telecommute, and 1% (or 40 employees) use the job-sharing option. New mothers working at S. C. Johnson & Son, Inc. are offered an additional 16 weeks of job-guaranteed leave for childbirth (over the 12 weeks guaranteed by the FMLA), with partial pay. New fathers are offered a total of six weeks paid leave for the birth of a child. Access to a lactation room is available to new mothers following childbirth. Adopting parents are afforded six weeks of paid leave with a $6000 stipend to help cover costs associated with the adoption. Finally, similar to the other companies highlighted in this review of the top 10 of the 100 best companies for working mothers, employees at S. C. Johnson & Son, Inc. have access to eldercare resources.

Some innovative policies at S. C. Johnson & Son, Inc. include a 'no meeting day policy', in which no scheduled meetings are allowed on two of the Fridays every month. The goal of this policy is to 'enable employees to be more productive heading into the weekends, decreasing the need to take work home' (Johnson, no date, p. 2). In addition, the company offers a partially paid (full benefits and partial pay) sabbatical, with the employee choosing how to spend this time (e.g., family time, volunteering, relaxing, traveling). Within the company park, employees have access to services designed to help reduce errands and hassles for parents: on-site banking, dry-cleaning pick-up, oil change for cars, intramural sports, fitness and social activities (e.g., indoor recreation center, aquatic complex, softball fields, tennis courts, golf driving range, miniature golf course) (Johnson, no date). Although this company is unique in that it is family owned and operated, it has definitely managed to demonstrate a great example of one comprehensive effort to alleviate the amount of conflict between work and family demands experienced by employees.

Wachovia Corporation

The Wachovia Corporation is a large financial services company that began as a small bank in North Carolina in 1879; with a century of growth and a 2001 merger with First Union Corporation, Wachovia now has over 89,000 employees. Wachovia was recognized by *Working Mother* magazine for their six company-sponsored childcare centers on or near site, with approximately 650 children enrolled. In addition, Wachovia Corporation attempts to provide sick childcare arrangements or backup childcare options for sick children. Approximately 2600 of the employees at Wachovia make use of the pretax dollars set aside to help aid their childcare expenses. When it comes to parental leave for childbirth and adoptions, Wachovia offers their employees an additional four weeks (beyond the mandated 12), at partial pay, for childbirth with their job guaranteed upon returning back to work; fathers are offered two weeks of paid leave for childbirth. Wachovia employees who adopt a child get a $1500 stipend to aid with expenses as well as four weeks of paid leave during the process. Finally, the Wachovia Corporation also reported that eldercare resources (e.g., access to a financial advisor who can discuss the financial implications of being a caretaker, flexible spending accounts where out-of-pocket pretax dollars can be used to cover caregiving expenses) and private nursing rooms are available to their employees. Wachovia was recognized in the *Working Mother* magazine article as best in class when it comes to having a family-friendly company culture:

[In 2002], Wachovia trained 2,178 managers on work/life issues and 2,083 on [flexible] scheduling; 7,200 employees used the company's employee assistance program, and 6,053 used the elder-care resource and referral service. While the company did not conduct an employee opinion survey [in 2002], it conducted three in the [previous] five years.

('Making It', 2003, p. 62)

When it comes to flexibility, Wachovia Corporation allows their employees to work with their supervisors in determining the hours and the location of work (Wachovia, no date). That is, the company policy is open to flexible workday start and stop times, working remotely or telecommuting, scheduling a 40-hour workweek in less than five workdays (compressed week schedules), allowing employees to be regular part-timers, engaging in job sharing, and having a phase-in period after coming back from a leave of absence. The company also developed what they call the 'LifeWorks Family Resource Program' (Wachovia, no date). This program is a combination of a telephone service and seminar series in which employees receive information on a variety of issues relating to dependant care (e.g., assistance finding childcare and eldercare, adoption information, planning for college). Thus, Wachovia definitely stands out for its dedication to help its employees manage work and family responsibilities in a healthy and productive manner.

International Business Machines Corporation (IBM): an in-depth analysis

IBM is a large high-tech manufacturer dedicated to the creation, development and manufacture of information technologies such as computer systems, software, networking systems, etc. Not only was IBM Corporation in the top 10 of the 100 best companies for working mothers, but it was also highlighted in their best of class section for their childcare benefits, policies and services ('Making It', October 2003, p. 62). Specifically, according to the report in *Working Mother* magazine, IBM sponsors 63 childcare centers either on or near site, with approximately 2324 children enrolled in these centers. In addition, they report having before or after school care available to their over 145,000 employees, having programs available for the teen-aged children of their employees, and sponsoring summer programs that are made available to their employees. In terms of flexible work options, the IBM Corporation reports that at least 70% of their employees use a flexitime schedule and at least 23% of their employees telework or complete some of their work from home.

When it comes to parental leave for new parents, IBM Corporation is one of the best. They offer an additional 13 weeks of job-guaranteed parental leave for childbirth, over and above the federally legislated 12 weeks demanded of employers with more than 50 employees. Six to eight of those weeks are fully paid leave for mothers. As for paternity leave and help with adoptions, the IBM Corporation offers two weeks of paid paternity leave as well as two weeks of paid leave for parents who are adopting, with $2800 in aid for adoption costs. Finally, the IBM Corporation offers eldercare resources to their workforce, including computer classes for retired employees and transportation for elderly relatives of employees.

One outstanding aspect of IBM's dedication to the work and family needs of its employees is its recent international focus. While their first work–life survey was conducted in the USA in 1986, and in a few other countries in 1998 (Europe and Latin America) and 1999 (the Asia–Pacific region), in 2001 they conducted their first global work–life survey (Childs, 2003). Childs reports that this survey was conducted in 20 languages and in 48 countries, with a response rate of 44%, or 25,000 employees. Based on the global survey results and employee comments, IBM recognized that their employees around the world are dealing with significant work–life responsibilities. As a result of this international recognition, the Global Work–Life Fund (GWLF), a $50 million fund to be invested over the years 2001–2005, was developed to address the dependant care and work–life needs of IBM employees worldwide (IBM, 2002). IBM already has active childcare and eldercare projects in at least 18 countries, and a full 60% of the GWLF is dedicated to additional projects outside the USA (Childs, 2003). We recognize IBM as a company demonstrating best practices because of its dedication to the dependant care needs of employees not only in the USA, but also of the potentially unique needs of its employees working in countries across the globe.

Compared to other companies, IBM also has scientific, empirical, published research documenting some of the positive effects of its work–family policies, benefits and services. Hill et al. (1997) believe that IBM employees perceive the flexibility of choosing when, where and how to complete their work as one of the most beneficial IBM practices for managing work and life demands (as cited in Hill et al., 2003). In fact, a recent study by Hill et al. (2003) revealed that approximately 100,000 IBM employees working in diverse locations across the globe use a virtual office instead of the traditional company-provided office space (as cited in Hill et al., 2003). These alternative work arrangements result in real estate savings of $75 million annually (Apgar, 1998). Despite these bottom-line savings for the corporation, a group of researchers and IBM employees recognized the importance of considering how these alternative work arrangements may impact organizational effectiveness and employees' well-being.

Hill and colleagues have extensively examined potential outcomes associated with these alternative work arrangements. Most IBM employees taking advantage of alternative work arrangements are engaged in telework and/or telecommuting as well as use of a virtual office. Telework can be defined as 'any form of substitution of information technologies (such as telecommunication and computers) for work-related travel; moving the work to the workers instead of moving the workers to work' (Nilles, 1998, p. 1). Nilles defines telecommuting as 'periodic work out of the principal office, one or more days per week either at home, a client's site, or in a telework center' (p. 1). Finally, the virtual office refers to the employer offering any portable means necessary for employees to conduct their job, where employees have the authority of choosing where and when the work can be done. Hence, employees in a virtual office have a flexibility of working from a variety of locations (e.g., satellite office, home office, customer sites) (Hill *et al.*, 2003). Most of the research on IBM employees' use of these alternative work arrangements focused on the effects of different work venues on several aspects of the employees' work and non-work life.

Research findings on alternative work arrangements at IBM

Different work options that have been studied among IBM employees include telework, telecommuting and the virtual office.

The research with IBM employees provides an empirical illustration of how different work venues affect such outcomes as working hours, job performance, teamwork, morale, workload success, job retention, job motivation and career opportunity. In general, employees working in a virtual or home office were found to work longer hours than employees in a traditional office (Hill *et al.*, 1998, 2003). The results of qualitative and quantitative analyses, used to explore the effects of virtual office employees ($N = 157$) and traditional office workers ($N = 89$), revealed that the virtual office had a positive effect on the perceived *work productivity* (Hill *et al.*, 1998). However, in a recent study, which compared IBM employees working in the traditional office (work from designated IBM facility, $N = 4316$), virtual office (work from a variety of venues, $N = 767$) or home office (work from home, $N = 441$), results of qualitative and quantitative analyses were ambivalent (Hill *et al.*, 2003). For example, on the one hand, the qualitative analysis indicated that both virtual and home office workers reported that their work arrangements increased their perceived job performance, with virtual office workers reporting significantly higher performance ratings than did workers in the home office. The authors suggested that since employees enjoy the flexibility provided to them by IBM, they may be responding positively to ensure the availability of alternative venues (Hill *et al.*, 2003). On the other hand, the results of multivariate analyses revealed that being in the virtual office, but not home or a traditional office, was a significant predictor of poorer perceived job performance. Hill *et al.* (2003) suggested that longer work hours found for employees in the virtual office accounted for the lower levels of perceived performance. In fact, when job hours were removed from the regression equation, the relationship between being in the virtual office and perceived job performance was no longer significant (Hill *et al.*, 2003).

The findings for *job motivation* revealed that flexible work options (either the virtual or home office) were associated with higher job motivation (Hill *et al.*, 2003). One of the possible explanations for these findings provided by authors was a feeling of autonomy in deciding where and when to work, which comes with an alternative work arrangement. Similarly, autonomy may explain the finding that employees working in either virtual or home offices had lower *turnover* intentions than employees in the traditional office (Hill *et al.*, 2003).

Interestingly, Hill *et al.* (1998) found that while qualitative data revealed negative effects of alternative work options on *teamwork*, the relationship between these variables was not significant in the multivariate analysis (Hill *et al.*, 1998). Hence, the authors concluded that the negative relationship between teamwork and virtual office arrangement was exaggerated, especially since employees, regardless of work arrangement, reported similar problems for working in teams.

Finally, the results for *workload success* (the ability to better manage workload as a result of telework) and *career opportunity* were promising. Working from a virtual office was positively related to workload success, while working in a traditional office was negatively related to workload success (Hill *et al.*, 2003). Furthermore, virtual office employees perceived their opportunity for advancement more optimistically compared to employees working in traditional offices (Hill *et al.*, 2003).

In sum, based on the reviewed research at IBM, it may be concluded that the impact of alternative work arrangements on organizational and employee outcomes is positive at IBM. Alternative work arrangements appear to be beneficial for IBM due to reduced real estate costs, increased employee motivation and reduced turnover intentions. One of the main benefits of alternative work arrangements for employees is autonomy in choosing when and where to work.

Research findings on work–life balance at IBM

One of the reasons IBM implemented alternative work arrangements was to enhance employees' flexibility and their ability to navigate work and life responsibilities. There are three studies that explored whether or not alternative work arrangements and perceptions of flexibility associated with these arrangements contributed to work–life balance among IBM employees. Overall, these studies revealed that perceived flexibility was related to higher work–life balance. However, levels of work–life balance differed for employees from various work venues.

Hill *et al.* (1998) provided evidence of the positive relationship between telework and flexibility. Telework employees believed that their alternative work arrangement assisted with meeting work (e.g., greater control over employees' time) and family (e.g., taking care of ill children, being available during family quality time) demands. In yet another study, it was found that employees with higher perceived job flexibility associated with telework also reported more work–family balance, and this effect was found after controlling for the effects of gender, marital status, occupation level, work hours and hours spent on unpaid household duties (Hill *et al.*, 2001). Moreover, not only did perceived flexibility mean more work–family balance, but employees with high perceived flexibility could also work longer hours before their work negatively impacted their work–family balance.

The other two studies examined whether or not perceived flexibility and work–life balance differed for employees in different work venues. Specifically, in a study comparing 157 telework and 89 office employees, the former reported having significantly more flexibility in choosing timing and location of work (Hill *et al.*, 1996). Written comments, however, showed that although some mobile workers described experiencing more work–life balance, others believed that telework had negative effects on work–family balance by diffusing the borders between these life domains. Interestingly, within the telework group, employees with preschool children reported experiencing more work–life balance than those without preschool children.

Finally, a recent study revealed a variation in perceived work–life balance for different work venues (Hill *et al.*, 2003). Although the qualitative analysis showed that virtual office workers viewed their work venue to have no impact on work–life balance, direct comparisons showed that virtual office employees experienced less work–life balance than both traditional office workers and home office workers. Further, a negative relationship between being a virtual office employee and poorer work–life balance was supported by multivariate analyses. One possible explanation for these findings is the lack of the boundary between work and family; that is, virtual office employees may not know when the work should end and home activities should take over (Hill *et al.*, 2003).

The results for home office employees were more positive. All methods of data analysis (qualitative and quantitative) showed that being a home office worker was associated with better work–life balance. Additionally, home office employees reported more work–life balance than either virtual office or traditional office employees.

In sum, there is some evidence that perceived flexibility associated with alternative work arrangements helped employees to have a better work–life balance at IBM. However, the results for the two studies examining work–life balance for different work venues are equivocal. Although home office employees perceived higher levels of work–life balance, the findings for virtual office employees were not consistent.

Corporate Voices for working families

The last work–family best practice reviewed here is a US-based national non-profit organization developed to bring together private sector corporations and public policy makers around issues affecting working families.

This is an effort to bring together private corporations, work–family expertise and national policy efforts to enhance the lives of working families. With a primary focus in four areas – children, eldercare, the work environment and family economic stability – Corporate Voices is developing policy statements to help policy makers understand the efforts that have been made and still need to be made on behalf of working families. For example, with the help of the Fannie Mae Foundation, Corporate Voices is developing tools for the business community to better understand the needs of low-wage workers. With the efforts of Donna Klein, President and CEO, Corporate Voices co-sponsored a survey with the Boston College Center for Work and Family focused on model programs and policies for hourly and lower-wage employees (Litchfield *et al.*, 2004). Released in April 2004, this report focused on the 52% of the US workforce making less than $25,000 annually, arguing that little is known about work–life needs and policies available to these lower-wage workers. General findings of the survey of 15 large employers indicated that types of programs for low-wage workers included subsidies for childcare, employee emergency loan programs, literacy programs and flexible work options. Although most of the programs identified were open to all full-time employees, some of the programs were limited to those employees under a specific wage. In addition, most of the programs highlighted in the report were relatively new, beginning sometime after 1998. This report is unique in its focus on lower-wage employees, a sector of the workforce frequently overlooked in many of the work–family best practices identified. It is these efforts that have led us to list Corporate Voices for Working Families as a unique approach to work–family best practices.

CONCLUSIONS

This chapter aimed to review some examples of organizational work–family best practices. These observations were mostly limited to larger US companies that could afford in-house programs. It should be recognized, however, that the majority of organizations are smaller than the ones reviewed here and thus they must either rely on the limited (e.g., USA) or not so limited (e.g., The Netherlands) government policies targeted to support working families. In addition, when companies are not large enough to have in-house practices, many of them may choose to make use of the vast amount of work–life consulting firms that have emerged over the past decade. These firms offer everything from childcare and eldercare resources and referral to larger-scale efforts at designing work–life programs that are tailored to a company's needs. Issues related to the implementation and evaluation of work–family programs are in need of further attention in the literature. Thus, what is presented here is a limited examination of work–life best practices in large-scale, resource-rich corporations.

Finally, for companies considering embarking on work–life interventions, we suggest conducting a needs assessment survey to help determine what types of programs would be useful in an effort to target the needs of the workforce to the particular practice being implemented. One possible resource is the Work–Family Sourcebook for Employers, available online, which provides a sample needs assessment survey (Neal and Hammer, 2001). In addition, without more information on the effectiveness of such practices, it is difficult to make recommendations to employers. As Hill and Weiner (2003) have identified, their suggested five-step model of evaluation of work–life programs may prove to be useful for companies that are implementing such programs, and for future benchmarking of work–life best practices.

REFERENCES

Allen, T. D. (2001). Family-supportive work environments: the role of organizational perceptions. *Journal of Vocational Behavior*, *58*, 414–435.

APA (American Psychological Association) (2003). Psychological Healthy Workplace Awards: 2003 Best Practices Honors.

Apgar, M. (1998). The alternative workplace: changing where and how people work. *Harvard Business Review*, *76*, 121–136.

Arthur, M. M. (2003). Share price reactions to work–family human resource decisions: an institutional perspective. *Academy of Management Journal*, *46*, 497–505.

Childs, T. (2003, July). Is work/life balance a global issue – or has the U.S. culture simply exported the issue? Retrieved 29 January 2004 from http://www.workfamily.com/Open/work-Life-Guest-ColumnChilds.asp

Fannie Mae (no date). Working at Fannie Mae: family and lifestyle. Retrieved 31 January 2004 from http://www.fanniemae.com/careers/working/index.jhtml;jsessionid=NOP5X0UK2UEZ1J2FECHSFGNHQUQJCIV5?p=Careers&s=Working+at+Fannie+Mae

Fredrikson-Goldsen, K., and Scharlach, A. E. (2001). *Families and work: New directions in the twenty-first century*. New York: Oxford University Press.

Hammer, L. B., Neal, M. B., Newsom, J., Brockwood, K. J., and Colton, C. (2005). A longitudinal study of the effects of dual-earner couples' utilization of family-friendly workplace supports on work and family outcomes. *Journal of Applied Psychology*, *90*, 799–810.

Hill, E. J., Campbell, A., and Koblenz, M. (1997). The art of employee surveys: using surveys for organizational change. Paper presented at the *1997 Conference Board Work and Family Conference*, New York.

Hill, E. J., Ferris, M., and Märtinson, V. (2003). Does it matter where you work? A comparison of how three work venues (traditional office, virtual office, and home office) influence aspects of work and personal/family life. *Journal of Vocational Behavior*, *63*, 220–241.

Hill, E. J., Hawkins, A. J., Ferris, M., and Weitzman, M. (2001). Finding an extra day a week: the positive influence of perceived job flexibility on work and family life balance. *Family Relations, 50,* 49–58.

Hill, E. J., Hawkins, A. J., and Miller, B. C. (1996). Work and family in the virtual office: perceived influences of mobile telework. *Family Relations, 45,* 293–301.

Hill, E. J., Miller, B. C., Weiner, S. P., and Colihan, J. (1998). Influences of the virtual office on aspects of work and work/life balance. *Personnel Psychology, 51,* 667–683.

Hill, E. J., and Weiner, S. P. (2003). Work/life balance policies and programs. In J. E. Edwards, J. C. Scott and N. S. Raju (eds), *The human resources program-evaluation handbook* (pp. 447–468). Newbury Park, CA: Sage.

IBM (International Business Machines Corporation) (2002). Corporate responsibility report. Retrieved 31 January 2004 from http://www.ibm.com/ibm/responsibility/

Johnson (no date). We offer an innovative environment. Retrieved 31 January 2004 from http://www.scjohnson.com/careers/car_aie.asp

Kossek, E. E., and Ozeki, C. (1998). Work–family conflict, policies, and the job-life satisfaction relationship: a review and directions for organizational behavior–human resources research. *Journal of Applied Psychology, 83,* 139–149.

Lanquestin, M., Laufer, J., and Letablier, M. (2000). Reconciliation policies from a comparative perspective. In L. Hantrais (ed.), *Gendered policies in Europe: Reconciling employment and family life* (pp. 49–67). London: Macmillan Press.

Litchfield, L. C., Swanberg, J. E., Sigworth, C. M. (2004). Increasing the visibility of the invisible workforce: model programs and policies for hourly and lower wage employees. Corporate Briefing, Corporate Voices for Working Family and Boston College Center for Work and Family, Carroll School of Management. Retrieved 8 June 2004 from http://www.cvworkingfamilies.org/

Making it: how we chose the 100 best companies for working mothers. (2003, October). *Working Mother,* 56–63.

Neal, M. B., Chapman, N. J., Ingersoll-Dayton, B., and Emlen, A. C. (1993). *Balancing work and caregiving for children, adults, and elders.* Newbury Park, CA: Sage.

Neal, M. B., and Hammer, L. B. (2001). Supporting employees with child and elder care needs: an employers' sourcebook. Portland State University. Retrieved 31 January 2004 from http://www.sandwich.pdx.edu/

Nilles, J. M. (1998). *Managing telework: Strategies for managing the virtual workforce.* New York: Wiley.

Perry-Smith, J. E., and Blum, T. C. (2000). Work–family human resource bundles and perceived organizational performance. *Academy of Management Journal, 43,* 1107–1117.

Stebbins, L. F. (2001). *Work and family in America: A reference handbook.* Santa Barbara, CA: ABC-CLIO.

Wachovia (no date). Balancing career and personal life. Retrieved 31 January 2004 from http://www.wachovia.com/inside/page/0,,137_363_412,00.html

12 Work–life policy and practice in the USA: gendered premise, radical potential?

Paulette R. Gerkovich

The history and uses of work–life programs in the USA are unique, particularly in comparison to the ways in which flexibility is articulated in the European context. US work–life programs, and even attitudes toward using them, are borne of a confluence of shifting demographics, economic necessity, and governmental and corporate policy that distinguish American approaches toward social action. For example, a reticence on the part of American governmental institutions to legislate and fund social programs – such as that related to working mothers – has left a space that the corporation often need to fill.

At the same time, American work–life programs have not entirely shed their history as an answer to the issues faced by working mothers (see Chapter 11). Despite increasing demands for flexible work arrangements on the parts of women who are not mothers, as well as men, flexibility is still largely seen as a women's issue.

This chapter, which will commence with a brief history of work–life policy and programs[1] in the USA, addresses the question of why they remain fixed in the realm of women's issues. While the history of work–life programs clearly is a contributor, there are more pervasive reasons that are grounded in the nature and structure of organizations, as well as in deeply embedded conceptions of the good manager. Specifically, the concept 'manager', as well as the organization itself, is a gendered entity that privileges men over women. I analogize this to liberal political ideology's conception of the good citizen as a way of further demonstrating the entrenchment of such concepts in western culture and public life.

Interventions that seek to redress this privilege – such as flexible work arrangements for working mothers – indelibly become 'women's issues'. I go on to argue that because men – and men's needs and capabilities – already are privileged in the modern organization, that which is seen as a women's issue will continue to render women marginalized.

The only solution that such a dilemma leaves us with is to subvert the gendered nature of the organization itself. In the last section of this chapter, I argue that work–life policies and programs can be used as tools to begin doing just that.

Again, rapidly increasing numbers of men and women without children desire to use – and are demanding that companies provide – flexible work. Many men are openly making these demands so that they can more fully participate in caretaking activities. At the same time, both women and men – particularly beginning with Generation X (those born between 1964 and 1975) – recognize that they want full work *and* personal lives. Working flexibly is a way to achieve that.

The work–life issue, then, is evolving away from being related solely to working mothers for two reasons. First, men increasingly are making it an issue related to working fathers. But, more importantly, employees of both sexes are envisioning work–life programs as mechanisms for achieving a higher quality of life.

Ultimately, offering work–life programs could become a standard way of doing business for those organizations that wish to remain highly competitive in the employee marketplace. The work–life issue would then no longer be a women's issue, but does include tools that can meet many women's needs. These tools would become embedded in the way that business is done, and require a concurrent reshaping of the organization – a subversion of the current organizational structure – to accommodate it. In this way, I argue, work–life policies and programs contain an element of radical potential.

THE HISTORY OF WORK–LIFE POLICY AND PRACTICE IN THE USA

While the history of work–life policies and programs does not follow a clear and linear path,[2] most experts would agree that they are grounded in governmental policy aimed at supporting working families with children. The sudden need for such legislation is a result of increasing numbers of women entering the paid labor force. Policies, including the 1978 passage of the Pregnancy Discrimination Act, along with 1981 changes in tax laws enabling parents to use pre-tax dollars for childcare, set a precedent for the flexibility issue to be treated as a working mother issue.

The terminology 'work–family', which was the common terminology referring to work–life policies and programs until the 1990s, is further indication that these efforts, at least initially (if not still), were seen as ways to address the needs of working mothers. In fact, in the late 1970s and throughout the 1980s, flexible work arrangements primarily *were* geared toward meeting the needs of new mothers. Employers, particularly Human Resources managers, recognized that these arrangements often were an effective way of transitioning mothers back into the workforce. Part-time work was seen as a particularly effective mechanism for doing this. The assumption, however, was that these arrangements were a temporary measure to ease transition, rather than a long-term business strategy (such as one aimed to increase recruitment or retention) (Catalyst, 2000).

Reinforcing the temporary nature of flexible work arrangements was general uncertainty amongst employees that one could work flexibly while significantly advancing one's career. This pessimism was not unfounded. Managers were unlikely to recognize the viability of working flexibly and contributing to the organization as fully as those working traditional, full-time schedules. So pervasive was this belief that, by 1989, many companies explicitly prohibited job-sharing teams and part-time employees from holding supervisory positions (Catalyst, 2000).

As the US government began to address issues of working families and the demographics of the American workforce diversified even more, research institutions began focusing on work–life issues and new institutes dedicated to its study began to crop up. In 1983, the Conference Board founded its Work–life Leadership Council, while that same year Elinor Guggenheimer founded the Child Care Action Campaign. One year later, in 1984, Work/Family Directions offered the first childcare resource and referral service. In 1989 the Families and Work Institute was founded (Catalyst, 2000).

At the same time, American workers were increasingly demanding attention to work–family issues from their employers. In addition to wanting more control over their work schedules, employees began talking about creating customized career paths – a sharp divergence from the traditional 'up or out' model predominant in many organizations (Catalyst, 2000).

In the late 1980s, work–life issues were still largely seen as women's issues and, in particular, mothers' issues. In 1985, *Working Mother* magazine began publishing its '100 Best Companies for Working Mothers' list (as discussed in Chapter 11). Business involvement came primarily in the form of making the case for excellent childcare and building on-site childcare centers. At this time, companies that understood the importance of on-site childcare were truly pioneering. For example, Catalyst presented its first annual Catalyst Award to outstanding efforts to recruit, develop and advance women in 1987. That year's winners included IBM's National Child Care Referral Program and the Connecticut Consortium for Child Care – a group of companies that had pooled resources to provide quality childcare to its employees (Catalyst, 2000).

The US workforce demographic changes that had started in the 1980s continued into the 1990s. Between 1989 and 1999, women's labor force participation increased from 56% to 59%, and almost three-quarters of mothers with children under the age of 18 were working in the paid labor force (US Department of Labor, Women's Bureau, 2000). In addition, economic shifts irrevocably changed the nature of American businesses as the mid to late 1980s ushered in an era of downsizing, rightsizing and re-engineering. Increasing demands – to work longer hours and be more productive – were placed on those in the paid labor force (Catalyst, 2000; see also Chapter 1).

During this time, American businesses became much more involved in work–life issues. Progressive employers began to understand the impact of working flexibly on morale and, in turn, recruitment and retention, and began to address the work–life needs of their employees. As cutting-edge companies established and used formal flexible work arrangement programs as strategic recruitment and retention tools, an understanding of the work–life issue as a key business issue was gaining credence (Catalyst, 2000).

However, voluntary flexible work arrangements for managers and professionals were still far from the norm by the late 1980s. A 1990 study of women in the workplace revealed that 40% of companies participating in the study did not offer flexible work arrangements to any level of exempt employees. Just over one-half (57%) offered part-time work options to their professional staff, 24% offered this option to managers and only 14% to senior managers (Catalyst, 1990).

As in the 1980s, corporate involvement occurred in conjunction with governmental policy. Most prominently, in 1993, President Bill Clinton signed into law the Family and Medical Leave Act requiring those employing 50 or more individuals to offer unpaid job-protected family or medical leave of up to 12 weeks to qualified employees (Catalyst, 2000) (see also Chapter 2).

Despite an increasing focus on work–life, conversations and corporate involvement in the early 1990s still remained focused primarily on child-care. Again, this is evidenced by the Catalyst Award being granted to the American Business Collaboration for Quality Dependent Care in 1992 (Catalyst, 2000).

However, the mid to late 1990s saw a tremendous change in approaches to work–life. That change is evidenced by shifts in terminology; for example, corporations and professionals in the flexibility field moved away from the term 'work–family' and employed the more egalitarian and accurate term 'work–life'. This terminology is not insignificant and marks increasing corporate and academic recognition that work–life was becoming a key consideration for women and men, parents and non-parents.

Companies that took the lead in this area include Baxter which, in 1994, undertook an employee needs assessment to understand how it could benefit from championing work–life balance. The following year, IBM launched its Global Women Leaders Task Force, which spearheaded the implementation of work–life surveys in its offices across the globe (Catalyst, 2000).

Foundations, associations and research firms also led the shift in thinking about work–life issues and policies. In 1994, the Alfred P. Sloan Foundation introduced a program focused on dual-career families. In 1996, the Alliance of Work–Life Professionals was founded, and Catalyst published the instructive guide *Making Work Flexible: From Policy to Practice* (Catalyst, 1996).

It is important to note that while at the end of the 20th century public discourse increasingly turned to issues of work–life, the fact remains that women are primary caretakers for children and the elderly; in short, they bear a disproportionate burden of family-related responsibilities. So, while work–life policies and programs have become mechanisms for addressing concerns that extend beyond family, there needs remain a focus on family. To that end, in 1997, MacDonald Communications and *Working Mother* held their first annual 'Work/Family Congress' and CEO Summit. In 1999, the Families and Work Institute and the Boston College Center for Work and Family convened the first 'Global Forum on Work and Family' (Catalyst, 2000).

At the same time, the business case for working flexibly became increasingly understood by progressive organizations who knew that quality of life for both women and men was at stake. In order to attract and retain these individuals, organizational programs and policies must address the work–life issue.

In fact, according to a 1997 survey of 614 employers across the globe, flexible schedules were the most highly ranked retention tool. (Other tools included training, above-market compensation and stock options.) Furthermore, of the banking, finance and insurance companies in the study, 81% reported that they planned to increase their use of flexible work arrangements within one year. Of manufacturing firms – which sometimes face great challenges implementing flexibility – 66% planned to increase telecommuting and 49% will increase the number of job shares (Watson Wyatt Worldwide, 1997). Giving the growing support and strengthening business case for working flexibly, it is not surprising that by 1999 about one-quarter of women in the US paid labor force worked part time (US Department of Labor, Women's Bureau, 2000).

The pioneering work of women who had used flexible work arrangements – and communicated their resulting success – also contributed to increasing acceptance. Women working on part-time arrangements, who participated in a 2000 Catalyst study, believe that the examples they set led to the formalization of work–life programs within their organizations, and their increasing use by both women and men (Catalyst, 2000). (In fact, an earlier Catalyst, 1998b, study on dual-career marriages found that almost one in four men surveyed already had used some type of formal flexible work schedule, and 83% use some type of flexible hours. There occurred a concurrent shift in opinions about those who work flexibly.) Women in this study report that colleagues' attitudes increasingly grew supportive, and discussions of new ways to work proliferated (Catalyst, 2000).

CURRENT ARTICULATIONS OF WORK–LIFE POLICIES AND PROGRAMS

Clearly, a tremendous amount of progress in the field of work–life has been made in a relatively short period of time. However, despite promising examples to the contrary, there remain significant challenges to attaining flexible work; to advancing in one's career even if it is attained; and, more generally, for widespread acceptance amongst organizational leaders of work–life as a business issue.

For example, although most large companies – and a good deal of smaller ones – have flexibility policies, many individuals cannot use them without jeopardizing their careers (see Chapter 10). While employees who fill lower-level positions often are doing the kinds of work that preclude working flexibly, many of those in more senior positions (often conducive to working flexibly) risk stigmatization should they do so. In a recent study of women and men executives, almost all respondents agreed that they could be flexible with their work schedules when they had a family or personal matter to attend to.[3] However, only 24% of women and 33% of men agreed that they 'can turn down a work opportunity for family/ personal reasons without jeopardizing [their] career advancement'. Only 15% of women and 20% of men agree that they 'can use a flexible work arrangement without jeopardizing [their] career advancement'. A mere 14% of women and men agree that they 'can use a parental leave or sabbatical without jeopardizing [their] career advancement' (Catalyst, 2004).

Despite fears that job advancement will be endangered by working flexibly, women and men desire to do so. More interestingly, they desire to work flexibly in relatively equal percentages, although very few of them actually do. The study cited above found that 39% of women and 32% of men want to take a leave or sabbatical, while only 7% and 2%, respectively, have done so. They also want to work in more non-traditional ways. Twenty-eight percent of women and 24% of men want to work a compressed week, while only 7% and 5%, respectively, have done so. Telecommuting/working from home was the only flexible work arrangement that did not evidence a huge disparity between those who want to utilize it and those who actually have. Twenty-three percent of women wish to telecommute, compared to 12% who actually have. Men seem to be faring even better in this arena; 15% of men wish to telecommute/work from home and 14% actually have (Catalyst, 2004). One of the interesting issues that these findings raise is that work–life – working flexibly – is clearly of concern to both women and men.

Yet the popular framing of the work–life issue as a women's issue remains. The views of executive women and men who want to work flexibly notwithstanding, both organizational programs and policies and conventional wisdom frame the work–life issue as a women's issue. Its link to mothers and future mothers remains quite a strong one.

Furthermore, as long as the work–life issue continues to be seen solely as a women's issue, it is unlikely that it will ever be widely accepted as an effective business tool. It *is* likely that women's commitment to their jobs will be suspect as the belief that they will always place personal and family life first persists.[4]

In fact, one of the challenges to women's advancement cited by both women and men in a recent study is a commitment to personal and family responsibilities.[5] This finding, however, likely has different meanings for women and men. While men often continue to question women's commitment to their jobs in light of their personal responsibilities, women are concerned about two things. First, they understand that the *perception* (not the reality) that they will be committed to their personal lives to the exclusion of their work lives is a barrier to advancement. Second, they recognize that as long as being committed to one's personal life stands in opposition to commitment to one's work, the struggle to the top will be a difficult one.

In light of this, the remainder of this chapter will address two issues. The first concerns the question of why the work–life issue – despite evidence to the contrary – largely remains a 'women's issue'. The second considers whether and how this might change, i.e., whether and how working flexibly becomes widely recognized as a business issue and a mechanism to achieving a better quality of life for both women and men.

THE GENDERED NATURE OF WORK–LIFE POLICIES AND PROGRAMS

In some ways, the question of why the work–life issue is still framed as a women's issue appears relatively easy to answer. The intentions of men who wish to participate in caretaking notwithstanding, the fact is that women continue to bear a disproportionate level of caretaking and household responsibilities (see Chapter 6). Quite simply, that means they will be the primary consumers of work–life programs.

This holds true even for women in executive positions. A recent study revealed that much higher percentages of women utilized specific strategies to achieve a balance between their work and personal lives than their male colleagues. Specifically, women were far more likely than men to rely on support from others (either from paid help or family and friends); curtail their personal interests; make decisions related to family (such as postponing having children or marriage); and using flexible work arrangements, including telecommuting and taking leave. The only 'balance strategy' that higher percentages of men than women used was pursuing personal interests (Catalyst, 2004).

The second reason that the work–life issue is still seen largely as a women's issue is that work–life programs and policies originally were designed to meet the needs of working mothers. The history of work–life *is* that of a women's issue. (Let us not forget the significance of the term 'work–family'.) Both governmental and corporate flexibility and work–life policies – beginning in the late 1970s – were enacted primarily to help mothers gain or maintain a role in the paid labor force.

These policies were not necessarily developed because of a moral imperative to drive workplace equality for women. Rather, they spoke to a need for more and increasingly skilled labor. Drawing on as much talent as possible was – and continues to be – the linchpin in the business case to develop and advance women (Catalyst, 1998a).

But there is a third and deeper reason that the work–life issue is still seen largely as a women's issue. The reason is that the body of the prototypical employee – particularly the executive – is a male body. While seemingly neutral, the employee and the organizational structure within which that employee operates are deeply gendered. According to Acker (1990), 'Since men in organizations take their behavior and perspectives to represent the human, organizational structures and processes are theorized as neutral. When it is acknowledged that women and men are affected differently by organizations, it is argued that gendered attitudes and behavior are brought into (and contaminate) essentially gender-neutral structures' (p. 142).

Therefore, because the gender of the employee is actually male, any policy, program or structure that is designed to account for the specificities of the female body (e.g., childbearing) will be strongly bound up with that very femaleness. It will be seen as upending the neutrality of the proto-typical employee and providing for special treatment. In other words, because the 'good employee' (particularly the good manager) is male, additional policies and programs to account for the uniqueness of the female body must be implemented. (One need only consider the nature of maternity leave to recognize this reality.) Going backward, and reconcep-tualizing those policies as for and about both women *and* men, is excep-tionally difficult.

The concept of the employee as male was first fully articulated by Moss Kanter (1977). She explores the characteristics of the effective manager and theorizes that they are characteristics traditionally seen as belonging to men. They include rationality, a 'tough' approach to problem resolution, abstract analytical abilities, and the willingness and ability to separate the emotional from work-related responsibilities (Moss Kanter, 1977). Men historically have been seen as possessing these traits, while women have been represented as just the opposite – irrational, emotional and 'soft'.

Not incidentally, feminist political theorists have made similar arguments about the 'good citizen'. The notion that women are irrational, and therefore incapable of citizenship, has been prevalent since ancient Greece.

The political ideology of liberalism, upon which US civic life is founded, features the universal, generalizable individual who ostensibly could be either male or female. But, just as Moss Kanter recognized in conceptions of the good employee, the universal citizen is actually a man. Because liberalism privileges the rational citizen – and women are seen as more closely tied to the irrational/nature/body – the liberal citizen, then, is actually male.

Pateman (1988) articulates this in her analysis of the western political canon. She observes that for all of the classical political theorists (except Thomas Hobbes), their stories of origin and contract rely on sexual differentiation. This differentiation is marked, most prominently, by men's ability and women's inability to think and act rationally. Only men innately possess the potential to fulfill the demands of civic life. As a result, women categorically are excluded from the conception of 'individual' established within western political philosophy.

In addition to this rationality, the liberal individual is construed as isolated and autonomous, and liberal society a collection of independent entities putting forth individual interests. These interests are seen as separate from and/or in opposition to the other individuals within that society. Again, feminist critics of liberalism demonstrate that such an individual can only be male because there is no accounting for the processes of giving birth and caring for children, not to mention the intricate web of relationships that would likely build as a result (Tong, 1989).

I argue elsewhere that it is this conception of the liberal individual as universal and generalizable when he is actually very much a man that compels women to frame political demands around issues related to their bodies – that which allows recognition of them as women. Put differently, because liberalism does not recognize the female, while saying it recognizes everybody, women must assert their specificity *as* women in order to be recognized (Gerkovich, 2002).

This is not unrelated to what women in organizations are forced to do. As Moss Kanter points out, the prototypical employee/manager is actually a man. I would go on to say that women must assert their specificity – their difference – as women in order to have their needs recognized. What this means, ultimately, is that until programs and policies that allow women to have and care for children are seen as part of the routine functioning of organizations, women will never be seen as employees in the same way that men are.

Acker (1990) takes this analysis even further, pointing out that Moss Kanter is correct to identify the employee as male. However, she goes on to note that this employee is operating within an organizational system that also is gendered. While Moss Kanter considers gender as standing *outside of* organizational structure, Acker posits that it is woven into its very fabric.

Acker (1990) points out that the gendered nature of organizations is borne of a variety of things. First, organizations feature a number of gender-based divisions, such as who does what work and where one works. This is evidenced by the location of men at the top of most organizational structures. They, in turn, reproduce a culture and structure that reflect their needs and desires. So, according to Acker, '[m]anagers' decisions often initiate gender divisions, and organizational practices maintain them' (Acker, 1990, p. 146).

Secondly, a system of symbols – which include language, dress and the media – support those gender divisions. Third, sanctioned or culturally acceptable interactions between the sexes establish and maintain gendered dynamics. This includes flow in conversation, such as who speaks, and when and how. This, in turn, impacts upon an individual's identity – how the individual sees him/herself and presents that self to the world. In the end, Acker observes, all of this acts to create and support social structures from the family to the organization (Acker, 1990).

It is here that Acker's (1990) analysis of organizations reflects the feminist analysis of the liberal political structure. For example, Acker takes the seemingly neutral and universal categories 'job' and 'hierarchy', and demonstrates that they are gendered in a way that privileges men over women. 'In organizational logic, filling the abstract job is a disembodied worker who exists only for the work. The closest the disembodied worker doing the abstract job comes to a real worker is the male worker whose life centers on his full-time, life-long job, while his wife or another woman takes care of his personal needs and children' (p. 149). In other words, the concept of 'job' is always and already premised on a certain sexual division of labor.

Similarly, hierarchies are gendered because they are premised on the notion that those who can commit to paid employment (as described above) are the most suited to that employment. Those who cannot be so fully committed must seek employ in the lower ranks of the hierarchy. Again, such a system certainly does not account for personal realities such as childbearing and caretaking. According to Acker (1990), '[t]he absence of sexuality, emotionality, and procreation in organizational logic and organizational theory is an additional element that both obscures and helps to reproduce the underlying gender relations' (p. 151). Once more, the good employee who sits atop the hierarchy must be male.

Work–life policies and programs were created within this paradigm of the gendered organization. They, too, are gendered concepts that reflect the nature of the employee and organizational structure. Even though – in fact, *because* – work–life policies and programs were created to allow activities such as childbearing, breastfeeding and caretaking, they are distinctly gendered. They seem to account for women's needs, and often do, but are a response to a system that inherently cannot account for women. Just like the liberal female citizen who must assert the specificity of her body, the employee must assert the specificity of *her* body to be able to work. The result, however, is that in systems that assume a disembodied and neutral subject men will always be privileged.

Because work–life policies and programs were designed to account for the specificities of the female body, they continue to be seen as women's issues. Furthermore, as long as these policies and programs are not part of the actual composition of organizations – but are, rather, additions – use of them will remain suspect.

THE TRANSFORMATIVE POTENTIAL OF WORK–LIFE POLICIES AND PROGRAMS

Feminist theorists who come to these types of conclusions often must pull up their reins at a stark reality. Entirely transforming existing organizations to reflect the realities of women's bodies is an overwhelming task. It will be achieved in small steps, if achieved at all.

I contend that if it is going to happen, work–life policies and programs could assist in transforming the gendered organization. Acker hints at this when she proposes her solution to the dilemma imposed by the gendered organization: 'The rhythm and timing of work would be adapted to the rhythms of life outside work' (Acker, 1990, p. 155). From my perspective, this means that what occurs in the private sphere (e.g., caretaking) must be synchronized to occur with what occurs in the public sphere (e.g., the workplace).

However, in order for public and private work to be seen as equally important – and for there to exist a harmony between public and private life – there need be a critical mass demanding that it does. That will occur only when men and women both agree that caretaking and paid labor are important, and they demand that their employers address the issue. In some ways, this already is beginning to happen, as men increasingly prioritize their personal lives.

A recent survey of the next generation of leaders (Generation X managers and professionals) revealed that while both women and men were very dedicated to their jobs, they placed a higher importance on personal values than on work-related values and achievements. For example, 86% of women and 79% of men reported that having a loving family was extremely important; 76% of women and 62% of men reported that obtaining and sharing companionship with family and friends was extremely important; and 74% of women and 65% of men reported that establishing a relationship with a significant other was extremely important (Catalyst, 2001).

While these individuals reported that work was a high priority for them, they placed much less emphasis on work-related values and goals. Specifically, 18% of women and 27% of men said that earning a great deal of money was extremely important; 13% of women and 22% of men said that becoming an influential leader was extremely important; and 5% of women and 10% of men said that becoming well known was extremely important (Catalyst, 2001).

Furthermore, this younger generation of women and men leaders is even more likely than the previous to want to work flexibly. Two-thirds (67%) want to use a compressed workweek (only 6% actually do); 59% want to telecommute (17% do); 46% want the ability to change their work schedule on an ad hoc basis (22% have it); 43% want the opportunity to take leave or a sabbatical (18% have it); and 36% want to work part time (4% do) (Catalyst, 2001).

The primary reason for wanting to work flexibly is childcare, as reported by large majorities of both women and men. Specifically, 79% of women and 68% of men who want to work flexibly want to do so to attend to children.

Generation X employees do, however, have a variety of other reasons for wanting to adopt flexible work arrangements. Thirty-seven percent of women and 47% men want to work flexibly to attend school;[6] 41% of women and 44% of men for personal health reasons; 31% of women and 39% of men for a personal interest unrelated to family; 33% of women and 35% to address overwork; and 26% of women and 20% of men to address adult care responsibilities (Catalyst, 2001).

These findings raise two important points that will indelibly impact the issue of work–life. First, large and unprecedented percentages of men have the need and desire to work flexibly so that they can assist with childcare responsibilities. Furthermore, one in five men envisions the need to work flexibly to care for elderly and dependant adults (Catalyst, 2001). This marks the possible beginning of a huge, historic shift in who performs caring work, and in how it is performed. If the intentions of male Generation X employees are even partially realized, conversations about flexibility (tied closely to those of caretaking as they are) could be pushed out of the realm of women's issues entirely.

The second important point is that both women and men desire to use work–life policies and programs to meet a whole variety of needs not related to family. While these policies and programs – just a few decades ago – were borne of the need to transition mothers into the workplace, their scope has widened considerably. They are no longer seen solely as mechanisms to support women so that they can perform paid as well as caretaking work. Rather, they are tools that can assist women and men in achieving their workplace aspirations, as well as a higher quality of life.

These are ambitious suppositions, and are premised on radical shifts in thinking about sexual divisions of labor. For change to occur, it is also necessary for organizations to account for those shifts. This is likely to happen only if women and men demand that it does, and if they frame those demands in ways that will affect an organization's bottom line.

There is some evidence that employee demands for work–life programs could have a profound impact on organizational structure and economics. For example, Generation X managers and professionals assert that they will leave their organizations if they cannot attain access to the flexibility programs that they desire. Of those who plan on leaving their organizations in less than three years, 64% will leave to work in an environment that is more supportive of their family and personal commitments, and 63% will leave to attain more control over their work schedules. Furthermore, about two-thirds (68%) of them reported that the perceived ability to balance their work and personal lives had been an extremely or very important factor in attracting them to their current organization. Finally, over three-quarters

(78%) of women and men report that flexible work policies and programs are extremely or very important to their advancement and job satisfaction (Catalyst, 2001).

It is these types of demands to use work–life programs, from women *and* men, that ultimately could compel organizations – at least those that wish to compete in the 'war for talent' – to adopt them as standard practice. While such programs clearly would need to be adapted to address the unique circumstances of industries, roles and jobs, their adoption as a customary business practice would do nothing short of requiring modifications to existing organizational structures. Not incidentally, they require modification of those structural elements that negate the specificities of the female body (e.g., the ability to bear children). In isolation, work–life policy and practice will not entirely transform the gendered organization. However, in the ways described above, they do have the potential to *begin* subverting a very entrenched, very gendered paradigm.

NOTES

1 In this chapter, I use the term work–life policies and programs primarily to refer to flexible work arrangements including, but not limited to, part-time, telecommuting, compressed workweeks, and paid and unpaid leave. I wish to acknowledge here that the term 'work–life' is much more than a synonym for flexible work arrangements, but also touches on issues related to the nature and quality of work, its contribution to one's social identity, and its integration into larger perceptions of how one conceives of and conducts one's entire life. In this conception, no one particular aspect of one's life (e.g., work) is given primacy; rather, one's life – which often includes performing paid labor – is treated holistically. Therefore, I also use the term 'work–life *issue*' when I am addressing this broader concept (of which flexible work arrangements are a subset).

2 The evolution of work–life policy and programs has been shaped by the changing intersection of household demographics, economics and governmental policy. This history is further complicated by realities of gender, class and sexuality, as each of these characteristics impacts the type of work one performs, as well as perceptions of an individual as a childbearer and caretaker. While the beginning of this chapter will address the evolution of work–life policies and programs, in general, my analysis and comments will focus primarily on the situations of executive-level women and men. In so doing, I do not wish to undermine the challenges of other positions and types of work, but rather, reinforce that there exist stark differences.

3 Specifically, 91% of women and 94% of men agreed with this statement.

4 The issue of whether one should *have to* prioritize spheres of their lives will be addressed subsequently.

5 Specifically, 67% of women and 54% of men agreed or strongly agreed that a commitment to personal or family responsibilities was a barrier to women advancing to senior levels within their organizations. All women and men surveyed were at the Vice President level or above, and employed within Fortune 1000 companies (Catalyst, 2004).

6 In this case, 'attend school' refers to the attendance of educational programs by survey respondents.

REFERENCES

Acker, J. (1990). Hierarchies, jobs, bodies: a theory of gendered organizations. *Gender and Society*, *4*, 139–158.

Catalyst (1990). *Women in corporate management*. New York: Catalyst.

Catalyst (1996). *Making work flexible: From policy to practice*. New York: Catalyst.

Catalyst (1998a). *Closing the gap: Women's advancement in corporate and professional Canada*. New York: Catalyst.

Catalyst (1998b). *Two careers, one marriage: Making it work in the workplace*. New York: Catalyst.

Catalyst (2000). *Flexible work arrangements III: A ten-year retrospective of part-time arrangements for managers and professionals*. New York: Catalyst.

Catalyst (2001). *The next generation: Today's professionals, tomorrow's leaders*. New York: Catalyst.

Catalyst (2004). *Women and men in U.S. corporate leadership*. New York: Catalyst.

Gerkovich, P. R. (2002). *Accessing power with the medicalized body: The paradox and implications of women's health demands* (doctoral dissertation, University of Maryland). ProQuest Digital Dissertations (UMI no. 3080270).

Moss Kanter, R. (1977). *Men and women of the corporation*. New York: Basic Books.

Pateman, C. (1988). *The sexual contract*. Stanford, CA: Stanford University Press.

Tong, R. (1989). *Feminist thought: A comprehensive introduction*. Boulder, CO and San Francisco, CA: Westview Press.

US Department of Labor, Women's Bureau (2000). *Employment characteristics of families*.

Watson Wyatt Worldwide (1997). *Strategic rewards survey report: Keeping your best talent from walking out the door*. Bethesda, MD: Watson Wyatt Worldwide.

Conclusion

Work and life: the road ahead

Fiona Jones, Ronald J. Burke and Mina Westman

It is clear from the diverse chapters included in this volume that achieving work–life balance and/or integration is a complex issue and currently many individuals are a long way from having optimal arrangements. It is also clear that too often the focus has been on work–family interventions that have no basis in research or theory. Furthermore, many such interventions have focused purely on the needs of employees with small children. There has been little consideration of the wider needs of all individuals for work–life balance regardless of family situation. Whatever people's living arrangements and domestic responsibilities, people should have scope to balance work with other activities, e.g., leisure and community activities and friendships. To achieve good work–life balance and integration for all, the issue needs to be addressed at many levels. There are implications for working individuals, their families and for organizations. Actions also need to be supported by legal and policy changes at a national and even international level.

At an individual level it may be necessary to improve family decision making and family communication processes to optimize working arrangements, to minimize damaging effects of role conflict (described in Chapter 5) and to reduce crossover of strains to other family members (see Chapter 7). The individual may also need to ensure that work does not disrupt behaviors essential for optimal health (Chapter 8) and to pay attention to ways in which activities may aid recovery from work (Chapter 9). However, for individuals to be able to achieve a satisfactory balance, the changes they make need to be supported by organizational policies and practices, including the availability and legitimization of such practices as flexible working hours, home-work and telework (Chapter 6). These need to be implemented in a context where they are not seen as marginal, catering purely for the needs of women with children. Organizational interventions, in turn, need to be supported by policy changes and legal frameworks at a national level. The ways in which laws in various countries are now addressing some of these issues were outlined in Chapter 2.

Underpinning all these changes, wide-ranging shifts in cultures, attitudes and values as well as policies are likely to be required (see Chapters 10 and 12). Overall, this requires communication between various levels of government, organizations, trade unions and professional associations, communities and individuals. Fundamental change in organizations may be required; however, in Chapter 12 it is argued that an increasing acceptance of these changes may start to challenge the gendered nature of organizations.

Throughout this book it is also argued that change needs to be supported by more knowledge and information, based on theory and research, into what interventions are effective in what circumstances. In the following sections we put forward some concluding thoughts elaborating what needs to be done by individuals, organizations and by researchers.

WHAT CAN INDIVIDUALS DO?

Implicit in a number of sections in the book is the notion that imbalance (and lack of integration) results from complex interactions between personal and family situational factors, and organizational and social factors. However, there is little research into what the individual might do to improve work–life balance. Instead, the emphasis in most writing is on the organizational pressures that restrict balance. Work by Kofodimos (1993), however, offers some suggestions concerning the role of the individual in colluding with these pressures. She argues that, in western society, our character formation emphasizes the centrality of work and the importance of a mastery orientation to life. Thus personal, as well as organizational and social forces, are at the root of the lack of work–personal life integration.

Kofodimos (1993) addresses three interrelated levels of imbalance:

1 *Time, energy and commitment.* At this level Kofodimos suggests that people typically put more time, energy and commitment into work than other areas of life.
2 *Attitudes and behaviors.* Central to this level of imbalance is the notion that attitudes inculcated in western society emphasize a striving for mastery and achievement and an avoidance of intimacy.
3 *Means and criteria for self-esteem.* Kofodimos suggests this is the deepest level at which many people have an image of the person we feel we should be. This is derived from people's upbringing and is reinforced by later environments, including work. Maintaining self-esteem is dependent on how much we can match up to this image. She argues that for many this is tied to the demonstration of mastery and the avoidance of intimacy.

Work relationships, with their emphasis on mastery and achievement, enable us to maintain the illusion that we measure up to our ideal self.

However, this idealized self is not necessarily consistent with our real selves, our needs and our talents. Intimacy may threaten this status quo and risk people revealing their real selves. The implication of this is that, while ultimately less fulfilling and likely to lead to long-term problems, colluding with the pressure to dedicate all one's time and energy to work may often seem the easiest option.

Kofodimos' work suggests that to achieve work–life integration, and ultimately a more fulfilling life, individual change must take place at three levels: firstly, balancing time, energy and commitment; secondly, integrating mastery and intimacy; and thirdly, becoming aware of one's real self-values and aspirations. While taking a very different approach, these ideas are not inconsistent with suggestions made in Chapter 9 that active involvement in leisure activities and family life has the potential to facilitate recovery from work much more than passive activities. Such activities involve an investment of time, energy and commitment in areas other than work.

These approaches suggest employees have some choice and should be able to improve their work–personal life balance by, for example, changing their behaviors and/or investments. Reich (2001), writing about knowledge workers, implies that this may not be easy. He suggests that employees may choose to behave in ways that limit work–personal life integration. These include accepting existing values about the primacy of work, the importance of face-time and the increasing emphasis on material goods and consumerism as indicators of one's personal value. They may therefore be reluctant to say no to additional work assignments and feel the need to invest heavily in work in the early career stage to guarantee later success. For these reasons individual efforts may not be effective without wider changes within organizations and society.

WHAT CAN ORGANIZATIONS DO?

As we have seen in Chapter 11, some organizations have tried out diverse and imaginative approaches in this area. However, as discussed above, such practices may be seen as programs for working mothers and not designed to encompass the entire workforce. They may not be viewed as a central part of the human resources policy of a company. Furthermore, people may feel discouraged from using such practices if their use is not consistent with cultures that encourage long hours and high visibility in the workplace. Giving the issue of work–life balance a much higher profile may be necessary to help promote organizational cultures that are more sensitive to employees' work and family needs.

The salience of work–life balance initiatives would be likely to be heightened by positioning family-friendly practices and other work–life initiatives as strategic human resource management (SHRM) practices. The last decade has produced increasing amounts of writing and research evidence on SHRM and organizational performance. Typically, SHRM involves bundles of HR practices including training and development, reward and incentive motivation programs, work redesign and performance management. The bulk of the evidence shows that organizations using a higher level of SHRM practices tend to be more productive and profitable (Burke and Cooper, 2005). Clearly, therefore, work–life policies would be strengthened if seen as part of such practices. Furthermore, these change efforts need to be pursued in the context of a dual agenda strategy: one aspect addressing the quality of personal life of employees, while the second addresses the organization's needs for performance.

The development of widespread good organizational practice is further dependent on the evaluation of interventions and the dissemination of good practice. Thus the promotion, involvement and dissemination of research need to go hand-in-hand with the above developments.

WHAT CAN RESEARCHERS DO?

We now have a well-established body of research into the impacts of work on home life and a range of theoretical frameworks (e.g., see Chapters 3, 5 and 7). We also increasingly have a good body of instruments for measurement (Chapter 4). However, we know too little about what it is that makes for effective interventions. While we have some examples of innovative practices in this area and such practices are increasingly being recognized (Chapter 11; see also Lewis and Cooper, 2005), there remains a dearth of good information.

There is information available to organizations wanting to address these issues in terms of policies and programs likely to be both relevant and useful. There is considerably less writing and research on how these change programs have benefited individuals and their families and even less on how organizations may have benefited through lessened turnover and higher performance. There is almost no research on how these change efforts were planned, introduced, implemented and evaluated (i.e., what worked well, what did not work) and what was learned from these experiments. More published action research interventions, such as those of Bailyn (1997) discussed in Chapter 10, are a promising way to produce both innovative interventions and good dissemination of practical information. Furthermore, research studies, such as those conducted by IBM, described in Chapter 11, are useful models.

There is also a need for increased academic research to establish good theoretical approaches on which companies can base interventions. Research into areas such as role conflict and spillover has shown cross-sectional relationships between perceptions of role conflicts and psychological well-being, but has told us little about the processes involved or the individual differences in reactions. Thus they lead to few practical suggestions for improving balance. What, for example, are the coping strategies used by those who are able to maintain a satisfactory work–life balance? These gaps in the literature are highlighted in a recent review of the work and family research covering the last 20 years (Eby *et al.*, 2005). Eby *et al.* argue for an increased emphasis on developing and testing models including mediated relationships. They further suggest that current approaches overemphasize variables from the work domain and argue for a greater emphasis on family variables.

Research reviewed in this book highlights the need also to include organizational level variables (such as aspects of culture; see Chapter 10) into our research models. Studies that can examine interactions between organizational and individual factors may lead to more sophisticated theorizing. Furthermore, we need longitudinal designs to shed light on directions of causation. The development of new statistical techniques of multilevel modeling has increased the possibilities for the analysis of data collected at a range of levels (e.g., Bryk and Raudenbush, 1992). It enables researchers to test models that include organizational-level variables, individual difference variables and longitudinal data collected from individuals and their families on a daily (or even more frequent) basis. While potential models may be complex, these approaches offer scope to shed new light on the processes by which individuals manage work–life boundaries and may suggest more practical implications for change.

Research is currently being conducted by academics in various disciplines (psychology, sociology, management, social work) and by a range of practitioners (HR specialists, and enlightened managers and professionals). Sometimes academic thinking and research are criticized as lacking practical relevance for the practitioner, while applied research may fail to be generalizable and to help develop approaches that others can use. More needs to be done to foster a dialogue between academics and practitioners to facilitate good research and dissemination of results.

Although much of the early work was done in the USA, research in these areas is increasingly being conducted in the UK, Europe and further afield. Clearly, as interest grows throughout the developed world there is scope for cross-cultural research and sharing of best practice internationally.

SOME CONCLUDING THOUGHTS

Typically, the focus in both research and practice so far has emphasized negative impacts such as psychological distress and poor family functioning. There is therefore a danger that achieving balance is seen in terms of avoiding such outcomes. This raises the question of whether this is all we can hope for. Might it be possible to aspire to a greater degree of pleasure and fulfillment in work and other aspects of life through greater balance or integration of these domains? The new positive approaches to exploring the ways in which one role may enrich or enhance another, which are described in Chapters 3 and 5, move us some way in that direction. Furthermore, it may be helpful to build bridges with the newly emerging field of positive organizational scholarship, which focuses on positive outcomes, processes and qualities, e.g., synergy, optimism, joy at work and engagement (Cameron *et al.*, 2003).

Following Bailyn and her colleagues (discussed in Chapter 10), it seems important to consider the structures and cultures around work practices to make a significant and lasting headway on the work and family front. Organizational members sometimes seem to work in ways that limit both job performance and work–family integration. For example, employers and managers may, on occasions, collude in ensuring that meetings are extended unnecessarily or that time is wasted on fruitless bureaucratic activities. In some cases people are encouraged to be highly visible at work or to work in open-plan offices, even though this may be inappropriate for the type of work they do. Norms that encourage individualism and competition, thereby discouraging cooperation, may also militate against efficient performance. Little research has focused on what work practices are effective and under what conditions. Too often work is organized according to the latest management fashion, which may not be appropriate for every type of job.

In the future, however, organizations may have little choice but to change as the values of society change. Conflicting forces currently seem to be pulling in opposite directions. Younger workers want to have a life beyond work and are resisting the work-dominated lives of their managers (Brannen *et al.*, 2002; Cooper *et al.*, 2001; Lewis *et al.*, 2003). However, they are working in an environment in which global forces are demanding more and more effort with little consideration of how this is affecting individuals, families or societies (Rapoport *et al.*, 2004: see also Chapter 1). A self-reinforcing cycle of global competition, intensified consumerism, greed (reflected in status and conspicuous consumption), increased individualism, a devaluing of care and community, all lead to reduced health and well-being. The challenges these forces raise for improving work–life balance are immense.

Given these conflicting pressures there is no easy solution and many questions remain unanswered. How do we increase our awareness of the effects of workplace structures, cultures and practices on work and family issues? How can we think for the long term instead of seeking quick fixes? How can we come to grips with the difficulties in bringing about deep and meaningful change? Although these questions are daunting, we are optimistic that continued advances will be seen in both research and practice. As this book has demonstrated, more research resources are now being devoted to understanding work–family integration and more organizations are realizing that improving the fit between individual and family needs and organizational requirements will have significant performance benefits.

REFERENCES

Bailyn, L. (1997). The impact of corporate culture on work–family integration. In S. Parasuraman and J. H. Greenhaus (eds), *Integrating work and family: Challenges and choices for a changing world* (pp. 299–219). Westport, CT: Quorum.

Brannen, J., Lewis, S., Nilsen, A., and Smithson, J. (2002). *Young Europeans, work and family*. London: Routledge.

Bryk, A., and Raudenbush, S. W. (1992). *Hierarchical linear models for social and behavioral research: Applications and data analysis methods*. Newbury Park, CA: Sage.

Burke, R. J., and Cooper, C. L. (2005). *Reinventing HRM: Challenges and new directions*. Oxford: Routledge.

Cameron, K. S., Dutton, J. E., and Quinn, R. E. (2003). *Positive organizational scholarship*. San Francisco: Berrett-Koehler.

Cooper, C. L., Lewis, S., Smithson, J., and Dyer, J. (2001). *Flexible futures: Flexible working and work–life integration*. London: Institute of Chartered Accountants in England and Wales.

Eby, L. T., Casper, W. J., Lockwood, A., Bordeaux, C., and Brinley, A. (2005). Work and family research in IO/OB: content analysis and review of the literature (1980–2002). *Journal of Vocational Behavior, 66*, 124–197.

Kofodimos, J. (1993). *Balancing act*. San Francisco: Jossey-Bass.

Lewis, S., and Cooper, C. L. (2005). *Work–life integration: Case studies of organizational change*. Chichester: Wiley.

Lewis, S., Rapoport, R., and Gambles, R. (2003). Reflection on the integration of paid work with the rest of life. *Journal of Managerial Psychology, 18*, 824–841.

Rapoport, R., Lewis, S., Bailyn, L., and Gambles, R. (2004). Globalization and the integration of work and personal life. In S. Poelmans (ed.), *Work and family: An international research perspective*. Mahwah, NJ: Lawrence Erlbaum Associates.

Reich, R. B. (2001). *The future of success*. New York: Alfred A. Knopf.

Author index

Note: page numbers in **bold** refer to information contained in tables and diagrams.

Subject index

Note: page numbers in **bold** refer to information contained in tables and diagrams.

Printed in the USA/Agawam, MA
December 13, 2013

583054.010